Contents

Colt 1400 GLX 3-door model

Colt 1400 GLX 5-door model

P3

Colt 1400 GLX
Owners
Workshop

This book is to be returned on or before the last date stamped below.

NCH: PB

TM - 671319   629.2 COL

Acknowledgements

Thanks are due to the Colt Car Company Limited for the supply of technical information and certain illustrations, to Castrol Limited who supplied the lubrication data and to the Champion Sparking Plug Company who supplied the illustrations showing the various spark plug conditions. The bodywork repair photographs used in this manual were provided by Holt Lloyd Limited who supply 'Turtle Wax', 'Dupli-Color Holts' and other Holts range products.

About this manual

Its aim

The aim of this manual is to help you get the best value from your car. It can do so in several ways. It can help you decide what work must be done (even should you choose to get it done by a garage), provide information on routine maintenance and servicing, and give a logical course of action and diagnosis when random faults occur. However, it is hoped that you will use the manual by tackling the work yourself. On simpler jobs it may even be quicker than booking the car into a garage and going there twice to leave and collect it. Perhaps most important, a lot of money can be saved by avoiding the costs the garage must charge to cover its labour and overheads.

The manual has drawings and descriptions to show the function of the various components so that their layout can be understood. Then the tasks are described and photographed in a step-by-step sequence so that even a novice can do the work.

Its arrangement

The manual is divided into twelve Chapters, each covering a logical sub-division of the vehicle. The Chapters are each divided into Sections, numbered with single figures, eg 5; and the Sections into paragraphs (or sub-sections), with decimal numbers following on from the Section they are in, eg 5.1, 5.2, 5.3 etc.

It is freely illustrated, especially in those parts where there is a detailed sequence of operations to be carried out. There are two forms of illustration; figures and photographs. The figures are numbered in sequence with decimal numbers, according to their position in the Chapter – eg Fig. 6.4 is the fourth drawing/illustration in Chapter 6. Photographs carry the same number (either individually or in related groups) as the Section or sub-section to which they relate.

There is an alphabetical index at the back of the manual as well as a contents list at the front. Each Chapter is also preceded by its own individual contents list.

References to the 'left' or 'right' of the vehicle are in the sense of a person in the driver's seat facing forwards.

Unless otherwise stated, nuts and bolts are removed by turning anti-clockwise, and tightened by turning clockwise.

Vehicle manufacturers continually make changes to specifications and recommendations, and these when notified are incorporated into our manuals at the earliest opportunity.

Whilst every care is taken to ensure that the information in this manual is correct, no liability can be accepted by the authors or publishers for loss, damage or injury caused by any errors in, or omissions from, the information given.

Introduction to the Colt 1400 GLX

Produced in Japan and imported into the UK by the Colt Car Company Limited, this car is one of the most European-styled cars yet to leave the Mitsubishi factories.

Although the unique Power/Economy speed range is the most obvious feature of the car, the ease of servicing and overhaul must not be overlooked.

The car is well built and finished and has adequate passenger and luggage accommodation.

General dimensions, weights and capacities

Dimensions

Overall length	149.2 in (3790 mm)
Overall width	62.4 in (1585 mm)
Overall height	53.0 in (1345 mm)
Wheelbase	90.6 in (2300 mm)
Front track	53.9 in (1370 mm)
Rear track	52.8 in (1340 mm)

Weights

Curb weight	1808 lb (820 kg)
Maximum trailer weight	1543 lb (700 kg)

Capacities

Engine oil:	
With filter change	6.2 Imp pt (3.5 litres, 3.7 US qt)
Without filter change	5.3 Imp pt (3.0 litres, 3.2 US qt)
Transaxle oil	4.0 Imp pt (2.3 litres, 2.4 US qt)
Fuel tank	8.8 Imp gal (40 litres, 10.6 US gal)
Cooling system	8.8 Imp pt (5.0 litres, 5.3 US qt)

Use of English

As this book has been written in England, it uses the appropriate English component names, phrases, and spelling. Some of these differ from those used in America. Normally, these cause no difficulty, but to make sure, a glossary is printed below. In ordering spare parts remember the parts list will probably use these words:

English	American	English	American
Aerial	Antenna	Layshaft (of gearbox)	Countershaft
Accelerator	Gas pedal	Leading shoe (of brake)	Primary shoe
Alternator	Generator (AC)	Locks	Latches
Anti-roll bar	Stabiliser or sway bar	Motorway	Freeway, turnpike etc
Battery	Energizer	Number plate	License plate
Bodywork	Sheet metal	Paraffin	Kerosene
Bonnet (engine cover)	Hood	Petrol	Gasoline
Boot lid	Trunk lid	Petrol tank	Gas tank
Boot (luggage compartment)	Trunk	'Pinking'	'Pinging'
Bottom gear	1st gear	Propeller shaft	Driveshaft
Bulkhead	Firewall	Quarter light	Quarter window
Cam follower or tappet	Valve lifter or tappet	Retread	Recap
Carburettor	Carburetor	Reverse	Back-up
Catch	Latch	Rocker cover	Valve cover
Choke/venturi	Barrel	Roof rack	Car-top carrier
Circlip	Snap-ring	Saloon	Sedan
Clearance	Lash	Seized	Frozen
Crownwheel	Ring gear (of differential)	Side indicator lights	Side marker lights
Disc (brake)	Rotor/disk	Side light	Parking light
Drop arm	Pitman arm	Silencer	Muffler
Drop head coupe	Convertible	Spanner	Wrench
Dynamo	Generator (DC)	Sill panel (beneath doors)	Rocker panel
Earth (electrical)	Ground	Split cotter (for valve spring cap)	Lock (for valve spring retainer)
Engineer's blue	Prussian blue	Split pin	Cotter pin
Estate car	Station wagon	Steering arm	Spindle arm
Exhaust manifold	Header	Sump	Oil pan
Fast back (Coupe)	Hard top	Tab washer	Tang; lock
Fault finding/diagnosis	Trouble shooting	Tailgate	Liftgate
Float chamber	Float bowl	Tappet	Valve lifter
Free-play	Lash	Thrust bearing	Throw-out bearing
Freewheel	Coast	Top gear	High
Gudgeon pin	Piston pin or wrist pin	Trackrod (of steering)	Tie-rod (or connecting rod)
Gearchange	Shift	Trailing shoe (of brake)	Secondary shoe
Gearbox	Transmission	Transmission	Whole drive line
Halfshaft	Axleshaft	Tyre	Tire
Handbrake	Parking brake	Van	Panel wagon/van
Hood	Soft top	Vice	Vise
Hot spot	Heat riser	Wheel nut	Lug nut
Indicator	Turn signal	Windscreen	Windshield
Interior light	Dome lamp	Wing/mudguard	Fender

Miscellaneous points

An 'oil seal' is fitted to components lubricated by grease!

A 'damper' is a 'shock absorber', it damps out bouncing, and absorbs shocks of bump impact. Both names are correct, and both are used haphazardly.

Note that British drum brakes are different from the Bendix type that is common in America, so different descriptive names result. The shoe end furthest from the hydraulic wheel cylinder is on a pivot; interconnection between the shoes as on Bendix brakes is most uncommon. Therefore the phrase 'Primary' or 'Secondary' shoe does not apply. A shoe is said to be 'Leading' or 'Trailing'. A 'Leading' shoe is one on which a point on the drum, as it rotates forward, reaches the shoe at the end worked by the hydraulic cylinder before the anchor end. The opposite is a 'Trailing' shoe, and this one has no self servo from the wrapping effect of the rotating drum.

Buying spare parts and vehicle identification numbers

Buying spare parts

Spare parts are available from many sources, for example: Colt garages, other garages and accessory shops, and motor factors. Our advice regarding spare parts is as follows:

Officially appointed Colt garages – This is the best source of parts which are peculiar to your car and are otherwise generally not available (eg complete cylinder heads, internal gearbox components, badges, interior trim etc). To be sure of obtaining the correct parts it will always be necessary to give the storeman your car's engine and chassis number, and if possible to take the old part along for positive identification. Remember that many parts are available on a factory exchange scheme – any parts returned should always be clean! It obviously makes good sense to go to the specialists on your car for this type of parts as they are best equipped to supply you.

Other garages and accessory shops – These are often very good places to buy material and components needed for the maintenance of your car (eg oil filters, spark plugs, bulbs, drivebelts, oil and grease, touch-up paint, filler paste etc). They also sell general accessories, usually have convenient opening hours, charge lower prices and can often be found not far from home.

Motor factors – Good factors will stock all of the more important components which wear out relatively quickly (eg clutch components, pistons, valves, exhaust systems, brake cylinders/pipes/hoses/seals/shoes and pads etc). Motor factors will often provide new or reconditioned components on a part exchange basis – this can save a considerable amount of money.

Vehicle identification numbers

The vehicle identification plate is attached to the engine compartment rear bulkhead (photo). The digits can be decoded as shown in the illustrations.

The engine number is stamped on a machined surface at the side of the exhaust manifold.

The chassis number is stamped on the engine compartment rear bulkhead.

The body colour label is affixed to the left-hand front wing valance under the bonnet (photo).

The transaxle number is stamped on the clutch housing pad of the transaxle case.

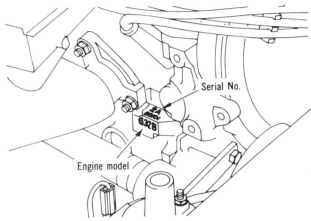

Location of engine number

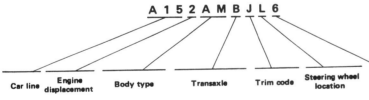

Car line	Engine displacement	Body type	Transaxle	Trim code	Steering wheel location	Destination
A15—Colt	2—1400 c.c.	AM—Hatch back	B—4x2-speed M/T	E—Low U—Medium J—High	L—Left hand R—Right hand	6—For Europe None— For other countries

A 1 5 2 A M B J L 6

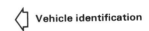

Vehicle identification

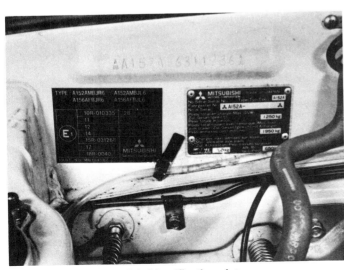

Vehicle identification plate

Paint colour label

Tools and working facilities

Introduction

A selection of good tools is a fundamental requirement for anyone contemplating the maintenance and repair of a motor vehicle. For the owner who does not possess any, their purchase will prove a considerable expense, offsetting some of the savings made by doing-it-yourself. However, provided that the tools purchased are of good quality, they will last for many years and prove an extremely worthwhile investment.

To help the average owner to decide which tools are needed to carry out the various tasks detailed in this manual, we have compiled three lists of tools under the following headings: *Maintenance and minor repair*, *Repair and overhaul*, and *Special*. The newcomer to practical mechanics should start off with the *Maintenance and minor repair* tool kit and confine himself to the simpler jobs around the vehicle. Then, as his confidence and experience grow, he can undertake more difficult tasks, buying extra tools as, and when, they are needed. In this way, a *Maintenance and minor repair* tool kit can be built-up into a *Repair and overhaul* tool kit over a considerable period of time without any major cash outlays. The experienced do-it-yourselfer will have a tool kit good enough for most repair and overhaul procedures and will add tools from the *Special* category when he feels the expense is justified by the amount of use these tools will be put to.

It is obviously not possible to cover the subject of tools fully here. For those who wish to learn more about tools and their use there is a book entitled *How to Choose and Use Car Tools* available from the publishers of this manual.

Maintenance and minor repair tool kit

The tools given in this list should be considered as a minimum requirement if routine maintenance, servicing and minor repair operations are to be undertaken. We recommend the purchase of combination spanners (ring one end, open-ended the other); although more expensive than open-ended ones, they do give the advantages of both types of spanner.

> Combination spanners - 10, 11, 12, 13, 14 & 17 mm
> Adjustable spanner - 9 inch
> Spark plug spanner (with rubber insert)
> Spark plug gap adjustment tool
> Set of feeler gauges
> Brake bleed nipple spanner
> Screwdriver - 4 in long x $\frac{1}{4}$ in dia (flat blade)
> Screwdriver - 4 in long x $\frac{1}{4}$ in dia (cross blade)
> Combination pliers - 6 inch
> Hacksaw (junior)
> Tyre pump
> Tyre pressure gauge
> Grease gun
> Oil can
> Fine emery cloth (1 sheet)
> Wire brush (small)
> Funnel (medium size)

Repair and overhaul tool kit

These tools are virtually essential for anyone undertaking any major repairs to a motor vehicle, and are additional to those given in the *Maintenance and minor repair* list. Included in this list is a comprehensive set of sockets. Although these are expensive they will be found invaluable as they are so versatile - particularly if various drives are included in the set. We recommend the $\frac{1}{2}$ in square-drive type, as this can be used with most proprietary torque spanners. If you

cannot afford a socket set, even bought piecemeal, then inexpensive tubular box wrenches are a useful alternative.

The tools in this list will occasionally need to be supplemented by tools from the *Special* list.

> Sockets (or box spanners) to cover range in previous list
> Reversible ratchet drive (for use with sockets)
> Extension piece, 10 inch (for use with sockets)
> Universal joint (for use with sockets)
> Torque wrench (for use with sockets)
> Mole wrench - 8 inch
> Ball pein hammer
> Soft-faced hammer, plastic or rubber
> Screwdriver - 6 in long x $\frac{5}{16}$ in dia (flat blade)
> Screwdriver - 2 in long x $\frac{5}{16}$ in square (flat blade)
> Screwdriver - 1$\frac{1}{2}$ in long x $\frac{1}{4}$ in dia (cross blade)
> Screwdriver - 3 in long x $\frac{1}{8}$ in dia (electricians)
> Pliers - electricians side cutters
> Pliers - needle nosed
> Pliers - circlip (internal and external)
> Cold chisel - $\frac{1}{2}$ inch
> Scriber
> Scraper
> Centre punch
> Pin punch
> Hacksaw
> Valve grinding tool
> Steel rule/straight-edge
> Allen keys
> Selection of files
> Wire brush (large)
> Axle-stands
> Jack (strong scissor or hydraulic type)

Special tools

The tools in this list are those which are not used regularly, are expensive to buy, or which need to be used in accordance with their manufacturers' instructions. Unless relatively difficult mechanical jobs are undertaken frequently, it will not be economic to buy many of these tools. Where this is the case, you could consider clubbing together with friends (or joining a motorists' club) to make a joint purchase, or borrowing the tools against a deposit from a local garage or tool hire specialist.

The following list contains only those tools and instruments freely available to the public, and not those special tools produced by the vehicle manufacturer specifically for its dealer network. You will find occasional references to these manufacturers' special tools in the text of this manual. Generally, an alternative method of doing the job without the vehicle manufacturers' special tool is given. However, sometimes, there is no alternative to using them. Where this is the case and the relevant tool cannot be bought or borrowed you will have to entrust the work to a franchised garage.

> Valve spring compressor
> Piston ring compressor
> Balljoint separator
> Universal hub/bearing puller
> Impact screwdriver
> Micrometer and/or vernier gauge
> Dial gauge
> Stroboscopic timing light

Dwell angle meter/tachometer
Universal electrical multi-meter
Cylinder compression gauge
Lifting tackle (photo)
Trolley jack
Light with extension lead

Buying tools

For practically all tools, a tool dealer is the best source since he will have a very comprehensive range compared with the average garage or accessory shop. Having said that, accessory shops often offer excellent quality tools at discount prices, so it pays to shop around.

Remember, you don't have to buy the most expensive items on the shelf, but it is always advisable to steer clear of the very cheap tools. There are plenty of good tools around at reasonable prices, so ask the proprietor or manager of the shop for advice before making a purchase.

Care and maintenance of tools

Having purchased a reasonable tool kit, it is necessary to keep the tools in a clean serviceable condition. After use, always wipe off any dirt, grease and metal particles using a clean, dry cloth, before putting the tools away. Never leave them lying around after they have been used. A simple tool rack on the garage or workshop wall, for items such as screwdrivers and pliers is a good idea. Store all normal spanners and sockets in a metal box. Any measuring instruments, gauges, meters, etc, must be carefully stored where they cannot be damaged or become rusty.

Take a little care when tools are used. Hammer heads inevitably become marked and screwdrivers lose the keen edge on their blades from time to time. A little timely attention with emery cloth or a file will soon restore items like this to a good serviceable finish.

Working facilities

Not to be forgotten when discussing tools, is the workshop itself. If anything more than routine maintenance is to be carried out, some form of suitable working area becomes essential.

It is appreciated that many an owner mechanic is forced by circumstances to remove an engine or similar item, without the benefit of a garage or workshop. Having done this, any repairs should always be done under the cover of a roof.

Wherever possible, any dismantling should be done on a clean flat workbench or table at a suitable working height.

Any workbench needs a vice: one with a jaw opening of 4 in (100 mm) is suitable for most jobs. As mentioned previously, some clean dry storage space is also required for tools, as well as the lubricants, cleaning fluids, touch-up paints and so on which become necessary.

Another item which may be required, and which has a much more general usage, is an electric drill with a chuck capacity of at least $\frac{5}{16}$ in (8 mm). This, together with a good range of twist drills, is virtually essential for fitting accessories such as wing mirrors and reversing lights.

Last, but not least, always keep a supply of old newspapers and clean, lint-free rags available, and try to keep any working area as clean as possible.

Jaw gap (in)	Spanner size
0.250	$\frac{1}{4}$ in AF
0.276	7 mm
0.313	$\frac{5}{16}$ in AF
0.315	8 mm
0.344	$\frac{11}{32}$ in AF; $\frac{1}{8}$ in Whitworth
0.354	9 mm
0.375	$\frac{3}{8}$ in AF
0.394	10 mm
0.433	11 mm
0.438	$\frac{7}{16}$ in AF
0.445	$\frac{3}{16}$ in Whitworth; $\frac{1}{4}$ in BSF
0.472	12 mm
0.500	$\frac{1}{2}$ in AF
0.512	13 mm
0.525	$\frac{1}{4}$ in Whitworth; $\frac{5}{16}$ in BSF
0.551	14 mm

Jaw gap (in)	Spanner size
0.563	$\frac{9}{16}$ in AF
0.591	15 mm
0.600	$\frac{5}{16}$ in Whitworth; $\frac{3}{8}$ in BSF
0.625	$\frac{5}{8}$ in AF
0.630	16 mm
0.669	17 mm
0.686	$\frac{11}{16}$ in AF
0.709	18 mm
0.710	$\frac{3}{8}$ in Whitworth, $\frac{7}{16}$ in BSF
0.748	19 mm
0.750	$\frac{3}{4}$ in AF
0.813	$\frac{13}{16}$ in AF
0.820	$\frac{7}{16}$ in Whitworth; $\frac{1}{2}$ in BSF
0.866	22 mm
0.875	$\frac{7}{8}$ in AF
0.920	$\frac{1}{2}$ in Whitworth; $\frac{9}{16}$ in BSF
0.938	$\frac{15}{16}$ in AF
0.945	24 mm
1.000	1 in AF
1.010	$\frac{9}{16}$ in Whitworth; $\frac{5}{8}$ in BSF
1.024	26 mm
1.063	$1\frac{1}{16}$ in AF; 27 mm
1.100	$\frac{5}{8}$ in Whitworth; $\frac{11}{16}$ in BSF
1.125	$1\frac{1}{8}$ in AF
1.181	30 mm
1.200	$\frac{11}{16}$ in Whitworth; $\frac{3}{4}$ in BSF
1.250	$1\frac{1}{4}$ in AF
1.260	32 mm
1.300	$\frac{3}{4}$ in Whitworth; $\frac{7}{8}$ in BSF
1.313	$1\frac{5}{16}$ in AF
1.390	$\frac{13}{16}$ in Whitworth; $\frac{15}{16}$ in BSF
1.417	36 mm
1.438	$1\frac{7}{16}$ in AF
1.480	$\frac{7}{8}$ in Whitworth; 1 in BSF
1.500	$1\frac{1}{2}$ in AF
1.575	40 mm; $\frac{15}{16}$ in Whitworth
1.614	41 mm
1.625	$1\frac{5}{8}$ in AF
1.670	1 in Whitworth; $1\frac{1}{8}$ in BSF
1.688	$1\frac{11}{16}$ in AF
1.811	46 mm
1.813	$1\frac{13}{16}$ in AF
1.860	$1\frac{1}{8}$ in Whitworth; $1\frac{1}{4}$ in BSF
1.875	$1\frac{7}{8}$ in AF
1.969	50 mm
2.000	2 in AF
2.050	$1\frac{1}{4}$ in Whitworth; $1\frac{3}{8}$ in BSF
2.165	55 mm
2.362	60 mm

A Haltrac hoist and gantry in use during a typical engine removal sequence

Jacking and towing

Jacking

The jack supplied in the car tool kit should only be used for changing a roadwheel. Do not use this jack if working under the car unless it is supported on axle stands.

When using a trolley, hydraulic or screw type jack for overhaul or repair operations, locate it only under the front and rear crossmembers or side frame. Never use a jack under the rear suspension crosstube. Always supplement the jacks with axle stands.

Towing

The hooks provided at the front and rear of the car (photos) are for tying the car down during moving on a transporter although they can be used for attaching a tow rope to another vehicle.

Whenever your car is being towed on its roadwheels by another vehicle, make sure that the steering column is unlocked.

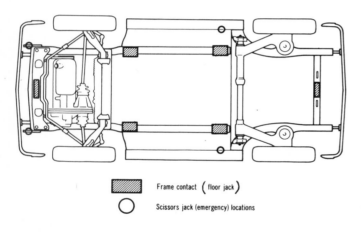

Frame contact (floor jack)

Scissors jack (emergency) locations

Workshop jacking points

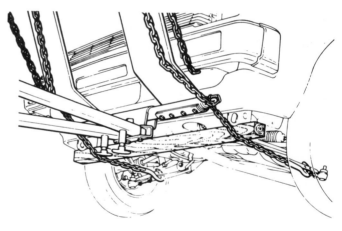

Front towing/lifting chain attachment

Front towing hook/jacking point

Rear towing hook

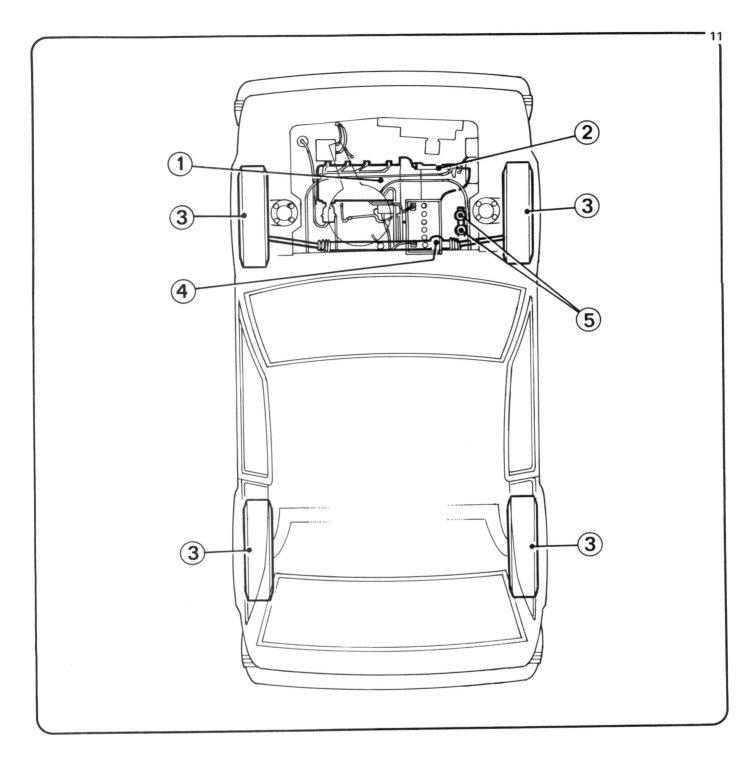

Recommended lubricants and fluids

Component or system	Lubricant type or specification	Castrol product
Engine (1)	20W/50 engine oil	Castrol GTX
Transaxle (2)	SAE 80 EP gear oil	Castrol Hypoy Light
Steering rack (3)	SAE J 310a general purpose grease	Castrol LM grease
Wheel bearings (4)	SAE J 310a general purpose grease	Castrol LM grease
Brake fluid (5)	SAE J 1703e hydraulic fluid	Castrol Girling Universal Brake and Clutch fluid

Note: *The above are general recommendations only. Lubrication requirements vary from territory to territory and depend on vehicle usage. If in doubt consult your nearest dealer or the operator's handbook supplied with the vehicle.*

Safety first!

Professional motor mechanics are trained in safe working procedures. However enthusiastic you may be about getting on with the job in hand, do take the time to ensure that your safety is not put at risk. A moment's lack of attention can result in an accident, as can failure to observe certain elementary precautions.

There will always be new ways of having accidents, and the following points do not pretend to be a comprehensive list of all dangers; they are intended rather to make you aware of the risks and to encourage a safety-conscious approach to all work you carry out on your vehicle.

Essential DOs and DON'Ts

DON'T rely on a single jack when working underneath the vehicle. Always use reliable additional means of support, such as axle stands, securely placed under a part of the vehicle that you know will not give way.

DON'T attempt to loosen or tighten high-torque nuts (e.g. wheel hub nuts) while the vehicle is on a jack; it may be pulled off.

DON'T start the engine without first ascertaining that the transmission is in neutral (or 'Park' where applicable) and the parking brake applied.

DON'T suddenly remove the filler cap from a hot cooling system — cover it with a cloth and release the pressure gradually first, or you may get scalded by escaping coolant.

DON'T attempt to drain oil until you are sure it has cooled sufficiently to avoid scalding you.

DON'T grasp any part of the engine, exhaust or catalytic converter without first ascertaining that it is sufficiently cool to avoid burning you.

DON'T syphon toxic liquids such as fuel, brake fluid or antifreeze by mouth, or allow them to remain on your skin.

DON'T inhale brake lining dust — it is injurious to health.

DON'T allow any spilt oil or grease to remain on the floor — wipe it up straight away, before someone slips on it.

DON'T use ill-fitting spanners or other tools which may slip and cause injury.

DON'T attempt to lift a heavy component which may be beyond your capability — get assistance.

DON'T rush to finish a job, or take unverified short cuts.

DON'T allow children or animals in or around an unattended vehicle.

DO wear eye protection when using power tools such as drill, sander, bench grinder etc, and when working under the vehicle.

DO use a barrier cream on your hands prior to undertaking dirty jobs — it will protect your skin from infection as well as making the dirt easier to remove afterwards; but make sure your hands aren't left slippery.

DO keep loose clothing (cuffs, tie etc) and long hair well out of the way of moving mechanical parts.

DO remove rings, wristwatch etc, before working on the vehicle — especially the electrical system.

DO ensure that any lifting tackle used has a safe working load rating adequate for the job.

DO keep your work area tidy — it is only too easy to fall over articles left lying around.

DO get someone to check periodically that all is well, when working alone on the vehicle.

DO carry out work in a logical sequence and check that everything is correctly assembled and tightened afterwards.

DO remember that your vehicle's safety affects that of yourself and others. If in doubt on any point, get specialist advice.

IF, in spite of following these precautions, you are unfortunate enough to injure yourself, seek medical attention as soon as possible.

Fire

Remember at all times that petrol (gasoline) is highly flammable. Never smoke, or have any kind of naked flame around, when working on the vehicle. But the risk does not end there — a spark caused by an electrical short-circuit, by two metal surfaces contacting each other, or even by static electricity built up in your body under certain conditions, can ignite petrol vapour, which in a confined space is highly explosive.

Always disconnect the battery earth (ground) terminal before working on any part of the fuel system, and never risk spilling fuel on to a hot engine or exhaust.

It is recommended that a fire extinguisher of a type suitable for fuel and electrical fires is kept handy in the garage or workplace at all times. Never try to extinguish a fuel or electrical fire with water.

Fumes

Certain fumes are highly toxic and can quickly cause unconsciousness and even death if inhaled to any extent. Petrol (gasoline) vapour comes into this category, as do the vapours from certain solvents such as trichloroethylene. Any draining or pouring of such volatile fluids should be done in a well ventilated area.

When using cleaning fluids and solvents, read the instructions carefully. Never use materials from unmarked containers — they may give off poisonous vapours.

Never run the engine of a motor vehicle in an enclosed space such as a garage. Exhaust fumes contain carbon monoxide which is extremely poisonous; if you need to run the engine, always do so in the open air or at least have the rear of the vehicle outside the workplace.

If you are fortunate enough to have the use of an inspection pit, never drain or pour petrol, and never run the engine, while the vehicle is standing over it; the fumes, being heavier than air, will concentrate in the pit with possibly lethal results.

The battery

Never cause a spark, or allow a naked light, near the vehicle's battery. It will normally be giving off a certain amount of hydrogen gas, which is highly explosive.

Always disconnect the battery earth (ground) terminal before working on the fuel or electrical systems.

If possible, loosen the filler plugs or cover when charging the battery from an external source. Do not charge at an excessive rate or the battery may burst.

Take care when topping up and when carrying the battery. The acid electrolyte, even when diluted, is very corrosive and should not be allowed to contact the eyes or skin.

If you ever need to prepare electrolyte yourself, always add the acid slowly to the water, and never the other way round. Protect against splashes by wearing rubber gloves and goggles.

Mains electricity

When using an electric power tool, inspection light etc which works from the mains, always ensure that the appliance is correctly connected to its plug and that, where necessary, it is properly earthed (grounded). Do not use such appliances in damp conditions and, again, beware of creating a spark or applying excessive heat in the vicinity of fuel or fuel vapour.

Ignition HT voltage

A severe electric shock can result from touching certain parts of the ignition system, such as the HT leads, when the engine is running or being cranked, particularly if components are damp or the insulation is defective. Where an electronic ignition system is fitted, the HT voltage is much higher and could prove fatal.

Routine maintenance

Maintenance is essential for ensuring safety and desirable for the purpose of getting the best in terms of performance and economy from your car. Over the years the need for periodic lubrication — oiling, greasing, and so on — has been drastically if not totally eliminated. This has unfortunately tended to lead some owners to think that because no such action is required, components either no longer exist, or will last for ever. This is a serious delusion. It follows therefore that the largest initial element of maintenance is visual examination. This may lead to repairs or renewals.

Every 250 miles (400 km) or weekly

Check the tyre pressures when the tyres are cold (Chapter 11)
Check the engine oil level and top up if necessary (photos)
Check the battery and coolant levels (Chapters 2 and 9)
Top up the washer fluid reservoir (photo)
Check the operation of the lights, direction indicators and horn
Check the operation of windscreen and tailgate wipers
Check the brake hydraulic fluid level

After the first 600 miles (1000 km)

Check the torque of the cylinder head bolts (cold) (Chapter 1)
Check the torque of the manifold bolts (Chapter 1)
Check the contact breaker points gap (Chapter 4)
Check the drivebelt tension
Check the torque of the engine mounting bolts (Chapter 1)
Change the transaxle oil level (Chapter 6)
Check the torque of the steering gear bolts (Chapter 10)
Check brake pipes, fuel pipes and hoses for leaks
Check the brake pedal free play (Chapter 8)
Check the clutch pedal free play (Chapter 5)
Change the engine oil
Check the valve clearances (Chapter 1)
Check the dwell angle and ignition timing (Chapter 4)
Check the idling speed (Chapter 3)
Check the handbrake operation (Chapter 8)

Every 6000 miles (10 000 km)

Check and clean the spark plugs (Chapter 4)
Check and clean the air filter element (Chapter 3)
Check the contact breaker points (Chapter 4)
Check the drivebelt tension
Check the front wheel bearings for play (Chapter 11)
Check the disc pads for wear (Chapter 8)
Check the hydraulic system for leaks
Check the fuel pipes and hoses for leaks
Check the steering and driveshaft boots (Chapters 7 and 10)
Check fuel fuel, water and oil leaks
Check the hydraulic fluid
Check the brake pedal free play (Chapter 8)
Check the clutch pedal free play (Chapter 5)
Lubricate all locks and hinges etc
Change the engine oil
Change the oil filter after the first 6000 miles (10 000 km) and then at every second oil change. In the case of cars used in severe conditions change the filter at every oil change
Check and adjust the dwell angle and ignition timing (Chapter 4)
Check and adjust the idling speed (Chapter 3)
Check the brake servo operation (Chapter 8)
Check the handbrake operations (Chapter 8)

Every 12 000 miles (20 000 km)

Check the torque of the cylinder head bolts (cold) (Chapter 1)
Check the torque of the manifold bolts (Chapter 1)
Lubricate the distributor (Chapter 4)
Check the fuel filter (Chapter 3)
Check the transaxle oil (photo) (Chapter 6)
Check the torque of the front suspension lower arm retaining bolts (Chapter 11)
Check the front and rear suspension for damage
Check the rear brake linings and drums for wear (Chapter 8)
Check the steering linkage for smooth operation
Change the brake fluid (Chapter 8)
Check the steering for free play
Check and adjust the valve clearances (Chapter 1)
Check the front wheel toe-in (Chapter 10)

Every 24 000 miles (40 000 km)

Change the transaxle oil (photos) (Chapter 8)
Change the wheel bearing grease (Chapter 11)
Check the wheel bearing nuts (Chapter 11)
Change the engine coolant (every two years) (Chapter 2)

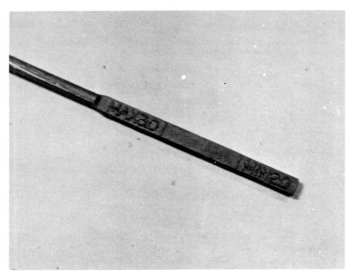

Engine oil dipstick markings

Coolant expansion tank (lower left) and washer fluid reservoir and pumps

Topping up the engine oil

Manual transmission filler/level plug

Manual transmission drain plug

Filling the manual transmission

Fault diagnosis

Introduction

The car owner who does his or her own maintenance according to the recommended schedules should not have to use this section of the manual very often. Modern component reliability is such that, provided those items subject to wear or deterioration are inspected or renewed at the specified intervals, sudden failure is comparatively rare. Faults do not usually just happen as a result of sudden failure, but develop over a period of time. Major mechanical failures in particular are usually preceded by characteristic symptoms over hundreds or even thousands of miles. Those components which do occasionally fail without warning are often small and easily carried in the car.

With any fault finding, the first step is to decide where to begin investigations. Sometimes this is obvious, but on other occasions a little detective work will be necessary. The owner who makes half a dozen haphazard adjustments or replacements may be successful in curing a fault (or its symptoms), but he will be none the wiser if the fault recurs and he may well have spent more time and money than was necessary. A calm and logical approach will be found to be more satisfactory in the long run. Always take into account any warning signs or abnormalities that may have been noticed in the period preceding the fault – power loss, high or low gauge readings, unusual noises or smells, etc – and remember that failure of components such as fuses or spark plugs may only be pointers to some underlying fault.

The pages which follow here are intended to help in cases of failure to start or breakdown on the road. There is also a Fault Diagnosis Section at the end of each Chapter which should be consulted if the preliminary checks prove unfruitful. Whatever the fault, certain basic principles apply. These are are follows:

Verify the fault. This is simply a matter of being sure that you know what the symptoms are before starting work. This is particularly important if you are investigating a fault for someone else who may not have described it very accurately.

Don't overlook the obvious. For example, if the car won't start, is there petrol in the tank? (Don't take anyone else's word on this particular point, and don't trust the fuel gauge either!). If an electrical fault is indicated, look for loose or broken wires before digging out the test gear.

Cure the disease, not the symptom. Substituting a flat battery with a fully charged one will get you off the hard shoulder, but if the underlying cause is not attended to, the new battery will go the same way. Similarly, changing oil-fouled spark plugs for a new set will get you moving again, but remember that the reason for the fouling (if it wasn't simply an incorrect grade of plug) will have to be established and corrected.

Don't take anything for granted. Particularly, don't forget that a 'new' component may itself be defective (especially if it's been rattling round in the boot for months), and don't leave components out of a fault diagnosis sequence just because they are new or recently fitted. When you do finally diagnose a difficult fault, you'll probably realise that all the evidence was there from the start.

Electrical faults

Electrical faults can be more puzzling than straightforward mechanical failures, but they are no less susceptible to logical analysis if the basic principles of operation are understood. Car electrical wiring exists in extremely unfavourable conditions – heat, vibration and chemical attack – and the first things to look for are loose or corroded connections and broken or chafed wires, especially where the wires pass through holes in the bodywork or are subject to vibration.

All metal-bodied cars in current production have one pole of the battery 'earthed', ie connected to the car bodywork, and in nearly all modern cars it is the negative (-) terminal. The various electrical components motors, bulb holders etc – are also connected to earth, either by means of a lead or directly by their mountings. Electric current flows through the component and then back to the battery via the car bodywork. If the component mounting is loose or corroded, or if a good path back to the battery is not available, the circuit will be incomplete and a malfunction will result. The engine and/or gearbox are also earthed by means of flexible metal straps to the body or subframe; if these straps are loose or missing, starter motor, generator and ignition trouble may result.

Assuming the earth return to be satisfactory, electrical faults will be due either to component malfunction or to defects in the current supply. Individual components are dealt with in Chapter 9. If supply wires are broken or cracked internally this results in an open-circuit, and the easiest way to check for this is to bypass the suspect wire temporarily with a length of wire having a crocodile clip or suitable connector at each end. Alternatively, a 12V test lamp can be used to verify the presence of supply voltage at various points along the wire and the break can be thus isolated.

If a bare portion of a live wire touches the car bodywork or other earthed metal part the electricity will take the low-resistance path thus formed battery to the battery: this is known as a short-circuit. Hopefully a short-circuit will blow a fuse, but otherwise it may cause burning of the insulation (and possibly further short-circuits) or even a fire. This is why it is inadvisable to bypass persistently blowing fuses with silver foil or wire.

Spares and tool kit

Most cars are only supplied with sufficient tools for wheel changing; the *Maintenance and minor repair* tool kit detailed in *Tools and working facilities*, with the addition of a hammer, is probably sufficient for those repairs that most motorists would consider attempting at the roadside. In addition a few items which can be fitted without too much trouble in the event of breakdown should be carried. Experience and available space will modify the list below, but the following may save having to call on professional assistance.

Spark plugs, clean and correctly gapped
HT lead and plug cap – long enough to reach the plug furthest from the distributor

Distributor rotor, condenser and contact breaker points (mechanical breaker type distributor)
Drivebelt(s) – emergency type may suffice
Spare fuses
Set of principal light bulbs
Tin of radiator sealer and hose bandage
Exhaust bandage
Roll of insulating tape
Length of soft iron wire
Length of electrical flex
Torch or inspection lamp (can double as test lamp)
Battery jump leads
Tow-rope
Ignition waterproofing aerosol
Litre of engine oil
Sealed can of hydraulic fluid

If spare fuel is carried, a can designed for the purpose should be used to minimise risks of leakage and collision damage. A first aid kit and a warning triangle, whilst not at present compulsory in the UK, are obviously sensible items to carry in addition to the above.

When touring abroad it may be advisable to carry additional spares which, even if you cannot fit them yourself, could save having to wait while parts are obtained. The items below may be worth considering:

Clutch and throttle cables
Cylinder head gasket
Alternator brushes
Fuel pump repair kit
Tyre valve core

One of the motoring organisations will be able to advise on availability of fuel etc in foreign countries.

Engine will not start

Engine fails to turn when starter operated
Flat battery (recharge, use jump leads, or push start)
Battery terminals loose or corroded
Battery earth to body defective
Engine earth strap loose or broken
Starter motor (or solenoid) wiring loose or broken
Automatic transmission selector in wrong position, or inhibitor switch faulty
Ignition/starter switch faulty

Major mechanical failure (seizure) or long disuse (piston rings rusted to bores)
Starter or solenoid internal fault (see Chapter 9)

Starter motor turns engine slowly
Partially discharged battery (recharge, use jump leads, or push start)
Battery terminals loose or corroded
Battery earth to body defective
Engine earth strap loose
Starter motor (or solenoid) wiring loose
Starter motor internal fault (see Chapter 9)

Starter motor spins without turning engine
Flat battery
Flywheel gear teeth damaged or worn
Starter motor mounting bolts loose

Engine turns normally but fails to start
Damp or dirty HT leads and distributor cap (crank engine and check for spark)
No fuel in tank (check for delivery at carburettor)
Excessive choke (hot engine) or insufficient choke (cold engine)
Fouled or incorrectly gapped spark plugs (remove, clean and regap)

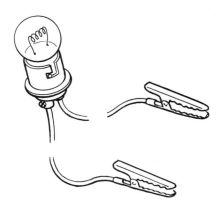

A simple test lamp is useful for checking electrical faults

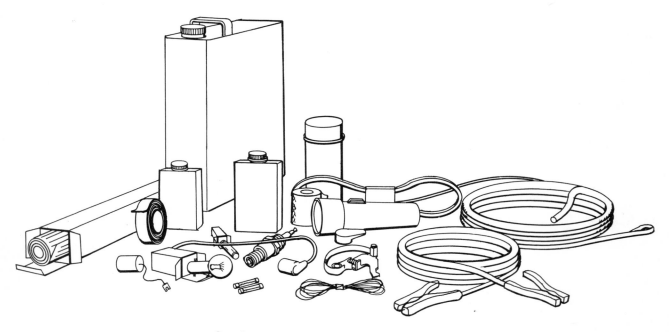

Carrying a few spares can save you a long walk

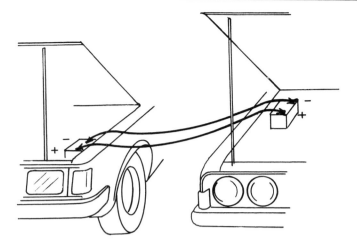

Correct way to connect jump leads. Do not allow car bodies to touch!

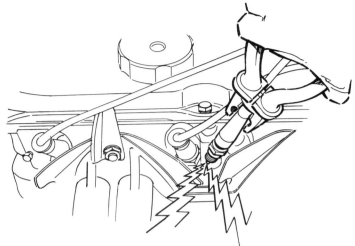

Crank engine and check for spark. Note use of insulated tool!

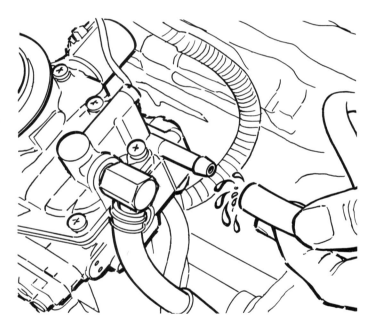

Check for fuel delivery at carburettor

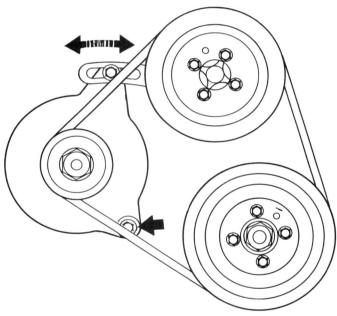

A slack drivebelt can cause overheating and battery charging problems. Slacken arrowed bolts to adjust

Other ignition system fault (see Chapter 4)
Other fuel system fault (see Chapter 3)
Poor compression (see Chapter 1)
Major mechanical failure (eg camshaft drive)

Engine fires but will not run
Insufficient choke (cold engine)
Air leaks at carburettor or inlet manifold
Fuel starvation (see Chapter 3)
Ballast resistor defective, or other ignition fault (see Chapter 4)

Engine cuts out and will not restart

Engine cuts out suddenly – ignition fault
Loose or disconnected LT wires
Wet HT leads or distributor cap (after traversing water splash)
Coil or condenser failure (check for spark) (mechanical breaker system)
Other ignition fault (see Chapter 4)
Fault in electronic system component

Engine misfires before cutting out – fuel fault
Fuel tank empty
Fuel pump defective or filter blocked (check for delivery)
Fuel tank filler vent blocked (suction will be evident on releasing cap)
Carburettor needle valve sticking
Carburettor jets blocked (fuel contaminated)
Other fuel system fault (see Chapter 3)

Engine cuts out – other causes
Serious overheating
Major mechanical failure (eg camshaft drive)

Engine overheats

Ignition (no-charge) warning light illuminated
Slack or broken drivebelt – retension or renew

Ignition warning light not illuminated
Coolant loss due to internal or external leakage (see Chapter 2)

Thermostat defective
Low oil level
Brakes binding
Radiator clogged externally or internally
Electric cooling fan not operating correctly
Engine waterways clogged
Ignition timing incorrect or automatic advance malfunctioning
Mixture too weak

Note: *Do not add cold water to an overheated engine or damage may result*

Low engine oil pressure

Gauge reads low or warning light illuminated with engine running
Oil level low or incorrect grade
Defective gauge or sender unit
Wire to sender unit earthed
Engine overheating
Oil filter clogged or bypass valve defective
Oil pressure relief valve defective
Oil pick-up strainer clogged
Oil pump worn or mountings loose
Worn main or big-end bearings

Note: *Low oil pressure in a high-mileage engine at tickover is not necessarily a cause for concern. Sudden pressure loss at speed is far more significant. In any event, check the gauge or warning light sender before condemning the engine.*

Engine noises

Pre-ignition (pinking) on acceleration
Incorrect grade of fuel
Ignition timing incorrect
Distributor faulty or worn
Worn or maladjusted carburettor
Excessive carbon build-up in engine

Whistling or wheezing noises
Leaking vacuum hose
Leaking carburettor or manifold gasket
Blowing head gasket

Tapping or rattling
Incorrect valve clearances
Worn valve gear
Worn timing chain or belt
Broken piston ring (ticking noise)

Knocking or thumping
Unintentional mechanical contact (eg fan blades)
Worn fanbelt
Peripheral component fault (generator, water pump etc)
Worn big-end bearings (regular heavy knocking, perhaps less under load)
Worn main bearings (rumbling and knocking, perhaps worsening under load)
Piston slap (most noticeable when cold)

Chapter 1 Engine

Contents

Specifications

Engine (general)

	4-cylinder in-line, overhead camshaft	
	J	**K**
Engine type		
Designation	1410 cc (86 cu in)	1597 cc (97.5 cu in)
Capacity		
Bore	2.91 in (74.0 mm)	3.03 in (76.9 mm)
Stroke	3.23 in (82.0 mm)	3.39 in (86.0 mm)
Compression ratio	9.0 : 1	8.5 : 1
Firing order	1-3-4-2 (No 1 at timing belt end)	

Crankshaft

Main journal diameter	1.8898 in (48.0 mm)	2.2441 in (57.0 mm)
Crankpin diameter	1.6535 in (42.0 mm)	1.7717 in (45.0 mm)
Maximum taper of crankpin or journals	0.0004 in (0.01 mm)	
Crankshaft end-float	0.002 to 0.007 in (0.05 to 0.18 mm)	
Journal and crankpin undersizes	0.010, 0.020, 0.030 in (0.25, 0.50, 0.75 mm)	
Main bearing running clearance	0.0008 to 0.0028 in (0.02 to 0.07 mm)	
Connecting rod big-end bearing running clearance	0.0004 to 0.0024 in (0.01 to 0.06 mm)	
Side clearance	0.004 to 0.01 in (0.1 to 0.25 mm)	

Cylinder block

Material	Cast iron
Maximum taper or out of round of cylinder bore	0.0008 in (0.02 mm)

Piston and piston rings

Piston diameter	2.91 in (74.0 mm)	3.0276 in (76.9 mm)
Piston oversizes	0.010, 0.020, 0.030, 0.039 in (0.25, 0.50, 0.75, 1.00 mm)	
Piston to bore clearance	0.0008 to 0.0016 in (0.02 to 0.04 mm)	
Clearance of piston ring in piston groove		
Top compression ring:		
Standard	0.0012 to 0.0028 in (0.03 to 0.07 mm)	
Maximum	0.006 in (0.15 mm)	0.004 in (0.10 mm)
Second compression ring:		
Standard	0.0008 to 0.0024 in (0.02 to 0.06 mm)	
Maximum	0.005 in (0.12 mm)	0.004 in (0.10 mm)
Compression ring end gap:		
Standard	0.008 to 0.016 in (0.2 to 0.4 mm)	
Maximum	0.039 in (0.1 mm)	0.039 in (0.1 mm)
Oil control ring side rail end gap:		
Standard	0.008 to 0.020 in (0.2 to 0.5 mm)	
Maximum	0.039 in (0.1 mm)	
Oversize piston rings	0.010, 0.020, 0.030, 0.039 in (0.25, 0.50, 0.75, 1.00 mm)	
Compression pressures, with starter motor running, throttle full open, coil HT lead disconnected	149 lbf/in² (10.48 kgf/cm²)	
Maximum variation between cylinders	15 lbf/in² (1.05 kgf/cm²)	

Cylinder head

Material	Light alloy
Maximum distortion of joint face	0.004 in (0.1 mm)

Camshaft

Number of bearings	Three	Five
Bearing running clearance	0.002 to 0.0035 in (0.05 to 0.09 mm)	
Height of cam lobe:		
Intake	1.50 in (38.1 mm)	1.4331 in (36.4 mm)
Exhaust	1.5039 in (38.2 mm)	1.4331 in (36.4 mm)
Wear limit	0.020 in (0.5 mm)	
Camshaft endfloat	0.002 to 0.008 in (0.05 to 0.2 mm)	0.002 to 0.006 in (0.05 to 0.15 mm)

Valves

Clearance (hot):		
Intake	0.006 in (0.15 mm)	
Exhaust	0.010 in (0.25 mm)	
Stem diameter:		
Intake	0.315 in (8.0 mm)	
Wear limit	0.004 in (0.1 mm)	
Exhaust	0.315 in (8.0 mm)	
Wear limit	0.006 in (0.15 mm)	
Clearance of valve stem in guide:		
Intake	0.0012 to 0.0024 in (0.03 to 0.06 mm)	
Wear limit	0.004 in (0.1 mm)	
Exhaust	0.002 to 0.0035 in (0.05 to 0.09 mm)	
Wear limit	0.006 in (0.15 mm)	
Valve guide oversizes	0.002, 0.010, 0.020 in (0.05, 0.25, 0.50 mm)	
Valve head edge minimum thickness after grinding in:		
Intake	0.028 in (0.7 mm)	0.039 in (1.0 mm)
Exhaust	0.039 in (1.0 mm)	
Valve seat contact width	0.035 to 0.051 in (0.9 to 1.3 mm)	
Valve seat angle	45°	
Oversize seat inserts	0.12, 0.24 in (0.3, 0.6 mm)	
Valve springs:		
Type	Coil	
Free length	1.697 in (43.1 mm)	1.823 in (46.3 mm)
Maximum reduction in free length before renewal	0.039 in (1.0 mm)	
Jet valves (North America):		
Valve clearance (hot)	0.006 in (0.15 mm)	
Valve stem diameter	0.1693 in (4.300 mm)	
Seat angle	45°	
Valve spring free length	1.1654 in (29.60 mm)	

Oil pump

Type	Eccentric gear or trochoid rotor
Clearances (Eccentric gear):	
Outer gear and casing	0.0039 to 0.0079 in (0.1 to 0.2 mm)
Crescent and outer gear	0.0087 to 0.0134 in (0.22 to 0.34 mm)
Crescent and inner gear	0.0083 to 0.0126 in (0.21 to 0.22 mm)
Gear endfloat	0.0016 to 0.0039 in (0.04 to 0.10 mm)
Clearances (Trochoid rotor):	
Between tips of rotors	0.0016 to 0.0047 in (0.04 to 0.12 mm)
Outer rotor to pump cover	0.0039 to 0.0063 in (0.10 to 0.16 mm)
Rotor endfloat	0.0024 to 0.0047 in (0.06 to 0.12 mm)
Oil pressure relief valve free length	1.850 in (47.0 mm)

Torque wrench settings

	lbf ft	Nm
Cylinder head bolts (cold engine):		
Stage 1	26	35
Stage 2	40	55
Stage 3	53	72
Camshaft bearing cap bolts (1597 cc engine)	15	20
Camshaft sprocket bolt	53	72
Rocker cover bolts:		
1410 cc engine	3	4
1597 cc engine	4	6
Main bearing cap bolts	38	52
Connecting rod cap nuts	25	34
Flywheel bolts	100	136
Driveplate bolts (automatic transmission)	30	40
Crankshaft pulley centre bolts	41	56
Crankshaft pulley outer bolts	7	10
Oil pump sprocket bolt (1597 cc engine)	26	36
Timing belt tensioner bolts	16	22
Sump oil pan bolts	4	6
Sump drain plug	44	60
Oil pump cover screws (1410 cc engine)	6	8
Intake manifold bolts	13	18
Exhaust manifold bolts	13	18
Exhaust downpipe flange bolts	17	24
Front casing bolts:		
1410 cc engine	10	14
1597 cc engine	12	17
Jet valves (North America)	15	20
Rocker arm shaft bolts (1410 cc engine)	18	25
Oil pump relief plug	35	48
Engine mounting bolts and nuts:		
Flexible mountings to crossmember	29	40
Flexible mountings to brackets	18	25
Brackets to crankcase	50	68
Transmission mounting bolts and nuts:		
Flexible mounting to frame	29	40
Flexible mounting to bracket	25	34
Mounting bracket to transmission	18	25
Damper rod bracket bolts	16	22
Damper rod pivot bolts	29	40
Clutch bellhousing or torque converter housing to engine:		
Flange bolts	35	48
Bolts with washer	25	34
Clutch cover bolts	15	20

Part A 1410 cc (86 cu in) engine

1 General description

The engine is of the four cylinder, in-line, overhead camshaft type. It is transversely mounted at the front of the car as an assembly in conjunction with the transmission.

The camshaft is supported in three bearings and it is driven by a toothed belt from a sprocket on the crankshaft. The camshaft has an integral drivegear for driving the distributor and also incorporates an eccentric cam for operating the fuel pump.

The rocker gear comprises separate shafts for the intake valves and the exhaust valves. The design of the rocker arm differs according to which type of valve it is operating. On North American models, the intake rocker arms operate two valves per cylinder, the extra one being the jet valve, which is fitted as an aid to exhaust emission control.

The valve gear comprises heat resistant steel valves, coil springs and split retaining collets. Oil seals are located in the valve guides.

The pistons are of tapered skirt elliptical type fitted with three piston rings — two compresssion and one oil control. The gudgeon pins are press fitted in the connecting rods but are floating in the pistons.

The crankshaft is a steel forging supported on five main bearings. It is fitted with an oil seal at the front and rear ends. The centre main bearing shells incorporate thrust flanges to control endfloat.

The lubrication system is based upon an oil pump driven from the front end of the crankshaft. The pump is of eccentric gear type and incorporates a pressure relief valve. The pressurised oil passes through a full flow, disposable, cartridge type oil filter which is screwed into the front face of the engine.

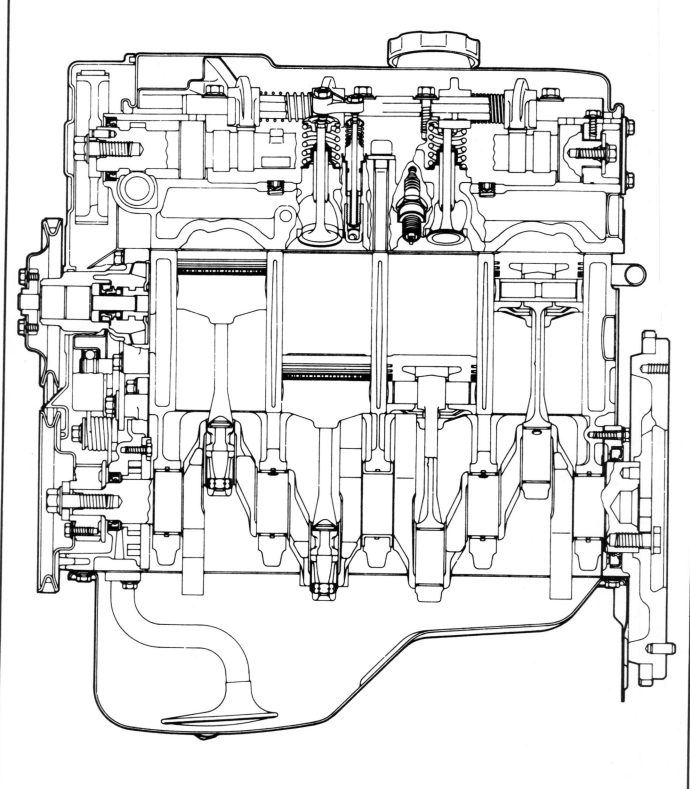

Fig. 1.1 Cutaway view of the 1410 cc engine (Sec 1)

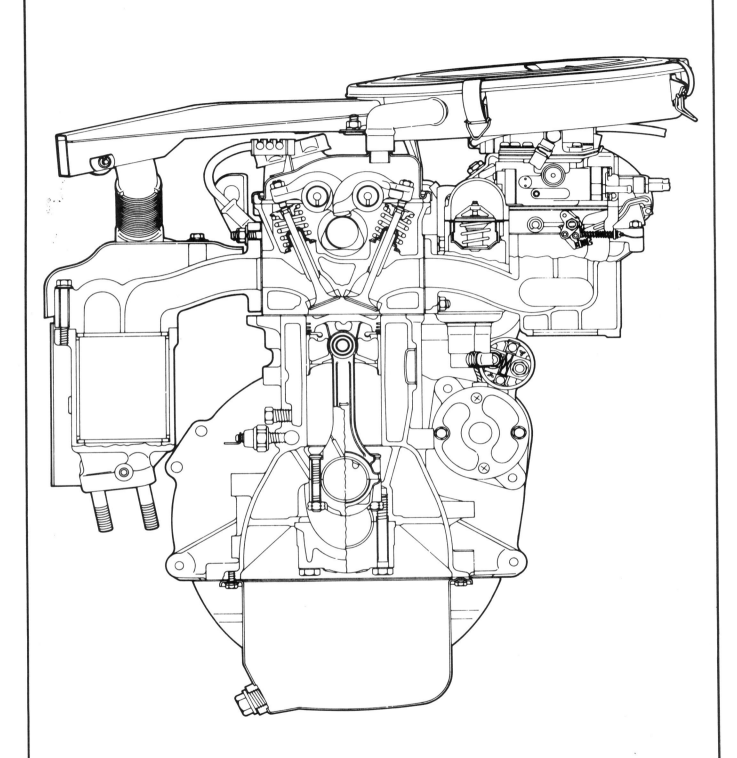

Fig. 1.2 Cutaway view of 1410 cc engine with N.American specification (temperature controlled air cleaner and catalytic converter) (Sec 1)

2 Major operations possible with engine in car

1   The following operations can be carried out without having to remove the engine/transmission from the car.

Removal and refitting of the rocker gear
Removal and refitting of the camshaft
Removal and refitting of the timing belt
Removal and refitting of the cylinder head
Removal and refitting of the engine oil sump
Removal and refitting of the engine front casing and oil pump
Removal and refitting of the pistons and connecting rods
Removal and refitting of the flywheel*
Removal and refitting of the crankshaft*

* As the transmission and clutch must first be withdrawn it is recommended that the engine/transmission is removed to gain access to these components.

3 Rocker gear – removal and refitting

1   Remove the breather hose which runs between the rocker cover and the air cleaner casing.
2   Remove the air cleaner.
3   On models with a two piece timing belt cover, remove the top half.
4   Unbolt and remove the rocker cover.
5   It is recommended that the crankshaft is now turned by means of the crankshaft pulley bolt until No 1 piston is at TDC. This can be verified by making sure that the notch in the pulley is aligned with the TDC mark on the timing index when both valves of No 1 cylinder are closed.
6   Unscrew the bolts which hold the rocker shafts in position and remove the rocker arm and shaft assemblies.
7   Refit the rocker gear by reversing the removal operations. The exhaust and intake rocker assemblies have different types of rocker arms and they are not equally spaced so they cannot be interchanged.

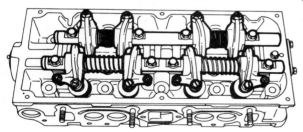

Fig. 1.3 The rocker gear (Sec 3)

8   Check the valve clearances on completion as described in Section 19 or 20 and use a new rocker cover gasket.

4 Timing belt – renewal

1   Release the alternator mounting and adjuster link bolts, push the alternator in towards the engine and remove the drivebelt. Unbolt and remove the pulley from the water pump. Using a ring spanner on the crankshaft pulley bolt, set the locating pin on the crankshaft sprocket opposite to the TDC mark on the belt cover with No 1 piston at TDC on its compression stroke. This can be checked by observing that the contact end of the distributor rotor arm is opposite the No 1 HT lead segment in the distributor cap.
2   Unbolt and remove the timing belt cover.
3   Release the belt tensioner pinch bolt, followed by the tensioner pivot mounting bolt. Lever the tensioner towards the water pump and retighten the bolts. This will have removed tension from the belt.
4   Slide the toothed belt from the camshaft pulley.
5   Remove the four small bolts from the crankshaft pulley. If the centre bolt is held while the small ones are unscrewed, the setting of the TDC mark will not be altered.
6   Pull off the pulley, remove the timing belt from the crankshaft sprocket. If it is to be used again, mark it with regard to the direction of running so that it can be refitted the correct way round; also as to tooth alignment with the sprockets.
7   For inspection details of the timing belt and sprockets refer to Part D of this Chapter.
8   Before fitting the belt, make sure that the crankshaft has not been moved from its TDC setting. To check this, observe that the sprocket roll pin aligns with the projection on the front casing. If by any chance, the crankshaft sprocket has been taken off, make sure that the belt flange which goes behind it has its convex face against the sprocket (photo).
9   Check that the timing mark on the camshaft sprocket is in alignment with the mark on the cylinder head (photo).
10   Fit the timing belt, making sure that the tension side of the belt is taut between sprockets.
11   Refit the crankshaft pulley.
12   Release the tensioner bolts to allow it to move and to apply tension to the belt. Tighten the tensioner pinch bolt followed by the pivot bolt, to the specified torque.
13   Using a spanner on the crankshaft pulley centre bolt, turn the crankshaft through one complete turn (360°) and re-align the TDC marks.
14   Release the tensioner pivot and pinch bolts in that order and then retighten them in the reverse order. The belt should now be correctly tensioned (photo).
15   Refit the timing belt cover and the water pump pulley. Fit and adjust the drivebelt, by referring to Section 17.

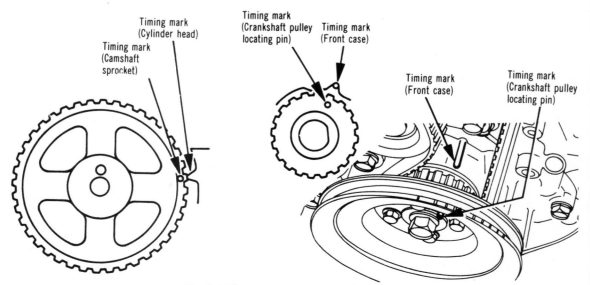

Fig. 1.4 The sprocket timing marks (Sec 4)

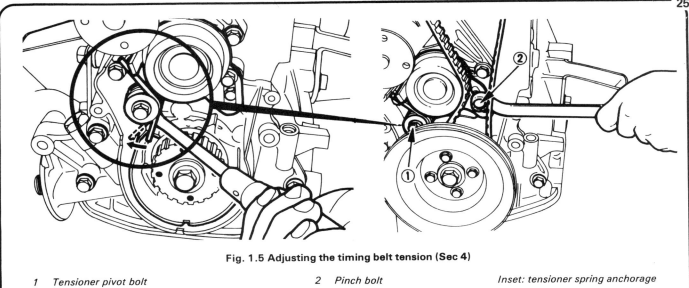

Fig. 1.5 Adjusting the timing belt tension (Sec 4)

1   Tensioner pivot bolt   2   Pinch bolt   Inset: tensioner spring anchorage

4.8 The crankshaft sprocket (TDC) alignment

4.9 The camshaft sprocket alignment

4.14 Timing belt fitted

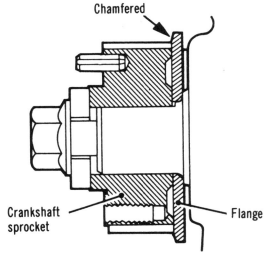

Fig. 1.6 Crankshaft sprocket flange (Sec 4)

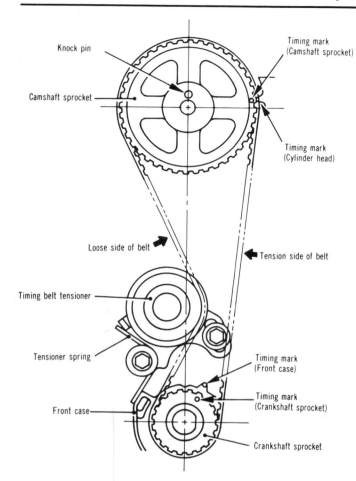

Fig. 1.7 Timing belt tensioning details (Sec 4)

5.5a Method of holding the camshaft to stop it from rotating

5.5b Removing the camshaft sprocket

5.7 The camshaft thrust housing cover plate

5 Camshaft – removal and refitting

1   Remove the breather hose which runs between the rocker cover and the air cleaner casing.

2   Remove the air cleaner.

3   Disconnect the timing belt from the camshaft sprocket by removing the belt cover and releasing the belt tensioner as described in Section 4. There is no need to release the belt from the crankshaft sprocket.

4   Unbolt and remove the rocker cover.

5   Unbolt and remove the camshaft sprocket. Hold the sprocket still to unscrew the bolt by either passing a lever through the spokes of the sprocket or by gripping the square 'nibs' provided for this purpose on the camshaft (photo).

6   Remove the rocker shaft assemblies as described in Section 3.

7   Unbolt and remove the small rectangular cover plate from the rear of the cylinder head (photo).

8   Unscrew and remove the camshaft anchor bolt and thrust casing tightening bolt (photos).

9   Remove the cooling system expansion tank. Withdraw the camshaft and thrust casing from the end of the cylinder head which is nearest the flywheel housing (photo).

10 Refer to Part D of this Chapter for inspection and renovation details.

11 Refitting is a reversal of removal but make sure that the threaded hole in the thrust casing is aligned with the bolt hole in the cylinder head. Refit the timing belt as descrbed in Section 4. Tighten the sprocket bolt to the specified torque (photo).

12 Check and adjust the valve clearances as described in Sections 19 or 20.

5.8a The camshaft anchor bolt

5.8b The camshaft thrust casing bolt

5.9 Removing the camshaft

5.11 Fitting the camshaft thrust casing

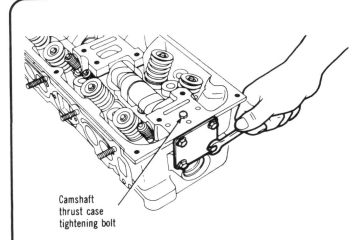

Camshaft
thrust case
tightening bolt

Fig. 1.8 Removing the camshaft cover plate (Sec 5)

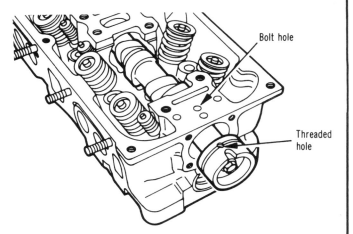

Bolt hole

Threaded
hole

**Fig. 1.9 Fitting the camshaft. Note the thrust casing bolt holes
(Sec 5)**

6.15a Fitting the cylinder head gasket

6.15b Fitting the cylinder head

6.15c Tightening the cylinder head bolts

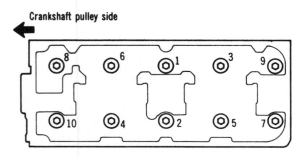
Fig. 1.10 Cylinder head bolt tightening sequence (Sec 6)

Crankshaft pulley side

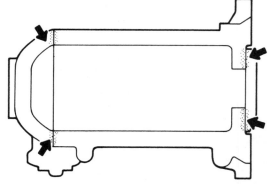
Fig. 1.11 Sealant application areas for sump fitting (Sec 7)

6 Cylinder head – removal and refitting

1 Drain the cooling system as described in Chapter 3.
2 Remove the air cleaner. Disconnect the engine upper stabiliser/damper by unscrewing its forward pivot bolt.
3 Remove the rocker cover.
4 Disconnect the radiator upper hose from the cylinder head.
5 Disconnect the brake servo vacuum hose from the intake manifold.
6 Disconnect the fuel hoses from the carburettor.
7 Disconnect the heater and choke heating hoses.
8 Pull the HT leads from the spark plugs, take off the distributor cap and place it to one side.
9 Disconnect the LT lead and vacuum pipe from the distributor and remove the distributor (see Chapter 4).
10 Unbolt and remove the intake manifold. Pull it away carefully without straining the accelerator control cable and tie the complete assembly with carburettor to the bulkhead.
11 Unbolt the heat collecting cowl and the exhaust manifold. Release the downpipe bracket. Provided the manifold is pulled carefully forward on the flexible mounting of the exhaust system, it will clear the cylinder head and can be wedged or tied back.
12 Release the timing belt from the camshaft sprocket as described in Section 4.
13 Unscrew the cylinder head bolts evenly and progressively by reversing the sequence shown in Fig. 1.10. The bolts are of socket headed type and a hexagon (Allen key) type wrench will be required.
14 For complete dismantling and renovation of the cylinder head, refer to Part D of this Chapter.
15 Refitting is a reversal of the removal operations but make sure that the head and block surfaces are absolutely clean and use a new gasket without jointing compound. Tighten all bolts progressively to the specified torque in the sequence shown in Fig. 1.10. Use new gaskets for the manifolds and apply sealant round the coolant hole in the gasket for the intake manifold (photos).
16 Adjust the valve clearances (Sections 19 or 20) and after refitting the distributor, check the ignition timing (see Chapter 4).

17 The timing belt is refitted as described in Section 4.
18 Fill the cooling system and check that all wires and hoses have been reconnected.

7 Engine sump – removal and refitting

1 Raise the front of the car on ramps or axle stands and drain the engine oil.
2 Unscrew and remove the sump securing bolts.
3 Remove the sump, clean it out and scrape away all old pieces of gasket from the mating flanges.
4 Refitting is a reversal of removal. Use a new gasket but before fitting it, apply sealant to the crankcase flange as shown.
5 Make sure that the drain plug is fully tightened.

8 Engine front casing and oil pump – removal and refitting

1 Remove the timing belt as described in Section 4.
2 Remove the engine oil sump as described in the preceding Section.
3 Peel away and remove the now exposed sump gasket.
4 Unscrew and remove the securing bolts from the front casing and withdraw the casing complete with oil pump, pick-up pipe and filter (photo).
5 Refer to Part D of this Chapter for details of oil pump overhaul and casing oil seal renewal.
6 Refitting is a reversal of the removal procedure.

9 Pistons and connecting rods – removal and refitting

1 Remove the cylinder head as described in Section 6.
2 Remove the engine sump (Section 7) and the oil pick-up pipe and filter screen.

8.4 Removing the front casing with the oil pump

9.4 Making the big-end identification marks

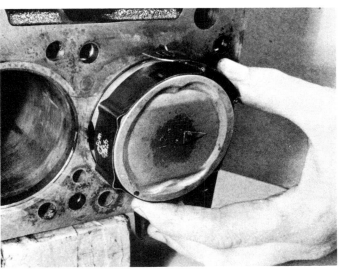
9.11a A piston with ring compressor

9.11b The piston crown directional arrow

9.12 Fitting a piston and connecting rod to the cylinder block

9.13a A connecting rod bearing shell

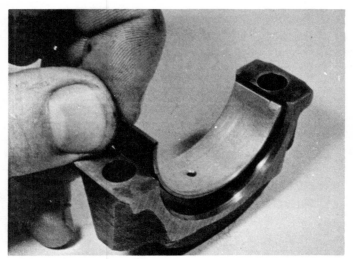
9.13b A connecting rod cap bearing shell

9.13c Tightening a big-end bearing nut

3   Turn the crankshaft until No 1 connecting rod big-end is at its lowest point. This is the one nearest the timing belt end of the engine.
4   Unfortunately, the rods and their caps are not marked and this should be done now by filing a single line across the adjacent surfaces of this first rod and cap joint (photo).
5   Unscrew and remove the big-end cap nuts, tap off the cap and retrieve the shell bearing.
6   Using a piece of wood or a hammer handle, placed against the connecting rod studs, tap the rod/piston out of the top of the block. If by any chance the piston stops abruptly during its upward travel, then this will be due to a wear ring at the top of the cylinder bore. Push the piston down again and very carefully scrape the ring away.
7   Once the assembly is withdrawn, retrieve the shell bearing for the rod. If the bearings are to be used again, tape them to their respective rod or cap.
8   Rotate the crankshaft as necessary to remove the remaining three piston/rod assemblies. Again mark them by filing, two marks for No 2, three marks for No 3 and four marks for No 4. A directional arrow is cast into the piston crown pointing to the timing belt end of the engine so make your file marks on the same side of the rod in each case and note to which side of the crankcase they face then if the piston/rod is dismantled, correct reassembly will be simplified.
9   Refer to Part D of this Chapter for details of piston and cylinder bore examination and renovation and for piston ring, gudgeon pin and connecting rod dismantling.
10 Refitting is a reversal of removal but after having staggered the piston ring end gaps at equidistant points of a circle, a piston ring clamp will have to be fitted and the rings compressed.
11 Insert the connecting rod into the cylinder bore and have the piston ring compressor resting squarely on the top face of the cylinder block. Make sure that the directional arrow on the piston crown points towards the timing belt and that the piston rings and the cylinder bores have been liberally oiled (photo).
12 Apply the wooden handle of a hammer to the piston crown and give the head of the hammer a sharp blow to drive the piston/rod down the bore (photo).
13 Pull the rod complete with bearing shell on to its crankshaft crankpin, fit the big-end cap complete with shell so that the filed lines are adjacent, screw on the nuts and tighten them to the specified torque (photos).
14 Refit the cylinder head and sump.

10 Engine/transmission – method of removal

1   The engine is removed complete with transmission by lifting the assembly up and out of the engine compartment so a suitable hoist or lifting gear will be required.

11.12 The alternator harness connector

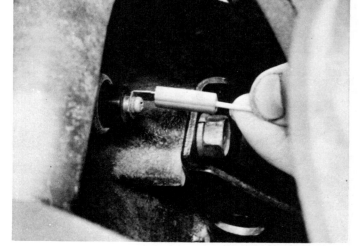
11.13 The oil pressure switch lead

11 Engine/transmission – removal

1 Open the bonnet, mark the position of the hinges on the underside. With the help of an assistant, unbolt the hinges, release the support strut retaining clip and lift the bonnet away to a safe place where it will not be damaged.

2 Disconnect the battery and then remove it from the engine compartment.

3 Drain the engine oil.

4 Drain the transmission oil.

5 Drain the coolant as described in Chapter 2, retaining it for further use if it contains fresh antifreeze.

6 Remove the engine undershield by unscrewing its retaining bolts.

7 Working within the engine compartment, remove the air cleaner.

8 Remove the radiator/electric fan. To reach the mounting bolts, the air grille will first have to be withdrawn after extracting its securing screws.

9 Disconnect the coil HT lead.

10 Disconnect the LT lead from the distributor.

11 Release the distributor cap spring retaining clips, pull the leads from the spark plugs and remove the cap. The lead outlets on the distributor cap are marked with the spark plug connecting numbers, No 1 plug being nearest the timing belt.

12 Disconnect the leads from the rear of the alternator. This is done at at the connector plug located behind the radiator grille blanking panel (photo).

13 Disconnect the oil pressure switch lead (photo).

14 Disconnect the wiring harness at the side of the battery support tray. A connector plug is used for this and incorporates the coolant temperature lead so the lead need not be further disconnected from the actual switch which is screwed into the underside of the intake manifold and is itself coolant heated (photo).

15 Disconnect the accelerator cable from the operating arm on the carburettor (photo).

16 Disconnect the brake servo vacuum pipe from the intake manifold.

17 Disconnect the heater hoses.

18 Disconnect the fuel flexible hose which runs between the rear bulkhead mounted fuel filter and the fuel pump.

19 Disconnect the fuel flow and return flexible hoses from the carburettor.

20 Disconnect the electrical leads from the fuel anti-run on solenoid valve on the carburettor, the washer pump harness and the reverse lamp switch (photos).

21 Disconnect the earth lead which runs between the transmission casing and bodyframe, also release the speedometer cable from the transmission casing.

22 Disconnect the clutch operating cable from the release lever on the clutch bellhousing. To do this, pull out the split pin and then the clevis pin.

23 Loosen the two bolts on the engine upper stabiliser/damper rod then disconnect the engine end of the rod. Push the rod up out of the way against the bulkhead.

24 Working underneath the car, disconnect the exhaust downpipe from the manifold joint and release the downpipe clip. Cut the locking wire which secures the pinch bolt at the coupling on the front end of the gearchange remote control rod. Unscrew the bolt and separate the coupling by pulling the remote control rod to the rear (refer to Chapter 6).

25 Disconnect the power/economy selector cable. To do this, two cable retaining brackets will have to be unbolted from the transmission casing and the circlip extracted from the clevis pin which retains the cable to the operating lever on the transmission. Once the cable retaining brackets are unbolted, it will be found that the gearchange stabiliser rod is also released as it is secured by one of these brackets.

26 Disconnect the earth strap from the rear face of the engine crankcase.

27 Disconnect the lower front engine stabiliser/damper rod from the crankcase by removing its pivot bolt.

28 Again working on the top of the engine, attach a suitable hoist to the two lifting eyes provided on the engine. These are so positioned to give the correct balance to the engine/transmission when the mountings are released. Take the weight of the engine but do not lift it.

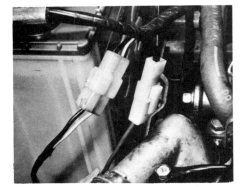

11.14 The engine harness connector plugs

11.15 A throttle cable clip

11.20a The fuel anti-run on valve lead

11.20b The washer pump lead connectors

11.20c The reverse lamp switch leads

11.31 Releasing the driveshaft from the transmission

29 Unscrew and remove the nut which connects the flexible mounting to the transmission bracket on the right-hand end of the transmission casing.

30 Unscrew and remove the nuts which connect the remaining two engine flexible mountings to their crankcase brackets.

31 Insert the blade of a strong screwdriver between the driveshaft and the transmission casing. Prise the shaft outward to release it by overcoming the resistance of its circlip (photo).

32 Raise the hoist slowly until the engine/transmission just clears the mounting studs. Now push the unit towards the left-hand side of the car as far as it will go and disconnect the right-hand driveshaft from the transmission. If it will not quite come out, raise the engine hoist slightly.

33 Gently swivel the engine/transmission diagonally across the engine compartment and push the transmission into the right-hand front corner until the left-hand driveshaft can be disconnected.

34 Raise the hoist and lift the engine/transmission out of the engine compartment.

12 Engine/transmission – separation

1 With the engine/transmission removed from the car and placed securely on the floor or a bench, now is a good time to clean away dirt and grease from the external surfaces by using a water soluble solvent or paraffin and a stiff brush.

2 With this done, support the engine oil sump on pieces of wood so that the transmission is not in contact with the floor.

3 Unscrew and remove all the clutch bellhousing bolts. As some of these are withdrawn from the lower part of the bellhousing, the starter motor and the lower cover plate will be released and they can be removed.

4 Take the weight of the transmission and draw it from the engine crankcase in a straight line.

13 Engine – complete dismantling

1 These operations describe complete dismantling of the engine for overhaul. If wear or damage is not evident in the crankshaft or flywheel components then the necessary work may be carried out with the engine in the car as described in Sections 3 to 9 of this Chapter.

2 Mark the relationship of the clutch cover to the flywheel (manual gearbox models) and then unbolt it and remove it, catching the driven plate which is sandwiched between the pressure plate and the flywheel.

3 As the distributor driven gear and the body have alignment marks (see Chapter 4) there is no need to mark the relative position of the rotor to the distributor body or the body to the cylinder head before withdrawing the unit.

4 Disconnect the distributor vacuum pipe and then release the

clamp bolt and remove the distributor (photo).

5 Unbolt and remove the intake manifold. As the manifold is withdrawn, disconnect the flexible fuel pipe which runs between the carburettor and the fuel pump, also the lead from the anti-run on valve of the carburettor.

6 Unbolt and remove the hot air collecting shroud and the exhaust manifold.

7 Withdraw the engine oil dipstick.

8 Release the alternator mounting pivot bolt and the adjuster link bolt, push the alternator in towards the engine and slip the drivebelt from the pulleys. Remove the alternator.

9 Unbolt and remove the fuel pump and catch the operating rod as it slips out of its hole in the cylinder head.

10 Unbolt the coolant distribution pipe and pull it from its O-ring sealed socket in the water pump housing (photo).

11 Unbolt and remove the pulley from the water pump. On 1597 cc engines a pulley and fan blades are fitted.

12 Unscrew the bolts and remove the timing belt cover.

13 Unscrew the timing belt tensioner pivot mounting and pinch bolts, push the tensioner away from the belt to remove the tension and retighten the pinch bolt.

14 Unscrew the crankshaft pulley centre bolt. To do this, the starter ring gear teeth on the flywheel will have to be jammed with a suitable lever to prevent the crankshaft turning. Once the bolt is removed, pull off the pulley complete with sprocket which is attached by means of a roll pin. Do not rotate the camshaft sprocket from this point onward.

15 Remove the timing belt, noting and marking its direction of normal rotation if it is to be used again. Remove the tensioner/spring assembly.

16 Take off the timing belt thrust washer from the front end of the crankshaft.

17 Unbolt and remove the water pump noting that the adjuster link for the alternator is located under its left-hand bolt.

18 Unscrew, remove and discard the oil filter. If it is stuck tight, use a filter strap wrench or if all else fails, drive a large screwdriver through the filter fairly near its sealed end so that it emerges from the other side and use this as a lever to unscrew it.

19 Unscrew the cylinder head socket headed bolts using a hexagon wrench (Allen key). Release the bolts evenly in the reverse order to that shown for tightening in Fig. 1.10.

20 Once the bolts are removed, if the head is stuck, use a piece of hardwood and a hammer to tap it upward. Place the wood under the projections provided, never try inserting a blade or lever in the gasket joint.

21 With the cylinder head removed, peel away and discard the old gasket.

22 To dismantle the cylinder head, remove the rocker gear by extracting the shaft bolts.

23 Remove the camshaft sprocket bolt by holding the sprocket with a lever passed through the sprocket spokes and then remove it from the camshaft.

13.4 The distributor vacuum pipe at the carburettor

13.10 The coolant distribution pipe and O-ring

13.27a Removing the engine mounting bracket bolts

13.27b Removing an engine mounting bracket bolt

13.29 Removing the oil sump bolts

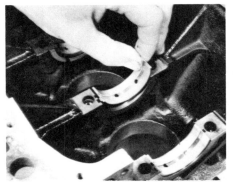

15.2a Fitting the main bearing shell to crankcase

15.2b The centre main bearing shell with thrust flanges

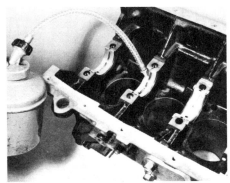

15.3a Lubricating the main bearing shells

24 Unbolt and remove the rectangular plate from the end of the cylinder head.

25 Unscrew the camshaft thrust casing tightening bolt and the camshaft anchor bolt, then withdraw the camshaft and the thrust casing from the cylinder head end face opposite to the camshaft sprocket.

26 Removal of the valve gear is covered in Section 62 of Part D, in conjunction with decarbonising.

27 Although not absolutely essential, it is best to unbolt the mounting brackets from the crankcase, especially if the engine is to be sent away for reboring or other work (photos).

28 Unbolt and remove the flywheel. Jam the starter ring gear on the flywheel to prevent it turning while the bolts are unscrewed.

29 Remove the securing bolts and withdraw the oil sump (photo).

30 Unbolt and remove the engine front casing complete with oil pump and oil pick-up pipe.

31 Unbolt the engine rear plate.

32 Remove the crankshaft rear oil seal retainer and plate.

33 Remove the piston/connecting rods by referring to Section 9, paragraphs 3 to 8.

34 The crankshaft main bearing caps are numbered 1 to 5 and incorporate a cast arrow pointing towards the timing belt end of the engine. Unscrew and remove the main bearing cap bolts, tap off the caps and keep their shell bearings tapered to the cap. Note that the centre bearing shell incorporates thrust flanges.

35 Lift the crankshaft from the crankcase and pick out the bearing shells. Keep these also with their respective caps.

36 With the engine now completely dismantled refer to Part D for examination and renovation procedure.

14 Engine reassembly – general

1 Before commencing reassembly, gather together the necessary tools, gaskets and other small items.

2 Observe absolute cleanliness during reassembly and lubricate each component before fitting with clean engine oil.

3 Do not use unnecessary force to fit a part but recheck clearances and tolerances where difficulties are encountered.

4 Tighten all nuts and bolts to the specified torque wrench settings.

15 Crankshaft and main bearings – refitting

1 Wipe out the bearing seats in the crankcase and the main bearing caps. Dirt left here will cause the bearing shell to bind on the crankshaft when it is fitted.

2 Fit the shells into the crankcase seats with the flanged shell at the centre position. If the old shells are being used again, make sure that they are returned to their original locations (photos).

3 Oil the bearing shells liberally and lower the crankshaft carefully into place (photo).

4 Fit the bearing shells into their caps and fit the caps in the correct numbered sequence with their cast arrows pointing towards the timing belt end of the engine (photos).

5 Tighten the cap bolts progressively, in stages, to the specified torque, working from the centre cap towards each end of the crankshaft (photo).

6 Check that the crankshaft turns smoothly and then using feeler blades, check the crankshaft endfloat. Do this by inserting the blades between the centre bearing shell flange and the thrust face of the crankpin, pushing the crankshaft first in one direction and then in the other to make sure that maximum endfloat has been obtained. If the endfloat is outside the specified tolerance it will be due to wear in the bearing shell flanges and is unlikely to occur if the shells have been renewed (photos).

7 Renew the crankshaft rear oil seal as a matter of routine. Remove the oil seal and fit the new one using a piece of tubing. Oil the seal lips and using a new gasket, bolt the seal retainer with support plate, into position (photo).

15.3b Fitting the crankshaft

15.4a The main bearing cap shell

15.4b The centre main bearing cap shell with thrust flanges

15.4c Fitting the front main bearing cap

15.5 Tightening a main bearing cap bolt

15.6 Testing for crankshaft endfloat

15.7a The crankshaft rear oil seal and retainer

15.7b Fitting the crankshaft rear oil seal

16.3a Fitting the flywheel

16.3b Method of jamming the flywheel starter ring gear

16.3c Tightening the flywheel bolts

17.9 The rocker gear correctly fitted

16 Flywheel — refitting

1   Refit the engine plate to the rear of the cylinder block.
2   Offer the flywheel to the crankshaft mounting flange so that the bolt holes line up.
3   Screw in the bolts and tighten them to the specified torque. Jam the starter ring gear if necessary to prevent the flywhel from turning (photos).

17 Engine — complete rebuilding

1   With the crankshaft and flywheel fitted, building up the rest of the engine is now as described in earlier Sections of this Chapter for 'in situ' overhaul.
2   The following reassembly sequence is recommended.
3   Always use new gaskets and tighten nuts and bolts to specified torque.
4   Fit the piston/connecting rods (Section 9).
5   Fit the front casing/oil pump complete with oil pick-up pipe (Section 8).
6   Fit the engine oil sump (Section 7).
7   Fit the cylinder head (Section 6).

17.10 Tightening the crankshaft sprocket bolt

17.11 Fitting the crankshaft pulley

17.13a Fitting the timing belt cover

17.13b Fitting the water pump pulley

17.16 Adjusting the drivebelt tension

8   Fit the camshaft (Section 5) and its sprocket, then refit the camshaft end plate.

9   Refit the rocker gear (photo).

10 Push the thrust washer and belt sprocket onto the crankshaft and fit and tension the timing belt (Section 4) (photo).

11 Fit the crankshaft pulley and tighten the four bolts to the specified torque (photo).

12 Fit the water pump.

13 Fit the timing belt cover and fit the pulley to the water pump flange (photos).

14 Refit the coolant distribution pipe using a new O-ring seal at its entry into the water pump.

15 Fit the fuel pump and its operating rod using new gaskets.

16 Fit the alternator loosely to its pivot mounting and connect the adjuster link. Slip the drivebelt round the crankshaft, water pump and alternator pulleys. Pull the alternator away from the cylinder block until when the adjuster link bolt is tightened, there is a total deflection at the centre point of the longest run of the belt of 0.4 in (10.0 mm) (photo).

17 Fit the exhaust manifold using new gaskets and connect the hot air collecting shroud.

18 Fit the intake manifold/carburettor using new gaskets (photo).

19 Refit the distributor (refer to Chapter 4). Provided No 1 piston is at TDC on its compression stroke, this is simply a matter of pushing the distributor into its recess so that the rotor and body alignment marks made during manufacture are lined up. A certain amount of trial and error may be required due to the fact that the rotor turns about 40 degrees as the unit is pushed into position. This must be anticipated by positioning the rotor in such a way to allow for this anti-clockwise rotation. On cars destined for operation in California, an electronic (breakerless) ignition system is used but this does not affect the method of refitting the distributor.

20 Refit the clutch, centralising the driven plate as described in Chapter 5.

21 Adjust the valve clearances as described in Section 19 or 20.

22 Refit the rocker cover using a new gasket (photo).

23 If the engine mounting brackets were removed from the crankcase, bolt them back into position.

24 If not already fitted, the engine rear plate should now be installed (photo).

18 Engine/transmission – reconnection

1   With the engine reassembled, support it in an upright position.

2   If not already done the clutch will have to be centralised and refitted to the flywheel (see Chapter 5).

17.18a Fitting the intake manifold

17.18b Tightening the intake manifold bolts

17.22 Fitting the rocker cover

17.24 Fitting the engine rear plate

18.3 Reconnecting the engine/transmission

18.4 Fitting the starter motor

3   Lift the transmission and connect it to the engine by passing the input shaft through the splined hub of the clutch driven plate. If there is any difficulty in engaging, have an assistant turn the crankshaft pulley slightly to re-align the splines on hub and shaft (photo).
4   Once the transmission has engaged the dowels on the crankcase, insert one or two upper bolts to take the strain and then locate the starter motor and bellhousing lower cover plate after which the remaining bolts can be screwed in and tightened to specified torque (photo).

19 Valve clearance – adjustment (except North America)

1   Where the clearances have to be set cold as a means of starting the engine after major overhaul the following procedure applies but they should be checked and adjusted again as soon as the engine reaches the normal operating temperature. Normal service checking and adjusting should be carried out with the engine at the normal operating temperature.
2   Remove the air cleaner, disconnect the breather hose and unbolt and remove the rocker cover.
3   One of two methods can be used to check and adjust the valve clearances.

Method A

4   Using a ring spanner on the centre bolt of the crankshaft pulley rotate the crankshaft until the rocker arms for No 1 cylinder are seen to be just 'rocking' – (one arm going down as the other one is just coming up) indicating that the inlet valve is opening and the exhaust valve is closing.
5   Insert the appropriate feeler blades between the face of No 4 rocker arm screws and the end of the valve stems, remembering that the exhaust and inlet clearances are different (photo).
6   The feeler blade should be a stiff sliding fit. If it is not, release the adjuster screw locknut and turn the screw. Once the correct adjustment has been achieved, tighten the locknut without altering the position of the screw.
7   Turn the crankshaft and with each pair of rocker arms in sequence, check and adjust the remaining valves.

Rocker arms rocking	Valves to adjust
No 1 cylinder	No 4 cylinder
No 2 cylinder	No 3 cylinder
No 3 cylinder	No 2 cylinder
No 4 cylinder	No 1 cylinder

Method B

8   Using a ring spanner on the crankshaft pulley centre bolt set No 1 piston at TDC on its compression stroke. This can be verified by observing that the two valves for this cylinder are closed.

19.5 Adjusting the valve clearance

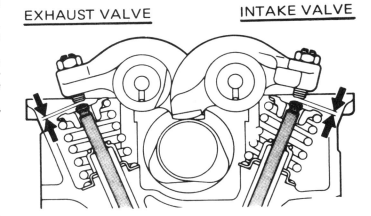

EXHAUST VALVE   INTAKE VALVE

Fig. 1.12 The valves correctly positioned prior to the clearances being checked (Sec 19)

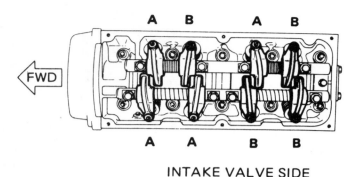

INTAKE VALVE SIDE

Fig. 1.13 Inlet and exhaust valve arrangement (Sec 19)

For key to A and B see text

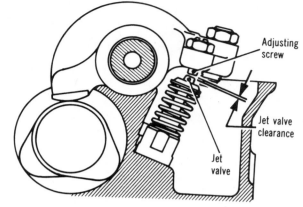

Fig. 1.14 Jet valve clearance (North American models) (Sec 20)

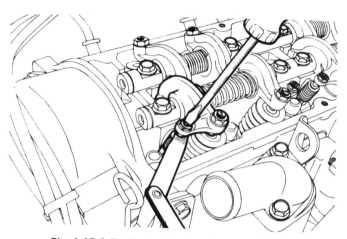

9   The valves marked A in the figure 1.13 can now be checked and adjusted in exactly the same way as described in paragraphs 5 and 6.
10   Now rotate the crankshaft through one full turn and check the clearances of valves marked B.
11   Check that all the locknuts have been tightened, refit the rocker cover and air cleaner and make sure that you have removed the ring spanner from the crankshaft pulley bolt.

20 Valve clearance – adjustment (North America)

1   On emission controlled vehicles (see Section 24 of this Chapter and also see Chapter 3) the intake rocker arms incorporate dual valve clearance adjusting screws. The extra one being for the jet valves.
2   On engines fitted with these devices, always check and adjust the jet valves before the intake valves.
3   Follow one of the methods described in the preceding Section to bring the intake valves into position for checking their clearances. Release the locknut and unscrew the adjuster screw which controls the intake valve clearance on the first rocker arm which is to be tackled. Unscrew it at least two turns to ensure that the jet valve can be adjusted without the presence of any overriding influence from the intake valve adjustment.
4   Release the locknut on the jet valve adjuster screw and use a feeler blade to set the gap between the end of the screw and the valve stem. Retighten the locknut without moving the position of the screw.
5   Set the intake valve clearance on this arm in the normal way and then repeat the operations on the remaining valve rocker arms, turning the crankshaft as necessary to bring the intake valves into their correct clearance checking positions. Set the exhaust valve clearances at the same time.
6   It will be appreciated that with the additional adjustments required on these emission controlled engines, you will have to work fast if the engine is not to cool down and spoil the accuracy of the setting.
7   Incorrect setting of the jet valve clearances will cause misfiring, poor performance and an incorrect exhaust gas CO content.

Fig. 1.15 Adjusting a jet valve clearance (Sec 20)

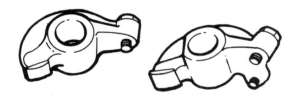

Fig. 1.16 Rocker arms with and without jet adjuster screws (Sec 20)

21 Oil filter – renewal

1   Using an oil filter wrench or small chain wrench unscrew the oil filter which is of sealed cartridge type. Be prepared for some loss of oil as the filter is withdrawn from the crankcase.
2   Lightly smear the rubber sealing ring of the new filter with oil and screw it into position as tightly as possible using only the hands, never a tool of any kind (photo).
3   When the engine is first started, it will take a few seconds for the oil pressure warning lamp to go out as the filter casing fills with oil. This is normal. A new filter absorbs about one pint (0.57 litre) of oil so make allowance for this when filling up with oil.

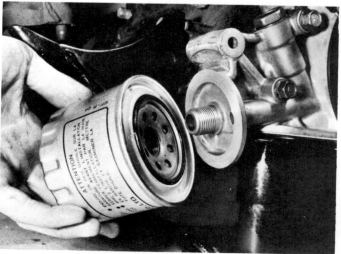

21.2 Fitting the oil filter cartridge

22 Engine/transmission – refitting

1 With the engine/transmission ready for refitting, connect the hoist to the lifting eyes and raise the unit over the engine compartment (photo).
2 Lower it carefully until the end of the transmission is tucked into the right-hand front corner. Engage the left-hand driveshaft with the transmission (photo).
3 Now push the engine/transmission as far to the left-hand side of the engine compartment as it will go and engage the right-hand driveshaft with the transmission. The engine/transmission may require lowering slightly to facilitate this.
4 Lower the engine/transmission onto the flexible mountings and screw on the retaining nuts. Note the heat shield on the front mounting (photo).
5 Connect the bracket at the transmission end mounting. Remove the hoist.

6 Connect the lower front engine stabiliser/damper (photos).
7 Grip each inboard driveshaft joint and push it towards the transmission to lock the retaining circlip. If sufficient force cannot be applied with the hand, fit a worm drive clip around the metal cover of the joint and use this as a striking point to drive the shaft inwards. On no account attempt to hammer on the flexible gaiter, you will only damage the joint and split the gaiter (photo).
8 Still working under the car, connect the earth strap to the rear face of the crankcase. Connect the Power/Economy selector cable and the gearchange selector rod.
9 Reconnect the exhaust downpipe flange and clip.
10 Now turn your attention to the top of the engine and reconnect the engine top stabiliser/damper rod (photo).
11 Reconnect the clutch cable and adjust it if necessary as described in Chapter 5 (photo).
12 Connect the earth lead between the transmission casing and the bodyframe.

22.1 Lowering the engine/transmission into position

22.2 The engine positioned for connecting the left-hand driveshaft

22.4a The engine rear mounting

22.4b The engine front mounting with heat shield

22.6a The engine lower front stabiliser bracket

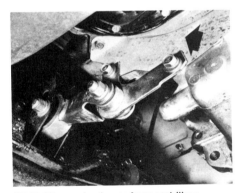

22.6b The engine lower front stabiliser connected note flywheel housing cover plate (arrowed)

22.7 Connecting a driveshaft to the transmission

22.10 The engine upper stabiliser/damper

22.11 The clutch cable connection to the release lever

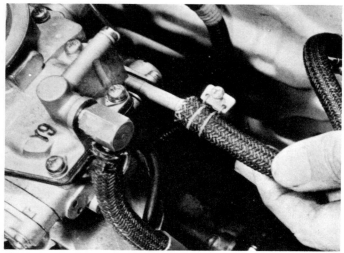

22.14 Fitting a fuel hose to the carburettor

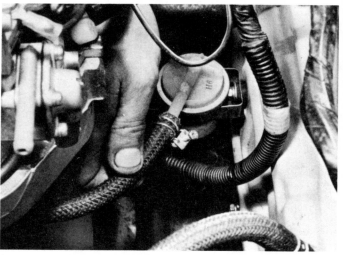

22.15 Fitting a fuel hose to the filter

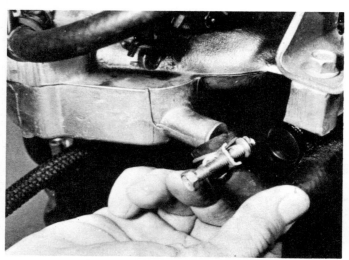

22.16 Connecting a heater hose

22.17 Brake servo vacuum hose (arrowed)

13 Connect the lead to the solenoid and anti-run on valve on the carburettor.
14 Connect the fuel flow and return hoses to the carburettor (photo).
15 Connect the fuel pipe between the bulkhead filter and the fuel pump (photo).
16 Reconnect the heater hoses (photo).
17 Reconnect the brake servo vacuum hose to the intake manifold and the vacuum pipe to the distributor.
18 Connect the accelerator cable to the carburettor.
19 Reconnect the wiring harness at the side of the battery tray.
20 Connect the lead to the oil pressure switch.
21 Reconnect the alternator leads.
22 Fit the distributor cap, reconnect the coil and spark plug leads.
23 Fit the radiator/electric fan followed by the radiator grille.
24 Fit the air cleaner and connect the breather hose.
25 A new oil filter should now be screwed into position. Earlier fitting is not recommended due to the possibility of damage occurring to it during engine installation. Fit the filter as described in Section 21.
26 Refit the engine undershield (photo).
27 Fit the battery and attach the connecting leads.
28 Fill the cooling system.
29 Fill the sump with engine oil.
30 Fill the transmission with the correct grade and quantity of oil.
31 Check for electrical leads and pipes and hoses which may have

22.26 The engine undershield

been overlooked and left disconnected. Check that all tools and rags have been removed.

32 With the help of an assistant, refit the bonnet.

23 Initial start-up after major overhaul

1 Turn the engine idle speed screw in about one $\frac{1}{2}$ turn more than normal to ensure that the engine will have a faster than normal idle speed during the first few hundred miles to offset the stiffness of new components.

2 Start the engine. This may take a little longer than usual due to the need for the fuel pump and carburettor bowl to fill.

3 As soon as the engine starts, let it run at a fast idle speed as set by the automatic choke.

4 Now check the engine for leaks. Any oil will probably be burning off the exhaust where it was handled during overhaul and need not cause alarm.

5 Run the engine on the road until it reaches normal operating temperature and then check the valve clearances and adjust.

6 Check and adjust the ignition timing (Chapter 4).

7 Where the engine bearings or components (pistons, rings etc) have been renewed then the operating speed should be restricted for the first 500 miles (800 km) and the engine oil changed at the end of this period.

8 After the first 1000 miles (1600 km) check the cylinder head bolt torque wrench settings (cold) and then check and adjust the valve clearances (hot).

24 Emission control and overhaul operations (North American models)

1 Apart from a temperature controlled air cleaner and the inclusion of a crankcase ventilation hose fitted between the engine rocker cover and the air cleaner on all models, emission control systems only complicate the engine overhaul operations on vehicles prepared for operation in North America. On Canadian specifications, some of the more involved devices are not insisted upon.

2 Reference should be made to Chapter 3 for complete details of the systems used but the following summary will indicate how the individual system affects the particular engine overhaul operation.

3 *Fuel evaporative emission control system.* Extra hoses to be disconnected from air cleaner.

4 *Catalytic converter.* Incorporated below the exhaust manifold.

5 *Secondary air supply system.* Reed valve and connecting hoses require disconnection from the exhaust manifold and air cleaner.

6 *Exhaust gas recirculation system.* Valves and connecting hoses require disconnection between the intake and exhaust manifolds.

7 *The carburettor* is modified to incorporate a coasting air valve, an air switching valve and a throttle valve closure delay dashpot.

8 *The ignition system* is of electronic type for California only.

Part B 1597 cc (97.5 cu in) engine without silent shaft

25 General description

The engine is very similar to the smaller 1410 cc (86 cu in) unit described in Part A of this Chapter to which reference should be made, but the following differences must be noted.

The camshaft is supported in five bearings and is driven through a toothed belt from the front end of the crankshaft. An eccentric cam on the front end of the camshaft drives the fluid pump while a gear at the same end drives the distributor.

The oil pump is of the trochoid type mounted on the timing belt end of the engine and driven by the belt through the sprocket.

Additional engine cooling is provided by an engine driven fan, the blades being mounted on the water pump pulley.

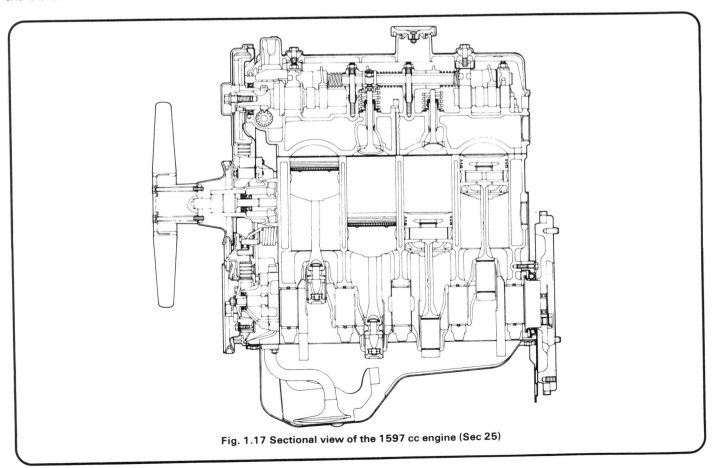

Fig. 1.17 Sectional view of the 1597 cc engine (Sec 25)

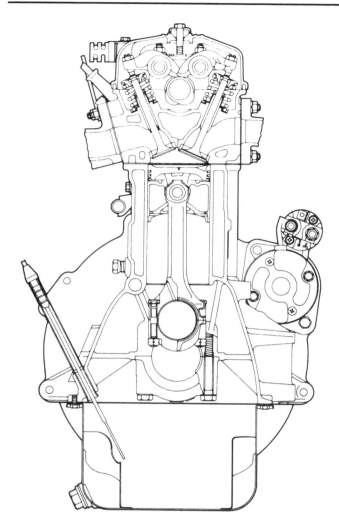

Fig. 1.18 Sectional view of the 1597 cc engine (Sec 25)

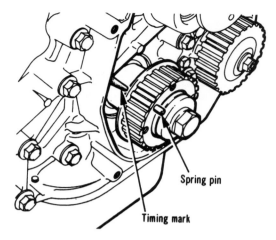

Fig. 1.19 Crankshaft sprocket timing mark alignment (Sec 28)

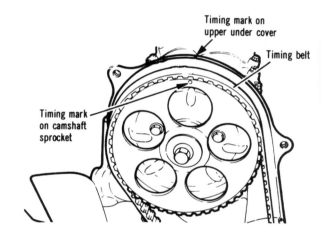

Fig. 1.20 Camshaft sprocket timing mark alignment (Sec 28)

26 Major operations possible with engine in car

1   These are identical with those listed in Section 2 of Part A of this Chapter.

27 Rocker gear – removal and refitting

1   Refer to Section 3, Part A of this Chapter.

28 Timing belt – renewal

1   Release the alternator mounting and adjuster link bolts, push the alternator in towards the engine and slip the drivebelt from the pulleys.
2   Unscrew the four small bolts and remove the crankshaft pulley. Unbolt and remove the water pump pulley and fan blades.
3   Remove the upper and lower sections of the timing belt cover.
4   Apply a ring spanner to the crankshaft sprocket bolt and turn the crankshaft until No 1 piston is at TDC on its compression stroke. This will be indicated when the roll pin in the crankshaft sprocket is aligned with the mark cast into the engine front casing and the dimple on the camshaft sprocket is at its highest point and in alignment with the mark on the belt cover backing plate.
5   Release the belt tensioner mounting pivot bolt and pinch nut, push the tensioner against the tension of the spring and tighten the pinch nut.

6   With the tension released, the timing belt can be slid from the sprockets but not before its running direction has been marked so that it can be refitted the same way round.
7   To fit a belt, first check that the crankshaft sprocket and camshaft marks are as originally aligned.
8   Engage the belt first with the crankshaft sprocket then round the oil pump sprocket and finally round the camshaft sprocket. Keep the belt taut between the crankshaft and camshaft pulleys as it goes round the oil pump sprocket.
9   Release the belt tensioner so that it applies tension to the belt. Gently push the tensioner against the tension of its spring. This will settle the belt teeth positively in mesh with the sprocket grooves. Release the tensioner and tighten the pinch nut followed by the mounting bolt.
10 Fit the crankshaft pulley for the purpose of retaining the belt on the sprocket as the crankshaft is turned in the next operation.
11 Apply the spanner to the crankshaft pulley centre bolt and turn the crankshaft one complete turn, smoothly, in the normal engine running direction.
12 Release the tensioner bolt and nut then retighten the nut followed by the bolt in that order. The bolt should now be correctly tensioned. This can be checked using pressure from the thumb as shown. With pressure exerted, the distance between the belt and the joint of the belt cover and backing plate should be 0.47 in (12.0 mm).
13 Remove the crankshaft pulley again so that the belt cover can be fitted, fit the pulley again. Fit the water pump pulley and fan blades.
14 Fit the drivebelt and tension it as described in Section 17 of Part A of this Chapter.

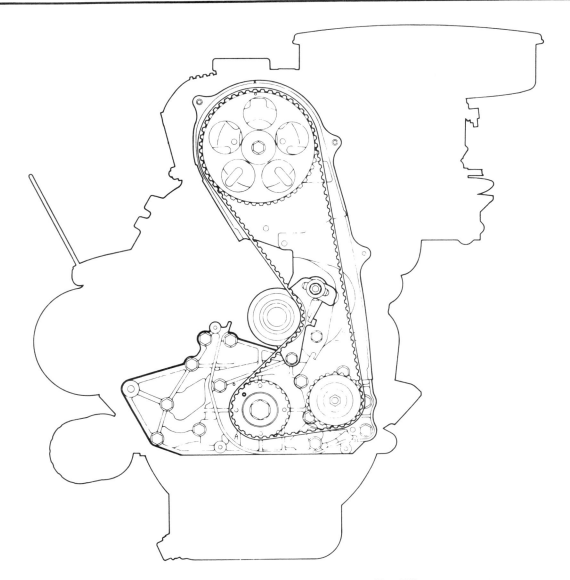

Fig. 1.21 The timing belt configuration (Sec 28)

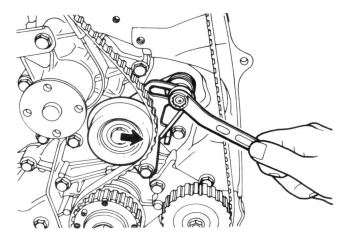

Fig. 1.22 Adjusting the timing belt tension (Sec 28)

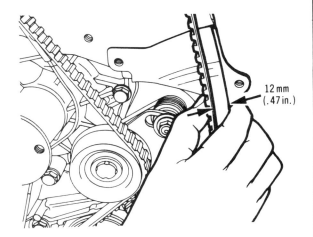

12 mm
(.47 in.)

Fig. 1.23 Checking the timing belt tension (Sec 28)

29 Camshaft – removal and refitting

1 Detach the breather and purge hoses and remove the air cleaner.
2 Pull the leads from the spark plugs.
3 Remove the upper section of the timing belt cover. Remove the alternator drivebelt.
4 Remove the rocker cover.
5 Using a ring spanner on the crankshaft pulley centre bolt, turn the crankshaft until No 1 piston is at TDC on its compression stroke. This can be verified in one of three ways. Either check that the dimple in the camshaft sprocket is in alignment with the mark on the timing belt cover backing plate, that both valves for No 1 cylinder are closed or by removing the distributor cap, observe whether the rotor is pointing to No 1 spark plug lead contact position in the cap and the notch in the crankshaft pulley is opposite the TDC mark on the scale. Mark the belt in relation to the camshaft sprocket dimple in case the belt slips round the sprocket.
6 Unscrew and remove the camshaft sprocket bolt and lift the sprocket from the camshaft keeping the timing belt taut. A sprocket holder is built into the lower section of the belt cover but if there is excessive clearance between the bottom of the sprocket and the holder, it will allow the timing belt to slip off the crankshaft and oil pump sprockets and complicate the procedure by adding all the belt renewal operations described in the preceding Section. To overcome any excessive clearance, pack the bottom of the sprocket with a strip of rubber.
7 Remove the camshaft spacer.
8 Extract the three securing bolts and remove the belt cover backing plate upper section.
9 Remove the camshaft bearing cap bolts and then lift away the rocker gear and the bearing caps as a complete assembly.
10 Remove the oil seal and the distributor drivegear from the camshaft.
11 Lift the camshaft from the cylinder head. There is no need to remove the fuel pump as its operating lever will be depressed when the camshaft is refitted.
12 Refer to Part D of this Chapter for inspection and renovation details.
13 To refit the camshaft, first oil the bearing surfaces and cam lobes and then lower it into its bearings seats so that the Woodruff key at its front end is at the 2 o'clock position.
14 Push the distributor drivegear onto the front end of the camshaft so that when it is engaged with the gear on the distributor shaft, the distributor rotor still aligns with No 1 spark plug contact in the distributor cap. This assumes that the crankshaft has not been disturbed from its TDC setting.
15 Lower the rocker gear/bearing cap assembly into position, screw in the cap bolts and tighten them in stages to the specified torque working from the centre ones towards each end.
16 Oil the lips of a new oil seal and tap it into position on the front end of the camshaft. Do not drive the seal in too far but enough to allow the camshaft spacer to pass through it and contact the distributor drivegear but at the same time not permitting the larger diameter step of the spacer to rub on the front face of the seal.
17 Fit the timing belt upper cover backing plate.
18 Oil the camshaft spacer and push it into position.
19 Grip the camshaft sprocket and pull it upward keeping the belt taut and locate it on the camshaft mounting flange. Any fractional adjustment to the camshaft position to enable the sprocket to engage with the dowel pin may be made by placing a screwdriver against the projecting cubes on the camshaft and tapping the handle sharply.
20 Tighten the sprocket bolt to the specified torque.
21 Make sure that you have removed the temporary packing piece, if fitted from the sprocket holder and then fit the belt cover upper section and spark plug cable clips. Reconnect the spark plug leads.
22 Refit the rocker cover and air cleaner, start the engine and bring it to normal operating temperature.
23 Check the valve clearances (hot) and adjust as described in Section 19 or 20, Part A of this Chapter.
24 Refit the rocker cover using a new gasket with sealant applied at the points indicated (Fig 1.29).

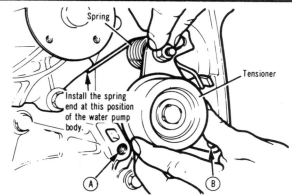

Fig. 1.24 The timing belt tensioner spring anchorage points (Sec 29)

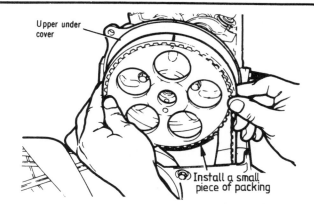

Fig. 1.25 Resting camshaft sprocket on sprocket holder (Sec 29)

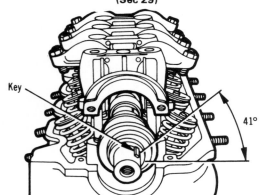

Fig. 1.26 Fitting the camshaft (Sec 29)

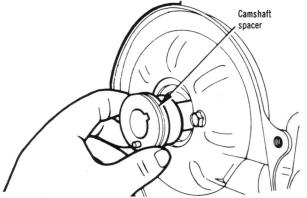

Fig. 1.27 Fitting the camshaft spacer (Sec 29)

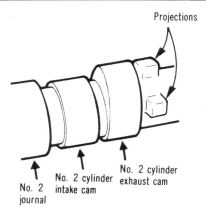

Fig. 1.28 Projections for turning the camshaft (Sec 29)

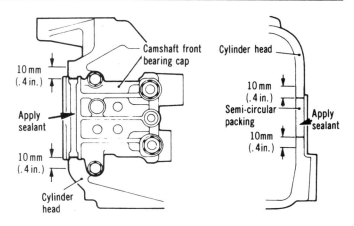

Fig. 1.29 Rocker cover sealant application points (Sec 29)

30 Cylinder head – removal and refitting

1   The operations are similar to those described in Section 6, Part A of this manual up to and including paragraph 9, then carry out the following procedure.
2   Unbolt and remove the intake manifold complete with carburettor.
3   Unbolt and remove the exhaust manifold.
4   Remove the upper section of the timing belt cover.
5   Unbolt and remove the fuel pump from the cylinder head.
6   Remove the timing belt and camshaft sprocket to the sprocket holder as described in Section 29, Paragraph 5 and 6.
7   Remove the timing belt cover upper section backing plate.
8   Remove the rocker cover.
9   Unscrew the socket headed type cylinder head bolts in the reverse sequence to that for tightening. A hexagonal type (Allen key) bit will be required for these bolts, which should be loosened progressively in stages.
10 Lift the cylinder head from the block. Do not attempt to tap the head sideways at it is located on dowels and must be removed directly upwards.
11 For complete dismantling and renovation of the cylinder head, refer to Part D of this Chapter.
12 Refitting is a reversal of the removal operations but make sure that the head and block surfaces are absolutely clean and use a new gasket without any jointing compound.
13 Tighten all bolts progressively to the specified torque in the sequence shown (Fig 1.30). Use new gaskets for the manifolds and apply sealant around the coolant hole in the intake manifold gasket but make sure that the sealant does not seep into the jet air passage.
14 Adjust the valve clearances (Section 19 or 20, Part A of this Chapter and after refitting the distributor check the ignition timing.
15 Fill the cooling system (Chapter 12).

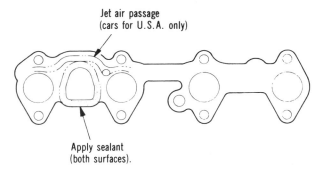

Fig. 1.30 Cylinder head bolt tightening sequence (Sec 30)

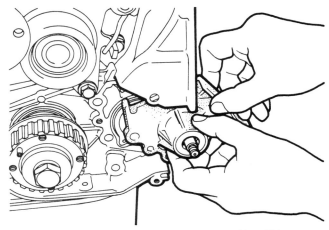

Fig. 1.31 Sealant application area on intake manifold gasket (Sec 30)

31 Engine sump pan – removal and refitting

1   The operations are as described in Section 7, Part A of this Chapter.

32 Engine front casing and oil pump – removal and refitting

1   Remove the timing belt as described in Section 28.
2   Remove the engine sump and then unbolt and remove the oil pick-up pipe with filter screen which is now exposed.
3   Remove the oil pump sprocket. In order to release the nut, the sprocket will have to be prevented from rotating. Take care not to grip the sprocket teeth with any tool as they will soon be damaged. The most satisfactory way to jam the sprocket is to use a thick soft-wood wedge inserted from above between the oil pump and crankshaft sprockets.
4   Remove the oil pump cover.
5   Remove the front casing complete with oil pump rotors. If the assembly is stuck to the crankcase, a large screwdriver can be inserted

Fig. 1.32 Removing oil pump cover (Sec 32)

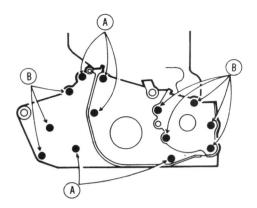

Fig. 1.33 Front casing bolt identification (Sec 32)

A   8 x 35 mm bolts
B   8 x 40 mm bolts

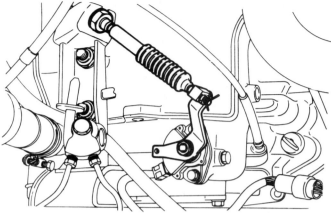

Fig. 1.34 Automatic transmission speed selector cable (Sec 36)

in the groove provided in the thick part of the flange. Do not strike the casing to jar it off.
6   Refer to Part D of this Chapter for details of oil pump overhaul.
7   Refitting is a reversal of removal but use a new front casing gasket and tighten the bolts to the specified torque. Note the different bolt lengths.
8   Tighten the oil pump sprocket nut to the specified torque, again jamming it by inserting the wooden wedge from below, between the crankshaft sprocket.

33 Pistons and connecting rods – removal and refitting

1   The operations are as described in Section 9, Part A of this Chapter.

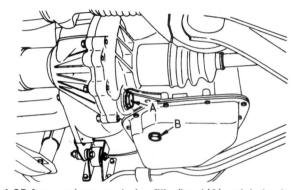

Fig. 1.35 Automatic transmission filler/level (A) and drain plugs (B) (Sec 36)

34 Engine/transmission – method of removal

1   This is identical to that described in Section 10, Part A of this Chapter for the 1410 cc engine. If the help of an assistant is not available then it will probably be easier to release the driveshafts from the transmission first by disconnecting the front suspension balljoints as described in Chapter 6 when removing the transmission independently.

35 Engine/manual transmission – removal

1   The operations are as described for the 1410 cc engine in Section 11, Part A of this Chapter except that additional cooling is provided by an engine-driven fan.
2   Take care as the engine is raised that the fan blades do not cat on anything on the sides of the engine compartment.

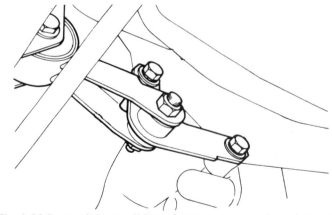

Fig. 1.36 Forward damper linkage (automatic transmission) (Sec 36)

36 Engine/automatic transmission – removal

1   Working within the engine compartment, disconnect and remove the battery and the air cleaner.
2   Remove the purge control valve bracket from the battery support.
3   Remove the windscreen washer reservoir.
4   Remove the radiator expansion reservoir.
5   Drain the coolant and disconnect the transmission fluid cooler pipes from the base of the radiator. Plug the pipes and holes and then remove the radiator.
6   Disconnect the throttle cable from the carburettor.
7   Disconnect the speedometer cable from the transmission.
8   Disconnect the heater hoses.
9   Disconnect the fuel hoses from the carburettor.
10   Disconnect the various emission control hoses from the carburettor and control valves (refer to Chapter 3).

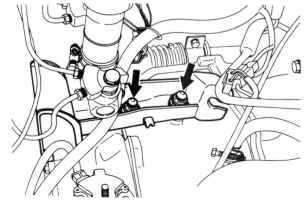

Fig. 1.37 Mounting bracket nuts (automatic transmission) (Sec 36)

11 Disconnect the speed selector control cable from the operating lever on the side of the transmission casing.
12 Separate the electrical harness at the connector plug.
13 Disconnect the engine/transmission earth leads.
14 Disconnect the leads from the starter motor, the alternator, the coolant temperature and oil pressure switches. If necessary, tag the leads with a piece of masking tape to identify their connection points.
15 Disconnect the HT and LT leads from the ignition coil.
16 Disconnect the lead from the high temperature sensor.
17 Remove the ignition coil.
18 Working under the car, remove the engine splash shield plate.
19 Remove the drain and filler/level plug and drain the transmission fluid. Drain the engine oil.
20 Now raise the front of the car and support it securely on stands placed under the frame side members so that the suspension hangs free. There is no need to remove the front roadwheels.
21 Withdraw both driveshafts from the transmission. To do this, first disconnect the suspension lower balljoints from the track control arms by unscrewing the two bolts from each side of the car. One of each of these pairs of bolts also secures the end of the radius rod.
22 Release the inboard ends of the driveshafts by inserting a flat blade (the end of the car hub cap remover will do) between the transmission casing and the driveshaft ball track casing and levering it sharply to overcome the tension of the circlip.
23 The hub carrier/driveshaft can now be pulled outwards sufficiently to enable the driveshaft end to be disconnected from the transmission. Support the disconnected driveshaft on blocks or tie it up with wire and take great care throughout the work not to strain the brake flexible hose.
24 Disconnect the opposite driveshaft in a similar way.
25 Disconnect the exhaust pipe at the engine end and support it to prevent strain.
26 Remove the bolts from the forward damper linkage.
27 Loosen the nuts on the transmission mounting bracket.
28 Working within the engine compartment, remove the bolts and nuts from the engine flexible mountings.
29 Disconnect the engine rear damper linkage.
30 Attach a suitable hoist to the engine lifting lugs and once the weight of the engine/transmission is taken, remove the previously loosened transmission mounting bracket nuts and lift the unit out of the engine compartment. Take care that the transmission casing does not damage the battery support as it is raised.

37 Engine/manual transmission – separation

1 Refer to Section 12, Part A of this Chapter.

38 Engine/automatic transmission – separation

1 With the engine/transmission removed from the car and placed securely on the floor or a bench, now is a good time to clean away any dirt and grease from the external surfaces by using a water soluble solvent or paraffin and a stiff brush.
2 Once this is done, support the engine sump on pieces of wood so that the transmission is not in contact with the floor.
3 Remove the cover plate from the lower face of the torque connector bellhousing.
4 The three special bolts which hold the torque convertor to the engine driveplate must now be removed. To bring each bolt into view, turn the crankshaft by fitting a ring spanner to the crankshaft pulley centre bolt. Jam the starter ring gear as each special bolt is released.
5 Have an assistant support the weight of the transmission while the bellhousing bolts are removed and the starter withdrawn.
6 Pull the transmission from the engine, in a straight line and support its weight, at the same time keeping the torque converter pressed fully into the bellhousing.
7 While the engine and transmission are separated, keep the torque converter fully into the bellhousing by bolting a suitable lever to one of the bellhousing flange bolt holes. Failure to do this will cause loss of fluid and may damage the oil seal.

39 Engine – complete dismantling

1 The following operations cover complete dismantling of the engine for overhaul. If wear or damage is not evident in the crankshaft or

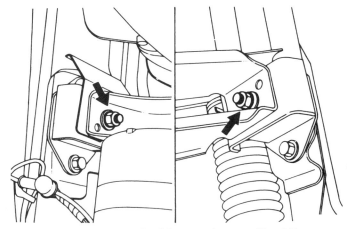

Fig. 1.38 Engine flexible mounting nuts (Sec 36)

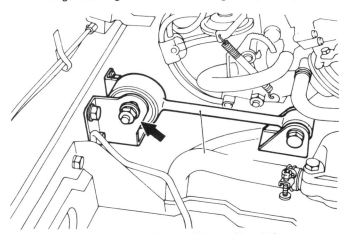

Fig. 1.39 Rear damper linkage (Sec 36)

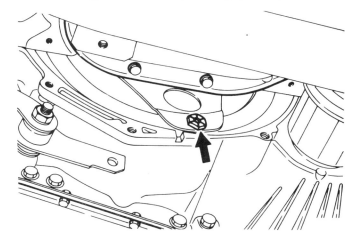

Fig. 1.40 Torque converter to driveplate bolts (Sec 38)

flywheel (driveplate – automatic transmission) components then the necessary work may be carried out without removing the engine from the car as described in Sections 27 to 33 of this Chapter.
2 On cars with manual transmission, mark the relationship of the clutch cover to the flywheel and then unbolt it and remove it, catching the driven plate which is sandwhiched between the pressure plate and the flywheel.
3 Drain the engine oil.
4 Remove the distributor as described in Chapter 4.
5 Unbolt and remove the intake manifold complete with carburettor. Remove the exhaust manifold and hot air collecting shroud.
6 Withdraw the engine oil dipstick.

7   Release the alternator mounting pivot bolt and the adjuster link bolt, push the alternator in towards the engine and slip the drivebelt from the pulleys.
8   Remove the alternator.
9   Remove the fan blades from the water pump pulley, if not done before the engine was removed.
10 Unbolt and remove the fuel pump from the cylinder head.
11 Remove the coolant distribution pipe from the water pump housing.
12 Remove the timing belt as described in Section 28.
13 Unbolt and remove the timing belt tensioner and the belt cover backing plate.
14 Remove the crankshaft sprocket.
15 Unbolt and remove the water pump.
16 Unscrew and discard the oil filter. If it is stuck tight, use a filter strap wrench or if all else fails, drive a large screwdriver through the filter fairly near its sealed end so that it emerges from the opposite side and then use this as a lever to unscrew it.
17 Remove the cylinder head as described in Section 30. With the head removed, peel away and discard the old gasket.
18 If necessary, remove the camshaft and rocker gear from the cylinder block as described in Sections 27 and 29.
19 Removal of the valves from the cylinder head is described in Part D, of this Chapter in conjunction with decarbonising.
20 Although not absolutely essential, it is best to unbolt the mounting brackets from the crankcase, especially if the engine is to be sent away for re-boring or other work.
21 On cars with manual transmission, unbolt and remove the flywheel. Jam the teeth of the starter ring gear on the flywheel to prevent it turning while the bolts are unscrewed.
22 On cars with automatic transmission, unbolt the driveplate from the crankshaft rear flange.
23 Remove the engine oil sump pan (Section 31).
24 Remove the front casing and oil pump (Section 32).
25 Unbolt and remove the engine rear plate.
26 Unbolt and remove the crankshaft rear oil seal retainer (five bolts).
27 Remove the piston and connecting rods as described in Section 9, paragraphs 3 to 8, Part A of this Chapter.
28 The crankshaft main bearings caps are numbered 1 to 5 and incorporate a cast arrow pointing towards the timing belt end of the engine. Unscrew and remove the main bearing cap bolts, tap off the caps and keep their shell bearings taped to the caps. Note that the centre bearing shell incorporates thrust flanges.
29 Lift the crankshaft from the crankcase, pick out the bearing shells and keep these also with their respective caps.
30 With the engine now completely dismantled, refer to Part D of this Chapter for the examination and renovation procedure.

40 Engine reassembly – general

1   Refer to Section 14, Part A of this Chapter.

41 Crankshaft and main bearings – refitting

1   Refer to Section 15 – Part A of this Chapter. The operations for both engines are similar.

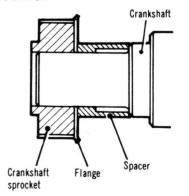

Fig. 1.41 Crankshaft sprocket, flange and spacer (Sec 41)

2   Fit new front and rear crankshaft oil seals as a matter of routine.
3   Fit the spacer, thrust flange and sprocket to the front end of the crankshaft. It is recommended that the sprocket bolt is tightened to the correct torque wrench setting after the flywheel has been fitted in order that the starter ring gear can be jammed to prevent the crankshaft from turning.

42 Flywheel (or driveplate – automatic transmission) – refitting

1   Refit the engine plate to the rear of the cylinder block.
2   Offer the flywheel to the crankshaft mounting flange so that the bolt holes line up.
3   Screw in the bolts and tighten to the specified torque.
4   Hold the camshaft sprocket with a ring spanner to prevent the flywheel from turning.

43 Engine – complete reassembly

1   With the crankshaft and flywheel fitted, building up the rest of the engine is as described in earlier Sections of this part of the Chapter for 'in situ' overhaul but the following reassembly sequence is recommended. Always use new gaskets and tighten all nuts and bolts to the specified torque.
2   Fit the piston and connecting rods.
3   Fit the front casing and oil pump with the oil pick-up pipe.
4   Fit the engine oil sump.
5   Fit the cylinder head.
6   Fit the crankshaft and rocker gear.
7   Fit the timing belt cover backing plates, then fit and tension the timing belt.
8   Fit the crankshaft pulley.
9   Fit the water pump.
10 Fit the timing belt cover sections. Fit the water pump pulley with fan blades.
11 Fit the alternator loosely to its pivot mounting and connect the adjuster link. Slip the drivebelt round the crankshaft, water pump and alternator pulleys, pull the alternator away from the engine so that when the adjuster link bolt is tightened, there is a total deflection at the centre point of the longest run of the belt of 0.38 in (10.0 mm).
12 Fit the manifolds using new gaskets.
13 Refit the distributor (refer to Chapter 4). Provided No 1 piston is at TDC on its compression stroke, this is simply a matter of pushing the distributor into its recess so that the rotor and body alignment marks made during manufacture are lined up. A little trial and error may be required due to the fact that the rotor turns about 40 degrees as the unit is pushed into position. This must be anticipated by positioning the rotor in such a way to allow for the anti-clockwise rotation. On cars destined for operation in California, an electronic (breakerless) ignition system is used but this does not effect the method of refitting the dstributor.
14 Refit the clutch, centralising the driven plate as described in Chapter 5.
15 Adjust the valve clearances (Section 19 or 20, Part A of this Chapter).
16 Refit the rocker cover using a new gasket.
17 Refit the engine mounting brackets to the crankcase.

44 Engine/manual transmission – reconnection

1   The operations are as described in Section 18, Part A of this Chapter.

45 Engine/automatic transmission – reconnections

1   Have the engine supported vertically with the driveplate bolted to the crankshaft rear flange.
2   Check that the torque converter is pushed fully into the bellhousing and keep it this way throughout the reconnection operations.
3   Remove any temporary retaining device from the torque converter.
4   With assistance lift the transmission to mate with the engine crankcase, keeping it level and obtaining the best alignment possible for the torque converter and driveplate bolt holes.

5   Once the transmission has engaged the positioning dowels, insert a couple of bolts at the top of the bellhousing to retain it.
6   Insert the first special bolt to join the torque converter and the driveplate. Use a ring spanner on the crankshaft pulley bolt to align the first bolt holes and to bring each bolt position into view within the bellhousing lower aperture.
7   Tighten all three bolts to the specified torque.
8   Fit the starter motor and the cover plate to the front face of the torque converter bellhousing and screw in and tighten remaining connecting bolts.

46 Valve clearance – adjustment

1   Refer to Sections 19 and 20, Part A of this Chapter.

47 Oil filter – renewal

1   Refer to Section 21, Part A of this Chapter.

48 Engine/transmission – refitting

1   The operations are similar to those described in Section 22, Part A of this Chapter.

49 Engine/automatic transmission – refitting

1   Raise the engine/transmission on the hoist until it can be lowered transversely into the engine compartment.
2   Lower the unit onto the flexible mountings and then connect the transmission mounting bracket.
3   Connect the engine rear damper linkage.
4   Remove the lifting gear.
5   Fit the nuts and bolts to the engine mountings.
6   Connect the engine front damper linkage.
7   Connect the exhaust pipe to the manifold.
8   Engage one driveshaft in the final drive taking care not to damage the oil seal.
9   The driveshaft must now be pressed inwards to snap the retaining clip into position. If this cannot be done with hand pressure then fit a large worm-drive clip round the metal cover of the inboard joint and use this as a striking point to drive the shaft inward. On no account attempt to hammer on the flexible gaiter, you will only damage the joint and split the gaiter.
10 Reconnect the hub carrier to the track control arm. The radius rod is also retained by one of each pair of bolts. The rod may need prising downward to engage the bolt.
11 Repeat the connection operations on the opposite driveshaft, then fit the engine undershield.
12 Refit the roadwheels and lower the car.
13 Working within the engine compartment, refit the ignition coil.
14 Reconnect all electrical leads including the earthing straps.
15 Connect the speed selector cable and 'kickdown' cable to the transmission.
16 Reconnect the emission control valves and hoses.
17 Connect the fuel hoses to the carburettor.
18 Connect the heater hoses.
19 Connect the speedometer cable to the transmission.
20 Connect the accelerator cable to the carburettor.
21 Refit the radiator and connect the transmission fluid cooler pipes.
22 Refit the coolant expansion tank and the windscreen washer reservoir.
23 Fit the purge control valve bracket to the battery support and then fit the battery and connect it.
24 Refit the air cleaner.
25 Check that all drain plugs are tight and a new filter has been fitted then fill up with coolant, engine oil and transmission fluid.

50 Initial start-up after major overhaul

1   Refer to Section 23, Part A of this Chapter.

51 Emission control and overhaul operations (North American versions)

1   Refer to Section 24, Part A of this Chapter.

Part C 1597cc (97.5 cu in) with silent shaft

52 General description

The main difference between this engine and the unit described in Part B is that two 'silent' shafts are incorporated within the crankcase.

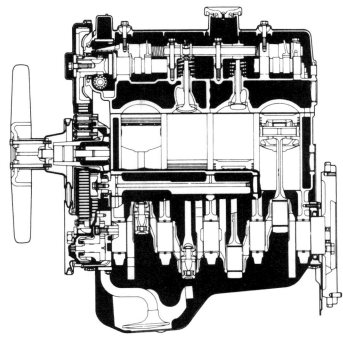

Fig. 1.42 Sectional view of 1597 cc engine with silent shafts (Sec 52)

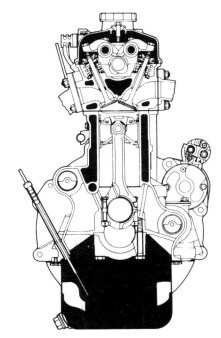

Fig. 1.43 Cross sectional view of 1597 cc engine with silent shafts (Sec 52)

These shafts are balance shafts, driven by the sprocket on the front end of the crankshaft and are designed to improve the smoothness of the engine throughout the engine speed range.

The timing belt configuration differs from the engine without silent shafts and apart from the Sections covering that in this part of the Chapter, all other operations are as described in Part B.

53 Toothed belts and sprockets – removal and refitting

1   Using a socket spanner on the crankshaft pulley centre bolt, turn the crankshaft until No 1 piston is at TDC on its compression stroke. This can be verified if the upper section of the timing belt cover is removed and the mark on the camshaft sprocket is aligned with the mark on the belt cover backing plate.
2   Mark which belt tooth is engaged in which camshaft sprocket notch.
3   Release the alternator mounting and adjuster link bolts, push the alternator in towards the engine and take off the drivebelt.
4   Unscrew the small bolts and withdraw the crankshaft pulley. Unbolt and remove the water pump pulley and fan blades.
5   Unbolt and remove the lower section of the timing belt cover.
6   Unscrew and remove the crankshaft sprocket bolt. The starter will have to be removed and the ring gear jammed to release the bolt.
7   Release the timing belt tensioner mounting bolt and adjuster nut and move the tensioner to relieve the belt of all tension, then retighten the adjuster nut.
8   Slip the timing belt from the sprockets.
9   Pull off the crankshaft outer sprocket. If it is very tight it may be necessary to use an extractor. Two tapped holes are provided in the sprocket for this purpose.
10 Unbolt and remove the tensioner.
11 Unscrew the plug from the base of the left-hand side of the cylinder block and insert a screwdriver (0.3 in (8.0 mm) diameter and at least 3.0 in (76.2 mm) long) into the hole. This will jam the silent shaft so that the nut which retains the oil pump sprocket can be unscrewed. Remove the oil pump sprocket.
12 Now remove the bolt which secures the sprocket to the opposite silent shaft.
13 Remove the silent shaft belt tensioner, and slip off the silent shaft toothed belt.
14 Remove the second (inner) crankshaft sprocket. If it is tight, again use an extractor.
15 Remove the sprocket from the silent shaft.
16 Commence reassembly by fitting the sprocket to the silent shaft and then the crankshaft inner sprocket. Turn the sprockets as necessary to align their marks with those on the front casing.

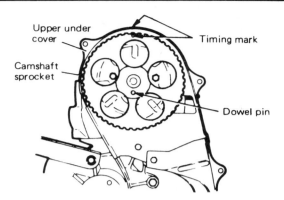

Fig. 1.44 Camshaft sprocket alignment marks (Sec 53)

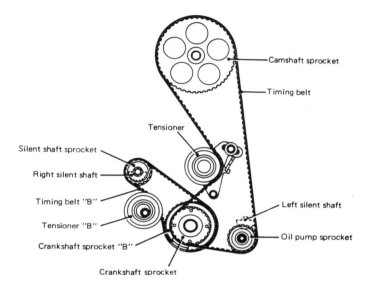

Fig. 1.45 Toothed belt configuration – 1597 cc engine with silent shafts (Sec 53)

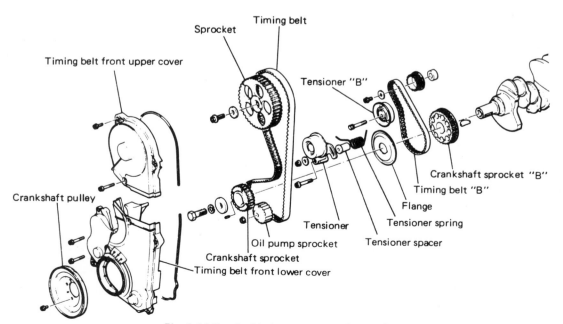

Fig. 1.46 Toothed belt components (Sec 53)

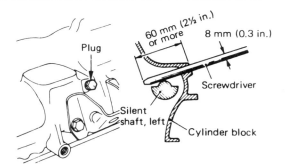

Fig. 1.47 Releasing the oil pump sprocket nut (Sec 53)

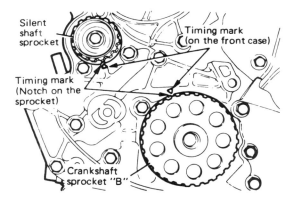

Fig. 1.49 Sprocket alignment marks (Sec 53)

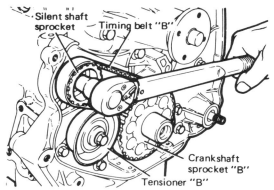

Fig. 1.48 Releasing the silent shaft sprocket bolt (Sec 53)

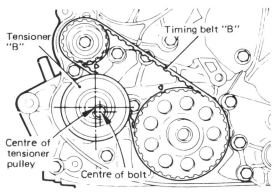

Fig. 1.50 Silent shaft belt tensioner installation (Sec 53)

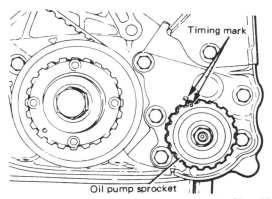

Fig. 1.51 Oil pump sprocket alignment marks (Sec 53)

17 Fit the timing belt B (Fig. 1.45) which drives the right-hand silent shaft and keep it taut between the sprockets on the side away from the tensioner.

18 Now fit the tensioner B making sure that the pulley flange is furthest from the front casing, and the centre of the bolt is offset towards the crankshaft sprocket (Fig. 1.45).

19 Fit the oil pump sprocket and screw on the nut.

20 Align the oil pump sprocket timing marks and then insert the screwdriver into the plug hole in the cylinder block as was done at dismantling. This time the purpose of the screwdriver is twofold. Firstly, the screwdriver must go in at least 2.36 in (60.0 mm) for the alignment to be correct. If it will only enter the hole by a distance of 1.0 in (25.4 mm) then withdraw the screwdriver and rotate the sprocket through one complete turn (360°) to ensure that the oil pump gear is meshed in the correct ratio phase. The second purpose of the screwdriver is to restrain the silent shaft while the oil pump sprocket nut is tightened.

21 Fit the timing belt tensioner, noting how the spring is engaged. Push the tensioner in the direction of the water pump and temporarily hold it in this position so that the timing belt can be fitted without any applied tension.

22 Fit the outer sprocket to the crankshaft and then check that all sprocket marks are in alignment with their marks on the front casing or (camshaft sprocket) with the mark on the belt cover backing plate.

23 Fit the timing belt by engaging it first with the crankshaft sprocket, then the oil pump sprocket, then the camshaft sprocket – in that order. Keep the belt taut between sprockets on the side away from the tensioner and make sure that the sprocket timing marks are not moved out of alignment. Make sure that if the original bolt is being refitted that the marked tooth is engaged in its original camshaft sprocket notch.

24 Make sure that the screwdriver is withdrawn from the hole and the plug refitted.

25 Fit the crankshaft pulley as a precaution against the timing belt riding off the sprockets during belt tensioning.

26 Release the tensioner nut so that it applies tension to the belt and then push the tensioner lightly towards the adjuster nut to make sure that the belt teeth are in full engagement with the sprockets.

27 Tighten the tensioner nut, followed by the bolt.

28 Using a spanner on the crankshaft pulley centre bolt turn the crankshaft through exactly 360° (one turn) in the normal engine rotational direction. Do not turn it backwards.

29 Release the tensioner bolt and nut and then retighten them, in the reverse order – nut first, followed by the bolt.

30 To verify the timing belt adjustment, apply thumb pressure as described in Section 28 of Part B of this Chapter.

31 Fit the two sections of the timing belt cover. The crankshaft pulley will have to be withdrawn again to do this. Fit the water pump pulley and fan blades.

32 Fit the alternator drivebelt and tension it as described in Section 17 of Part A of this Chapter.

54 Silent shafts – removal and refitting

1   Remove the engine oil sump pan (refer to Part B of this Chapter).
2   Unbolt and remove the oil pick-up pipe and filter screen.
3   Remove the toothed belts and sprockets as described in Section 53.

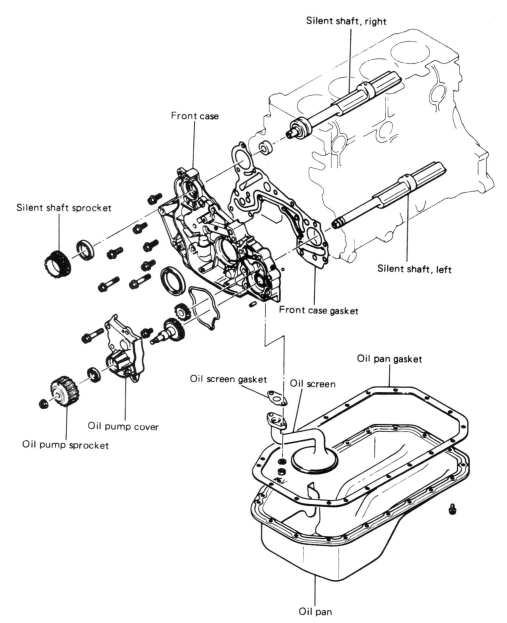

Silent shaft, right

Front case

Silent shaft sprocket

Silent shaft, left

Front case gasket

Oil pan gasket

Oil screen gasket

Oil screen

Oil pump cover

Oil pump sprocket

Oil pan

Fig. 1.52 Front casing and silent shafts (Sec 54)

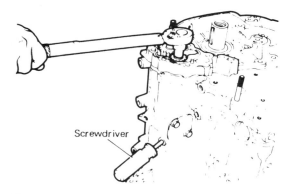

Screwdriver

Fig. 1.53 Releasing the oil pump sprocket nut (Sec 54)

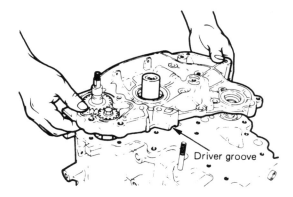

Driver groove

Fig. 1.54 Removing the front casing (Sec 54)

4   Unbolt and remove the oil pump cover.
5   With the screwdriver used to stop the silent shaft from rotating still inserted in its hole, release the oil pump driven gear securing bolt.
6   Extract the holding bolts and remove the front casing complete with the left-hand silent shaft.
7   The oil pump driven gear and the silent shaft can now be withdrawn from the front casing.
8   The right-hand silent shaft can now be pulled out of the crankcase if required.
9   Inspection and renewal of the silent shafts and their bearings is described in Part D, Section 56.
10 Reassembly and refitting is a reversal of the removal and dismantling procedure but observe the following points.
11 Use new gaskets and tighten all bolts and nuts to the specified torque.
12 When fitting the spacer onto the end of the right-hand silent shaft, make sure that the chamfered face enters first and that the oil seal lips are not trapped or rolled over.
13 Sprocket alignment and belt tensioning details are given in Section 53.

Part D Examination and renovation

55 Examination and renovation – general

This part of the Chapter describes the inspection of components and what action should be taken if wear or damage is evident. The dismantling of sub-assemblies is also covered here where it is necessary to reconditioning of the main component.
Never be tempted to refit worn parts or make do with worn oil seals or old gaskets. The purpose of the overhaul will be wasted. Use these Sections in conjunction with the Specifications at the beginning of the Chapter.

56 Crankcase, cylinder block and mountings

1   Examination of the cylinder block and crankcase should be carried in conjunction with examination of the cylinder bores. Obviously if any faults or damage are visible, it will be a waste of money having the block rebored.
2   Check for cracks especially between the cylinder bores. Repair of cast iron is a specialized job and it may be more economical to purchase a new assembly or one in good condition from a breakers yard.
3   Examine stud and bolt holes for stripped threads. New spiral type thread inserts can often be used to overcome this problem but the manufacturer's fitting instructions must be strictly observed.
4   Probe all oil and water passages with a piece of wire to ensure freedom from obstruction.
5   Check the engine and transmission flexible mountings. Although the mountings can be renewed with the engine still in position in the car if its weight is taken on a hoist or jack, take this opportunity to purchase new ones if the original ones are perished or show signs of deformation.
6   The cylinder bores must be examined for taper, ovality, scoring and scratches. Start by carefully examining the top of the cylinder bores. If they are at all worn a very slight ridge will be found on the thrust side. This marks the top of the piston ring travel. The owner will have a good indication of the bore wear prior to dismantling the engine, or removing the cylinder head. Excessive oil consumption accompanied by blue smoke from the exhaust is a sure sign of worn cylinder bores and piston rings.
7   Measure the bore diameter just under the ridge with a micrometer and compare it with the diameter at the bottom of the bore, which is not subject to wear. If the difference between the two measurements is more than 0.008 in (0.2 mm) then it will be necessary to fit special pistons and rings or to have the cylinders rebored and fit oversize pistons.
8   The standard clearance between a piston and the cylinder walls is between 0.0010 and 0.0018 in (0.025 and 0.045 mm). The easiest way to check this is to insert the piston into its bore with a feeler blade 0.0016 in (0.04 mm) in thickness inserted between it and the cylinder wall. Attach the feeler blade to a spring balance and note the force

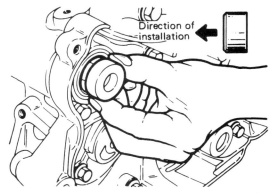

Fig. 1.55 Fitting the silent shaft spacer (Sec 54)

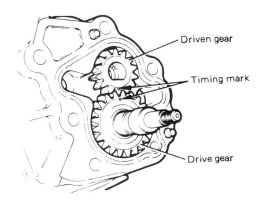

Fig. 1.56 The oil pump gears fitted (Sec 54)

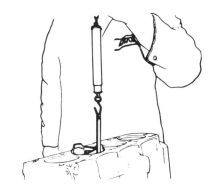

Fig. 1.57 Checking piston to cylinder bore clearance (Sec 56)

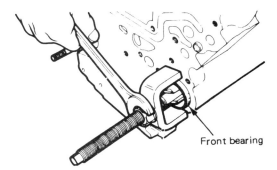

Fig. 1.58 Removing a silent shaft bearing (Sec 56)

required to extract the blade while pulling vertically upwards. This should be between 0.4 and 3.3 lb (0.2 and 1.5 kg). The ambient temperature during this test should be around 68°F (20°C).

9   Where less than the specified force is required to withdraw the feeler blade, then remedial action must be taken. Oversize pistons are available as listed in the Specifications.

10 These are accurately machined to just below the indicated measurements so as to provide correct running clearances in bores bored out to exact oversize dimensions.

11 If the bores are slightly worn but not so badly worn as to justify reboring them, then special oil control rings and pistons can be fitted, which will restore compression and stop the engine burning oil. Several different types are available and the manufacturer's instructions concerning their fitting must be followed closely.

12 If new pistons are being fitted and the bores have not been reground, it is essential to slightly roughen the hard glaze on the sides of the bores with fine glass paper so the new piston rings will have a chance to bed in properly.

13 Refer to Section 59 for piston/connecting rod dismantling.

14 The silent shafts fitted to certain 1597 cc engines run in renewable bearings in the crankcase.

15 Although it is recommended that new bearings are fitted by your dealer it is possible to do the work yourself. Draw the bearings out of their crankcase webs using a length of threaded studding or rod and suitable spacers. Refit the bearings using the same method but make sure that the lubrication holes in the bearing align with the ones in the crankcase.

57 Crankshaft and main bearings

1   Examine the crankpin and main journal surfaces for signs of scoring or scratches. Check the ovality of the crankpins at different positions with a micrometer. If more than 0.001 in (0.03 mm) out of round, the crankpin will have to be reground. It will also have to be reground if there are any scores or scratches present. Also check the journals in the same fashion.

2   If it is necessary to regrind the crankshaft and fit new bearings your local dealer or engineering works will be able to decide how much metal to grind off and the size of new bearing shells.

3   Full details of crankshaft regrinding tolerances and bearing under-sizes are given in the Specifications.

4   Temporarily refit the crankshaft to the crankcase having refitted the upper halves of the shell main bearings in their locations. Fit the centre main bearing cap only, complete with shell bearing and tighten the securing bolts to 50 lbf ft (68 Nm). Using a feeler gauge, check the endfloat by pushing and pulling the crankshaft. Where the endfloat is outside the specified tolerance, the renewal of the shells will normally correct it. Undo the bolts.

5   Finally examine the input shaft bearing in the centre of the flywheel on 1597 cc models. If it is worn, a new one will have to be fitted.

58 Connecting rods and big-end bearings

1   Big-end bearing failure is indicated by a knocking from within the crankcase and a slight drop in oil pressure.

2   Examine the big-end bearing surfaces for pitting and scoring. Renew the shells in accordance with the sizes specified in the Specifications. Where the crankshaft has been reground, the correct undersize big-end shell bearings will be supplied by the repairer.

3   Should there be any suspicion that a connecting rod is bent or twisted or the small-end bush no longer provides an interference fit for the gudgeon pin then the complete connecting rod assembly should be renewed.

4   Finally check that the big-end thrust (side) clearance is within the specified tolerance.

5   Refer to Section 59 for piston and connecting rod dismantling.

59 Pistons, connecting rods and piston rings

1   Where as a result of examination described in Sections 56 and 58, the pistons or connecting rods must be renewed, carry out the following operations.

Piston rings – removal and refitting

2   Piston rings should be removed over the top (crown) of the piston. Slide two or three old feeler blades behind the top ring and using a twisting motion remove the ring. Repeat on the remaining rings. The feeler blades will prevent the rings dropping into an empty groove (photo).

3   Before fitting new compression rings to a piston, push each ring down its cylinder bore, squarely and checks its end gap with a feeler blade. Correct if necessary by careful grinding.

4   Now test the fit of each compression ring in its piston groove. Slight tightness may be rectified by rubbing the ring on abrasive paper held flat on a piece of plate glass. Excessive tightness can only be corrected by having the grooves in the piston machined out.

5   Fit the new rings to the piston by using the removal method. Fit the three piece oil ring first followed by No 2 and then No 1 compression rings.

59.2 Removing a piston ring

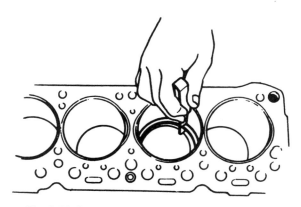

Fig. 1.59 Checking a piston ring end gap (Sec 59)

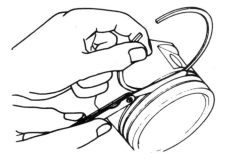

Fig. 1.60 Checking a piston ring to groove clearance (Sec 59)

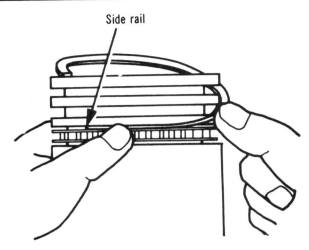

Fig. 1.61 Fitting an oil control ring side rail (Sec 59)

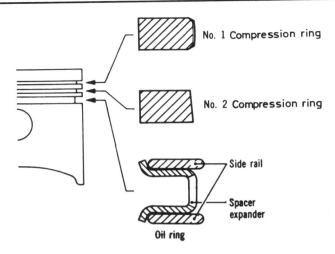

Fig. 1.62 Piston ring installation diagram (Sec 59)

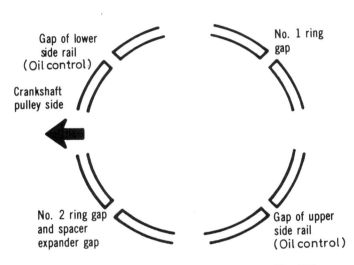

Fig. 1.63 Piston ring end gap fitting diagram (Sec 59)

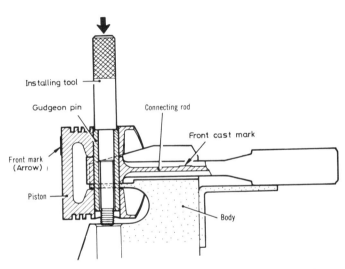

Fig. 1.64 Inserting a gudgeon pin using a press (Sec 59)

6   Check that the side rails of the oil control ring can be turned smoothly and ensure that the markings on the rails are visible when viewed from the top of the piston.

7   Both compression rings must be fitted so that their markings are also visible from the top of the piston but note that the top ring is chamfered.

8   When all rings are fitted, set the ring end gaps in accordance with Fig. 1.63.

Pistons and connecting rods – separation

9   Due to the need for a press and special guide tools, it is recommended that removal and refitting of a gudgeon pin is left to your dealer. For those having the necessary equipment, it should be noted that the cast mark on the connecting rod must be towards the same side as the front (arrow) mark on the piston crown when the two components are assembled.

10 Although the gudgeon pin is a press fit in the connecting rod small-end bush it should be a sliding fit, using finger pressure, in the piston bosses at normal room temperature. The use of special guide tools ensures that the gudgeon pin is accurately located centrally in the connecting rod otherwise side thrust would soon cause excessive wear to the piston and bore (photo).

59.10 The piston and connecting rod components

60 Camshaft and bearings

1   Inspect the camshaft journal bearing surfaces; if they are scored, the camshaft will have to be renewed. Check the condition of sprockets and drivegears.

2   If you possess a micrometer, check the height of the cam lobes. If they have been reduced by wear below the specified limit, again the camshaft will have to be renewed or the lobes re-profiled.

3   If the camshaft bearings have worn, then a new cylinder head is the only answer as they are machined directly onto it.

4   Before refitting the camshaft on 1410 cc engines locate the thrust casing on the end of the shaft and check the clearance as shown in Fig. 1.66. If it is too large, renew the thrust casing.

5   On 1597 cc engines, excessive camshaft endfloat can normally be overcome by fitting a new spacer.

6   Renew the camshaft oil seals (photo).

61 Rocker gear

1410 cc engines

1   The rocker arms and springs can be removed from their shafts as soon as the shafts are unbolted from the cylinder heads and the bolts withdrawn from the shafts.

60.6 Camshaft oil seal

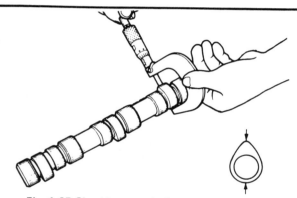

Fig. 1.65 Checking camshaft lobe height (Sec 60)

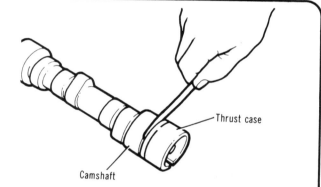

Fig. 1.66 Checking camshaft to thrust casing clearance (Sec 60)

Identification mark	Installation position
1-3	No.1 and 3 cylinders (positions A and C in illustration shown below)
2-4	No.2 and 4 cylinders (positions B and D in illustration shown below)

Identification mark

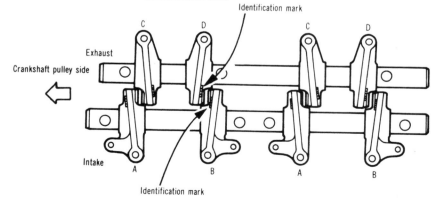

NOTE: Rocker arm for intake valves on engine for U.S.A. is shown.
On other engines rocker arm for intake valves is the same as that for exhaust valves.

Fig. 1.67 Rocker gear arrangement (1410 cc engine) (Sec 61)

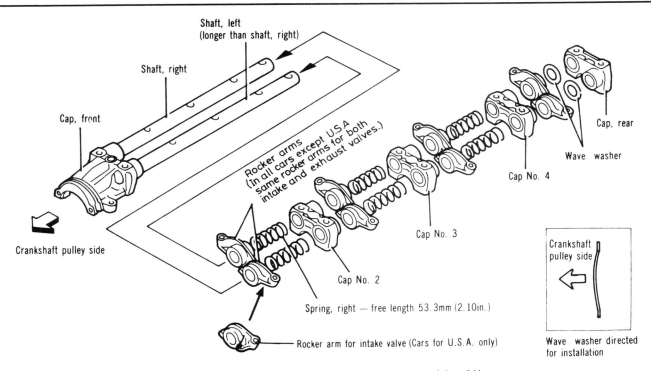

Fig. 1.68 Rocker gear arrangement (1597 cc engine) Sec 61)

2   Keep each component in strict sequence as it is withdrawn from its shaft and do not mix the shafts from side to side or the rocker arms with regard to shaft or position on that shaft.

3   The shafts are hollow to act as oil galleries and any wear in the rocker arm bushes will allow excessive oil to escape with a consequent drop in oil pressure.

4   Wear or scoring on the rocker arm to lobe contact faces should be rectified by renewal. Grinding out marks will reduce the adjustment range of the valve clearance screw and remove the hardened bearing surface from the arm.

5   On certain North American models the intake valve rocker arms incorporate a second adjuster screw for adjusting the emission control jet valve clearances.

1597 cc engine

6   The design of the rocker gear differs from that used on the smaller engine in that the rocker shafts run in the camshaft bearing caps.

7   The inspection and renovation details described for the smaller engine apply but when reassembling, make sure that the longer shaft is positioned on the intake valve side and that both the shaft cut-outs are uppermost.

8   As with the 1410 cc engine, the intake valve rocker arms on certain North American models incorporate a second adjuster screw for adjusting the emission control jet valve clearances.

62 Cylinder head and valves – servicing and decarbonising

1   With the cylinder head removed, use a blunt scraper to remove all trace of carbon and deposits from the combustion spaces and ports. Remember that the cylinder head is aluminium alloy and can be damaged easily during the decarbonising operations. Scrape the cylinder head free from scale or old pieces of gasket or jointing compound. Clean the cylinder head by washing it in paraffin and take particular care to pull a piece of rag through the ports and cylinder head bolt holes. Any dirt remaining in these recesses may well drop onto the gasket or cylinder block mating surfaces as the cylinder head is lowered into position and could lead to a gasket leak after reassembly is complete (photo).

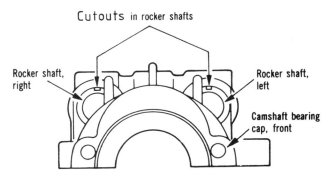

Fig. 1.69 Rocker shaft to bearing cap alignment (1597 cc engine) (Sec 61)

62.1 Cylinder head with one valve removed. Inlet valves have larger heads

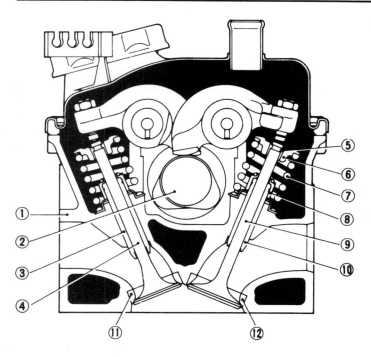

Fig. 1.70 Valve arrangement (1410 cc engine) (Sec 62)

1	Cylinder head	7	Valve spring
2	Camshaft	8	Oil seal
3	Exhaust valve guide	9	Intake valve
4	Exhaust valve	10	Intake valve guide
5	Split collet	11	Exhaust valve seat
6	Valve spring retainer	12	Intake valve seat

62.6a Compressing a valve spring

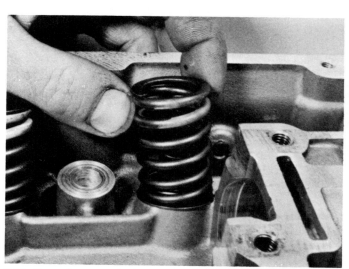

62.6b Removing a valve spring retainer

2   On North American models, clean the jet air passage and the EGR gas passage free from carbon.

3   With the cylinder head clean, test for distortion if a history of coolant leakage has been apparent. Carry out this test using straight edge and feeler gauges or a piece of plate glass. If the surface shows any warping in excess of 0.0039 in (0.1 mm) then the cylinder head will have to be resurfaced which is a job for a specialist engineering company.

4   Clean the pistons and top of the cylinder bores. If the pistons are still in the block then it is essential that great care is taken to ensure that no carbon gets into the cylinder bores as this could scratch the cylinder walls or cause damage to the piston and rings. To ensure this does not happen, first turn the crankshaft so that two of the pistons are at the top of their bores. Stuff rag into the other two bores or seal them off with paper and masking tape. The waterways should also be covered with small pieces of masking tape to prevent particles of carbon entering the cooling system and damaging the water pump.

5   Before scraping the carbon from the piston crowns, press grease into the gap between the cylinder walls and the two pistons which are to be worked on. With a blunt scraper carefully scrape away the carbon from the piston crown, taking great care not to scratch the aluminium. Also scrape away the carbon from the surrounding lip of the cylinder wall. When all carbon has been removed, scrape away the grease which will now be contaminated with carbon particles, taking care not to press any into the bores. To assist prevention of carbon build-up the piston crown can be polished with a metal polish. Remove the rags or masking tape from the other two cylinders and turn the crankshaft so that the two pistons which were at the bottom are now at the top. Place rag or masking tape in the cylinders which have been decarbonised and proceed as just described.

6   The valves can be removed from the cylinder head by the following method. Compress each spring in turn with a valve spring compressor until the two halves of the collets can be removed. Release the compressor and remove the spring retainer and spring. On all engines, a single spring only is used on both the exhaust and inlet valves (photos).

62.6c Removing a valve spring

62.9a Removing a valve spring seat

62.9b Removing a valve

62.9c Valve components

62.9d Removing a valve stem oil seal

7 If, when the valve spring compressor is screwed down, the valve spring retaining cap refuses to free to expose the split collet, do not continue to screw down the compressor as there is a likelihood of damaging the valve stem.

8 Gently tap the top of the tool directly over the cap with a light hammer. This will free the cap. To avoid the compressor jumping off the valve spring retaining cap when it is tapped, hold the compressor firmly in position with one hand.

9 Slide the valve spring seat off the top of each valve stem and then drop out each valve through the combustion chamber. Remove the valve stem oil seals (photos).

10 It is essential that the valves are kept in their correct sequence unless they are so badly worn that they are to be renewed.

11 Examine the heads of the valves for pitting and burning, especially the heads of the exhaust valves. The valve seatings should be examined at the same time. If the pitting on valve and seat is very slight the marks can be removed by grinding the seats and valve together with coarse, and then fine, valve grinding paste.

12 Where bad pitting has occurred to the valve seats it will be necessary to recut them and fit new valves. If the valve seats are so worn that they cannot be recut, then it will be necessary to fit new valve seat inserts. These two jobs should be entrusted to your local dealer or engineering works. In practice it it very seldom that the seats are so badly worn that they require renewal. Normally, it is the valve

that is too badly worn for replacement, and the owner can easily purchase a new set of valves and match them to the seats by valve grinding.

13 Valve grinding is carried out as follows: Clean off all carbon deposits from the valve head and stem using a scraper then a wire brush. Smear a trace of coarse carborundum paste on the seat face and apply a suction grinder tool to the valve head. With a semi-rotary motion, grind the valve head to its seat, lifting the valve occasionally to redistribute the grinding paste. When a dull matt even surface is produced on both the valve seat and the valve, wipe off the paste and repeat the process with fine carborundum paste, lifting and turning the valve to redistribute the paste as before. A light spring placed under the valve head will greatly ease this operation. When a smooth unbroken ring of light grey matt finish is produced, on both valve and valve seat faces, the grinding operation is completed.

14 Carefully clean away every trace of grinding compound, taking great care to leave none in the ports or in the valve guides. Clean the valves and valve seats with a paraffin soaked rag then with a clean rag, and finally, if an air line is available, blow the valves, valve guides and valve ports clean.

15 Test each valve in its guide for wear. After a considerable mileage, the valve guide bore may wear oval. This can best be tested by inserting a new valve in the guide and moving it from side to side. If the tip of the valve stem deflects by more than that given in the

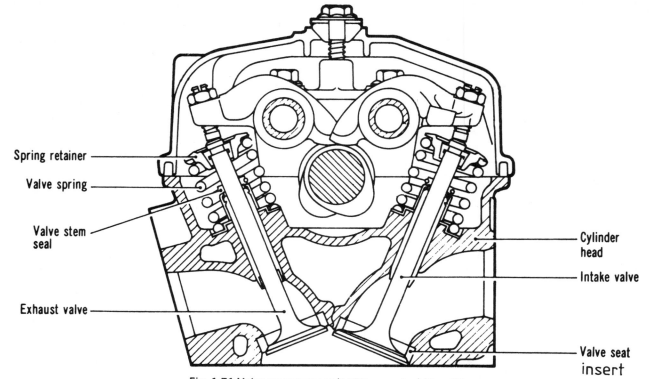

Spring retainer

Valve spring

Valve stem
seal

Exhaust valve

Cylinder
head

Intake valve

Valve seat
insert

Fig. 1.71 Valve arrangement (1597 cc engine) (Sec 62)

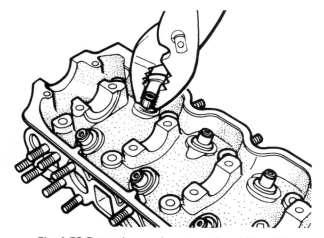

Fig. 1.72 Removing a valve stem oil seal (Sec 62)

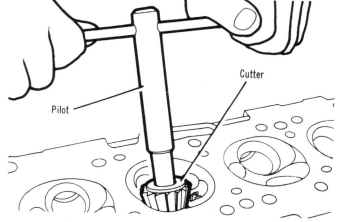

Cutter

Pilot

Fig. 1.73 Re-cutting a valve seat (Sec 62)

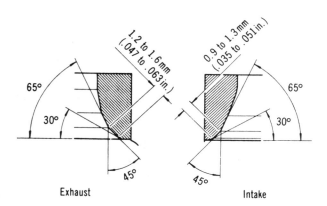

1.2 to 1.6mm
(.047 to .063 in.)

0.9 to 1.3mm
(.035 to .051 in.)

65°

30°

65°

30°

45°

45°

Exhaust

Intake

Fig. 1.74 Valve seat cutting diagram (1410 cc engine) (Sec 62)

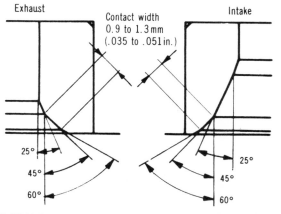

Exhaust

Intake

Contact width
0.9 to 1.3mm
(.035 to .051 in.)

25°

45°

60°

25°

45°

60°

Fig. 1.75 Valve seat cutting diagram (1597 cc engine) (Sec 62)

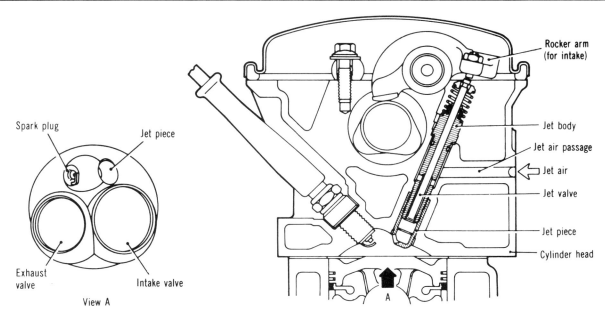

Fig. 1.76 Jet valve arrangement (1410 cc engine) (Sec 62)

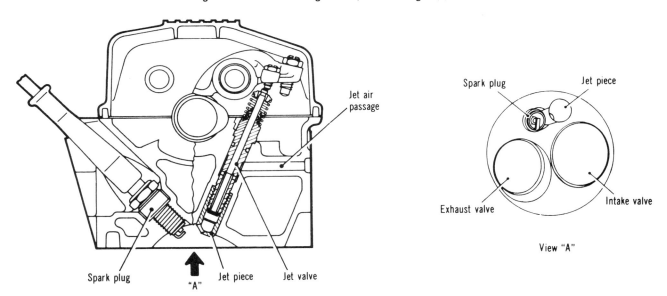

Fig. 1.77 Jet valve arrangement (1597 cc engine) (Sec 62)

Specifications then it must be assumed that the tolerance between the stem and guide is greater than the permitted maximum. Oversize valve guides can be fitted but as the original hole in the cylinder head must be reamed to accept the new guides and then the guides must be pressed in to a critical depth using a special installing tool, it is best to leave this work to your dealer.

16 Finally check the free-length of the valve springs and renew them if they are much less than specified or if they have been in operation for 30 000 miles (48 000 km) or more.

17 Using a piece of tubing, press the new oil seals onto the ends of the valve guides. Oil the first valve and return it to the seat into which it was ground. Using the compressor, fit the spring and other valve retaining components. The painted coils of the valve spring should be furthest from the head of the valve.

Jet valves (USA only)

18 The jet valve assemblies can be removed from the cylinder head using a long socket or box spanner. Do not tilt the socket or box spanner while unscrewing it or the jet valve stem may bend.

19 The jet valve assembly can be dismantled if the spring is carefully compressed and the split collets extracted.

20 The valve stem oil seal can be renewed but do not dismantle any further. A burnt seat or valve head should be rectified by complete renewal.

21 When refitting the jet valve assembly, oil the threads and fit a new O-ring seal. Tighten to the specified torque.

63 Timing belt, sprockets and tensioner

1 Before removing a timing belt, it is recommended that its teeth are marked in relation to its engagement with those of each sprocket and which way round it is fitted. A belt will have run-in after a short period and moving its position in any way will not only cause increased wear but will also generate extra noise.

2 If the belt has covered 30 000 miles (48 000 km) or more at the time of overhaul, discard it and fit a new one.

3 If the belt is observed to be frayed, hard or cracked with worn or missing teeth, renew it immediately regardless of mileage covered.

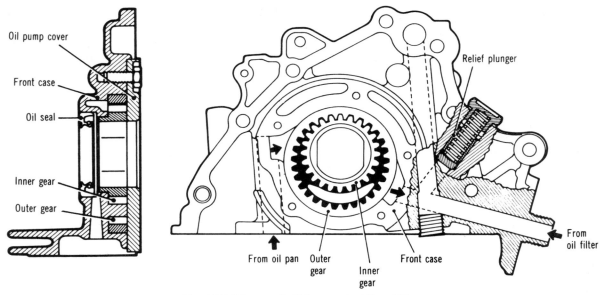

Fig. 1.78 Oil pump (1410 cc engine) (Sec 63)

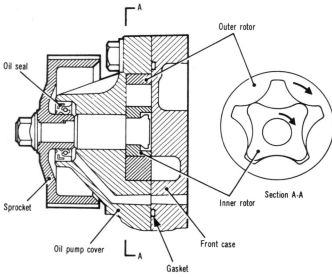

Fig. 1.79 Sectional view of oil pump (1597 cc engine) (Sec 63)

63.4 Anchoring the belt tensioner spring

4   The timing belt sprocket teeth rarely wear but check the roller on the tensioner. If this is grooved or does not spin freely it must be renewed (photo).
5   The foregoing remarks apply equally to the silent shaft belt and tensioner on 1597 cc engines so equipped.

64 Front casing and oil pump

1410 cc engine
1   With the oil pump cover plate removed from the front casing, mark the exposed faces of the gears so that they can be refitted in their original positions (photo).
2   Remove the gears, clean them and examine for worn or chipped teeth (photo).
3   Refit the gears and using feeler gauges, check the clearance between (a) the outer gear and casing (b) the crescent and outer gear and (c) the crescent and inner gear (photos).
4   Using a straight edge laid across the casing check the gear end clearance (photo).
5   If any dimension exceeds the specified tolerance renew the pump.
6   Unscrew the pressure relief valve plug and extract the spring and valve (photo).
7   The free length of the spring should be 1.85 in (47 mm). If it has been reduced to less than this, renew it. The valve plunger should slide smoothly.
8   Always renew the oil seal in the front casing (photo).

1597 cc engine
9   With the front casing removed and the oil pump cover detached, mark the visible faces of the inner and outer rotors with tape or a grease pencil so that they will be refitted the same way round.
10   Remove the rotors and check for scoring or chipping to their tips.
11   Refit the rotors and using feeler gauges check the following clearances between (a) the tips of inner and outer rotor (b) the outer rotor to pump cover and (c) the rotor endfloat in the oil pump cover using a straight edge across the cover flanges.
12   Also check for wear in the shaft bush in the cover.
13   Remove the pressure relief valve plug, extract the spring and plunger. The free length of the spring should be 1.85 in (47 mm). If it has been reduced to less than this, renew it. The valve plunger should slide smoothly.
14   Always renew the oil seal in the pump cover, and fit it flush with the narrow face of the cover.
15   On engines fitted with silent shafts, renew the shaft oil seal on the right-hand side of the front casing.

64.1 Removing the oil pump cover plate

64.2 Removing the oil pump gears

64.3a Checking the oil pump outer gear clearance

64.3b Checking the oil pump crescent clearance

64.3c Checking the oil pump inner gear clearance

64.4 Checking the oil pump gear endfloat

64.6 The oil pump pressure relief valve

64.8 The front casing oil seal

65 Flywheel and starter ring gear

1   Examine the clutch driven plate contact area on the flywheel for scoring or cracks. If these are severe or extensive then the flywheel should be renewed. Surface grinding is not recommended as the balance of the crankshaft/flywheel assembly will be upset.

2   If the teeth on the flywheel starter ring are badly worn, or if some are missing then it will be necessary to remove the ring and fit a new one, or preferably exchange the flywheel for a reconditioned unit.
3   On cars equipped with automatic transmission, the driveplate should be inspected for cracks especially at the bolt holes. The starter ring gear on these models is welded to the torque converter.

Part E Fault diagnosis

66 Fault diagnosis – engine

Symptom	Reason(s)
Engine will not start when the starter switch is operated*	Flat battery Bad battery connections Bad connections at solenoid switch and/or starter motor Defective starter motor
Engine turns over normally but fails to start*	No spark at plugs No fuel reaching engine Too much fuel reaching the engine (flooding)
Engine starts but runs unevenly and misfires	Ignition and/or fuel system faults Incorrect valve clearances Burnt out valves Worn out piston rings
Lack of power	Ignition and/or fuel system faults Incorrect valve clearances Burnt out valves Worn out piston rings
Excessive oil consumption	Oil leaks from crankshaft rear oil seal, crankshaft front oil seal, rocker cover gasket, oil filter gasket, sump gasket, sump plug washer, camshaft or oil pump oil seals Worn piston rings or cylinder bores resulting in oil being burnt by engine Worn valve guides and/or defective valve stem seals
Excessive mechanical noise from the engine	Wrong valve rocker clearances Wrong crankshaft bearings Worn cylinders (piston slap) Slack or worn timing belt and sprockets

Note: *When investigating starting and uneven running faults do not be tempted into snap diagnosis. Start from the beginning of the check procedure and follow it through. It will take less time in the long run. Poor performance from an engine in terms of power and economy is not normally diagnosed quickly. In any event the ignition and fuel systems must be checked first before assuming any further investigation needs to be made*

* Refer also to quick-reference chart at the front of this manual

Chapter 2 Cooling, heating, ventilation and air conditioning systems

Contents

Specifications

System type .... Liquid cooled, pressurised with radiator, electric cooling fan and belt driven coolant pump. Additional fan on coolant pump pulley of 1597 cc engine

Thermostat
Type .... Wax
Opens .... 82°C (180°F) or 88°C (190°F) depending upon operating territory
Full open .... 95°C (203°F) or 100°C (212°F) depending upon opening temperature

Fan thermal switch
Actuates fan .... 85°C (185°F)
Switches fan off .... 81°C (178°F)

Coolant temperature switch
Resistance at:
    80°C (176°F) .... 69.4 ohms
    100°C (212°F) .... 36.4 ohms
    120°C (248°F) .... 26.8 ohms

Coolant capacity .... 4.4 Imp qts (5.0 litres, 5.3 US qts)

Refrigerant type .... Carline 32 oz (907 g)

Torque wrench settings	lbf ft	Nm
Cooling system		
Water pump bolts	22	30
Thermostat cover bolts	20	27
Alternator link bolt	10	14
Alternator mounting bolt	18	24
Coolant temperature switch	25	34
Electric fan thermal switch	14	19
Heater		
Heater mounting bolt and nut	25	34

1 General description

The cooling system is of pressurised type and incorporates a radiator with remotely mounted expansion tank, a belt driven coolant pump and a thermostat.

An electric radiator fan is fitted to all models. Additional cooling is provided on 1597 cc engined models by fan blades mounted on the coolant pump pulley hub.

The car interior heating system is supplied with coolant from the engine cooling system as is also the intake manifold.

On 1597 cc engined models with automatic transmission, a transmission fluid cooler is built into the base of the radiator.

An air conditioner is available as a factory fitted option on cars destined for operation in North America and some other territories.

2 Coolant level – checking

1 Whenever you have occasion to open the bonnet with the engine warm and idling, it is a worthwhile habit to get into, to check the coolant level in the expansion tank.
2 This is done visually and the level should be between the LOW and FULL marks.
3 Normally, the addition of coolant should never be required between complete coolant changes but if the level does fall then this will indicate a leak in the system either from a component, a hose or gasket.
4 Any topping up which may be required as the result of a loose hose clip or similar should be made into the expansion tank with an antifreeze mixed in similar proportions to the original.

3 Cooling system – draining, flushing and refilling

1 Move the heater control lever to 'HOT'.
2 Remove the radiator cap. If the engine is hot, cover the cap wth a cloth and unscrew it only to its first stop to release the pressure before turning it fully anti-clockwise and removing it. Failure to observe this precaution may cause scalding.
3 Place a container under the radiator and unscrew the small top to drain the coolant (photo).
4 Provided the antifreeze mixture is renewed at the specified intervals or, on cars operating only in tropical climates a good quality corrosion inhibitor is used in the cooling system, rust and sediment should not occur and the system can be refilled with fresh coolant without any further action.
5 When the coolant being drained appears dirty, discoloured or rusty then the system must be flushed with cold water until it runs clear from the drain tap. In severe cases, it may be necessary to remove the radiator, turn it upside down and reverse flush it to dislodge the sediment.
6 Chemical cleaners are not recommended and scaling is not usually a problem as even in hard water areas the only lime introduced into the system is at initial filling as there is little subsequent topping up.
7 Tighten the radiator drain tap.
8 Refill the system by pouring in fresh coolant into the radiator until it is completely full.
9 Refit the radiator cap.
10 Start the engine and run it at a fast idle speed until the radiator top hose feels hot indicating that the thermostat has opened.
11 Switch off the engine, remove the radiator cap carefully making sure that it is covered with a cloth to prevent scalding from escaping steam. Add more coolant to bring the level to the top of the radiator filler neck and then refit the cap.
12 Fill the expansion tank to the FULL mark with coolant mixed in similar proportions to the main quantity.
13 Refer to Section 4 for details of coolant mixtures.

4 Coolant mixtures

1 Never use water alone in the engine cooling system. Apart from the danger of frost, corrosion of the aluminium components will occur, also rusting of the iron and steel content.

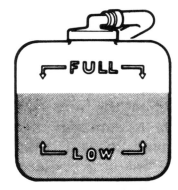

Fig. 2.1 Expansion tank markings (Sec 2)

3.3 Radiator drain tap and electric fan switch

Temperate and cold climates
2 To maintain maximum corrosion resistance, it is recommended that a minimum of 50% (by volume) of a good quality glycol type antifreeze is used. In extremely cold climates, this concentration can be exceeded by increasing the quantity of antifreeze up to a maximum of 70%.
3 A 50% concentration of antifreeze gives protection against freezing down to -36°C (-32.8°F).
4 Where a suitable hydrometer is available, the coolant concentration (50%) can be checked. At 20°C (68°F) the specific gravity should be 1.082.
5 When handling antifreeze mixture, take care not to spill it on the car paintwork as it will damage it if it is not wiped off immediately.

Tropical climates
6 Where antifreeze mixtures are not needed because of favourable climatic conditions, a good quality corrosion inhibitor should always be mixed with the cooling water – never use plain water in the system.

All climates
7 The cooling system should be drained and refilled with fresh coolant annually to maintain maximum protection. Mixtures used for longer periods tend to lose their effectiveness due to the deterioration in their chemical content.

5 Thermostat – removal, testing and refitting

1 Drain about half the contents of the cooling system into a clean container. Approximately 3.5 Imp pts (2.0 litres, 4.2 US pts) will do.
2 Disconnect the coolant hose from the thermostat housing.

5.3 Removing the thermostat housing cover

5.4 Removing the thermostat

5.7 Thermostat correctly fitted

3   Unscrew the two bolts and remove the cover from the thermostat housing (photo).
4   Withdraw the thermostat. If it is stuck tight, cut round its edge with a sharp knife to release it (photo).
5   To test the thermostat, suspend it in a saucepan of water and then heat the water. The thermostat valve should start to open when the water temperature reaches the level given in the Specifications and continue to open as the water approaches boiling point.
6   If the thermostat fails to operate as indicated or if it is stuck open when cold or stuck closed when hot, it must be renewed with one of the correct rating.
7   When fitting the thermostat, note that its mounting plate is offset and can only be installed one way to locate the jiggle pin (rapid warm-up by-pass) correctly (photo).

8   Make sure that the thermostat housing cover flanges are clean and use a new gasket.
9   Tighten the securing bolts to the specified torque.

6   Radiator – removal and refitting

1   The radiator on all models incorporates an electric fan and thermostatic switch.
2   Drain the cooling system as previously described.
3   Disconnect the coolant hoses from the engine.
4   Disconnect the fan and switch wiring harness at the connector plug.
5   On cars equipped with automatic transmission, disconnect the

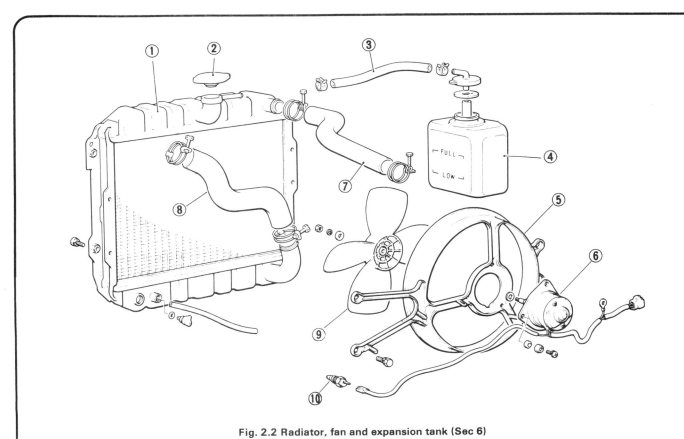

Fig. 2.2 Radiator, fan and expansion tank (Sec 6)

1	Radiator	4	Expansion tank	7	Radiator top hose	9	Fan
2	Pressure cap	5	Shroud	8	Radiator bottom hose	10	Fan thermal switch
3	Hose	6	Electric motor				

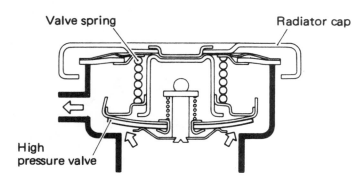

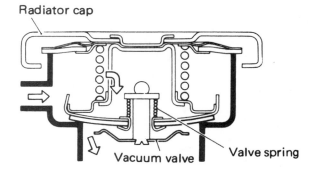

Fig. 2.3 Radiator pressure cap operating modes (Sec 6)

A   Overflow (pressure) condition   *B   Return (vacuum) condition*

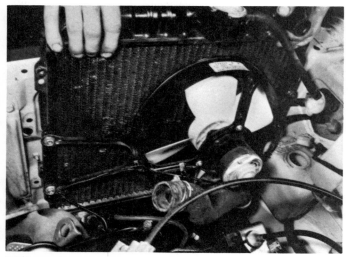

6.6 Removing the radiator

6.7 Radiator/electric fan assembly

pipe lines from the fluid cooler at the base of the radiator and quickly plug the openings to prevent loss of fluid and dirt entering.

6   Unscrew the four radiator mounting bolts and lift the radiator complete with electric fan from the engine compartment (photo).

7   With the radiator removed, the electric fan assembly may be unbolted and removed if necessary (photo).

8   A leaking radiator is best repaired by specialists or by fitting a reconditioned unit.

9   If the radiator fins are choked with dirt or flies, brush them off and then use compressed air or a strong jet of water from a hose to remove them completely.

10 A faulty radiator cap can cause overheating and a rise in the coolant level in the expansion tank and if these symptoms have occurred, renew the cap for one of identical rating.

11 Refitting the radiator is a reversal of removal.

12 Refill the cooling system (refer to Section 3) and on cars with automatic transmission, check and top up the transmission fluid.

---

7   Coolant temperature switch and electric fan switch

1   The coolant temperature switch is screwed into the underside of the intake manifold which is coolant heated (photo).

2   Removal of the switch will necessitate prior draining of about half the system coolant.

7.1 Coolant temperature sender switch

3   The switch which controls the operation of the radiator cooling fan is of thermostatic type and is screwed into the bottom tank of the radiator.

4   Both switches can be tested by removing them and suspending them in water being heated. If a test bulb and battery are then connected between the fan switch terminal and the switch body (earth) then the test lamp should come on and go off at the temperature levels shown in the Specifications. If it does not, then the switch will have to be renewed.

5   The coolant temperature switch can only be satisfactorily checked with an ohmmeter. Again as the temperature of the water is raised, the relative resistance should match the levels given in the Specifications.

6   If the temperature and fuel gauges both become faulty at the same time, suspect the instrument voltage regulator (refer to Chapter 10).

8   Water pump – removal and refitting

1   Disconnect the battery negative lead and drain the cooling system.
2   Disconnect the radiator hose from the coolant pump.
3   Release the alternator mounting and adjuster bolts, push the alternator in towards the engine and slip the drivebelt from the pulleys (photo).

4   Unbolt the water pump pulley (1410 cc engine) or the pulley and fan blades (1597 cc engine).

5   Remove the timing belt, camshaft sprocket and belt tensioner as described for the respective engines in Parts A, B or C of Chapter 1.

6   Unbolt and remove the water pump.

7   If the pump is leaking or noisy in operation, renew the pump complete as repair bits and spare parts are not available.

8   Refitting is a reversal of removal. Make sure that the mating surfaces of engine and pump are quite clean and use a new gasket smeared with jointing compound. Also use a new O-ring at the coolant distribution pipe joint (photo).

9   Note the locations of the different types of bolt and to which bolt the alternator adjuster link is attached by referring to the appropriate diagram according to engine type (photo).

10   Refit the timing belt and other components again as described in Chapter 1.

11   Reconnect the radiator hose.

12   Refit the water pump pulley and fan blades (1597 cc engine).

13   Fit and tension the water pump drivebelt.

14   Reconnect the battery and fill the cooling system.

8.3 Water pump showing drivebelt and water distribution pipe

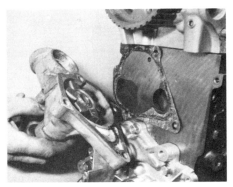
8.8 Refitting the water pump

8.9 Alternator adjuster link attached to water pump

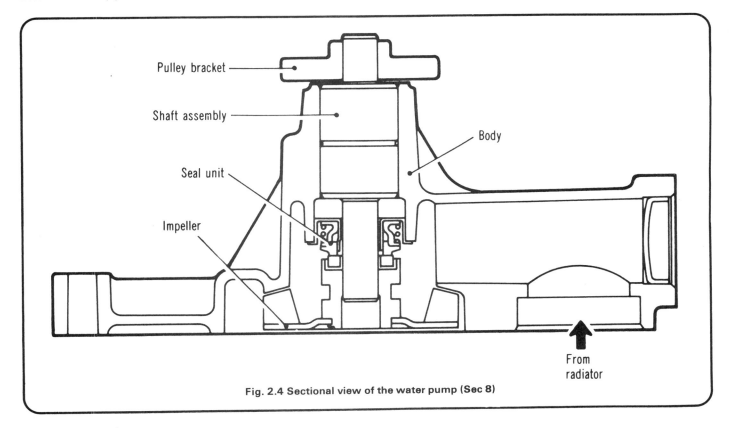
Fig. 2.4 Sectional view of the water pump (Sec 8)

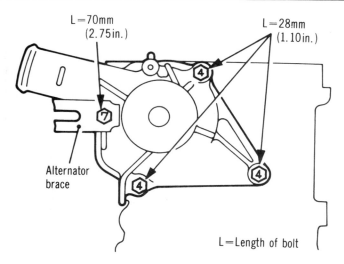

L=70mm (2.75in.)

L=28mm (1.10in.)

Alternator brace

L=Length of bolt

Fig. 2.5 Water pump bolt fitting diagram (1410 cc engine) (Sec 8)

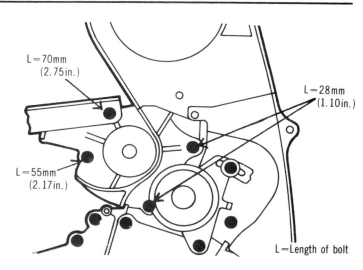

L=70mm (2.75in.)

L=28mm (1.10in.)

L=55mm (2.17in.)

L=Length of bolt

Fig. 2.6 Water pump bolt fitting diagram (1597 cc engine) (Sec 8)

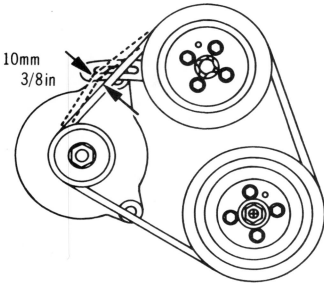

10mm 3/8in

Fig. 2.7 Water pump drivebelt tensioning diagram (Sec 8)

9 Heater/ventilator – general description

The heater unit is mounted centrally behind the facia panel within the car.

The heater matrix uses coolant from the engine cooling system. An electric booster motor and fan increase the air flow when the car is stationary or moving slowly.

Fresh air for the heater enters through the grille immediately below the windscreen.

Air flow can be regulated and directed by means of the levers and knob on the control panel to cover all requirements. These include temperature level, the particular outlet from which the air is to be ejected and whether fresh or recirculated air is desired.

10 Heater blower motor – removal and refitting

1 Disconnect the battery earth lead.
2 Remove the centre console and the parcels shelf as described in Chapter 12. Remove the centre ventilation duct and defroster dusts now exposed.
3 Remove the instrument panel trim also as described in Chapter 12.
4 Remove completely the two top heater securing nuts but only loosen the bottom mounting nut.
5 Disconnect the lead from the heater and then tilt the heater unit forward so that the three heater blower motor bolts can be extracted and the motor withdrawn.
6 Refitting is a reversal of removal.

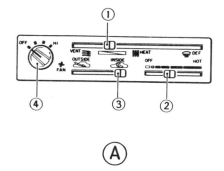

(A)

(B)

Fig. 2.8 Heater controls and air vents (Sec 9)

A	Control panel	2	Temperature control lever	4	Blower fan switch
1	Air deflection and direction lever	3	Fresh air (outside) or recirculated (inside) lever	B	Air outlet vents

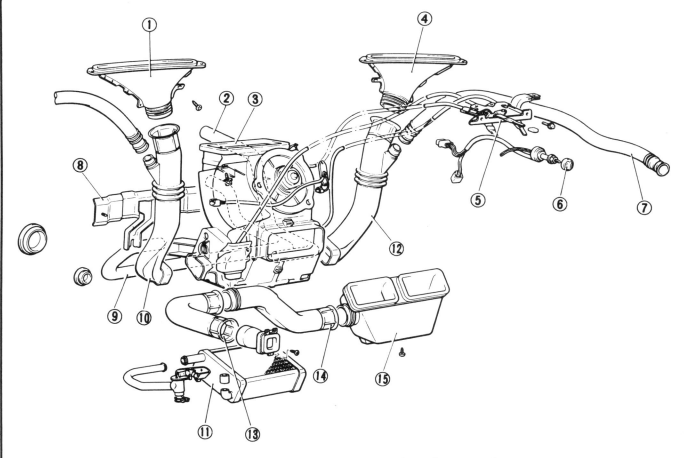

Fig. 2.9 Heater components (Sec 9)

1	Demister nozzle	5	Control lever assembly	9	Coolant hose (return)	13	Side ventilator duct
2	Heater air intake	6	Heater blower switch	10	Demister duct	14	Side ventilator duct
3	Heater casing	7	Side demister duct	11	Heater matrix	15	Centre ventilator duct
4	Demister nozzle	8	Mounting bracket	12	Demister duct		

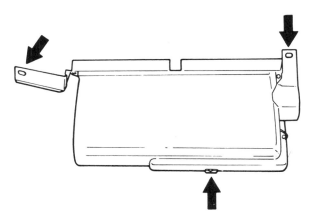

Fig. 2.10 Centre ventilator duct mounting points (Sec 10)

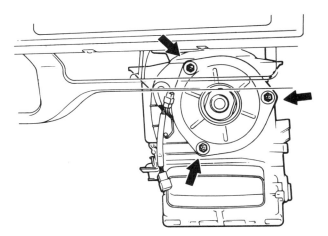

Fig. 2.11 Heater motor mounting bolts (Sec 10)

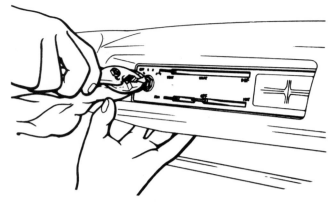

Fig. 2.12 Pulling heater control panel forward (Sec 11)

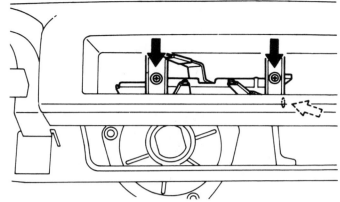

Fig. 2.13 Heater control lever mounting screws (Sec 11)

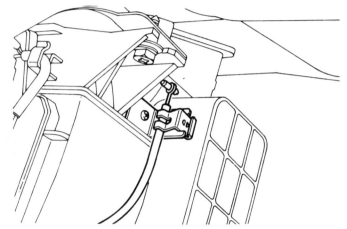

Fig. 2.14 Air control cable (Sec 11)

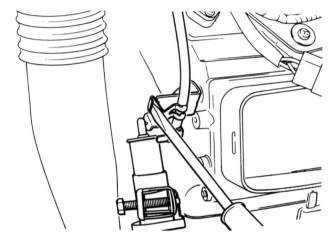

Fig. 2.15 Coolant valve cable (Sec 11)

11 Heater controls – removal, refitting, adjustment

1   Remove the centre console and the parcels shelf as described in Chapter 12.
2   Remove the now exposed centre ventilator duct.
3   Remove the instrument panel trim as described in Chapter 12.
4   Disconnect the control cables from the heater.
5   Pull the control knobs from the levers and the booster fan switch.
6   Disconnect the heater electrical harness at the multi-pin plug.
7   Grip the fan switch spindle with a pair of pliers and pull the heater control panel forward at the same time assisting removal by pushing with the fingers inserted from the rear.
8   Once the panel is partially withdrawn, extract the three panel securing screws and remove the control lever assembly from below the instrument panel.
9   Refit by reversing the removal operations but make sure that the springs and claws on the panel are securely engaged in the instrument pad.
10 Once the control panel is refitted, connect and adjust the control cables in the following way.

Fresh/Recirculated air control lever
11 Set the control lever to INSIDE and hold the fresh air flap on the heater closed but with the air outlets open. Clip the control cable securely in position.

Coolant valve lever
12 Set the temperature control lever to OFF. Set the coolant valve so that it is fully closed. Clip the control cable securely in position.

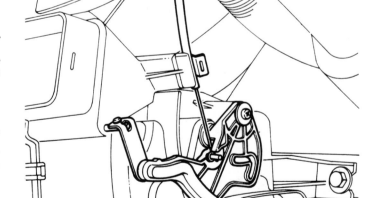

Fig. 2.16 Air flow direction cable (Sec 11)

Air flow direction lever
13 Set the control lever to the DEF position and then hold the flap valve on the heater downward to deflect air to the windscreen demister nozzles. Clip the control cable securely in position.

12 Heater unit – removal and refitting

1   Disconnect the battery negative lead.
2   Set the heater temperature control to HOT.
3   Drain the cooling system.

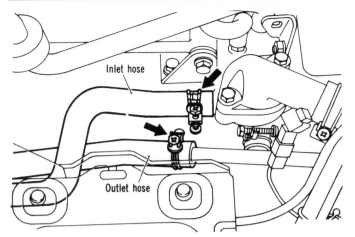

Fig. 2.17 Heater hose connections (Sec 12)

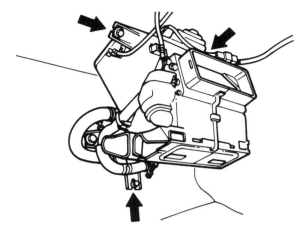

Fig. 2.18 Heater mounting bolts (Sec 12)

4   Working inside the car, remove the centre console and the parcels shelf as described in Chapter 12.
5   Remove the now exposed centre ventilator duct and the windscreen demister duct.
6   Remove the instrument panel trims as described in Chapter 12.
7   Disconnect the control cables from the heater.
8   Disconnect the heater hoses from the engine.
9   Disconnect the heater wiring at the multi-pin plug.
10 Remove the two upper and one lower heater mounting bolts and nut and remove the heater from the car interior. As the heater is withdrawn, make sure that the heater hoses and the bulkhead grommet are drawn through at the same time. Avoid spilling coolant which may be in the heater, on the carpets.
11 If the heater matrix is leaking, it must be removed from the casing and either repaired professionally or a new or reconditioned unit obtained.
12 Refitting is a reversal of removal but adjust the control cables as described in Section 11.
13 Refill the cooling system on completion.

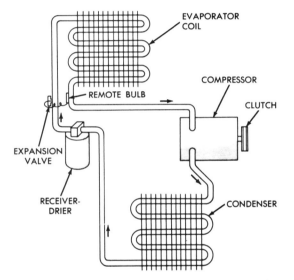

Fig. 2.19 Diagrammatic view of air conditioning system (Sec 13)

13 Air conditioner – general description

1   The optionally fitted air conditioner is of a conventional design incorporating a belt driven compressor, condensor and evaporator.

Fig. 2.20 Air conditioner wiring diagram (Sec 13)

2   Due to the dangerous type of refrigerant used in the system, *no* part of the air conditioning system must ever be disconnected unless it has been professionally discharged by your dealer or a refrigeration engineer.

3   In order to undertake some major engine overhaul operations, the compressor and other components may have to be moved. Provided that they can be unbolted and moved within the range of their flexible connecting hoses then this is acceptable. Where the air conditioning components still cause obstruction, then the refrigerant must be discharged by your dealer *before* disconnecting them.

4   Always have the air conditioner recharged with refrigerant by your dealer when the work is completed.

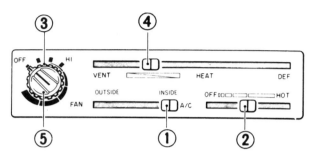

Fig. 2.21 Air conditioner control panel (Sec 14)

1   Fresh air (outside) or recirculated air (inside) lever
2   Heater temperature control lever (OFF for air conditioner)
3   Air conditioner temperature control ring
4   Air deflector lever
5   Fan switch

14 Air conditioner – operation and precautions

1   The system only operates when the ignition switch is ON.

2   To operate the air conditioner, set the air selector lever to INSIDE and the temperature control lever to OFF.

3   Set the air deflector lever as desired.

4   The air temperature control ring may now be rotated to the desired setting and the fan switch actuated (low, medium, high) to meet individual preference.

5   To obtain the best performance from the system when in use, observe the following:

(a)   Park the car in the shade
(b)   On cars with automatic transmission, during low roadspeeds, downshift to increase engine speeds
(c)   If you wish to operate the air conditioner while the car is stationary, set the gearchange lever in neutral and increase the idle speed to improve the engine cooling and compressor speed rotational level
(d)   When ascending a very long gradient, switch off the air conditioner from time to time to prevent the engine overheating
(e)   Keep the condenser free from flies and dirt by brushing the fins with a soft brush or blowing through the condenser in the reverse direction to normal airflow with a compressed air line
(f)   At the specified service intervals have your dealer check the refrigerant level and the compressor oil level
(g)   Maintain the correct compressor drivebelt tension
(h)   Periodically check the security of all component mounting bolts
(i)   Regularly check the condition of the system flexible hoses for deterioration. If evident have the system discharged and renew the hoses immediately

6   When the car has been left standing in hot weather, a pool of water may be observed under the vehicle. This is normal and is condensate draining from the evaporator.

7   If the refrigerant flow in the sight glass of the receiver-drier shows evidence of bubbles or foaming then the refrigerant level in the system is low or contains gas. This condition should be rectified by your dealer immediately.

15 Air conditioning system major components – removal and refitting

1   Although it is recommended that the renewal of system components and flexible and rigid pipelines is left to your dealer, there is no reason why the following operations cannot be carried out by the home mechanic.

2   Having said this, the following precautions must be observed:

Have the refrigerant discharged by your dealer or refrigeration engineer
Observe absolute cleanliness
Plug ports and hoses as quickly as possible after disconnection to prevent the admission of moisture

On completion, have the system pressure tested for leaks and recharged by your dealer.

Compressor – removal and refitting

3   Remove the engine air cleaner.

4   On 1597 cc engines release the drivebelt idler pulley.

5   Disconnect the suction and discharge hoses from the compressor by unscrewing the unions. Plug or cap all openings immediately to prevent the entry of moisture or dirt.

6   Remove the distributor cap and the rotor arm.

7   Disconnect the LT lead from the distributor.

8   Disconnect the lead to the compressor cut-out switch by separating it at its snap connector.

9   On 1410 cc engined models, unscrew the bolts which hold the compressor to the adjuster links, then remove the lower mounting bolts. Lift the compressor from its mounting bracket, slipping off the drivebelt as it is removed.

10   On 1597 cc engined models, loosen all mounting bolts, then remove the upper ones and swivel the compressor downwards. Unscrew the lower mounting bolts and remove the compressor from its bracket, slipping off the drivebelt as it is removed.

11   Refitting is a reversal of the removal operations but engage the drivebelt in the pulley groove before lowering the compressor into its mounting bracket. On 1410 cc engines, the compressor drivebelt is tensioned by moving the compressor on its mountings. On 1597 cc engines tensioning is made by moving the idler pulley. The belt is correctly tensioned when it can be deflected by 0.38 in (9.5 mm) using moderate thumb pressure at the centre of the longest run of the belt.

12   When connecting the hoses to the compressor, smear the union threads with refrigerant oil (nothing else) to ensure a good seal.

13   Do not operate the air conditioner until the compressor has been topped with oil and the system recharged with refrigerant by your dealer.

Condenser – removal and refitting

14   This is mounted at the front of the engine compartment to the left of the radiator.

15   Disconnect the pipelines from the condenser and immediately plug or cap the open ends to prevent the entry of moisture or dirt.

16   Unbolt and remove the condenser from the engine compartment.

17   Refitting is a reversal of removal. Smear the threads of the pipeline unions with refrigerant oil – nothing else.

Evaporator

18   Disconnect the battery earth lead.

19   Remove the high pressure cut-out switch from the discharge port on the compressor.

20   Remove the centre console from inside the car (see Chapter 12).

21   Remove the parcels shelf, the instrument lower panel and bezel (see Chapter 12).

22   From just above the evaporator, disconnect the plug from the control box and also disconnect the earth lead.

23   Disconnect the lead from the temperature sensor in the evaporator coil.

24   Remove the side cowl bracket.

25   Unbolt the evaporator and lower it until the pipelines can be disconnected from the evaporaator coil and the expansion valve.

26   Remove the condensate drain tube and then withdraw the evaporator from the car interior.

27   Refitting is a reversal of removal. Apply a smear of refrigerant oil to the threads of the pipeline unions before screwing them up.

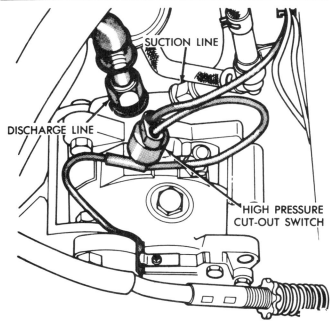

Fig. 2.22 Typical compressor connections (Sec 15)

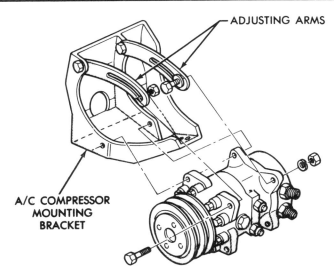

Fig. 2.23 Compressor mounting (1410 cc engine) (Sec 15)

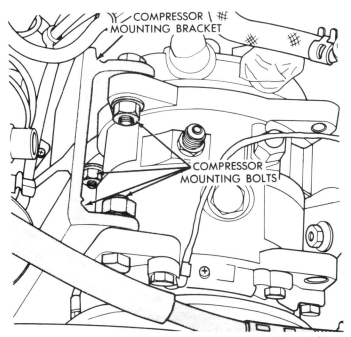

Fig. 2.24 Compressor mounting (1597 cc engine) (Sec 15)

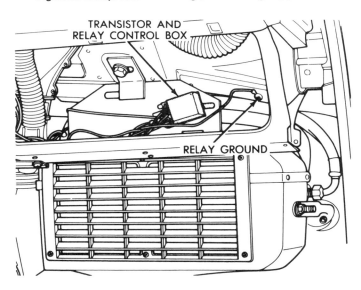

Fig. 2.25 Evaporator mounting (Sec 15)

Receiver/drier

28 Removal is simply a matter of disconnecting the pipelines and capping the openings and releasing the mountings.

29 Refit by reversing the removal operations but apply refrigerant oil to the threads of the pipeline unions before screwing them up.

16 Throttle opener – air conditioner

1 In order to compensate for a reduction in the engine idling speed which occurs when the air conditioner is switched on, a vacuum diaphragm unit is fitted to the carburettor which automatically opens the throttle slightly to maintain the specified idle speed.

2 Refer to Chapter 3, Section 10, for details and adjustment procedure.

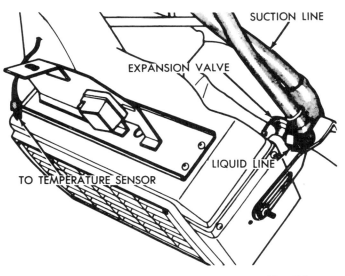

Fig. 2.26 Pipeline connections to evaporator (Sec 15)

17 Fault diagnosis – cooling system

Symptom	Reason(s)
Heat generated in cylinders not being successfully disposed of by radiator	Insufficient water in cooling system Drivebelt slipping (accompanied by a shrieking noise on rapid engine acceleration) Radiator core blocked or radiator grille restricted Bottom water hose collapsed, impeding flow Thermostat not opening properly Ignition advance and retard incorrectly set (accompanied by loss of power and perhaps misfiring) Carburettor incorrectly adjusted (mixture too weak) Exhaust system partially blocked Oil level sump too low Blown cylinder head gasket (coolant/steam being forced down the radiator overflow pipe under pressure) Engine not yet run-in Brake binding Inoperative electric fan Faulty fan thermostatic switch
Too much heat being dispersed by radiator	Thermostat jammed open Incorrect grade of thermostat fitted allowing premature opening of valve Thermostat missing
Leaks in system	Loose clips on coolant hoses Top or bottom coolant hoses perished and leaking Radiator core leaking Thermostat gasket leaking Pressure cap spring worn or seal ineffective Blown cylinder head gasket (pressure in system forcing coolant steam down overflow pipe Cylinder wall or head cracked
Oil in coolant	Blown engine gasket or leak in fluid cooler (automatic trans.)

18 Fault diagnosis – heating and ventilation systems

Symptom	Reason(s)
Insufficient heat	Faulty thermostat Blocked coolant flow control valve Blocked or collapsed heater hose Air pocket in heater hose or matrix
Poor air flow or incorrect distribution	Incorrectly adjusted heater control cables Disconnected ducts

19 Fault diagnosis – air conditioning system

Symptom	Reason(s)
No cooling	Blown fuse Disconnected electrical lead Defective relay Faulty compressor or clutch Leak in system Defective pressure switch
Intermittent cooling	Excessive moisture in system Excessive system pressure Slipping compressor drivebelt Expansion valve stuck open

Symptom	Reason(s)
Insufficient cooling	Defective temperature sensor
	Compressor clutch slipping
	Fresh air vents open
	Condenser fins clogged
	Evaporator fins clogged
	Low refrigerant level
	Receiver-drier clogged
	Excessive oil in system
	Air or moisture in system
	Defective expansion valve
Noisy operation	Worn or slack compressor drivebelt
	Loose compressor mountings
	Low compressor oil level
	Drivebelt idler pulley worn (1597 cc engine)
	Excessive moisture in system
	Defective expansion valve
	Too much or too little refrigerant in system

Chapter 3 Fuel, exhaust and emission control systems

Contents

Specifications

System type .... Rear mounted fuel tank, mechanical pump and dual barrel carburettor

Fuel type
Without catalytic converter .... 90 to 94 RON
With catalytic converter .... Unleaded

Carburettor application (1400 models)
UK .... Mikuni 26-30DIDTA-20
North America except California .... Mikuni 28-32DIDTA-181 or 28-32DIDTA-191
California .... Mikuni 28-32DIDTA-180 or 28-32DIDTA-190
Canada .... Mikuni 28-32DIDTA-132 or 28-32DIDTA-137

Carburettor application (1600 models)
North America except California
    Manual transmission .... Mikuni 28-32DIDSA-4, 28-32DIDSA-5, 28-32DIDSA-24, 28-32DIDSA-25, 28-32DIDTA-183, or 28-32DIDTA-193
    Automatic transmission .... Mikuni 28-32DIDTA-196
California:
    Manual transmission .... Mikuni 28-32DIDTA-138, 28-32DIDTA-182 or 28-32DIDTA-193
    Automatic transmission .... Mikuni 28-32DIDTA-194
Canada:
    Manual transmission .... Mikuni 28-32DIDTA-133
    Automatic transmission .... Mikuni 28-32DIDTA-139

Carburettor data (1400 models)

	26-30DIDTA-20	28-32DIDTA-132	28-32DIDTA-137	28-32DIDTA-180	28-32DIDTA-181	28-32DIDTA-190	28-32DIDTA-191
Throttle bore: Primary	1.02 in (26 mm)	1.10 in (28 mm)	1.10 in (28 mm)	1.10 in (28 mm)	1.10 in (28 mm)	1.10 in (2.8 mm)	1.10 in (28 mm)
Secondary	1.18 in (30 mm)	1.26 in (32 mm)	1.26 in (32 mm)	1.26 in (32 mm)	1.26 in (32 mm)	1.26 in (32 mm)	1.26 in (32 mm)
Main jet: Primary	92.5	101.3	101.3	96.3	95	97.5	98.8
Secondary	175	190	185	185	185	180	180
Pilot jet: Primary	60	60	60	52.5	52.5	55	55
Secondary	60	60	60	60	60	60	60
Enrichment jet	40	40 x 2	40 x 2	60	50	40	40
Float level (from top of body)	0.75 in (19 mm)	0.75 in (19 mm)	0.75 in (19 mm)	0.75 in (19 mm)	0.75 in (19 mm)	0.75 in (19 mm)	0.75 in (19 mm)
Choke valve set temperature	23°C (73°F)	23°C (73°F)	23°C (73°F)	23°C (73°F)	23°C (73°F)	23°C (73°F)	23°C (73°F)
Choke valve to bore clearance at choke breaker	0.055 in (1.4 mm)	0.055 in (1.4 mm)	0.055 in (1.4 mm)	0.055 in (1.4 mm)	0.055 in (1.4 mm)	0.055 in (1.4 mm)	0.055 in (1.4 mm)
Fast idle opening	12°	12°	12°	12°	12°	12°	12°
Idle speed	800 to 900 rpm	800 to 900 rpm	800 to 900 rpm	650 to 750 rpm	650 to 750 rpm	650 to 750 rpm	650 to 750 rpm
Idle CO	0.5 to 2.0%	0.5 to 2.0%	0.5 to 2.0%	Less than 0.1%	Less than 0.1%	0.5 to 1.5%	0.5 to 1.5%
Throttle opener setting	—	—		800 to 900 rpm	800 to 900 rpm	800 to 900 rpm	800 to 900 rpm

Carburettor details (1600 models)

	28-32DIDSA-4, 28-32DIDSA-5, 28-32DIDSA-25	28-32DIDTA-133	28-32DIDTA-138	28-32DIDTA-139	28-32DIDTA-182
Throttle bore: Primary	1.10 in (28 mm)	1.10 in (28 mm)	1.10 in (28 mm)	1.10 in (28 mm)	1.10 in (28 mm)
Secondary	1.26 in (32 mm)	1.26 in (32 mm)	1.26 in (32 mm)	1.26 in (32 mm)	1.26 in (32 mm)
Main jet: Primary	92.5	101.3	101.3	101.3	95
Secondary	190	190	185	185	185
Pilot jet: Primary	55	60	60	60	52.5
Secondary	70	60	60	60	60
Enrichment jet	60	40 x 2	40 x 2	40 x 2	50
Float distance from top of body	0.75 in (19 mm)	ADJUSTMENT BY WASHERS UNDER NEEDLE VALVE TO CENTRE FUEL LEVEL IN SIGHT GLASS			
Choke valve set temperature	23°C (73°F)				
Fast idle opening	18°	ALL CLEARANCES PRE-SET DURING MANUFACTURE			
Idle speed	650 to 750 rpm	800 to 900 rpm	800 to 900 rpm	800 to 900 rpm	650 to 750 rpm
Idle CO	Less than 0.1%	0.5 to 2.0%	0.5 to 2.0%	0.5 to 2.0%	Less than 0.1%
Throttle opener setting	800 to 900 rpm	—	—	—	800 to 900 rpm

	28-32DIDTA-183	28-32DIDTA-193	28-32 DIDTA-194	28-32DIDTA-195	28-32DIDTA-196
Throttle bore: Primary	1.10 in (28 mm)	1.10 in (28 mm)	1.10 in (28 mm)	1.10 in (28 mm)	1.10 in (28 mm)
Secondary	1.26 in (32 mm)	1.26 in (32 mm)	1.26 in (32 mm)	1.26 in (32 mm)	1.26 in (32 mm)
Main jet: Primary	96.3	98.8	98.8	97.5	97.5
Secondary	185	98.8	180	180	180
Pilot jet: Primary	52.3	55	55	55	55
Secondary	60	60	60	60	60
Enrichment jet	60	40	40	40	40
Float distance from top of body	ADJUSTMENT BY WASHERS UNDER NEEDLE VALVE TO CENTRE FUEL LEVEL IN SIGHT GLASS				
Choke valve set temperature					
Fast idle opening	ALL CLEARANCES PRE-SET DURING MANUFACTURE				
Idle speed	650 to 750 rpm	650 to 750 rpm	700 to 800 rpm	650 to 750 rpm	700 to 800 rpm
Idle CO	Less than 0.1%	0.5 to 1.5%	0.5 to 1.5%	0.5 to 1.5%	0.5 to 1.5%
Throttle opener setting	800 to 900 rpm	800 to 900 rpm	850 to 950 rpm	800 to 900 rpm	850 to 950 rpm

Torque wrench settings

	lbf ft	Nm
Intake manifold bolts	13	18
Exhaust manifold bolts	13	18
Exhaust manifold to downpipe flange nuts	17	24
Fuel tank mounting nuts	18	25
Carburettor mounting nuts	14	19

1 General description

The fuel system comprises a rear mounted fuel tank, flow and return fuel pipes, a mechanically operated fuel pump and a twin barrel downdraught carburettor.

All models have a crankcase emission control system but the number of other emission control devices employed depends upon the operating territory for which the vehicle is destined, refer to Section 13.

2 Fuel pump – description, removal and refitting

1   The fuel pump is operated by a short pushrod on 1410 cc engines or directly by its rocker arm on 1597 cc engine from an eccentric cam on the camshaft.

2   The pumps are of the sealed, disposable type and cannot be cleaned or repaired and in the event of a fault developing, a new pump must be fitted.

3   If a fuel pump is suspected of having failed due to the fact that there is no fuel at the carburettor, test the pump in the following way.

4   Disconnect the fuel inlet pipe from the carburettor and place its open end in a container. Operate the starter when regular well defined spurts of fuel should be seen to be ejected from the end of the pipe. If fuel is not ejected, check the following possibilities before renewing the pump.

   Fuel tank empty
   In-line fuel filter clogged (see next section)
   Fuel lines or tank breather hoses crushed or collapsed
   Faulty filler cap (USA only)

5   To remove the pump on the 1410 cc engine, disconnect the fuel hoses and then remove the securing bolts and lift the pump from the engine. Catch the operating rod as it slides out of its hole. On the 1597 cc engine, disconnect the fuel hoses and simply unbolt and remove the pump (photos).

6   When refitting a fuel pump, use new gaskets fitted one to each side of the insulating spacer.

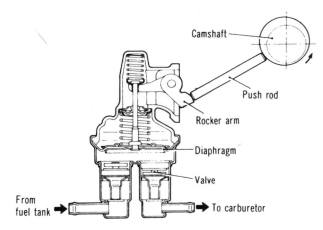

Fig. 3.1 Fuel pump (1410 cc engine) (Sec 2)

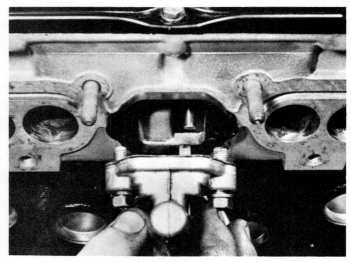

2.5a Removing the fuel pump (1410 cc engine)

2.5b The fuel pump operating rod

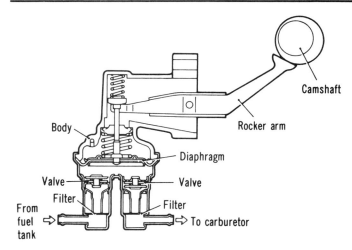

Fig. 3.2 Fuel pump (1597 cc engine) (Sec 2)

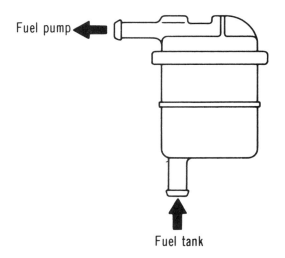

Fig. 3.3 Fuel filter connections (Sec 3)

3 In-line fuel filter – cleaning and renewal

1   At the intervals specified in the Routine maintenance Sections at the beginning of this manual remove the fuel filter and hold it in such a position that the fuel outlet nozzle is pointing down and apply compressed air or air from a tyre pump to the other nozzle. This will remove any accumulations of water from the filter (photo).
2   At the specified mileages, renew the filter making sure that it is reconnected the correct way round.

4 Air cleaner – servicing, removal and refitting

Engines without emission control system
1   This type of air cleaner has a manually controlled flap valve in the air intake spout which can be set to WINTER or SUMMER positions by moving a lever (photo). In the WINTER position air for the carburettor is drawn into the air cleaner from the area adjacent to the exhaust manifold (photo).
2   To remove the air cleaner element, prise down the toggle clips, remove the wing nut and lift off the lid. At the specified mileage intervals, the element should be renewed but at intermediate services, remove the element and tap it hard on a bench or apply compressed air to the inner surface of the element to dislodge any surface dirt. Never attempt to clean the element in water or any type of solvent (photos).
3   Always wipe the casing clean from grit or flies before fitting the element.
4   The air cleaner casing is bolted to the supporting brackets and if removed, only withdraw it far enough at first to be able to disconnect the flexible connecting hoses. regularly check the condition of the lid and casing sealing washers (photos).

Engines with emission control systems
5   On these engines, an automatic temperature controlled air cleaner is fitted. The temperature of the intake air is maintained at a constant level by means of a thermostatically controlled flap valve which mixes the air in the correct proportions as it is drawn from two sources, outside air and air from the vicinity of the exhaust manifold.
6   The correct operation of the flap valve can be observed by holding a mirror at the end of the intake spout. If the engine is cold the valve should be closed against cold air and when hot open, or partially open, to cold air.
7   Servicing of the element is carried out as described for the non-temperature-controlled air cleaner in paragraphs 2 to 4.

3.1 The fuel filter

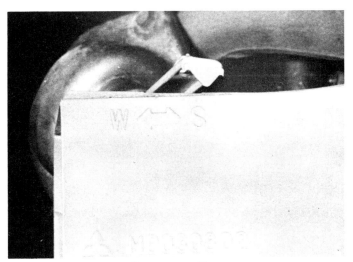

4.1 The air cleaner Winter/Summer markings

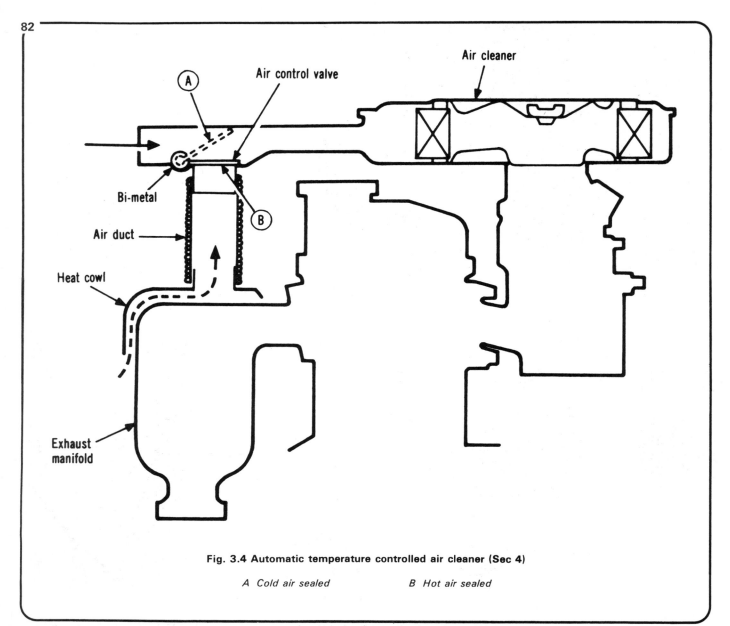

Fig. 3.4 Automatic temperature controlled air cleaner (Sec 4)

A Cold air sealed   B Hot air sealed

4.2a Undoing one of the air cleaner toggle clips

4.2b Removing the air cleaner element

4.4a The air cleaner to carburettor seal

4.4b The air cleaner lid alignment marks

5.3 The fuel tank flexible filler pipe

5.4 Fuel tank supporting strap

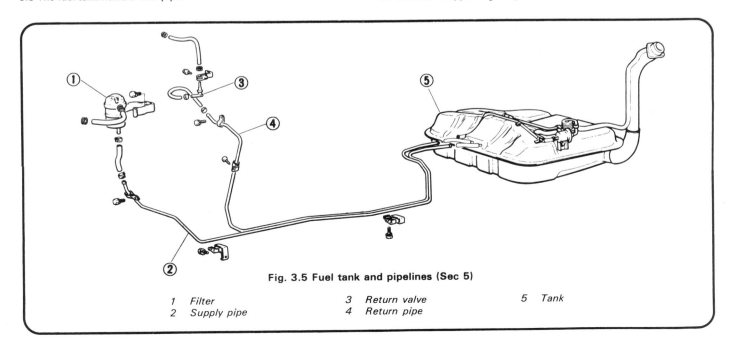

Fig. 3.5 Fuel tank and pipelines (Sec 5)

1	Filter	3	Return valve	5	Tank
2	Supply pipe	4	Return pipe		

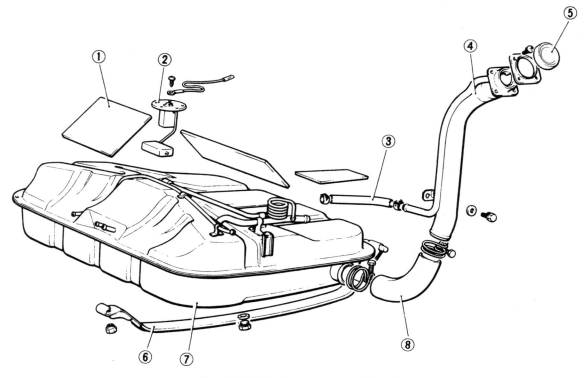

Fig. 3.6 Fuel tank components (Sec 5)

1 Insulation pad	3 Breather hose	5 Filler cap	7 Tank
2 Fuel level transmitter	4 Filler neck	6 Tank support strap	8 Flexible connecting hose

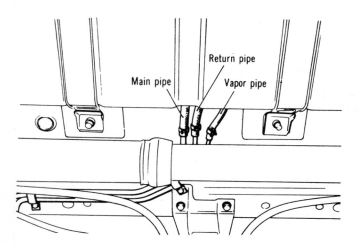

Fig. 3.7 Fuel hose identification at tank (Sec 5)

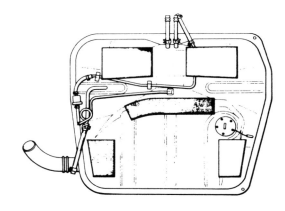

Fig. 3.8 Fuel tank insulating pad locations (Sec 5)

5 Fuel tank – removal and refitting

1   The rear mounted fuel tank is supported on metal straps. On cars built for operation in North America, the fuel system incorporates an evaporative control circuit (refer to Section 6).
2   To remove the tank, first disconnect the battery and drain the fuel into a container which can be sealed. On some models, a drain plug is fitted but if not the fuel will have to be syphoned out. Never drain fuel with the car over an open pit as the vapour will accumulate in the pit and take a long time to disperse.
3   Disconnect the fuel flow, return and breather hoses from the tank also the flexible hoses from the filler neck (photo).
4   Support the tank and unscrew the nuts from the support straps.

Lower the tank enough to be able to disconnect the leads from the tank sender unit, then remove the tank from under the car (photo).
5   The tank unit can be carefully withdrawn after extracting the securing screws.
6   If the tank contains sediment or water, it can be cleaned by vigourously shaking it (after first removing the sender unit) using several changes of paraffin and finally allowing it to drain.
7   If the tank is leaking or has rusted, repair is a job for experts as welding or soldering must never be carried out until the tank has been thoroughly purged by steam cleaning or an industrial type cleansing agent and degreaser.
8   Refitting is a reversal of removal, make sure that the insulating strips and pads are securely in position.

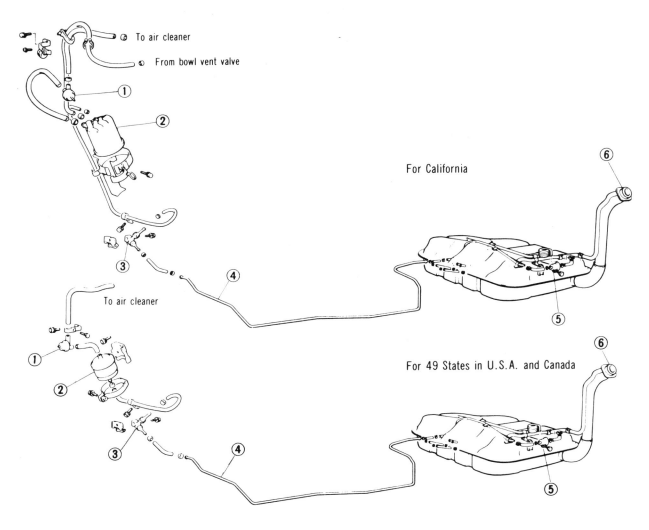

To air cleaner

From bowl vent valve

To air cleaner

For California

For 49 States in U.S.A. and Canada

Fig. 3.9 Fuel evaporative control system (Sec 6)

1   Purge control valve
2   Charcoal canister
3   Fuel check valve
4   Fuel vapour pipe
5   Two-way valve
6   Sealed filler cap

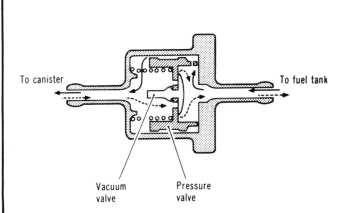

To canister

To fuel tank

Vacuum valve

Pressure valve

Fig. 3.10 Fuel evaporative control system two-way valve (Sec 6)

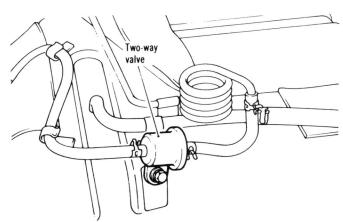

Two-way valve

Fig. 3.11 Location of fuel evaporative system two-way valve (Sec 6)

For 49 States in U.S.A. and Canada

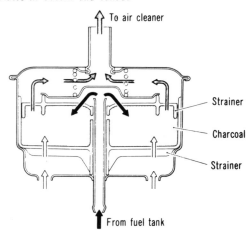

For California

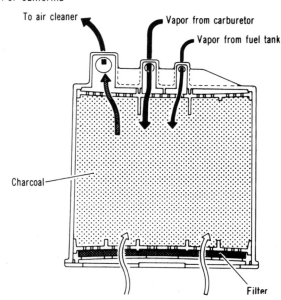

Fig. 3.12 Fuel evaporative control system charcoal canistr (Sec 6)

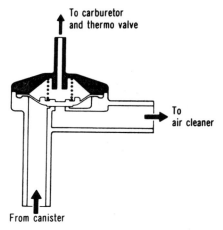

Fig. 3.13 Fuel evaporative control system purge control valve (Sec 6)

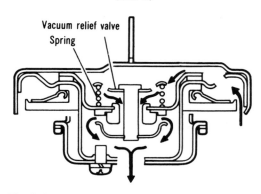

Fig. 3.14 Sealed type fuel tank filler cap (Sec 6)

---

6   Fuel evaporative control system (North America) – description and servicing

1   This system is used to control the fuel vapour which escapes from the vehicle fuel tank.

2   Components of the system include a charcoal canister, a purge control valve and a special fuel filler cap which incorporates a vacuum relief valve. On Californian models, a further refinement is in the form of a carburettor bowl vent valve to control any evaporation of fuel vapour from that area as well.

3   When the engine is not running, fuel vapour from the tank accumulates in the upper part of the tank where it then flows through a spirally wound tube into a two-way valve. At a pre-set vapour pressure the valve opens and the vapour passes into the charcoal canister where it is stored.

4   Once the engine is started and running, air is drawn into the canister and carries away the trapped fuel vapour into the air cleaner and to the intake manifold where it is burned during the normal combustion process.

5   As fuel in the tank is consumed, a two-way valve opens momentarily to allow air to be drawn into the tank through the charcoal canister in order to prevent a vacuum being created within the tank.

Servicing – two-way valve

6   At the intervals specified in the Routine maintenance section at the beginning of this manual, remove the valve and blow into it from either end. If the air passes through after an initial slight resistance then the valve is in good condition.

Servicing – charcoal canister

7   The canister should be renewed at the intervals specified in the Routine maintenance Section at the beginning of this manual. At the same time check the condition of all canister connecting hoses.

8   Mark the hoses and their connections on the canister to ensure that they are reconnected correctly.

Servicing – purge control valve

9   The purge control valve is designed to prevent fuel vapour from entering the air cleaner when the engine is idling otherwise an excessively high CO emission level would be detected from the exhaust.

10   Once the intake vacuum increases above a pre-set level at which the purge control valve diaphragm operates, then the fuel vapour begins to be purged from the canister as previously explained.

11   To check the valve, make sure that the temperature of the engine coolant is between 80 and 90°C (180 and 190°F).

12   Disconnect the purge hose from the air cleaner and blow into the hose. The valve should be closed.

13   Now start the engine and increase its speed to between 1500 and 2000 rpm and again blow into the purge hose. The valve should be open. If it is not, check for a clogged or split vacuum hose or a faulty thermo valve.

Fuel tank filler cap

14   The filler cap on cars built for operation in the USA is of the sealed type and incorporates a vacuum relief valve to admit air from outside as necessary to maintain a constant pressure within the fuel tank.

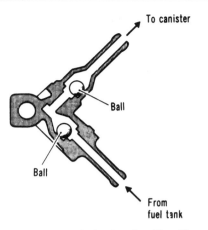

Fig. 3.15 Fuel check valve (Sec 7)

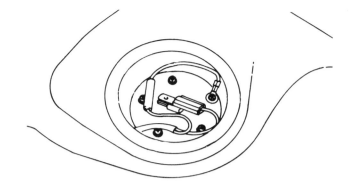

Fig. 3.16 Fuel tank transmitter inspection hole (Sec 8)

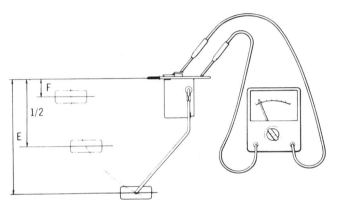

Fig. 3.17 Testing fuel tank transmitter (Sec 8)

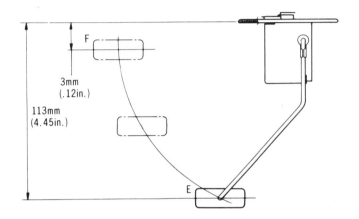

Fig. 3.18 Tank transmitter float positions (Sec 8)

7 Fuel check valve (North America)

1   This device is used on certain models to prevent the leakage of fuel in the event of the car turning over.
2   The valve is located in the fuel vapour line between the charcoal canister and the two-way valve and is mounted on the engine compartment rear bulkhead.
3   Under normal circumstances, the valve passages are open but if the car turns over then one of the bulbs will close the fuel passage from the tank.

8 Fuel level tank transmitter unit

1   An incorrect reading on the fuel gauge may be due to a faulty gauge or instrument voltage stabiliser (see Chapter 10). Where this has been proved not to be the case, turn your attention to checking the transmitter in the fuel tank.
2   Disconnect the battery and remove the spare wheel.
3   Detach the small cover plate from the floor of the spare wheel compartment to expose the tank transmitter unit.
4   Disconnect the electrical leads, remove the transmitter securing screws and withdraw the unit carefully from the tank. Cover the hole immediately to prevent dirt entering and fuel vapour escaping.
5   A tester will now be required to check the resistance of the unit at various float positions. Connect the tester between the terminal on the transmitter and the unit mounting plate. With the float arm in the fully raised position, the indicated resistance should be between 14.9 and 19.1 ohms. With the float arm fully lowered the resistance should be between 113.5 and 126.5 ohms. As the float arm is moved from fully lowered to fully raised so the resistance should alter smoothly in a consistently increasing series of increments.
6   If necessary, the float arm can be bent very gently to make the float positions agree with those shown in Fig. 3.18.

9 Carburettors – general

1   All models have a twin-barrel downdraught carburettor with automatic choke, accelerator pump and enrichment device (photos).
2   The exact version of the carburettor fitted to each particular vehicle depends upon the engine capacity, the type of transmission and the operating territory. The ancillary devices described in this Chapter may not therefore be found on all carburettors.

9.1a Carburettor (float chamber side)

9.1b Carburettor (fuel cut off solenoid side) – tamperproof mixture screw arrowed

9.1c Carburettor (automatic choke side)

3   When renewing a carburettor, always replace it with one of identical type by referring to the reference number or tag on the original units.

Automatic choke (cold start)

4   The choke valve plate is controlled by a thermo-wax element which senses the engine coolant temperature. At cold starts, with the coolant cold, the valve plate is closed. As the coolant temperature rises so the valve plate opens progressively to the full open position when normal engine temperature is reached.

5   The position of the valve plate is overridden by a choke breaker which is actuated by intake manifold vacuum to prevent over rich mixture.

6   The position of the cold start sensor and the choke valve plate also sets the fast idle cam to give a faster than normal engine idle speed when the engine is cold.

Primary metering system

7   This consists of the primary main jet, pilot jet, idle mixture screws and main nozzle for idling, part throttle also full throttle at low speeds.

9.1d Carburettor (vacuum diaphragm unit side)

Secondary metering system

8   This consists of the secondary main jet, pilot jet, main nozzle and diaphragm chamber. When power requirement exceeds that provided by the primary barrel, the secondary throttle comes into action, being actuated by venturi depression applied to the diaphragm.

Enrichment system

9   This is based upon the diaphragm chamber being connected to manifold vacuum. When the engine is operating at part throttle, the diaphragm is drawn to the right to close the enrichment valve. At wide throttle openings, the drop in manifold pressure allows the diaphragm to move in the opposite direction, by means of its spring, and to open the enrichment valve. Extra fuel then passes through the enrichment jet into the emulsion well.

Accelerator pump

10 This is of typical mechanical construction and comprises a flexible diaphragm, linkage and spring. The pump is charged with fuel when the throttle is closed and when the throttle is opened, the pump pushrod compresses the diaphragm spring and ejects fuel into the primary venturi.

Fuel inlet system

11 This comprises the usual needle valve and float. A small filter is located in the fuel inlet passage.

9.1e Top view of the carburettor

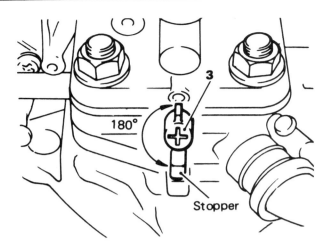

Fig. 3.19 Typical idle speed screw limiter cap (Sec 10)

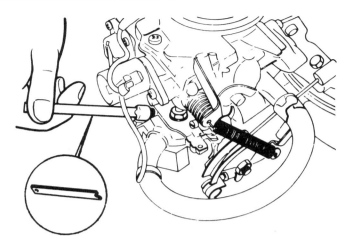

Fig. 3.20 Adjusting mixture screw with special tool (Sec 10)

Anti-overfill device

12 This is a steel ball located in the float bowl which will apply pressure to the float in the event of the car turning over, to hold the fuel inlet valve closed.

Fuel cut-off device

13 This is a small solenoid operated valve which is held open when the ignition key is ON, so penetrating the free flow of fuel.
14 When the ignition key is turned OFF the solenoid is de-energised and the valve cuts off the fuel flow immediately to prevent the engine running on (dieseling) due to fuel continuing to bleed into the intake manifold.

Throttle opener (air conditioned cars)

15 This device is fitted to cars equipped with an air conditioner to compensate for the reduction in engine idle speed which occurs when the air conditioner is switched on.

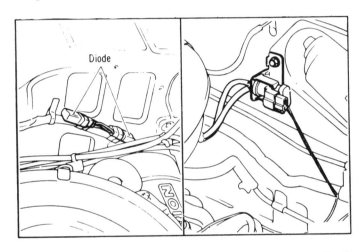

Fig. 3.21 Location of diode and solenoid – throttle opener circuit (Sec 10)

10 Idle speed and mixture – adjustment

Except USA models

1 On all models, the only adjustment which should require occasional alteration is the idle speed screw. The mixture adjustment screw is pre-set during production and should not be tampered with unless the carburettor has been completely overhauled and new parts ftted.
2 To adjust the idle speed have the engine at the normal operating temperature, idling with the transmission in neutral.
3 Make sure that all electrical accessories, lights and the air conditioner, if fitted, are off.
4 If the car is not already so equipped, connect a tachometer to the engine in accordance with the maker's instructions.
5 Turn the idle speed screw in or out as necessary to bring the engine speed to the level given in the Specifications for the particular engine and transmission. On some carburettors, a limiter cap is fitted to the screw.
6 A tamperproof cap is fitted to the mixture screw requiring the use of a special pronged tool to turn the screw.
7 With the engine at the normal operating temperature and a tachometer connected, turn the mixture screw in until the engine speed just starts to drop as indicated on the tachometer. Now unscrew it slightly until the engine runs smoothly.
8 Adjust the idle speed to that specified by means of the idle speed screw.
9 This should be regarded as a basic setting and an exhaust gas analyser should be used for precise adjustment to bring the exhaust emission level to within the specified CO level.
10 Switch off the engine, remove the tachometer and the exhaust gas analyser.

USA models

11 Have the engine at the normal operating temperature with the transmission in neutral and all lights and electrical accessories off.
12 Connect an exhaust gas analyser in accordance with the manufacturer's instructions.
13 Disconnect the air hose which runs between the reed valve and the air cleaner (see Section 14) at the reed valve end. Plug the inlet of the reed valve. Start the engine.
14 Using the idle speed and mixture adjusting screws, set the idle speed and CO level to the tolerance given in the Specifications according to engine capacity and transmission type.
15 Unplug the reed valve and reconnect the air hose.
16 Readjust the idle speed if necessary by using the idle speed screw.
17 On cars with an air conditioner, a throttle opener is fitted to the carburettor and this must now be adjusted by fully raising the throttle opener lever while the throttle opener setting screw is turned to give the speed again shown in the Specifications according to engine capacity and transmission type. The normal engine idle speed should not be affected by this adjustment.
18 On many later models, the tamperproof cap fitted to the idle mixture adjustment screw is retained by a lock screw which is only accessible after the carburettor has been removed.

11 Carburettor – removal and refitting

1 Do not remove the carburettor if the engine is hot, allow it to cool down first.

2   Disconnect the battery and drain the cooling system.
3   Remove the air cleaner.
4   Disconnect the fuel hoses from the carburettor.
5   Disconnect the throttle cable.
6   Disconnect the leads from the fuel cut-off solenoid valve and the coolant hose to the throttle body.
7   Unscrew and remove the carburettor mounting nuts and lift the unit from the intake manifold (photo).
8   Remove the old flange gaskets and clean the carburettor manifold and carburettor mating flanges.
9   Refit by reversing the removal procedure using new flange gaskets. It is possible to fit the gasket incorrectly so match the holes in the gasket with those in the base of the carburettor.
10 Refill the cooling system. Check the idle speed on completion. Do not operate the engine with the air cleaner removed as it is possible for the engine to backfire and cause ignition of fuel in the carburettor throat. Top up the cooling system (Chapter 2).

12 Carburettor – overhaul

1   Do not dismantle the carburettor needlessly. Unless the float chamber is contaminated with sediment or water or the jets require cleaning or the float level needs adjusting, there should really be little cause for stripping.
2   Where the unit has covered a high mileage and the throttle valve spindle and other pivots and linkage are worn, it is recommended that a new carburettor is fitted rather than attempt to renew small individual components.
3   With the carburettor removed from the engine, clean away any external dirt. Paraffin and a brush should be adequate for this job. Take care not to allow dirt to enter the fuel pipe connections or venturis.
4   Remove the throttle return spring and the damper spring.
5   Remove the throttle adjuster lever spring and the secondary return spring.
6   On USA cars, disconnect the lower end of the throttle opener link from the lever, extract the two screws and remove the throttle opener.
7   Prise off the circlip and disconnect the choke unloader link.
8   Disconnect the vacuum hose.
9   Disconnect the lower end of the diaphragm chamber link and then remove the chamber by unscrewing the nut at the top of the chamber.
10 On USA cars, extract the two screws and remove the air switching valve.
11 Remove the float chamber cover (five screws). Tap it off with a plastic-faced hammer, do not try and lever it off with a screwdriver. Once the cover is off, do not turn the carburettor upside down unless you are prepared to catch the check ball and accelerator pump discharge weight which will be ejected (photos).
12 Peel away the float chamber cover gasket.
13 Push out the float lever pivot pin and remove the float.
14 Unscrew and remove the fuel inlet needle valve, gasket and small filter.
15 On USA cars remove the mixture control valve nut do not disturb the orifice.
16 Unless absolutely essential, do not remove the automatic choke as this is set during production. If it is removed, watch for the ejection of the steel ball from the anti-overfill device.

11.7 Removing the carburettor

17 Remove the fuel cut-off solenoid valve.
18 The jets can be removed using screwdrivers which are a close fit in the jet grooves. Clean the jets only by blowing through them with air from a tyre pump or probing with a nylon bristle. Never use wire or the calibration of the jet will be ruined. Do not tamper with the by-pass or adjuster screws which are sealed with white paint. Take care that the primary and secondary jets are not mixed up when refitting them.
19 Remove the enrichment assembly.
20 Disconnect the pump rod from the throttle shaft lever and withdraw the accelerator pump assembly.
21 On USA models, remove the sub-EGR valve link retaining clip and after extracting the washer and spring, disconnect the link. Do not touch the EGR adjusting screw which is pre-set during production.
22 With the carburettor inverted, extract the two screws which hold the main carburettor body to the throttle body. Separate the components and peel off the gasket (photo).
23 If the idle speed or mixture screws must be removed, count the number of turns which they are screwed in when removing them so that they can be set in their approximate original positions when reassembling so the engine can at least be started.
24 Clean out the carburettor bowl and the small mesh filter.
25 Commence reassembly by gently screwing in the idle mixture screw to its original position. If this was not recorded at dismantling, turn it right in lightly with the fingers and then unscrew it 1½ turns as a basic starting point.
26 Using a new gasket, fit the throttle body.
27 Where applicable fit the sub-EGR valve link.
28 Connect the accelerator pump rod.
29 Fit the fuel cut-off valve.
30 Using a new gasket fit the enrichment assembly.
31 Fit the accelerator pump and the ball and counterweight.

12.11a Carburettor interior

12.11b Carburettor cover with float

12.22 Extracting a throttle body screw

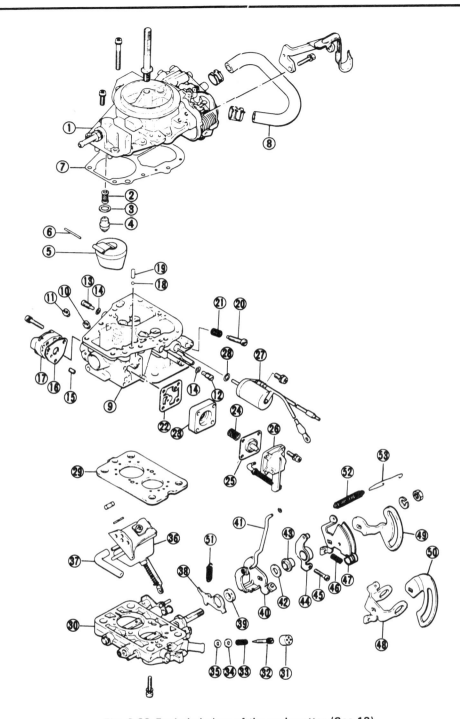

Fig. 3.22 Exploded view of the carburettor (Sec 12)

1 Float chamber cover
2 Filter mesh
3 Washer
4 Fuel inlet needle valve
5 Float
6 Pivot pin
7 Gasket
8 Coolant hose
9 Carburettor body
10 Primary main jet
11 Secondary main jet
12 Primary pilot jet
13 Secondary pilot jet
14 O-ring
15 Enrichment assembly
16 Gasket
17 Enrichment assembly
18 Check valve ball
19 Check valve weight
20 Idle speed screw
21 Spring
22 Gasket
23 Pump body
24 Spring
25 Diaphragm
26 Pump cover
27 Anti-run-on solenoid valve
28 O-ring
29 Insulator
30 Throttle body
31 Tamperproof cap
32 Mixture adjusting screw
33 Spring
34 Washer
35 Seal
36 Vacuum diaphragm unit
37 Hose
38 Intermediate lever
39 Spacer
40 Lever
41 Rod
42 Spacer
43 Collar
44 Fast idle lever
45 Fast idle adjusting screw
46 Spring
47 Throttle lever (RHD)
48 Throttle lever (LHD)
49 Lever (automatic transmission – RHD)
50 Lever (automatic transmission – LHD)
51 Throttle return spring
52 Pull-off spring
53 Damper spring

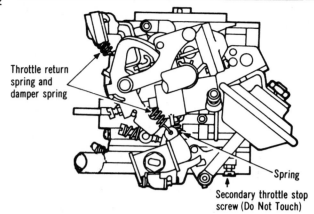

Throttle return spring and damper spring

Spring

Secondary throttle stop screw (Do Not Touch)

Fig. 3.23 Carburettor spring arrangement (Sec 12)

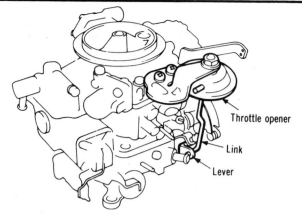

Throttle opener

Link

Lever

Fig. 3.24 Throttle opener (North American models) (Sec 12)

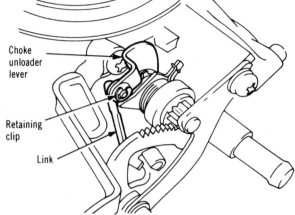

Choke unloader lever

Retaining clip

Link

Fig. 3.25 Choke unloader link (Sec 12)

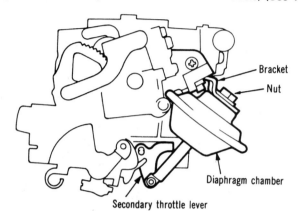

Bracket

Nut

Diaphragm chamber

Secondary throttle lever

Fig. 3.26 Removing diaphragm chamber (Sec 12)

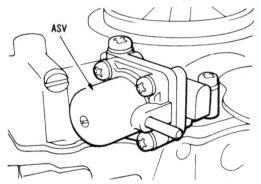

ASV

Fig. 3.27 Air switching valve (North American models) (Sec 12)

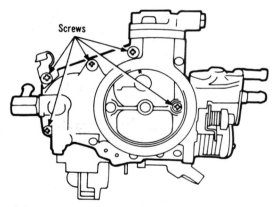

Screws

Fig. 3.28 Float chamber cover securing screws (Sec 12)

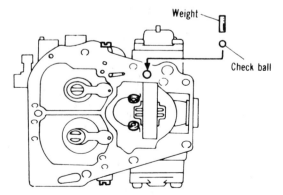

Weight

Check ball

Fig. 3.29 Location of accelerator pump discharge ball and weight (Sec 12)

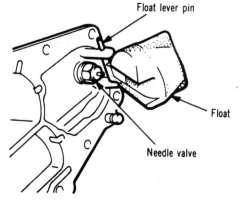

Float lever pin

Float

Needle valve

Fig. 3.30 Float arrangement (Sec 12)

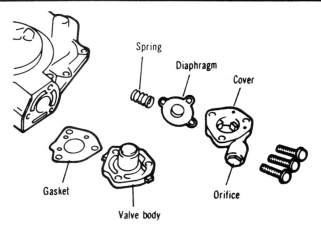

Fig. 3.31 Mixture control valve (North American models) (Sec 12)

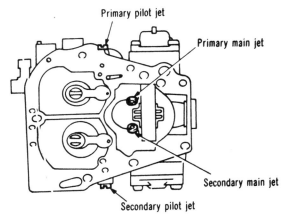

Fig. 3.32 Location of carburettor jets (Sec 12)

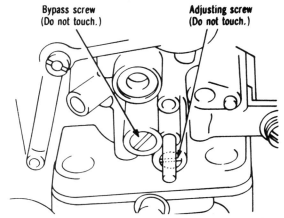

Fig. 3.33 Sealed adjuster screws not to be disturbed (Sec 12)

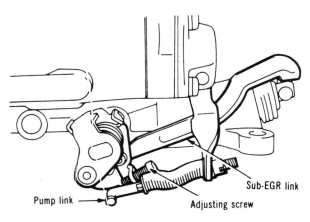

Fig. 3.34 Sub EGR valve link (North American models) (Sec 12)

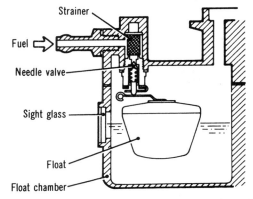

Fig. 3.35 Cut-away view of float chamber (Sec 12)

32 Fit the steel ball to the bottom of the float chamber making sure that the brass blade is face downward.
33 Fit the filter and fuel inlet needle valve.
34 Fit the float assembly.
35 Using a new gasket, fit the float chamber cover, tightening the screws evenly.
36 Where applicable, fit the mixture control valve using a new gasket and the air switching valve.
37 Fit the return springs.
38 Once the carburettor has been refitted to the engine, check the idle speed and mixture adjustment as previously described and check the fuel level in the float bowl sight glass. The level of the fuel should be within 0.16 in (4.0 mm) of the dot on the sight glass. If it is outside this tolerance, the cover will have to be removed from the float chamber and the thickness of washer under the fuel inlet needle valve either reduced or increased in size.

13 Emission control systems – general

1 In order to reduce the emissions from the engine and exhaust system, various devices are used, their number and complexity differing according to the operating territory of the particular vehicle.
2 All engines are fitted with a carburettor and a distributor designed to give 'clean' engine operation.
3 All engines have a crankcase ventilation system but the design differs according to operating territory.
4 Models having a temperature controlled air cleaner, jet valves and a fuel tank with vapour control have been described in earlier parts of this manual.
5 Other emission control devices and systems are briefly described and servicing procedures outlined in the next Section.

14 Emission control systems – description and testing

Crankcase emission control system (except California)
1 This is a closed type system which draws blow-by gas from the crankcase into the air cleaner and the intake manifold by means of hoses connected to the rocker cover. At small throttle openings, the blow-by gas is drawn from the rear of the cover into the manifold while fresh air enters the rocker cover from the air cleaner. At wide throttle openings, the blow-by gas is drawn from both ends of the rocker cover.

Crankcase emission control system (California)
2 On these vehicles, the system incorporates a positive crankcase ventilation (PCV) valve fitted to the rocker cover. Fresh air is drawn into the crankcase through the air cleaner and mixes with the blow-by gases which then pass through the PCV valve into the intake manifold. The PCV valve is a metering device responsive to intake manifold

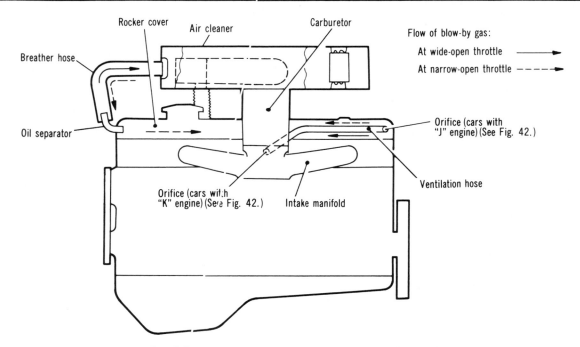

Fig. 3.36 Typical crankcase ventilation system (Sec 14)

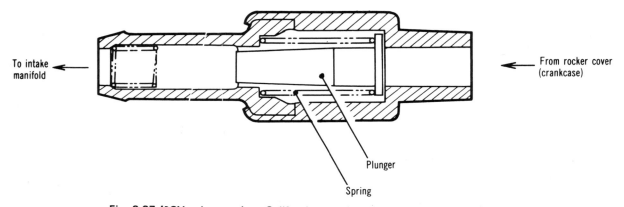

Fig. 3.37 PCV valve used on Californian crankcase ventilation system (Sec 14)

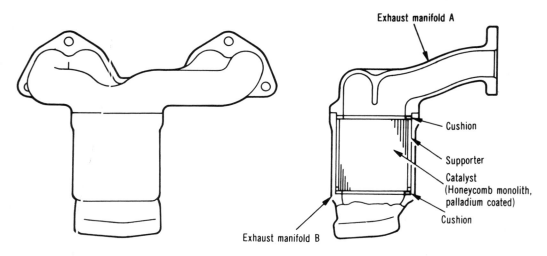

Fig. 3.38 Catalytic converter (Sec 14)

vacuum. Under conditions of heavy acceleration or high speed driving when manifold vacuum is low, and the blow-by gases exceed the PCV valve capacity, the gases accumulate in the air cleaner which they enter through the breather hose.

Catalytic converter (North America only)

3   This is basically a container of coated ceramic catalytic elements which oxidise the hydrocarbons and carbon monoxide in the exhaust gases, turning them into harmless water and carbon dioxide.
4   Unusually, the converter is mounted directly to the exhaust manifold within the engine compartment and to avoid overheating, observe the following precautions.
5   Do not allow the engine to idle if it is inclined to misfire.
6   Use only unleaded fuel.
7   Keep the engine in perfect tune.
8   Do not switch off the ignition when the car is moving in gear.
9   If the catalytic converter must be renewed due to damage or corrosion, note that the converter and the lower manifold have to be renewed as an assembly (Fig. 3.39).
10   To remove the converter, withdraw the air cleaner, the air duct and the heat cowl.
11   Disconnect the exhaust downpipe.
12   Unbolt the exhaust manifold from the cylinder head and pull it away from the head.
13   Unbolt the manifold from the catalytic converter casing.
14   Fit the new converter making sure that a new cushion is fitted to the top and bottom flanges also a new stainless steel gasket so that it fits within the cushion. Tighten the bolts to the specified torque.

Secondary air supply system

15   This is fitted in conjunction with a catalytic converter and incorporates a reed valve which feeds secondary air into the exhaust manifold to improve oxidation of the noxious exhaust gases. The reed valve pulsates by exhaust vacuum in the exhaust manifold and draws air in through the air cleaner.
16   Periodically check the operation of the reed valve by having the engine idling and then disconnecting the air hose from the reed valve. Place the hand lightly on the inlet port of the reed valve and if suction is felt, the valve is satisfactory. Also check that no exhaust gas can be detected being blown back from the valve.

Deceleration device

17   This prevents over rich mixture during deceleration when the throttle is closed causing an increase in exhaust hydrocarbon emissions.
18   The device incorporates a coasting air valve (CAV) and an air switching valve (ASV) both valves being attached to the carburettor.
19   The CAV is only used on North American cars and is actuated by carburettor vacuum to supply additional air to the intake manifold. A speed sensor and a solenoid valve are used in conjunction with the valve to suspend its action at low engine speeds to prevent the possibility of the engine stalling.
20   The ASV is again actuated by carburettor vacuum and it cuts off the fuel flow to the carburettor by-pass holes and pilot outlet by feeding extra air into the slow passage. At low engine speeds the valve action is suspended in a similar manner to that described for the CAV. The ASV as well as reducing emission levels also improves fuel economy.

Dashpot

21   This device shows the closure of the throttle to its idling position to reduce the volume of hydrocarbon emitted. A servo valve is incorporated to detect the vacuum in the intake manifold. If the vacuum exceeds a pre-set level, the valve is closed and the air trapped in the dashpot diaphragm cannot escape so the particular throttle valve opening is retained. Once the vacuum falls below the pre-set valve, the servo valve opens and the dashpot operates normally by the gentle escape of the trapped air from the diaphragm.
22   To adjust the dashpot, first make sure that the engine idle speed is correct.
23   With the engine idling, push the dashpot operating rod up as far as it will go and with the vehicle tachometer or one connected temporarily, check the engine speed. This should be between 1900 and 2100 rpm. Now release the operating rod suddenly and count the

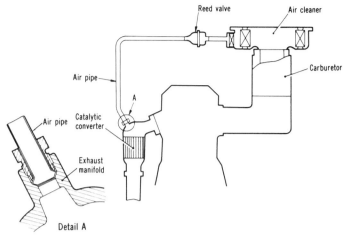

Fig. 3.39 Secondary air supply system (Sec 14)

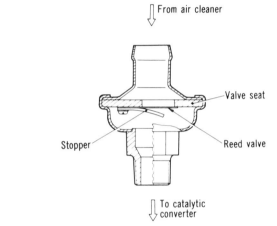

Fig. 3.40 Reed valve (Sec 14)

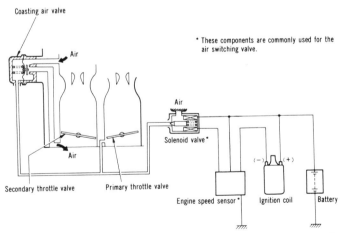

Fig. 3.41 Coasting air valve system (North American models) (Sec 14)

number of seconds taken for the engine speed to drop to 900 rpm. This should be between 3 and 6 seconds.
24   Adjust as necessary by means of the screw to bring the engine speed down to the specified level in the required time interval.

Exhaust gas recirculation (EGR) system (Canada)

25   With this system, the exhaust gases are partially recirculated in order to dilute oxides of nitrogen present in the gases resulting from the normal process of combustion.

26 Two valves are incorporated in the system, a control valve and a thermal valve.

27 The EGR control valve is vacuum operated from the intake manifold and responds to variations in engine load to reduce or increase the flow of recirculated exhaust gas.

28 The thermo valve senses the engine coolant temperature and keeps the EGR valve closed at low coolant temperatures to prevent any adverse effect upon cold starting and during warm up which the admission of recirculated exhaust gas might cause.

29 Periodically, check the operation of the system. To do this, start the engine from cold and then increase its speed from idle to 2500 rpm holding the finger under the EGR control valve to check the operation of the diaphragm. When the engine is cold (coolant below 55°C (131°F) the diaphragm should not move. If it does move, then probably the green striped vacuum hose which runs between the EGR control valve and the thermo valve is clogged or the thermo valve itself is defective.

30 If the control valve operates correctly with the engine cold, warm

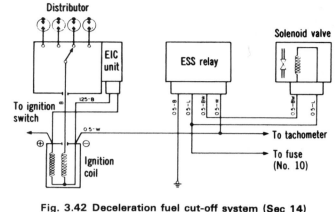

Fig. 3.42 Deceleration fuel cut-off system (Sec 14)

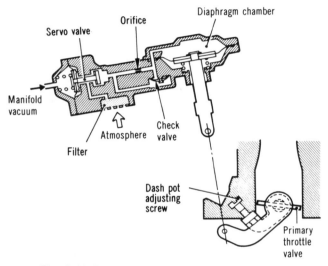

Fig. 3.43 Dashpot for throttle closure (Sec 14)

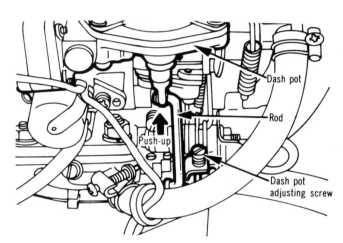

Fig. 3.44 Dashpot adjusting screw (Sec 14)

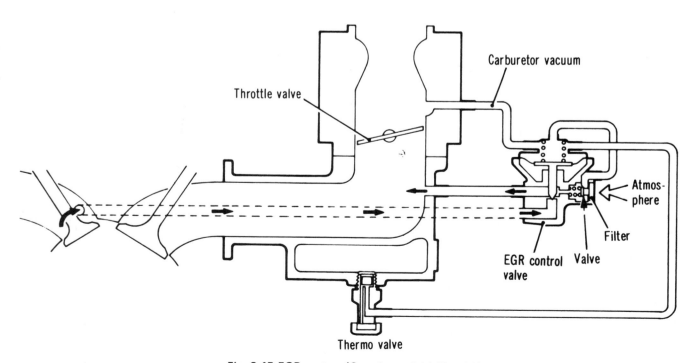

Fig. 3.45 EGR system (Canada models) (Sec 14)

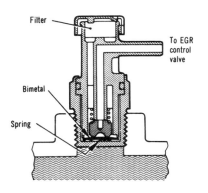

Fig. 3.46 EGR system thermo valve (Sec 14)

up the engine and repeat the test. If the diaphragm operates correctly, then the system is functioning satisfactorily. If it does not, either the vacuum hose, the thermo valve or the EGR valve diaphragm are probably at fault. Inspect and renew as necessary.

Exhaust gas recirculation (EGR) system (North America)
31 The purpose of the system is basically the same as that just described but the recirculated gas is more strictly controlled by extra complicated valve combinations.
32 On cars operating in California, a dual EGR control valve is used. This valve incorporates primary and secondary valves which are controlled by different vacuum sources according to the position of the throttle valve plate. A thermo valve is connected to the EGR valve to suspend or actuate the EGR valve according to engine coolant temperature but the EGR valve is always closed to gas flow at idle or full throttle conditions.
33 On cars operating outside California the EGR control valve is of a

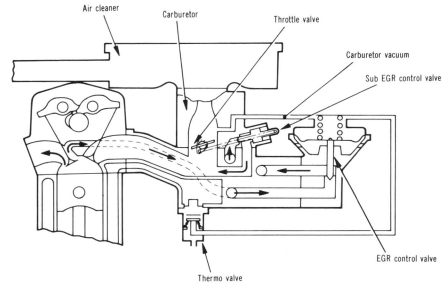

Fig. 3.47 EGR system (North America except California) (Sec 14)

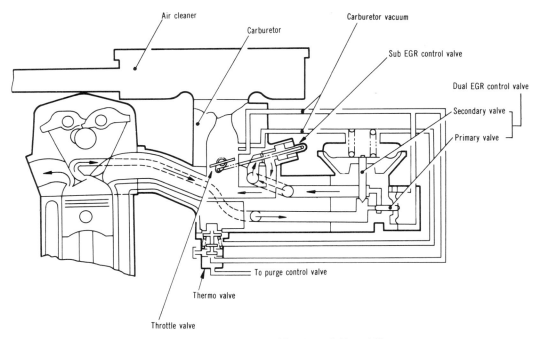

Fig. 3.48 EGR system (California) (Sec 14)

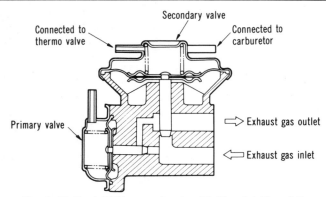

Fig. 3.49 Dual EGR control valve (California) (Sec 14)

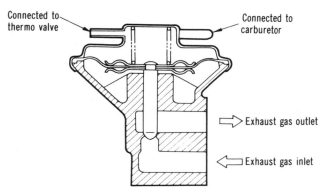

Fig. 3.51 EGR control valve (North America except California)
(Sec 14)

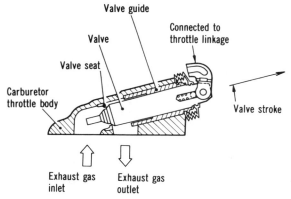

Fig. 3.53 Sub EGR control valve (Sec 14)

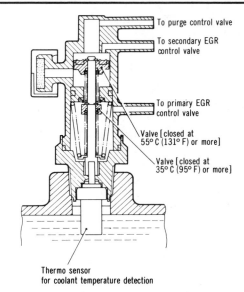

Fig. 3.50 EGR system thermo valve (California) (Sec 14)

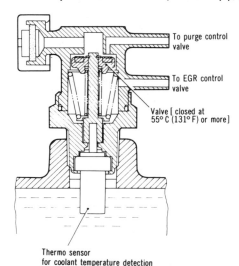

Fig. 3.52 EGR system thermo valve (North America except
California) (Sec 14)

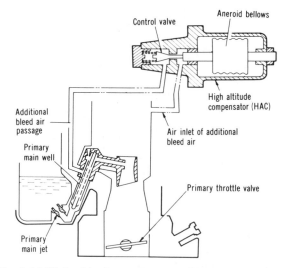

Fig. 3.54 High altitude compensator (California) (Sec 14)

more simple design serving the same purpose and again controlled by a thermo valve.

34 On all models, a sub EGR control valve is incorporated in the system. The valve opens and closes by direct linkage from the throttle valve to further modulate the EGR flow which is initially regulated by the EGR valve.

35 Periodically check the operation of the system. To do this, start the engine from cold and let it idle.

36 Raise the engine speed to 2500 rpm and check that the secondary EGR valve does not operate. If it does, renew the thermo valve.

37 Now warm up the engine until the coolant temperature exceeds 55°C (131°F). Again raise the engine speed to 2500 rpm and check that the secondary valve operates. If it does not, it may be the EGR valve or the thermo valve which is at fault.

38 Operate the sub EGR valve by hand to see that it operates smoothly. If it is stiff, remove it and try cleaning away carbon and dust deposits and lubricating it. If it is still very stiff, renew it.

39 If the sub EGR valve is very hard to remove, withdraw the rubber dust excluder and spray easing fluid around the valve to free it.

High altitude compensator (California)
40 This consists of a high altitude compensator (HAC), an additional air bleed passage and an air passage from the carburettor to the HAC. By this arrangement, the engine fuel/air mixture ratio is maintained at the same level irrespective of operating altitude by bleeding additional air into the carburettor primary main well which in turn is controlled by aneroid bellows reacting to changes in atmospheric pressure.

---

15 Accelerator linkage – removal and refitting

---

1 The control arrangement comprises a cable, pivot or cross-shaft, pedal and arm.
2 Working under the bonnet, remove the air cleaner and detach the accelerator cable from the clamps.
3 Release the locknut at the bulkhead and turn the adjusting screw to slacken the cable.
4 Disconnect the cable from the lever on the carburettor and the anchorage at the accelerator pedal arm.
5 Turn the cable adjusting screw to release the assembly from the bulkhead and withdraw the cable complete from the bulkhead into the engine compartment.

Right-hand drive models
6 Extract the split pin from the pedal arm pivot, unhook the return spring and remove the pedal.

Left-hand drive models
7 Remove the parcels shelf and the pedal cover.
8 Unhook the pedal return spring, extract the cross-shaft circlips and

Fig. 3.55 Accelerator pedal (right-hand drive models) (Sec 15)

unbolt the left-hand cross-shaft bracket. The accelerator pedal assembly can now be withdrawn.

All models
9 Refitting is a reversal of removal but apply grease to the friction surfaces.
10 On completion, adjust the cable by means of the bulkhead adjuster nut and locknut to give a free play not exceeding 0.04 in (1.0 mm).

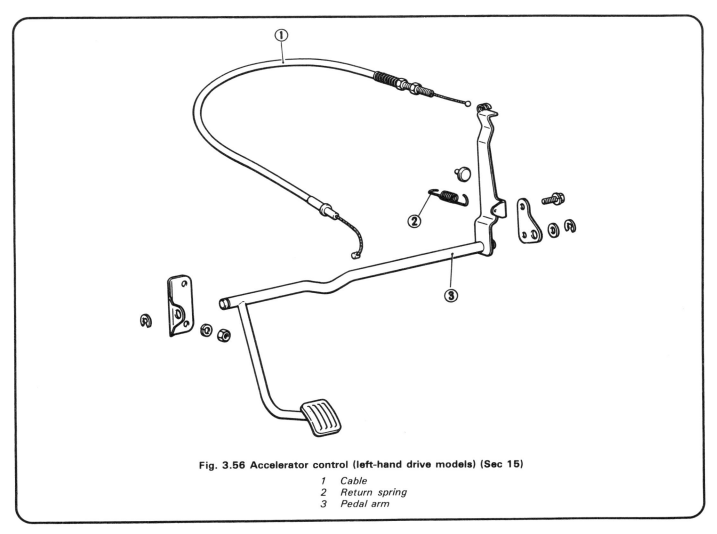

Fig. 3.56 Accelerator control (left-hand drive models) (Sec 15)

1 Cable
2 Return spring
3 Pedal arm

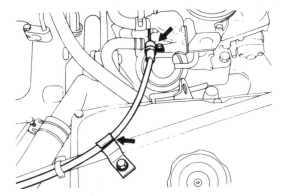

Fig. 3.57 Accelerator cable clips (Sec 15)

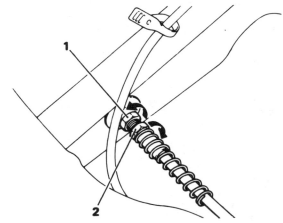

Fig. 3.58 Accelerator cable at bulkhead (Sec 15)

1   Locknut   2   Adjuster

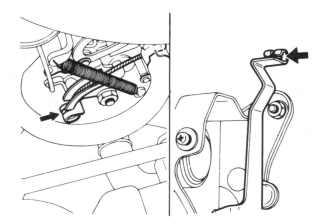

Fig. 3.59 Accelerator cable connections (Sec 15)

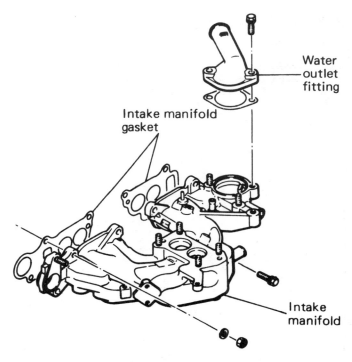

Fig. 3.60 Intake manifold (Sec 16)

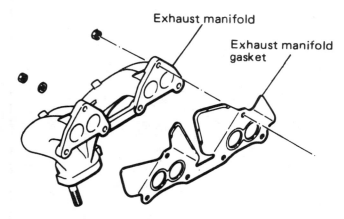

Fig. 3.61 Exhaust manifold (Sec 16)

16 Manifolds and exhaust system

Intake manifold

1   The intake manifold is constructed of light alloy and bolted to the side of the cylinder head.

2   In order to provide pre-heating for the carburettor, the intake manifold has coolant passages from the cylinder head. Before the intake manifold can be removed, the cooling system must be drained, also the hose from the thermostat housing disconnected.

3   The distributor passes through a cut-out in the intake manifold flange and the distributor must therefore be removed before the manifold can be withdrawn (refer to Chapter 4).

4   When refitting the intake manifold, always use a new gasket and smear gasket cement around the coolant passage cut-out.

Exhaust manifold

5   This is bolted to the cylinder head on the side opposite to the intake manifold and is of cast-iron construction. The heat shield for the collection of heated air for the air cleaner is located on the manifold and the flange gaskets are designed to form heat defecting shields at their upper edges (photo).

Exhaust system

6   This is of two section construction but may vary in design according to the operating territory.

7   The system is attached to the exhaust manifold by a flanged joint while the downpipe is supported by a bracket.

8   Inspect the system regularly for corrosion. The two sections may be renewed independently by unbolting the central flanged joint (photo).

9   The exhaust system is flexibly mounted (photos).

10   Refer to Section 14 of this Chapter for details of North American models equipped with a catalytic converter.

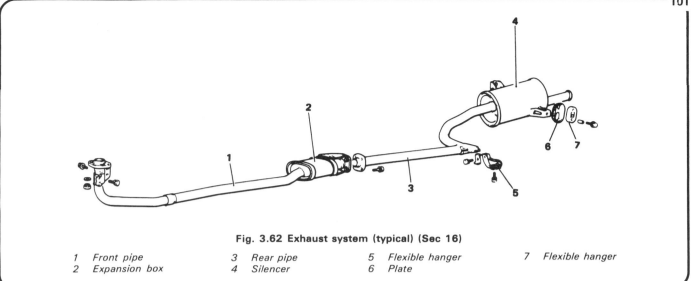

Fig. 3.62 Exhaust system (typical) (Sec 16)

1 Front pipe	3 Rear pipe	5 Flexible hanger	7 Flexible hanger
2 Expansion box	4 Silencer	6 Plate	

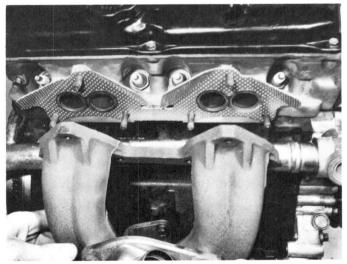

16.5 Fitting the exhaust manifold

16.8 Exhaust system flanged joint

16.9a Exhaust system centre mounting

16.9b Exhaust system rear mounting

17 Fault diagnosis – fuel and emission control

Symptom	Reason(s)
Fuel consumption excessive	Air cleaner choked and dirty giving rich mixture
	Fuel leaking from carburettor, fuel pump, or fuel lines
	Float chamber flooding
	Needle valve or float fault
	Generally worn carburettor or loose jets
	Distributor condenser faulty
	Balance weights or vacuum advance mechanism in distributor faulty
	Carburettor incorrectly adjusted, mixture too rich
	Idling speed too high
	Contact breaker gap incorrect
	Valve clearances incorrect
	Faulty automatic cold start device
	Incorrectly set spark plugs
	Tyres under-inflated
	Wrong spark plugs fitted
	Brakes dragging
	Emission control system faulty (see later in this Section)
Insufficient fuel delivery or weak mixture	Partially clogged filters in pump and carburettor or fuel line
	Faulty fuel pump
	Faulty tank filler cap (USA)
	Incorrectly adjusted mixture screw
	Too little fuel in fuel tank (prevalent when climbing steep hills)
	Union joints on pipe connections loose
	Split in fuel pipe on suction side of fuel pump
	Inlet manifold to block or inlet manifold to carburettor gaskets leaking
	Faulty anti-run-on solenoid valve
Power reduced	Clogged main jets
	Accelerator linkage requires adjustment
	Fuel filteer blocked
	Air cleaner blocked
	Accelerator pump fault
Erratic idling	Slow jet clogged
	Secondary throttle valve operating incorrectly
	Worn throttle valve shafts
	Broken carburettor flange gasket
	Incorrectly adjusted mixture screw
Flat spot or hesitation	Clogged jets
	Accelerator pump fault
	Secondary throttle valve operating incorrectly
Engine will not start	Fuel level too high
	Lack of fuel
	Incorrect setting of mixture screw
	Faulty anti-dieseling (anti-run-on) solenoid
	Incorrect fast idle adjustment

Emission control system faults

Erratic idling	Dash pot incorrectly adjusted
	Carbon canister purge line disconnected
	Faulty deceleration device (USA)
	Faulty EGR valve
Power reduced	Faulty altitude compensator (California)
	Faulty EGR valve

Chapter 4 Ignition system

Contents

Specifications

Firing order 1-3-4-2

Distributor (mechanical breaker type)
Rotation .... Clockwise
Contact breaker points gap .... 0.018 to 0.021 in (0.45 to 0.55 mm)
Dwell angle .... 49 to 55°
Condenser capacity .... 0.22 microfarad

Distributor (electronic breakerless type)
Rotation .... Clockwise
Air gap .... 0.008 to 0.024 in (0.2 to 0.6 mm)

Ignition timing
All models except California:
    Manual transmission models .... 4 to 6° BTDC at 650 to 750 rpm
    Automatic transmission models .... 4 to 6° BTDC at 700 to 800 rpm
Canadian models .... 4 to 6° BTDC at 800 to 900 rpm

Ignition coil
Californian models:
    Type .... LB 119
    Primary coil resistance .... 0.7 to 0.85 ohm
    Secondary coil resistance .... 9 to 11 k ohm
Canadian models:
    Type .... LB 63
    Primary coil resistance .... 1.26 to 1.54 ohm
    Secondary coil resistance .... 9 to 11 k ohm
    Ballast resistor .... 1.22 to 1.49 ohm
All other models:
Type .... LB 615
Primary coil resistance .... 0.95 to 1.15 ohm
Secondary coil resistance .... 15 to 20 k ohm
Ballast resistor .... 1.53 to 1.87 ohm

Spark plugs
Type:
    UK models .... NGK BPR-5ES or Champion RN12Y
    North American models .... NGK BPR-6ES-11, BP-6ES-11 or BUR-6EA or Champion N9Y or RN9Y
    Canadian models .... NGK BPR-6ES or Champion RN9Y
Gap:
    All models except North America .... 0.028 to 0.031 in (0.7 to 0.8 mm)
    North American models .... 0.039 to 0.043 in (1.0 to 1.1 mm)

Torque wrench settings

	lbf ft	Nm
Spark plugs	18	25

1 General description

All models except California

The ignition system comprises the battery, a coil with ballast resistor, a distributor driven from a gear on the camshaft and the spark plugs.

In order that the engine can run correctly it is necessary for an electrical spark to ignite the fuel/air mixture in the combustion chamber at exactly the right moment in relation to engine speed and load. The ignition system is based on feeding low tension (LT) voltage from the battery to the coil where it is converted to high tension (HT) voltage. The high tension voltage is powerful enough to jump the spark plug gap in the cylinders many times a second under high compression pressures, providing that the system is in good condition and that all adjustments are correct.

The ignition system is divided into two circuits: the low tension circuit and the high tension circuit.

The low tension (sometimes known as the primary) circuit consists of the battery lead to the ignition switch, lead from the ignition switch to the low tension or primary coil windings (terminal +) and the lead from the low tension coil windings (coil terminal -) to the contact breaker points and condenser in the distributor.

The high tension circuit consists of the high tension or secondary coil windings, the heavy ignition lead from the centre of the coil to the centre of the distributor cap, the rotor arm, and the spark plug leads and spark plugs.

The system functions in the following manner. Low tension voltage is changed in the coil into high tension voltage by the opening and closing of the contact breaker points in the low tension circuit. High tension voltage is then fed via the carbon brush in the centre of the distributor cap to the rotor arm of the distributor cap, and each time it comes in line with one of the four metal segments in the cap, which are connected to the spark plug leads, the opening and closing of the contact breaker points causes the high tension voltage to build up, jump the gap from the rotor arm to the appropriate metal segment and so via the spark plug lead to the spark plug, where it finally jumps the spark plug gap before going to earth.

The ignition is advanced and retarded automatically, to ensure the spark occurs at just the right instant for the particular load at the prevailing engine speed.

The ignition advance is controlled both mechanically and by a vacuum operated system. The mechanical governor mechanism comprises two weights, which move out from the distributor shaft as the engine speed rises due to centrifugal force. As they move outward they rotate the cam relative to the distributor shaft, and so advance the spark timing. The weights are held in position by two light springs and it is the tension of the springs which is largely responsible for correct spark advancement.

The vacuum control consists of a diaphragm, one side of which is connected via a small bore tube to the carburettor, and the other side to the contact breaker plate. Depression in the inlet manifold and carburettor, which varies with engine speed and throttle opening, causes the diaphragm to move, so moving the contact breaker plate, and advancing or retarding the spark. A fine degree of control is achieved by a spring in the vacuum assembly.

A ballast resistor is incorporated in the ignition circuit and it is located adjacent to the ignition coil. During low speed operation when primary current flow is high, the temperature of the ballast resistor rises to increase resistance and so reduce the current flow. This prolongs the life of the contact points. During high speed operation, when primary current is low, the ballast resistor cools to permit greater current flow which is required for high speed operation. When the starter motor is operated, the ballast resistor is by-passed to allow full battery voltage to the ignition primary circuit.

Californian models

On vehicles built for operation in California, a transistorized ignition system is used. The essential difference between this and the mechanical type is that the mechanical type 'make-and-break' contact points are replaced by a reluctor and coil which carries out the function electronically by interruption of a magnetic field and signal generation.

The electronic system comprises a battery, switch, coil, pointless breaker, control unit and spark plugs. Primary current is switched by the electronic ignition control unit in response to signals produced by a magnetic pick-up in conjunction with a reluctor in the distributor.

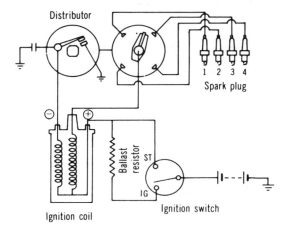

Fig. 4.1 Ignition circuit (mechanical breaker) (Sec 1)

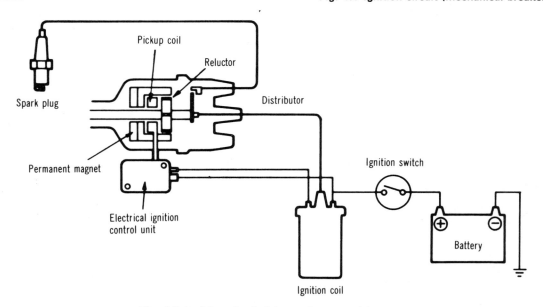

Fig. 4.2 Ignition circuit (electronic system) (Sec 1)

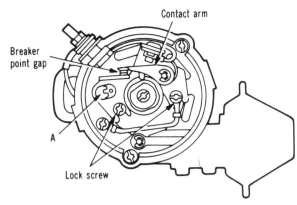

Fig. 4.3 Contact breaker points adjustment (Sec 2)

A   Adjuster eccentric cam

2   Mechanical contact breaker – adjustment

1   At the intervals specified in the Routine maintenance Section, remove the distributor cap by prising down the two holding clips. Remove the rotor arm.
2   Apply a ring spanner to the crankshaft pulley centre bolt and turn the crankshaft until the contact breaker points are wide open with the heel of the contact arm on the high point of the distributor cam.
3   Open the points and inspect the contact faces for erosion. If it is severe then the contact breaker set will have to be removed and cleaned or renewed as described in the next Section.
4   If they are in good condition, check the gap with a feeler blade. If the gap is outside that specified, loosen the two lockscrews and prise the eccentric adjuster to correct. Retighten the two lockscrews. Refit the rotor.
5   This method of adjustment should only be regarded as an initial, emergency type of adjustment and for optimum performance, check the dwell angle as described in Section 4.
6   Check the distributor cap for cracks and the condition of the central carbon brush before refitting it.
7   Check the ignition timing (refer to Section 5) after checking the dwell angle.

3   Mechanical contact breaker points – removal and refitting

1   If as the result of inspection described in the preceding Section, the contact points are badly eroded, remove them.
2   Take off the distributor cap and remove the rotor.
3   Release the spring arm of the moving contact arm by unscrewing the LT terminal nut on the distributor body.
4   Unscrew the two fixing screws from the fixed contact arm and withdraw the contact breaker points.
5   If the points are not too badly pitted, they can be dismantled by extracting the E clip which secures the moving arm to its pivot. Dress the points flat and square on an oilstone or abrasive paper.
6   If the points are so severely burned that excessive rubbing will be required to remove the condition, then renew them.
7   Severe pitting or burning of the contact points may be due to a poor engine or battery earth or a faulty condenser.
8   Refit the points, applying a trace of oil to the points pivot post and vacuum link pivot also smear the distributor cam high points with a little high melting point grease – don't overdo this or it may be thrown out onto the points during rotation.
9   Adjust the points initially to get the car running as described in the preceding Section and then check the dwell angle and the ignition timing as described in following Sections.

4   Dwell angle – checking and adjusting

1   On modern engines fitted with mechanical contact breaker points, adjustment of the contact breaker points gap should be made using a dwell meter to ensure optimum engine performance.

2   The dwell angle is the number of degrees through which the distributor cam turns during the period between the instants of closure and opening of the contact breaker points.
3   The dwell angle method not only provides a more accurate setting of the contact breaker points gap but also evens out any variations in gap which might be caused by wear in the distributor shaft bushes or differences in height of any of the four cam peaks.
4   Connect the dwell meter in accordance with the maker's instructions, start the engine and check that the dwell angle is within the specified tolerance.
5   If the angle is too large, increase the points gap. If the angle is too small, reduce the points gap.
6   The dwell angle should always be checked and adjusted before checking and adjusting the ignition timing.

5   Ignition timing (mechanical breaker distributor)

Initial setting with test lamp

1   Turn the engine until No 1 piston is rising on its compression stroke. This may be checked by removing No 1 spark plug and placing a finger over the plug hole to feel the compression being generated or alternatively, removing the distributor cap and observing that the rotor arm is coming up to align with the position of No 1 contact segment in the distributor cap.
2   There is a notch on the rim of the crankshaft pulley and a scale on the timing cover. Continue turning the crankshaft until the notch on the pulley is opposite the appropriate static ignition setting mark on the scale. Refer to the Specifications for this setting (photo).
3   Slacken the distributor clamp plate bolt
4   Connect a test lamp between the LT terminal of the distributor and a good earth and switch on the ignition.
5   Turn the distributor body to the position where even the slightest further movement will illuminate the test bulb.
6   Tighten the distributor clamp plate bolt, remove the test lamp and switch off the ignition.

Final setting with stroboscope

7   Mark the notch on the crankshaft pulley with chalk or white paint.
8   Mark in a similar manner the appropriate line on the timing cover scale (see the Specifications for static timing figure according to engine and vehicle type).
9   If an air conditioner is fitted make sure that it and all vehicle lights are turned off.
10   Connect a stroboscope in accordance with the maker's instructions (usually interposed between No 1 spark plug and HT lead). Connect a tachometer unless one is fitted as standard.
11   Start the engine (which should previously have been run to normal operating temperature) and let it idle (see the recommended speeds in

5.2 Ignition timing marks

the Specifications) otherwise the mechanical advance mechanism will operate and give a false ignition timing.

12 Point the stroboscope at the ignition timing marks when they will appear stationary and if the ignition timing is correct, in alignment. If the marks are not in alignment, loosen the distributor clamp plate screw and turn the distributor.

13 Switch off the ignition, tighten the distributor clamp plate screw and remove the stroboscope.

14 Remove the tachometer.

15 A supplementary use for the stroboscope is to check the operation of the distributor mechanical and vacuum advance. With the stroboscope connected as previously described, disconnect the distributor vacuum pipe. With the engine idling, suddenly open the throttle and observe that the timing marks move away from each other and by approximately what distance. Now connect the vacuum pipe and repeat the operation increasing the engine speed to as near as possible the same level as previously. The timing marks should again move away from each other but by a greater distance proving that both the centrifugal and vacuum advance is working.

---

6 Condenser (capacitor) mechanical breaker distributors – removal, testing and refitting

---

1 The condenser ensures that with the contact breaker points open, the sparking between them is not excessive to cause severe pitting. The condenser is fitted in parallel and its failure will automatically cause failure of the ignition system as the points will be prevented from interrupting the low tension circuit.

2 Testing for an unserviceable condenser may be effected by switching on the ignition and separating the contact points by hand. If this action is accompanied by a blue flash then condenser failure is indicated. Difficult starting, missing of the engine after several miles running or badly pitting points are other indications of the faulty condenser.

3 The surest test is by fitting a new unit.

4 Removal of the condenser is by means of withdrawing the screw which retains it to the distributor. Fitting is a reversal of this procedure.

---

7 Distributor (mechanical breaker type) – removal and refitting

---

1 Disconnect the battery negative lead.

2 Unclip the distributor cap and move it to one side. Disconnect the spark plug leads if necessary to facilitate this.

3 Disconnect the LT lead from the terminal on the side of the distributor body (photo).

4 Disconnect the vacuum hose from the distributor.

5 Remove the distributor clamp plate mounting nut and withdraw the distributor.

6 To refit the distributor, turn the crankshaft by means of its pulley centre bolt until No 1 piston is at TDC on its compression stroke. This can be verified as described in Section 5, paragraph 1.

7 Set the punch mark of the driven gear opposite the mark on the distributor body projecting sleeve (Fig. 4.4).

8 Hold the clamp plate in such a position that it will pass centrally over the retaining stud and push the distributor into position. As the distributor gear meshes with the drive gear on the camshaft, the rotor arm will turn in an anti-clockwise direction through approximately 40° (photos).

9 The contact end of the rotor should now be in alignment with No 2 spark plug lead contact if the distributor cap is fitted.

10 Adjust the position of the distributor until the mating mark on the clamp plate flange is aligned with the centre of the fixing stud. Tighten the clamp plate nut.

11 Reconnect the LT lead and the vacuum hose and refit the distributor cap.

12 Reconnect the battery.

13 Check the ignition timing as described in Section 5.

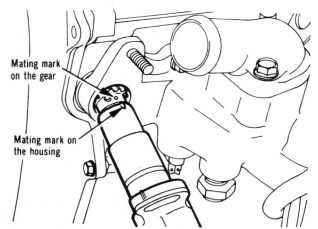

Fig. 4.4 Distributor gear to body alignment marks (Sec 7)

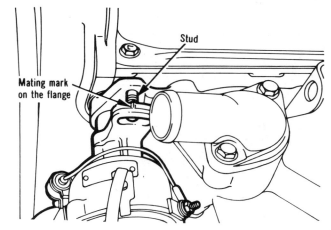

Fig. 4.5 Distributor clamp plate to stud alignment mark (Sec 7)

7.3 Distributor LT terminal

7.8a Rotor arm position before fitting the distributor

7.8b Rotor arm position after fitting the distributor

Measuring plug gap. A feeler gauge of the correct size (see ignition system specifications) should have a slight 'drag' when slid between the electrodes. Adjust gap if necessary

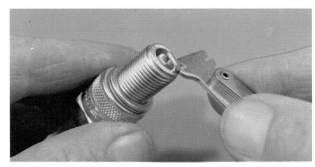

Adjusting plug gap. The plug gap is adjusted by bending the earth electrode inwards, or outwards, as necessary until the correct clearance is obtained. Note the use of the correct tool

Normal. Grey-brown deposits lightly coated core nose. Gap increasing by around 0.001 in (0.025 mm) per 1000 miles (1600 km). Plugs ideally suited to engine and engine in good condition

Carbon fouling. Dry, black, sooty deposits. Will cause weak spark and eventually misfire. Fault: over-rich fuel mixture. Check: carburettor mixture settings, float level and jet sizes; choke operation and cleanliness of air filter. Plugs can be re-used after cleaning

Oil fouling. Wet, oily deposits. Will cause weak spark and eventually misfire. Fault: worn bores/piston rings or valve guides; sometimes occurs (temporarily) during running-in period. Plugs can be re-used after thorough cleaning

Overheating. Electrodes have glazed appearance, core nose very white - few deposits. Fault: plug overheating. Check: plug value, ignition timing, fuel octane rating (too low) and fuel mixture (too weak). Discard plugs and cure fault immediately

Electrode damage. Electrodes burned away; core nose has burned, glazed appearance. Fault: initial pre-ignition. Check: as for 'Overheating' but may be more severe. Discard plugs and remedy fault before piston or valve damage occurs

Split core nose (may appear initially as a crack). Damage is self-evident, but cracks will only show after cleaning. Fault: pre-ignition or wrong gap-setting technique. Check: ignition timing, cooling system, fuel octane rating (too low) and fuel mixture (too weak). Discard plugs, rectify fault immediately

Fig. 4.6 Exploded view of mechanical breaker type distributor (Sec 8)

1   Cap
2   Carbon contact
3   Rotor arm
4   Earthing lead
5   Condenser
6   Contact breaker set
7   Low tension internal
    lead
8   Baseplate
9   Circlip
10 Vacuum control unit
11 Low tension terminal
12 Cam
13 Counterweight spring
14 Counterweight
15 Shaft
16 Oil seal
17 Washer
18 Cap clip
19 Gasket
20 Body
21 O-ring
22 Washers
23 Lockpin
24 Driven gear

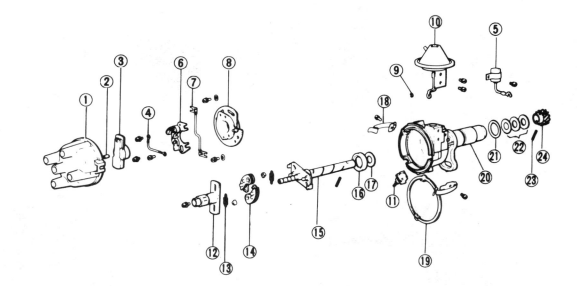

8   Distributor (mechanical breaker type) – overhaul

1   If a distributor becomes so badly worn that the shaft has side movement in the body then it is recommended that a new distributor is obtained. Make sure that the new one bears exactly the same serial number as the original otherwise the ignition advance curves for the particular engine will be altered and engine performance spoiled.
2   The other smaller components are usually available as spares and dismantling may be carried out in the following way.
3   With the distributor removed from the engine as described in the preceding Section, take off the cap and pull off the rotor.
4   Loosen the LT terminal nut on the side of the distributor, remove the E clip from the pivot post on which the moving contact breaker arm is fitted.
5   Remove the moving contact and then release the two fixing screws and withdraw the fixed contact. Remove the internal leads.
6   Extract the vacuum advance unit securing screws, disconnect the link by extracting the E clip. Remove the baseplate by extracting two screws.
7   Remove the cam assembly by extracting the single screw from the recess at the top of the distributor shaft.
8   If the cam assembly is to be dismantled, it is very important that the relative positions of the counterweight and the springs is noted with reference to the cam. Use a dab of quick drying paint or numbered masking tape to do this.
9   Mark the relative position of the driven gear to the distributor shaft before driving out the lock pin.
10 Renew worn parts also the oil seal and O-ring as a matter of routine.
11 Lubricate the shaft and friction surfaces sparingly during re-assembly with clean engine oil.
12 Check the cap and rotor arm for cracks and renew if eroded. At the time of major overhaul, it is worth renewing the condenser and the points unless they have been changed very recently.

9   Ignition coil (mechanical breaker system)

1   The high tension current should be negative at the spark plug terminals. To ensure this, check that the LT connections to the coil are correctly made.
2   The LT wire from the distributor must connect with the negative (-) terminal on the coil.

9.4 Ignition coil with ballast resistor

3   The coil positive (+) terminal is connected to the ignition/starter switch through a ballast resistor.
4   The ballast resistor is mounted on the side of the ignition coil, its purpose being as described in Section 1 (photo).
5   Unless an ohmmeter is available to check the primary and secondary resistance of the ignition coil and that of the ballast resistance, the only method of testing is by substitution of new units.

10 Ignition timing (electronic system)

1   With the engine idling at the normal operating temperature, connect a stroboscope and tachometer in accordance with the maker's instructions.
2   If an air conditioner is fitted make sure that it and all the vehicle lights are turned off.
3   Using the stroboscope as desired in Section 5, check the timing is

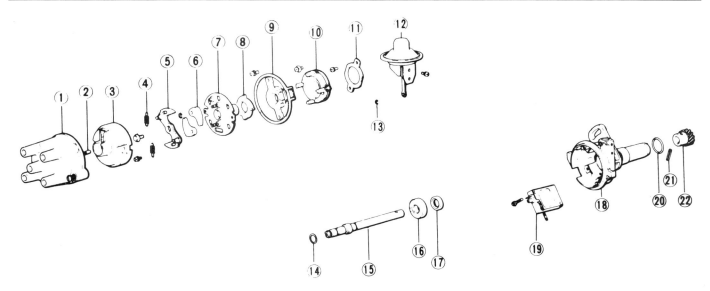

Fig. 4.7 Exploded view of the electronic type distributor (Sec 12)

1 Cap	7 Baseplate	13 E-clip	18 Body
2 Carbon contact	8 Reluctor	14 Washer	19 Control unit
3 Rotor arm	9 Pick-up coil	15 Shaft	20 O-ring
4 Counterweight spring	10 Stator	16 Ball bearing	21 Roll pin
5 Mounting plate	11 Plate	17 Oil seal	22 Driven gear
6 Counterweights	12 Vacuum control unit		

in accordance with that specified. If not, release the distributor to bring the timing marks into alignment.
4   Tighten the nut, switch off the engine and remove the stroboscope and tachometer.

---

11 Distributor (electronic type) – removal and refitting

1   The operations are very similar to those described in Section 7 for the mechanical breaker distributor except that the wiring harness must also be disconnected from the electronic control unit.
2   The distributor body, gear and clamp alignment marks are exactly the same as for the mechanical breaker type distributor.

---

12 Distributor (electronic type) – overhaul

1   Refer to paragraphs 1 and 2 of Section 8.
2   With the distributor removed from the engine, extract the two screws and pull the control unit from the distributor body. Do not clean away the silicone grease which coats the mating surfaces of the control unit and the distributor body.
3   Depress the spring-loaded cap fixing screws and turn to release the securing hooks. Remove the cap.
4   Extract the mounting screws and remove the rotor arm.
5   Extract the single screw and withdraw the governor assembly with the reluctor.
6   Remove the pick-up coil (two screws).
7   Unscrew the two mounting screws for the vacuum unit, extract the E-Clip from the vacuum unit link rod and withdraw the vacuum unit.
8   Remove the baseplate assembly.
9   Mark the relative position of the driven gear to the distributor shaft and drive out the locking pin.
10 Withdraw the shaft.
11 Reassembly is a reversal of dismantling.

---

13 Electronic (breakerless) system – fault testing

1   In the event of complete ignition failure or erratic operation, the following tests and checks can be carried out to establish the cause.

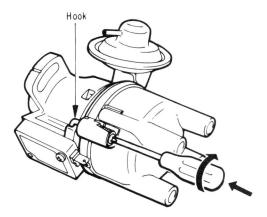

Fig. 4.8 Distributor cap securing hook and method of releasing (Sec 12)

Secondary ignition test
2   Check the security of all system wiring connections.
3   Remove the distributor cap and unscrew and lift out the rotor arm.
4   Switch on the ignition.
5   Disconnect the HT lead from the centre terminal of the distributor cap and then hold the end of the cable about 0.25 in (6.0 mm) from the cylinder block.
6   Insert a screwdriver between the reluctor and the stator. If a spark is produced at the end of the disconnected HT lead, then the control unit, pick-up coil, ignition coil or secondary connecting cable may be faulty. Have them checked out by your dealer or by substitution of new units or by carrying out the following test procedure.

Pick-up coil test
7   A circuit tester will be required for this test. With the probes applied as shown in Fig. 4.10, measure the resistance of the pick-up coil, this should be between 1000 and 1100 ohms.

Control unit test
8   Check for continuity between terminal C on the control unit and its metallic backplate. If the test is being carried out with the control unit

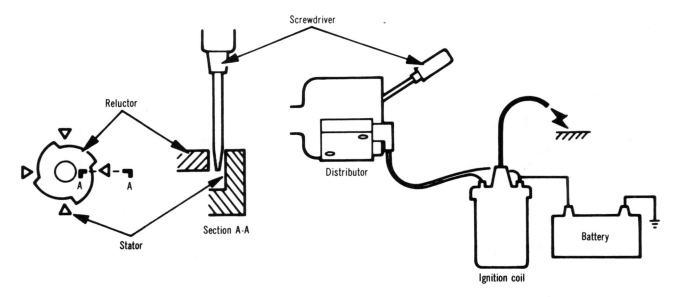

Fig. 4.9 Testing the electronic secondary ignition circuit (Sec 13)

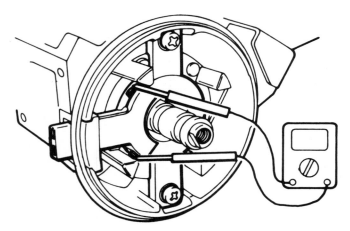

Fig. 4.10 Checking the pick-up coil on electronic type distributor (Sec 13)

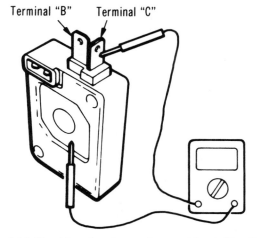

Fig. 4.11 Checking the electronic control unit (Sec 13)

still attached to the distributor then the check should be made between terminal C and the distributor body. Conduct the test in a similar way to that for testing a diode by alternately reversing the probes of the circuit tester. If continuity or an open circuit is indicated in both directions then the control unit is defective and it should be renewed.

Ignition coil
9   The method of testing is similar to that described in Section 9.

14 Spark plugs and HT leads

1   The correct functioning of the spark plugs is vital for the correct running and efficiency of the engine. The plugs fitted as standard are listed in the Specifications.
2   At the specified intervals, the plugs should be removed, examined, cleaned and, if worn excessively, renewed. The condition of the spark plug will also tell much about the overall condition of the engine.
3   If the insulator nose of the spark plug is clean and white with no deposits, this is indicative of a weak mixture, or too hot a plug. (A hot plug transfers heat away from the electrode slowly – a cold plug transfers it away quickly).

4   If the top and insulator nose is covered with hard black looking deposits, then this is indicative that the mixture is too rich. Should the plug be black and oily, then it is likely that the engine is fairly worn, as well as the mixture being too rich.
5   If the insulator nose is covered with light tan to greyish brown deposits, then the mixture is correct and it is likely that the engine is in good condition.
6   If there are any traces of long brown tapering stains on the outside of the white portion of the plug, then the plug will have to be renewed, as this shows that there is a faulty joint between the plug body and the insulator, and compression is being allowed to leak away.
7   Plugs should be cleaned by a sand blasting machine, which will free them from carbon more thoroughly than cleaning by hand. The machine will also test the condition of the plugs under compression. Any plug that fails to spark at the recommended pressure should be renewed.
8   The spark plug gap is of considerable importance, as, if it is too large or too small the size of the spark and its efficiency will be seriously impaired. The spark plug gap should be set to between 0.039 and 0.043 in (1.0 to 1.1 mm) for the best results.
9   To set it, measure the gap with a feeler gauge, and then bend open, or close, the outer plug electrode until the correct gap is achieved. The centre electrode should never be bent as this may crack

the insulation and cause plug failure, if nothing worse.
10 When fitting the plugs, remember to fit plug washers and replace the leads from the distributor in the correct firing order, No 1 cylinder being the one nearest the timing belt.

11 The plug leads require no routine attention other than being kept clean and wiped over regularly (photo).
12 The distributor cap is marked with the HT lead numbers to avoid any confusion when reconnecting them (photo).

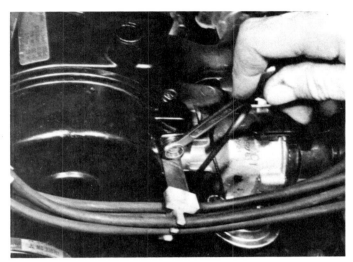

14.11 HT lead support bracket

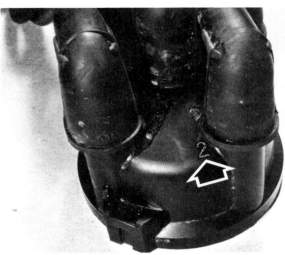

14.12 Distributor cap showing HT lead fitting sequence

15 Fault diagnosis – ignition system

Symptom	Reason(s)
Mechanical breaker system	
Engine fails to start	Discharged battery
	Oil on points
	Loose battery connections
	Disconnected ignition leads
	Faulty condenser
	Damp leads or distributor cap
	Faulty anti-run on valve
Engine misfires	Faulty spark plug
	Cracked distributor cap
	Cracked rotor arm
	Worn advance mechanism
	Incorrect spark plug gap
	Incorrect points gap
	Faulty condenser
	Faulty coil
	Incorrect timing
	Poor earth connections
Engine overheats or lacks power	Seized centrifugal counterweights
	Perforated or disconnected vacuum pipe
	Incorrect ignition timing
Engine 'pinks'	Timing too advanced
	Advance mechanism stuck in the advance position
	Broken counterweight spring
	Low fuel octane rating

Transistorised 'breakerless' system
All the foregoing symptoms and reasons apply except for those referring to the condenser and contact breaker points which apply only to the mechanical type system
In addition, the following apply only to the breakerless system

Engine fails to start	Faulty control unit
	Faulty pick-up coil
	Faulty ignition coil
	Disconnected secondary cable
Engine misfires	Reluctor to pick-up air gap incorrect due to wear in shaft or bushes

Chapter 5 Clutch

Contents

Specifications

Type .... Single dry plate, diaphragm spring with cable actuation

Clutch disc diameter .... 7.25 in (184. 2 mm)

Number of cushion springs 4

Clutch pedal free movement .... 0.8 to 1.2 in (20.0 to 30.0 mm)

Torque wrench settings

	lbf ft	Nm
Pedal cross-shaft nut	15	20
Bellhousing cover plate bolts	14	19
Clutch cover bolts	15	20
Transmission to engine bolts:		
Without washer (marked 7)	37	50
With washer (marked 10)	34	46

1 General description

The clutch is of single dry plate type with diaphragm spring. Actuation is by means of a cable.
The release bearing is of sealed ball type.

2 Clutch – adjustment

1 At the intervals specified in the Routine maintenance Section check the clutch pedal free movement and adjust if necessary.
2 First make sure that the height of the upper surface of the clutch pedal pad from the toe board is between 7.1 and 7.3 in (180 and 185 mm). If it is not, adjust by means of the screw and locknut at the upper part of the pedal arm.
3 Now working under the bonnet at the engine compartment rear bulkhead, gently pull the clutch·outer cable and check the clearance between the adjusting nut at the end of the spring sleeve. This should be between 0.20 and 0.24 in (5.0 to 6.0 mm). If it is not, turn the adjusting nut as necessary.

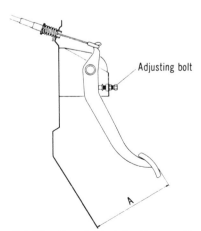

Fig. 5.1 Clutch pedal height diagram (Sec 2)

A = 7.1 to 7.3 in (180 to 185 mm)

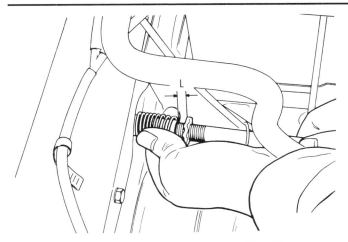

Fig. 5.2 Clutch cable adjustment (Sec 2)

L = 0.20 to 0.24 in (5.0 to 6.0 mm)

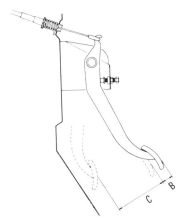

Fig. 5.3 Clutch pedal free movement diagram (Sec 2)

B (free play) = 0.8 to 1.2 in (20 to 30 mm)
C (stroke) = 5.7 in (145 mm)

4   The clutch pedal free movement should now be between 0.8 to 1.2 in (20.0 to 30.0 mm). This can be felt if the pedal is gently depressed with the fingers until the firmer resistance is encountered indicating that the clutch is being withdrawn.

3   Clutch cable – renewal

1   Fully release the clutch cable tension by turning the adjuster wheel at the engine compartment rear bulkhead.
2   Unscrew the bolt on the clutch pedal arm as far as it will go to create more slack in the clutch cable.
3   Slip the ends of the cable from the release lever and the clutch pedal and withdraw the cable through the bulkhead and from the transmission bracket (photo).
4   Refitting is a reversal of removal, apply a little grease to the cable ends at their contact points on the pedal arm and release lever and then adjust the free movement as described in Section 2.

4   Clutch pedal – removal and refitting

Left-hand drive models
1   Remove the clutch cable as described in the preceding Section.

3.3 Combined transmission mounting and clutch cable bracket

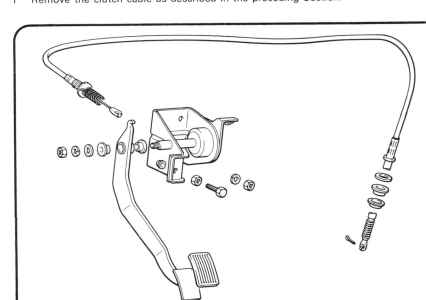

Fig. 5.4 Clutch pedal components (LHD) (Sec 4)

2   Unscrew the nut from the end of the pedal pivot shaft and withdraw the pedal complete with bushes.
3   Refit by reversing the removal operations but smear the pedal bushes with grease and tighten the pivot shaft nut to specified torque.
4   Adjust the pedal free movement as described in Section 2.

Right-hand drive models
5   Refer to Chapter 8 for removal in conjunction with the brake pedal.

5   Clutch – removal

1   Access to the clutch is obtained by removing the transmission as described in Chapter 6.
2   Unscrew and remove the clutch cover securing bolts. Do this evenly, a turn at a time in a diagonal sequence until the spring pressure is relieved.
3   Lever the cover from the locating dowels, catching the driven plate as it falls from the flywheel.

6   Clutch – inspection and renovation

1   Due to the slow wearing qualities of the clutch, it is not particularly easy to decide when the clutch is in need of renewal. Positive indication that something needs doing is when it starts to slip or when squealing noises on engagement indicate that the friction lining has worn down to the rivets. In such instances it can only be hoped that the friction surfaces on the flywheel and pressure plate have not been badly worn or scored. A clutch will wear according to the way in which it is used. Much intentional slipping of the clutch while driving – rather than the correct selection of gears – will accelerate wear.
2   Examine the surfaces of the pressure plate and flywheel for signs of scoring. If this is only light it may be left, but if very deep the pressure plate unit will have to be renewed. If the flywheel is deeply scored it should be taken off and advice sought from an engineering firm. Providing it may be machined completely across the face the overall balance of engine and flywheel should not be too severely upset. If renewal of the flywheel is necessary the new one will have to be balanced to match the original.

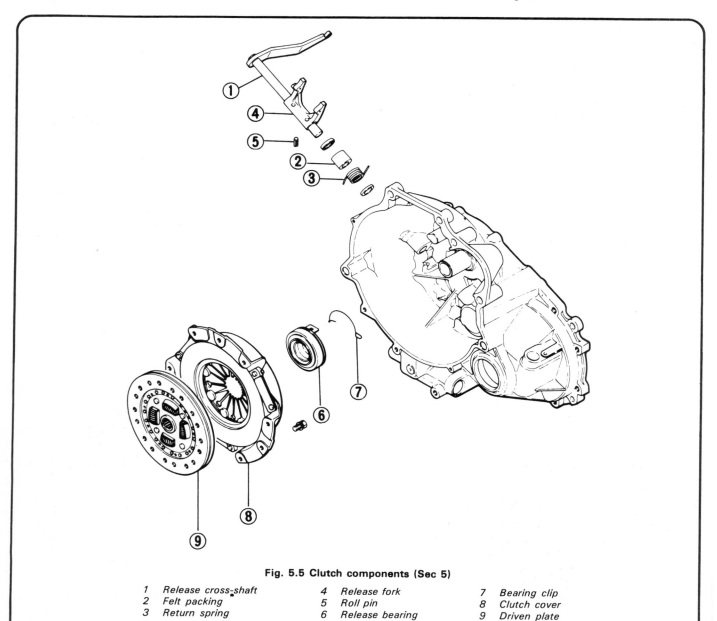

Fig. 5.5 Clutch components (Sec 5)

1	Release cross-shaft	4	Release fork	7	Bearing clip
2	Felt packing	5	Roll pin	8	Clutch cover
3	Return spring	6	Release bearing	9	Driven plate

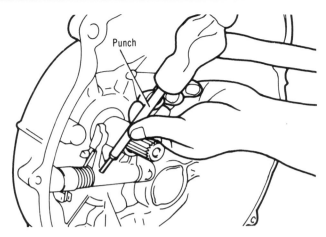

Fig. 5.6 Removing the release fork roll pin (Sec 7)

3 Sometimes, close examinatiion of the flywheel will reveal extensive fine cracking of the friction surface caused by overheating. Provided this is not deep then grinding or machining may remove it.
4 The friction plate lining surfaces should be at least 0.03 in (0.8 mm) above the rivets, otherwise the disc is not worth putting back. If the lining material shows signs of breaking up or black areas where oil contamination has occurred it should also be renewed. If facilities are readily available for obtaining and fitting new friction pads to the existing disc this may be done but the saving is relatively small compared with obtaining a complete new disc assembly which ensures that the shock absorbing springs and the splined hub are renewed also. The same applies to the pressure plate assembly which cannot be readily dismantled and put back together without specialised riveting tools and balancing equipment. An allowance is usually given for exchange units.
5 Where oil has caused contamination of the clutch, make sure that the faulty oil seal is renewed before refitting the transmission.

7 Release bearing and mechanism – inspection, dismantling and reassembly

1 The release bearing is of the ball bearing, grease sealed type and although designed for long life it is worth renewing at the same time as the other clutch components are being renewed or serviced.
2 Deterioration of the bearing should be suspected when there are signs of grease leakage or the unit is noisy when spun with the fingers.

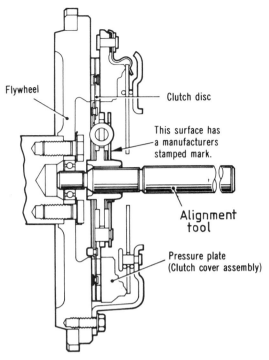

Fig. 5.7 Cut away view showing driven plate centralising (Sec 8)

3 The release bearing can be withdrawn once its retaining spring clips have been extracted (photo).
4 The release fork and cross-shaft can be dismantled if the spring pins are driven out with a suitable punch. Note the location of spring ends and the felt packings (photo).
5 When refitting the release bearing clips, make sure that the ends of the clips pass through the holes in the bearing into the arms of the release fork. The hoops of the spring clip engage in the bearing groove.

8 Clutch – fitting and centralising

1 Make sure that the clutch mating face of the flywheel is quite clean. Use solvent to wipe away any grease or oil.
2 Hold the driven plate against the flywheel so that the projecting plate which contains the torsion springs is not against the flywheel.

7.3 Clutch release bearing and spring clip

7.4 Clutch release fork, cross-shaft spring and felt spacers

3   Locate the pressure plate cover on the dowels and tighten the retaining bolts evenly in a diagonal sequence but only finger tight at this stage.

4   The driven plate must now be centralised otherwise it will be quite impossible to mate the transmission with the engine due to the fact that the splines of the input shaft will not pass through the hub of the driven plate.

5   To centralise the plate, insert a special clutch aligning tool (available from motor parts factors) or an old input shaft into the driven plate hub (photo). This will have the effect of displacing the driven plate sideways and centralising it. Now tighten the cover bolts to the specified torque and withdraw the alignment tool.

6   The transmission should be refitted as described in Chapter 6.

8.5a Clutch aligning tool (cover removed for clarity)

8.5b Clutch driven plate correctly centralised

9 Fault diagnosis – clutch

Symptom	Reason(s)
Judder when taking up drive	Loose engine or gearbox mountings Badly worn friction surfaces or contaminated with oil Worn splines on gearbox input shaft or driven plate hub Worn input shaft spigot bush in flywheel (1597 cc only)
Clutch spin (failure to disengage) so that gears cannot be meshed	Incorrect release bearing to diaphragm spring finger clearance Driven plate sticking on input shaft splines due to rust. May occur after vehicle standing idle for long period Damaged or misaligned pressure plate assembly
Clutch slip (increase in engine speed does not result in increase in vehicle road speed – particularly on gradients)	Incorrect release bearing to diaphragm spring finger clearance Friction surfaces worn out or oil contaminated
Noise evident on depressing clutch pedal	Dry, worn or damaged release bearing Insufficient pedal free travel Weak or broken pedal return spring Weak or broken clutch release lever return spring Excessive play between driven plate hub splines and input shaft splines
Noise evident as clutch pedal released	Distorted driven plate Broken or weak driven plate cushion coil springs Insufficient pedal free travel Weak or broken clutch pedal return spring Weak or broken release lever return spring Distorted or worn input shaft Release bearing loose on retainer hub

Chapter 6 Manual and automatic transmission

Contents

Specifications

Manual transmission
Type .... 8 forward speeds with 2 reverse. Front mounted, incorporating final drive, in unit with engine. Floor mounted gearchange and range selector levers

Ratios

	Power	Economy
1st	4.226 : 1	3.272 : 1
2nd	2.365 : 1	1.831 : 1
3rd	1.467 : 1	1.136 : 1
4th	1.105 : 1	0.855 : 1
Reverse	4.109 : 1	3.181 : 1
Final drive ratio	3.470 : 1	3.470 : 1

Tolerances
Synchro baulk ring to cone clearance .... 0.0315 in (0.8 mm) max
Selector fork to synchro sleeve groove:
    Clearance .... 0.0039 to 0.0118 in (0.1 to 0.3 mm)
    Wear limit .... 0.020 in (0.5 mm)
Width of synchro sleeve groove (unworn) .... 0.2756 in (7.0 mm)
Differential to pinion gear gear tooth backlash in direction of forward rotation .... 0.0022 to 0.0068 in (0.055 to 0.173 mm)
    Wear limit .... 0.0079 in (0.2 mm)
Differential side gear to pinion backlash .... 0 to 0.0030 in (0. to 0.076 mm)
Shaft tapered roller bearing outer track end play in rear cover .... 0 to 0.0020 in (0 to 0.05 mm)

Differential side gear spacers
Thickness
0.0429 to 0.0457 in (1.090 to 1.161 mm)
0.0398 to 0.0425 in (1.011 to 1.080 mm)
0.0366 to 0.0394 in (0.930 to 1.001 mm)
0.0327 to 0.0362 in (0.831 to 0.919 mm)
0.0295 to 0.0323 in (0.749 to 0.820 mm)

Input shaft bearing circlips
Plain ....
Blue ....
Brown ....

Thickness
0.0870 to 0.0894 in (2.210 to 2.271 mm)
0.0898 to 0.0921 in (2.281 to 2.339 mm)
0.0925 to 0.0949 in (2.350 to 2.410 mm)

Differential endplay spacers
E ....
Plain ....
C ....
B ....
A ....
F ....

Thickness
0.0516 in (1.31 mm)
0.0551 in (1.40 mm)
0.0587 in (1.49 mm)
0.0622 in (1.58 mm)
0.0657 in (1.67 mm)
0.0693 in (1.76 mm)

Output and intermediate shaft rear bearing track spacers (to rear cover)

Identification:	Thickness
84	0.0724 in (1.84 mm)
87	0.0736 in (1.87 mm)
90	0.0748 in (1.90 mm)
93	0.0760 in (1.93 mm)
96	0.0772 in (1.96 mm)
99	0.0783 in (1.99 mm)
02	0.0795 in (2.02 mm)
05	0.0807 in (2.05 mm)
08	0.0819 in (2.08 mm)
11	0.0831 in (2.11 mm)
14	0.0843 in (2.14 mm)
17	0.0854 in (2.17 mm)
20	0.0866 in (2.20 mm)
23	0.0878 in (2.23 mm)
26	0.0890 in (2.26 mm)
29	0.0902 in (2.29 mm)
32	0.0913 in (2.32 mm)
35	0.0925 in (2.35 mm)
38	0.0937 in (2.38 mm)
41	0.0949 in (2.41 mm)
44	0.0961 in (2.44 mm)
47	0.0972 in (2.47 mm)
50	0.0984 in (2.50 mm)
53	0.0996 in (2.53 mm)
56	0.1008 in (2.56 mm)
59	0.1020 in (2.59 mm)
62	0.1031 in (2.62 mm)
65	0.1043 in (2.65 mm)
68	0.1055 in (2.68 mm)

Torque wrench settings

	lbf ft	Nm
Transmission to engine bolts:		
Without washer (mark 7)	37	50
With washer (mark 10)	34	46
Bellhousing cover plate	8	11
Oil filler and drain plugs	24	33
Input shaft bearing retainer bolts	14	19
Input shaft staked nut	75	102
Output shaft staked nut	75	102
Rear cover bolts	15	20
Mounting bracket bolts	25	34
Crownwheel bolts	50	68
Reverse selector lever bracket	14	19
Range selector detent plug	22	30
Reverse lamp switch	22	30

Automatic transmission

Type .... KM 170. 3 element, 2 phase torque converter with planetary gear train to provide three forward and 1 reverse speed

Ratios

1st	2.551 : 1
2nd	1.488 : 1
3rd	1.000 : 1
Reverse	2.176 : 1

Approximate shift speeds*

	mph	km/h
At minimum throttle opening:		
1 to 2 upshift	7 to 12	12 to 19
2 to 3 upshift	11 to 16	18 to 25
3 to 1 downshift	5 to 9	8 to 15
At wide throttle opening:		
1 to 2 upshift	30 to 37	49 to 59
2 to 3 upshift	58 to 64	93 to 103
Kickdown limit:		
3 to 2 downshift (wide open throttle)	52 to 58	84 to 94
3 to 2 downshift (part throttle)	32 to 40	51 to 64
3 to 1 downshift (wide open throttle)	24 to 29	38 to 47

*Wide variations from these speeds will indicate the need for checking the line pressure and adjustment, a job for your dealer using special equipment

Torque wrench settings

	lbf ft	Nm
Driveplate to torque converter	30	40
Torque converter housing to engine:		
Flange bolt	35	48
Bolt with washer	25	34
Fluid filter bolts	5	7
Mounting bracket to transmission	18	25
Damper rod pivot bolts	29	39
Drain plug	24	33
Fluid cooler hose connectors	15	20
Fluid sump pan bolts	8	11

Part A Manual transmission

1 General description and maintenance

The transmission incorporates the gear train and the final drive/differential and is mounted transversely at the front of the car in unit with the engine.

One of eight forward speeds may be selected (two ranges of four) with two reverse speeds.

Power from the engine is transmitted through a conventional clutch to the transmission input shaft. This shaft incorporates two different ratio gears which may be selected by moving the range selector lever adjacent to the gearchange lever. Smooth and quiet change of ratio is accomplished by a synchroniser unit on the input shaft.

Once the Power or Economy gear range has been selected, power is transmitted through an intermediate and an output shaft and finally through open driveshafts to the front roadwheels.

This unique design of transmission provides a large number of gear ratios within one of the most compact units in production.

The final drive and the gearbox share a common lubrication system. Although checking and topping up the oil level is recommended by Mitsubishi, routine renewal of the transmission oil is not, as it

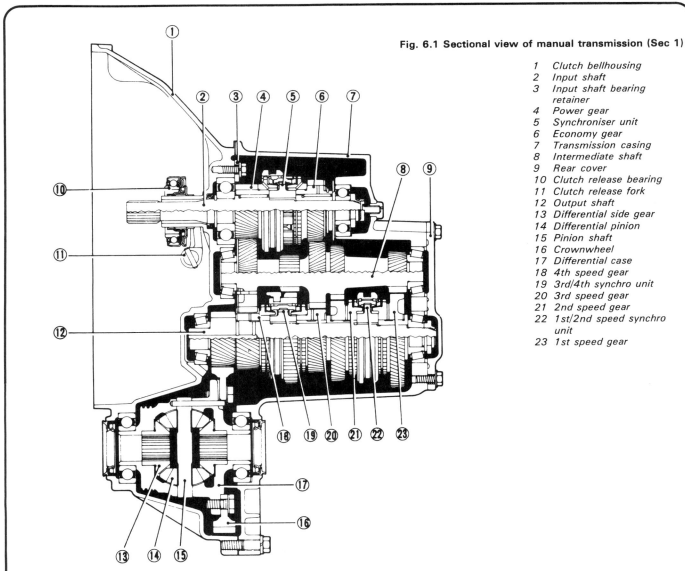

Fig. 6.1 Sectional view of manual transmission (Sec 1)

1   Clutch bellhousing
2   Input shaft
3   Input shaft bearing
   retainer
4   Power gear
5   Synchroniser unit
6   Economy gear
7   Transmission casing
8   Intermediate shaft
9   Rear cover
10 Clutch release bearing
11 Clutch release fork
12 Output shaft
13 Differential side gear
14 Differential pinion
15 Pinion shaft
16 Crownwheel
17 Differential case
18 4th speed gear
19 3rd/4th synchro unit
20 3rd speed gear
21 2nd speed gear
22 1st/2nd speed synchro
   unit
23 1st speed gear

is 'filled for life' during production. From experience however, it has proved a wise precaution to renew the oil at the intervals specified in the Routine maintenance Section if only to offset the deterioration which must occur in extreme pressure additive and viscosity strengths. The cost of an oil change at present day extended mileage intervals is small when compared with the cost of a new transmission.

2 Gearchange lever – removal and refitting

1   Release the locknut and unscrew and remove the gearchange lever knob. Some knobs do not have a locknut.
2   Extract the grub screw and pull off the knob from the range selector lever.
3   The console fixing screws can now be extracted and the console slid up the gear levers and removed. Disconnect electrical leads as necessary as the console is withdrawn.
4   Unscrew and remove the nuts from the studs of the lever mounting plate.
5   Working under the car, remove the cover plate.
6   Unscrew and remove the pivot bolt from the stabiliser strut which supports the gearchange rod.
7   Cut the locking wire, remove it and then unscrew the pinch bolt which holds the gearchange rod coupling to the operating rod of the transmission (photo).
8   Remove the exhaust heat protecting shield and then withdraw the gearchange rod and stabiliser strut together from under the car.
9   The rod assembly can be dismantled by extracting the E ring at the base of the gear lever and then removing the screws which hold the stabiliser strut to the gearchange rod plate.
10   The gear lever can be removed if the pin is driven out of the ball pivot.
11   Renew any worn components. If the free length of the gearchange lever coil spring is other than 1.23 in (31.2 mm), renew it.
12   When reassembling, pack the ball assembly with grease.
13   Refitting is a reversal of removal but make sure that the pinch bolt is locked with a new wire.

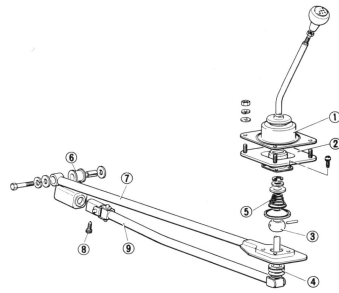

Fig. 6.2 Gearchange control linkage (Sec 2)

1   Cover   6   Bush
2   Insulator   7   Stabiliser bar
3   Fulcrum ball   8   Lock screw
4   Cover   9   Gear change remote
5   Coil spring   control rod

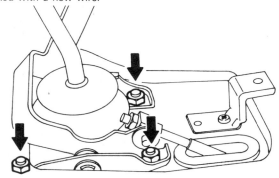

Fig. 6.3 Gearchange lever bracket nuts (Sec 2)

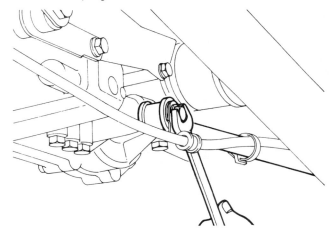

Fig. 6.4 Releasing gearchange rod stabiliser bolt (Sec 2)

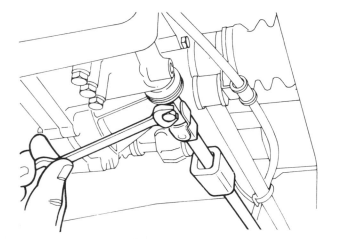

Fig. 6.5 Removing gearchange rod lock screw (Sec 2)

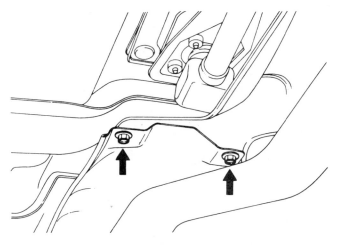

Fig. 6.6 Exhaust heat shield nuts (Sec 2)

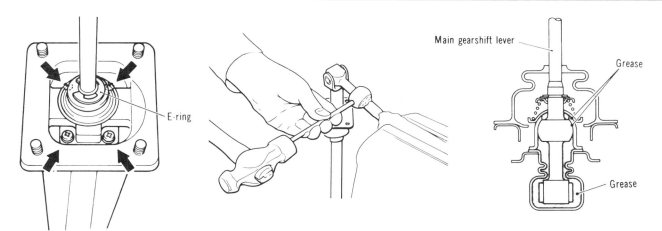

Fig. 6.7 Attachment of stabiliser strut and gearchange remote control rod using screws and E-ring (Sec 2)

Fig. 6.8 Gear lever fulcrum ball pin (Sec 2)

Fig. 6.9 Gear lever grease application points (Sec 2)

2.7 Transmission selector rod (arrowed)

3.2 Power/Economy range selector cable connection to hand control lever (arrowed)

3.8 Range selector lever indicator lamp switch (arrowed)

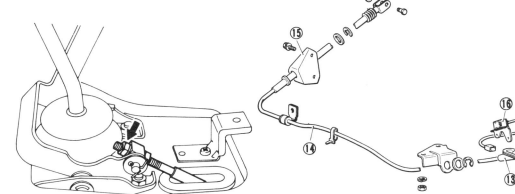

Fig. 6.10 Range selector cable attachment at centre console (Sec 3)

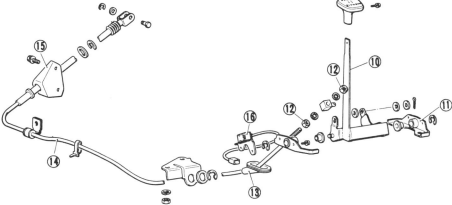

Fig. 6.11 Range selector cable components (Sec 3)

10 Hand control lever   14 Operating cable
11 Mounting bracket   15 Cable bracket
12 Cable adjuster   16 Range indicator switch
13 Dust excluding gaiter

3 Range selector lever – removal and refitting

1 Remove the centre console as described in the preceding Section.
2 Release the selector cable from the trunnion by unscrewing the nut (photo).
3 Working under the car, remove the cover plate.
4 Remove the retaining clips from the selector cable.
5 Extract the small circlip and remove the clevis pin to detach the

cable from the operating lever on the transmission.
6 Unbolt the cable support bracket from the transmission casing.
7 Unbolt the cable support bracket from below the selector lever, pull the cable from the trunnion and remove it.
8 Refitting is a reversal of removal then adjust the cable length by means of the two trunnion nuts so that when the selector hand control lever is pulled into the 'Economy' position, the back of the lever is just in contact with the floor. Adjust the indicator lamp switch if necessary (photo).

4   Transmission – removal and refitting

1   If the engine is to be the subject of major overhaul at the same time as the gearbox, the engine/transmission should be removed together and then separated as described in Chapter 1.
2   If the clutch or transmission is to be overhauled independently, then remove the transmission in the following way leaving the engine in position in the car.
3   Remove the battery and the shield from under the engine compartment.
4   Disconnect the clutch cable at the transmission.
5   Disconnect the speedometer cable from the transmission.
6   Disconnect the electrical leads from the reversing lamp switch and the starter motor.
7   Unbolt and remove the starter motor.
8   Disconnect the engine front stabiliser/damper rod.
9   Disconnect the gearchange rod and its stabiliser rod also the range selector cable as described in earlier Sections of this Chapter.
10   Drain the transmission lubricant.
11   Raise the front of the car and support it securely on stands placed under the side members so that the suspension hangs free. It is not necessary to remove the two front roadwheels.
12   Disconnect the front suspension balljoints from the track control arms by unscrewing the two bolts from each side. One of each of these pairs of bolts also secures the radius strut.
13   Release the inboard end of each driveshaft. To do this, insert a flat blade (the end of the car hub cap remover will do) between the transmission casing and each driveshaft ball track casing and then lever it sharply, to overcome the tension of the retaining circlip.
14   Each hub carrier/driveshaft can now be pulled outwards sufficiently to be able to disconnect the shaft inboard end from the transmission. Take care not to strain the brake flexible hoses. Support the driveshafts on blocks or axle stands.
15   Unbolt and remove the cover plate from the lower part of the clutch bellhousing
16   Connect a suitable hoist to the engine lifting eyes and take its weight.
17   Support the transmission on a trolley jack and then disconnect and remove the mounting bracket from the transmission. Lower the hoist slightly to enable the end of the gearbox to tilt downward and to the rear.
18   Unscrew and remove the engine to clutch bellhousing connecting bolts.
19   With the help of an assistant take the weight of the transmission and draw it from the engine. Keep it in a straight line and as soon as the input shaft clears the clutch driven plate, lower the transmission and remove it from under the car.
20   Refitting is a reversal of removal but make sure that the hollow dowels are in position on the crankcase mating flange. If the clutch has been disturbed, make sure that the driven plate has been centralized (Chapter 5), otherwise it will be impossible to pass the transmission shaft through the splined hub of the driven plate when the transmission is offered to the engine. Engage the bellhousing flange with the hollow dowels and pull the transmission casing tight against the engine.
21   Fit the bellhousing to engine connecting bolts, also the transmission mounting bracket.
22   Fit the cover plate to the lower part of the bellhousing.
23   Engage the driveshaft retaining circlips by pressing the driveshafts inwards. If engagement cannot be obtained with hand pressure then fit a large worm drive clip round the metal cover of the inboard joints and use the clip as a striking point to drive the shaft inward. On no account attempt to hammer on the flexible gaiter, you will only damage the joint and split the gaiter.
24   Reconnect the hub carriers to the track control arms. The radius rods may require prising down at their ends to enable the bolts to be fitted.
25   Lower the front of the car.
26   Reconnect the gearchange and range selector controls.
27   Reconnect the engine front damper rod.
28   Refit the starter motor.
29   Reconnect the electrical leads, refit the battery and reconnect the speedometer cable.
30   Reconnect the clutch operating cable and adjust the clutch (Chapter 5).

31   Refill the transmission with the correct grade and quantity of lubricant.

5   Transmission – dismantling into gear trains

1   With the transmission removed from the car, clean away external dirt using paraffin and a stiff brush or a water soluble solvent.
2   Unbolt and remove the mounting/clutch cable bracket from the transmission casing.
3   Unscrew and remove the reverse lamp switch and ball. Extract the latter with a pencil magnet or by tipping the casing.
4   Unbolt and remove the rear cover.
5   Remove the spacers from the now exposed bearing outer tracks. Identify the spacers as to location.
6   Unbolt the transmission casing and slide it off the gear assemblies.
7   Check that the gears are set in the neutral mode, moving the selector rods as necessary.
8   Unscrew the detent plugs and withdraw the springs and balls. The spring for reverse selector is shorter than the other two.
9   Pull out the reverse idler shaft, lift away reverse idler gear.
10   Remove the reverse shift lever.
11   Remove the reverse selector shaft.
12   Remove the 3rd/4th selector shaft sleeve.
13   Using a pin punch, drive out the roll pins from the 3rd/4th and 1st/2nd selector forks.
14   Withdraw the 1st/2nd selector shaft followed by the 3rd/4th selector shaft. To do this, prise the dogs at the base of the shafts upwards and then withdraw the shafts sideways. Note the interlock pin at the base of the 3rd/4th selector shaft. Pull the forks from the shafts.
15   Using a pencil magnet, withdraw the two interlock plungers from the selector shaft holes in the webs of the transmission casing. A blanking plug is provided in the wall of the transmission casing for direct access to these plungers but it should not have to be removed if a magnet is used.
16   Push the synchroniser sleeve at the bottom of the output shaft downward. This is the sleeve next to the pinion gear and controls the 3rd/4th speed selector. Remove the output shaft.
17   Unbolt and remove the speedometer cable drive gear and then lift out the crownwheel/differential.
18   Unscrew the range selector detent plug, ball and spring. To gain access to the screwdriver slot in the plug, the sealant will first have to be cleaned away with a sharp knife.
19   Unbolt the input shaft bearing retainer.
20   Withdraw the input shaft, the intermediate shaft and the Power/Economy ratio selector rod and fork together as one assembly.
21   Remove the spring retainer from the selector finger.
22   Using a pair of pliers, pull the roll pin from the selector finger.
23   Using a thin rod inserted into the selector finger shaft, rotate the shaft back and forth to extract the shaft. Watch for ejection of the spring loaded ball as the shaft is withdrawn from the finger. Remove the selector finger, springs and ball.
24   The clutch release mechanism can be removed from the bellhousing if required by referring to Chapter 5.
25   With the three shaft/gear assemblies removed, further dismantling will be dictated by the wear in the gears and synchronisers and whether there has been a history of noisy gear changing and whether the synchromesh could be easily 'beaten'. Dismantling of the shafts is covered in the following Sections but before attempting the work you must be in possession of a vice, a two-legged puller and preferably have access to a press. If the basic tools are not available, leave gear and bearing removal and refitting to your dealer.

6   Input shaft – dismantling and reassembly

1   Using soft wooden protection, grip the splined end of the input shaft in the jaws of the vice.
2   Unscrew and remove the staked nut.
3   Using a suitable puller, draw the ball type bearing from the shaft.
4   Remove the thrust washer.
5   Pull off the Economy gear, noting the anti-backlash plate held to its face by a circlip.
6   Remove the gear bush.
7   Remove the synchro baulk ring.

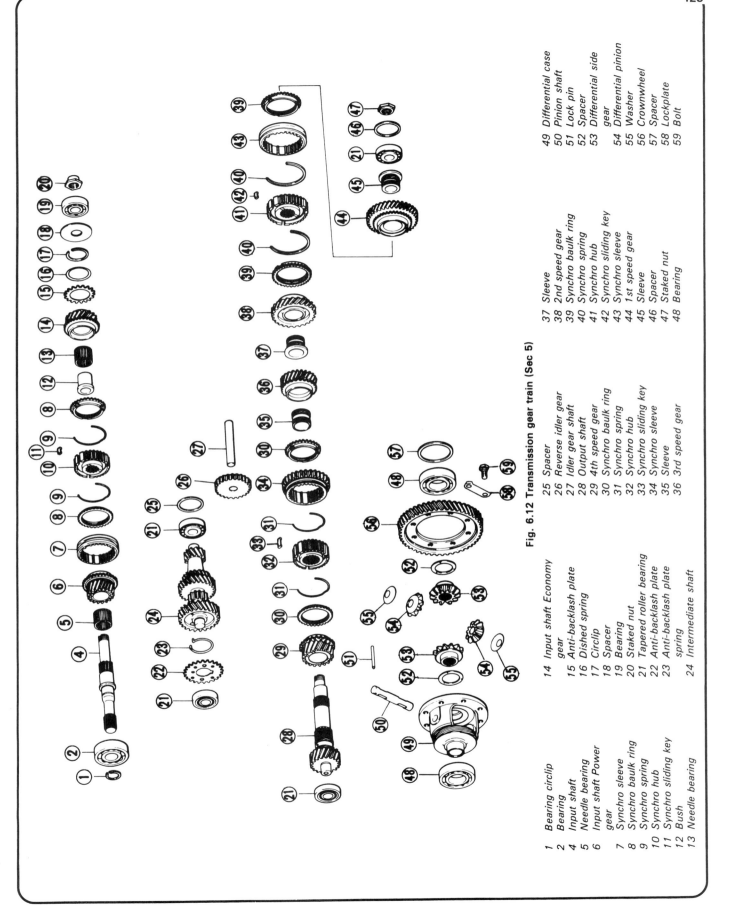

Fig. 6.12 Transmission gear train (Sec 5)

1 Bearing circlip
2 Bearing
4 Input shaft
5 Needle bearing
6 Input shaft Power gear
7 Synchro sleeve
8 Synchro baulk ring
9 Synchro spring
10 Synchro hub
11 Synchro sliding key
12 Bush
13 Needle bearing
14 Input shaft Economy gear
15 Anti-backlash plate
16 Dished spring
17 Circlip
18 Spacer
19 Bearing
20 Staked nut
21 Tapered roller bearing
22 Anti-backlash plate
23 Anti-backlash plate spring
24 Intermediate shaft
25 Spacer
26 Reverse idler gear
27 Idler gear shaft
28 Output shaft
29 4th speed gear
30 Synchro baulk ring
31 Synchro spring
32 Synchro hub
33 Synchro sliding key
34 Synchro sleeve
35 Sleeve
36 3rd speed gear
37 Sleeve
38 2nd speed gear
39 Synchro baulk ring
40 Synchro spring
41 Synchro hub
42 Synchro sliding key
43 Synchro sleeve
44 1st speed gear
45 Sleeve
46 Spacer
47 Staked nut
48 Bearing
49 Differential case
50 Pinion shaft
51 Lock pin
52 Spacer
53 Differential side gear
54 Differential pinion gear
55 Washer
56 Crownwheel
57 Spacer
58 Lockplate
59 Bolt

123

124

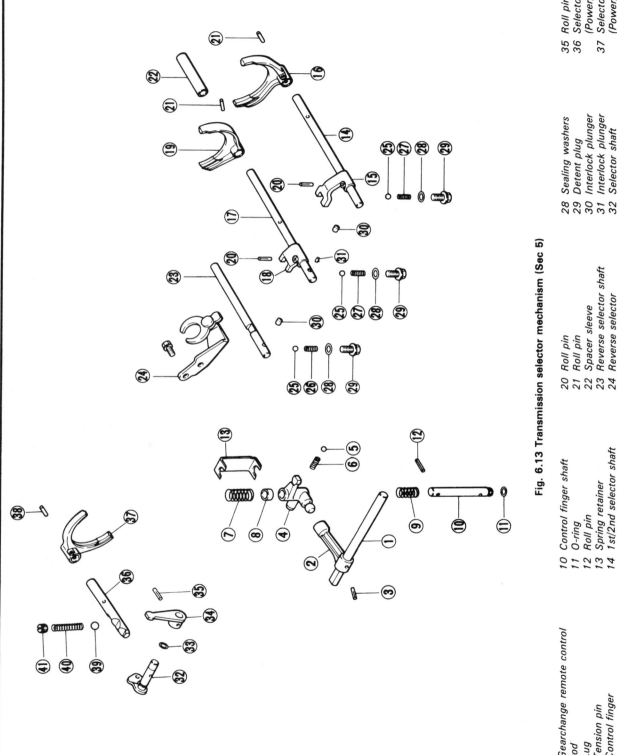

Fig. 6.13 Transmission selector mechanism (Sec 5)

1 Gearchange remote control
  rod
2 Lug
3 Tension pin
4 Control finger
5 Ball
6 Spring
7 Neutral return spring
8 Spacer
9 Reverse restrict spring

10 Control finger shaft
11 O-ring
12 Roll pin
13 Spring retainer
14 1st/2nd selector shaft
15 Selector dog
16 Selector fork
17 3rd/4th selector shaft
18 Selector dog
19 Selector fork

20 Roll pin
21 Roll pin
22 Spacer sleeve
23 Reverse selector shaft
24 Reverse selector
25 Detent ball
26 Reverse detent spring
27 1st/2nd and 3rd/4th
   detent springs

28 Sealing washers
29 Detent plug
30 Interlock plunger
31 Interlock plunger
32 Selector shaft
   (Power/Economy)
33 O-ring
34 Selector finger
   (Power/Economy)

35 Roll pin
36 Selector shaft
   (Power/Economy)
37 Selector fork
   (Power/Economy)
38 Roll pin
39 Detent ball
40 Spring
41 Detent plug

8   Now reverse the shaft in the jaws of the vice and extract the circlip which holds the bearing at the splined end of the shaft.

9   With a suitable puller, draw off the bearing.

10 Again reverse the position of the shaft in the vice and draw off the synchro unit and the Power gear from the threaded end of the shaft (photo).

11 Examine all components for wear and damage.

12 It is unlikely that the synchro unit will be worn or require renewal as it does not normally have to ensure the wear of the units on other shafts. However if it has been failing to provide quiet smooth range changes, renew it (photo).

13 The synchro baulk rings should be fitted to the cones and the clearance checked with feeler blades. If the clearance is less than 0.0315 in (0.8 mm) or the serrations on the ring contact surface are worn away, renew the baulk ring.

14 The clearance between the shift fork and the synchro sleeve groove should not exceed 0.020 in (0.5 mm). If it does, renew the synchro unit or the shift fork or both. This can be determined by

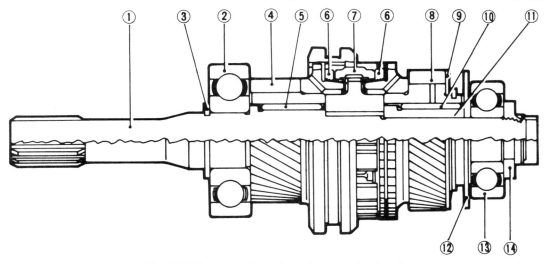

Fig. 6.14 Cutaway view of the input shaft (Sec 6)

1 Shaft	5 Needle bearing	9 Anti-backlash plate	12 Spacer
2 Bearing	6 Synchro baulk ring	10 Needle bearing	13 Bearing
3 Circlip	7 Synchro sliding key	11 Sleeve	14 Staked nut
4 Power gear	8 Economy gear		

6.10 Input shaft

6.12a Synchro hub showing teeth in good condition

6.12b Synchro sleeve showing teeth in good condition

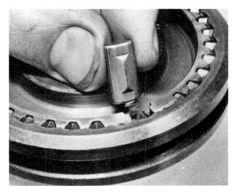

6.16a Synchro sliding key

6.16b Fitting a synchro spring

6.17 Fitting the input shaft ball bearing

6.18 Fitting the input shaft bearing circlip

6.19 Fitting the Power gear to the input shaft

6.20a Fitting the first baulk ring to the input shaft

6.20b Fitting the synchro to the input shaft

6.20c Fitting the second baulk ring to input shaft

6.20d Fitting the gear bush to the input shaft

6.20e Fitting the Economy gear to the input shaft

6.20f Economy gear backlash plate and circlip

6.22 Input shaft thrust washer and second bearing

6.23a Tightening the input shaft nut

6.23b Staking the input shaft nut

6.23c Input shaft completely assembled

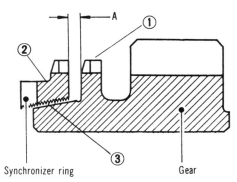

Fig. 6.15 Synchro baulk ring clearance diagram (Sec 6)

1 Splines
2 Baulk ring
3 Core of gear

A Clearance not exceeding
0.0315 in (0.8 mm)

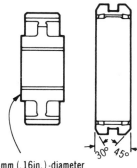

4mm (.16in.)-diameter
slot in oil groove

Fig. 6.16 Input shaft synchro assembly diagram (Sec 6)

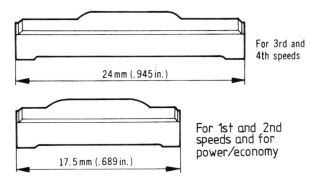

For 3rd and
4th speeds

24mm (.945in.)

For 1st and 2nd
speeds and for
power/economy

17.5mm (.689in.)

Fig. 6.18 Synchro sliding key identification (Sec 6)

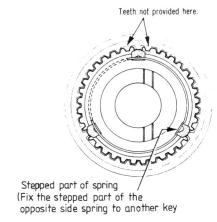

Fig. 6.17 Synchro spring installation diagram (Sec 6)

measuring the width of the sleeve groove which when new is 0.2756 in (7.0 mm) wide.

15 If a synchro unit falls apart inadvertently, observe the following points when reassembling. Make sure that the hub to sleeve relationship is correct (refer to Fig 6.16 showing sleeve chamfers).

16 Insert the sliding legs and engage the springs. The spring on one side must run in the opposite direction to the one on the other side. The stepped part of the springs must not engage in the same key even though they are fitted on opposite sides of the unit (photo).

17 Commence reassembly by fitting the bearing to the splined end of the shaft using a piece of tubing applied to the inner track of the bearing. Fit the bearings so that the engraved numbers are visible when the bearing is viewed from the end of the shaft onto which it is fitted (photo).

18 Fit the bearing circlip. These are available in three different thicknesses. Always select the thickest one which will fit into the shaft groove (photo).

19 Continue reassembly by fitting the Power gear onto the threaded end of the shaft. Make sure that the needle bearing race is in position (photo).

20 Fit the first synchro baulk ring, the synchro unit, the second baulk ring, the gear bush and the Economy gear. If the anti-backlash plate was removed when dismantling, smear the face of the gear with gear oil and then locate the dished spring against the gear so that the concave side is against the gear. Compress the spring with a piece of tubing and fit the retaining circlip. Take care that the spring does not slip into the circlip groove during this operation (photo).

21 Fit the thrust washer with its projecting boss towards the threaded end of the shaft.

22 Again using a piece of tubing, fit the ball bearing assembly as described in paragraph 18 (photo).

23 Screw a new nut onto the shaft and tighten it to the specified torque. Stake the nut into its groove (photo).

Fig. 6.19 Selecting a bearing circlip (Sec 6)

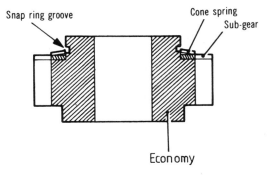

Snap ring groove

Cone spring
Sub-gear

Economy

Fig. 6.20 Input shaft anti-backlash plate (Sec 6)

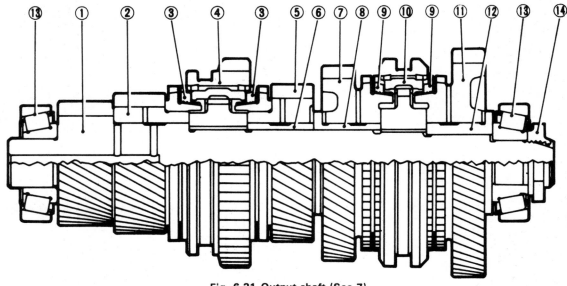

Fig. 6.21 Output shaft (Sec 7)

1 Shaft	5 3rd speed gear	9 Synchro baulk ring	12 Sleeve
2 4th speed gear	6 Sleeve	10 1st/2nd speed synchro	13 Tapered roller bearing
3 Synchro baulk ring	7 2nd speed gear	unit	14 Staked nut
4 3rd/4th synchro unit	8 Sleeve	11 1st speed gear	

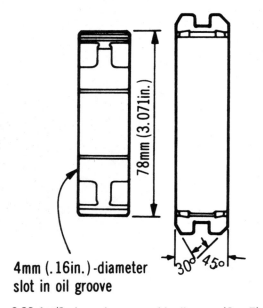

4mm (.16in.)-diameter
slot in oil groove

Fig. 6.22 1st/2nd synchro assembly diagram (Sec 7)

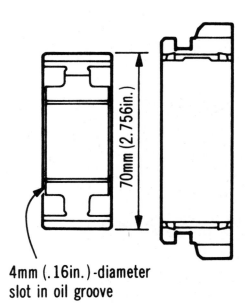

4mm (.16in.)-diameter
slot in oil groove

Fig. 6.23 3rd/4th synchro assembly diagram (Sec 7)

7   Output shaft – dismantling and reassembly

1   If the bearing at the pinion gear end of the shaft is worn, remove it with a suitable bearing puller, then using soft wooden protectors, grip the pinion gear teeth of the output shaft in the jaws of a vice.
2   Unscrew and remove the staked nut from the end of the shaft.
3   Using a two legged puller with its claws engaged under the 1st gear, draw off the tapered roller bearing with the gear bush together with 1st gear.
4   Remove the baulk ring.
5   Now engage the puller under the 2nd gear and withdraw the 1st/2nd synchro with the 2nd gear from the shaft.
6   Remove the 2nd gear bush.
7   Take the 3rd gear from the shaft followed by the baulk ring.
8   Remove the 3rd gear bush.

9   Remove the 3rd/4th synchro which incorporates the reverse gear.
10 Take the 4th gear from the shaft.
11 Remove the output shaft with pinion gear from the vice. The shaft cannot be further dismantled (photo).
12 Inspect the gear teeth for chipping and the shafts and bushes for wear. Renew as necessary.
13 Check the synchro units as described in Section 6, paragraphs 13 to 16.
14 Commence reassembly by fitting the 4th speed gear and the first of the 3rd/4th synchro baulk rings (photo).
15 Fit the 3rd/4th synchro unit noting carefully the way it is assembled and the position of the sleeve chamfers once it is installed on the shaft (photo).
16 Fit the second of the synchro baulk rings and the 3rd speed gear bush (photo).
17 Fit the 3rd speed gear (photo).

7.11 The output shaft

7.14a Fitting the 4th gear to the output shaft

7.14b Fitting the first 3rd/4th synchro baulk ring to the output shaft

7.15 Fitting the 3rd/4th synchro with reverse gear to the output shaft

7.16a Fitting the 3rd/4th synchro second baulk ring to the output shaft

7.16b Fitting the 3rd speed gear bush to the output shaft

7.17 Fitting the 3rd speed gear to the output shaft

7.18 Fitting the 2nd speed gear bush to output shaft

7.19a Fitting the 2nd speed gear to output shaft

7.19b Fitting the first baulk ring for the 1st/2nd synchro

7.19c Fitting the 1st/2nd synchro to the output shaft

7.20 Fitting the second baulk ring for the 1st/2nd synchro

7.21 Fitting the 1st gear and bush to the output shaft

7.22 Fitting the output shaft bearing

7.23 Staking the output shaft nut

7.24 Output shaft completely assembled

8.1a The intermediate shaft

8.1b The intermediate shaft anti-backlash plate

18   Fit the 2nd speed gear bush (photo).
19   Fit the 2nd speed gear followed by the 1st/2nd synchro baulk ring. Then fit the synchro unit which must again be correctly assembled in respect of its hub to sleeve relationship also with regard to the position of the sleeve chamfers when the unit is fitted to the shaft (photos).
20   Fit the second of the 1st/2nd synchro baulk rings (photo).
21   Fit the gear bush and the 1st speed gear (photo).
22   Using a piece of tubing applied to the centre track of the tapered roller bearing, drive the bearing onto the shaft so that the smaller diameter of the bearing is towards the end of the shaft (photo).
23   Screw on a new nut, tighten to the specified torque and stake it into its shaft groove (photo).
24   If the bearing at the pinion end of the shaft was removed, press on the new one in a similar way to that described in paragraph 22 (photo).

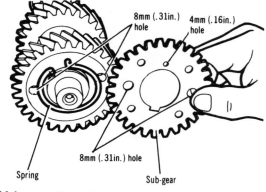

Fig. 6.24 Intermediate shaft anti-backlash plate and spring (Sec 8)

8   Intermediate shaft – dismantling and reassembly

1   The bearings anti-backlash plate and spring can all be removed from the shaft. Other than this, the assembly must be renewed complete in the event of wear or damage occurring (photo).
2   Remove the bearings using a suitable puller. The anti-backlash gear can now be removed.
3   When refitting the spring for the anti-backlash plate ensure that the longer leg engages in the 0.16 in (4.0 mm) hole in the gear.
4   Fit the plate to the gear, engaging the remaining spring end in the same sized hole in the plate.
5   New bearings must now be pressed onto the shaft.

9   Oil seals

1   At this stage in the overhaul, all O-rings and oil seals should be renewed as a matter of routine.

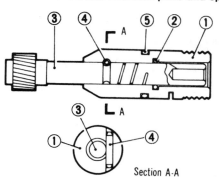

Fig. 6.25 Sectional view of speedometer driven gear (Sec 9)

1 Sleeve	4 Roll pin
2 O-ring	5 O-ring
3 Driven gear	

9.2 Driveshaft seal in final drive housing

10.1 Differential/final drive. Note speedometer drivegear

11.1 Fitting the differential/final drive

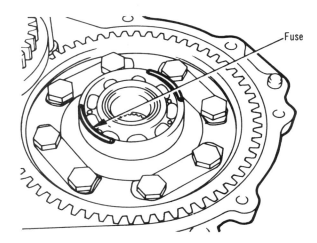

Fig. 6.26 Location of fuse wire for measuring differential endplay (Sec 10)

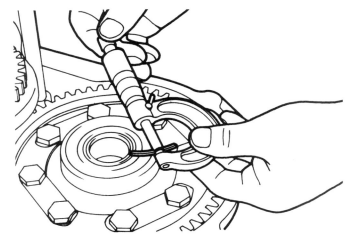

Fig. 6.27 Measuring thickness of compressed fuse wire to establish thickness of endfloat spacers (Sec 10)

2   These include the seals for the speedometer driven gear, the gearchange control shaft and the input shaft, also the driveshaft seals in the final drive housing (photo).

10 Differential/final drive – examination

1   Excessive wear in the differential or backlash in the crownwheel or pinion gear should be rectified by your dealer as the side gears will have to be removed and new spacers fitted (photo). Due to the need for special gauges this work is not within the scope of the home mechanic.
2   If as the result of wear, a new final drive is required then a matching pinion gear must be fitted which as it is part of the output shaft, means a new output shaft as well. When these problems occur it is recommended that a new or reconditioned transmission is considered as an economic alternative.
3   If new components are fitted to the final drive or new bearings are fitted, then the endplay must be calculated in the following way and the appropriate new spacers selected and fitted.
4   Fit the differential into the transmission casing.
5   Place two short lengths of soft lead wire (thick fuse wire will do) on the ball bearing outer track (Fig 6.26).
6   Fit the gear casing with gasket and tighten the six casing bolts around the differential to the specified torque.
7   Carefully unbolt and remove the casing.
8   Measure the thickness of the crushed wire using a micrometer. Select spacers from those available to make up a total thickness equal to that of the crushed wire. It is permissible to have spacers slightly thinner than the thickness of the crushed wire as long as the difference does not exceed 0.0059 in (0.15 mm) otherwise the endfloat which will be introduced as a result of this will exceed the specified tolerance.

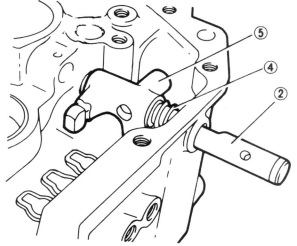

Fig. 6.28 Selector finger installation (Sec 11)

2   Gearchange rod   5   Control finger
4   Reverse restrict spring

11 Transmission – reassembly

1   With the casing clean, install the final drive/differential. The next step is to set the anti-backlash plate on the intermediate shaft. To do this, a bolt or bar will be required 0.31 in (8.0 mm) in diameter and 1.38 in (35.0 mm) in length. Turn the anti-backlash plate against spring pressure until the holes in the plate and gear are in alignment and insert the bolt or bar.

11.2a Shaft bearing tracks and recesses in final drive casing

11.2b Fitting the input and intermediate shafts with the range selector shaft and fork

11.2c Range selector dog in shaft cut-out

11.2d Bolting down the input shaft bearing retainer

11.3 Removing the anti-backlash plate setting rod

11.4a Inserting the control finger spring

11.4b Control finger ball

11.4c Inserting the shaft into the control finger. Note the coil spring and O-ring

11.5 Inserting the control finger roll pin

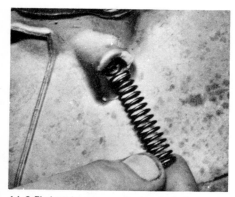
11.6 Fitting the range selector shaft detent ball and spring

11.7a Fitting the speedometer cable drivegear

11.7b Speedometer drive gear retainer

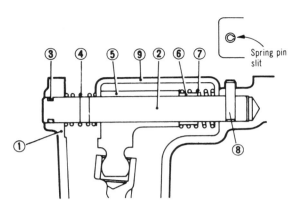

Fig. 6.29 Sectional view of selector finger (Sec 11)

1 *Transmission casing*	6 *Spacer collar*
2 *Gearchange rod*	7 *Neutral return spring*
3 *O-ring*	8 *Roll pin*
4 *Reverse restrict spring*	9 *Spring retainer*
5 *Control finger*	

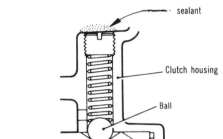

Fig. 6.31 Poppet ball, spring and plug (Sec 11)

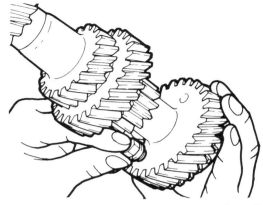

Fig. 6.30 Setting anti-backlash plate to intermediate shaft gear (Sec 11)

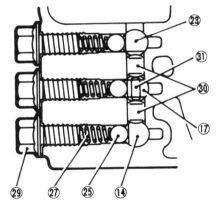

Fig. 6.32 Sectional view of detents (Sec 11)

14 *1st/2nd selector shaft*	27 *Detent spring*
17 *3rd/4th selector shaft*	29 *Detent plug*
23 *Reverse selector shaft*	30 *Interlock plunger*
25 *Detent ball*	31 *Lock pin*

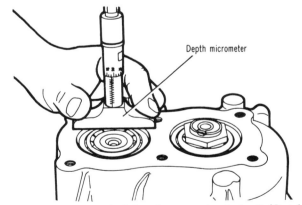

Fig. 6.33 Checking shaft bearing outer track depth (Sec 11)

2   The input and intermediate shafts must be fitted together into their bearing recesses in the transmission casing. Mesh the gears together and have the Power/Economy selector shaft and fork engaged in the synchro sleeve groove of the input shaft. As the two gear shafts and the selector shaft are fitted simultaneously, make sure that the Power/Economy selector dog engages in the cut-out of the selector shaft. Pin the fork to the shaft using the roll pin (photo). Bolt the input shaft bearing retainer into position.

3   Remove the temporary rod or bolt which was fitted to the anti-backlash plate (photo).

4   Continue reassembly by fitting the gearchange selector finger and shaft. The detent ball and spring will have to be inserted into the finger and then kept depressed with a rod as the selector rod is pushed through the casing and into the finger. Make sure that the coil springs are located on the shaft at each side of the control finger, also that the shaft has been fitted with a new O-ring seal (photos).

5   Once the finger and shaft holes are in alignment, tap the roll pin into position. Fit the spring retainer (photo).

6   Insert the Power/Economy range selector detent ball and spring into the hole in the casing and screw in the plug until the end of the plug is flush with the casing. Seal over the end of the plug with RTV sealant to prevent it unscrewing (photo).

7   Fit the speedometer drivegear and its retainer (photo).

8   Hold the output shaft ready for fitting and push the 3rd/4th synchro sleeve at the bottom of the shaft downward. Now fit the output shaft gear train into the casing (photo).

9   Using a pencil magnet or pair of long-nosed pliers, insert the two interlock plungers between the selector shafts into the holes in the webs of the casing (photo).

10 Fit the 3rd/4th selector shaft making sure that the interlock pin is correctly located at the base of the shaft and the fork is located in the synchro (photo).

11 Fit the 1st/2nd selector shaft, complete with fork correctly located in the synchro sleeve groove.

12 Supporting the selector shaft/fork assemblies, align the holes and tap the securing roll pins into position (photos).

13 Fit the 3rd/4th selector shaft sleeve (photo).

14 Fit the reverse selector shaft (photo).

15 Fit the reverse selector lever (photo).

16 Fit the reverse idler shaft and idler gear (photo).

17 Fit the detent balls, springs and plugs. Note that the spring for reverse is shorter than the other two (photos). The springs must be fitted with the small diameter end against the steel ball.

18 Move the selector forks as necessary to set the gears in the neutral

11.8 Fitting the output shaft

11.9 Fitting a selector shaft interlock plunger

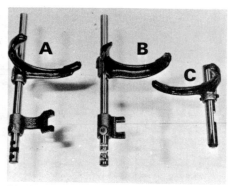

11.10a Selector shafts and forks. A-1st/2nd B-3rd/4th C-Power/Economy

11.10b 3rd/4th selector shaft interlock pin

11.10c 1st/2nd and 3rd/4th selector shafts installed

11.12a 3rd/4th selector shaft, fork and roll pin

11.12b 1st/2nd selector shaft, fork and roll pin

11.13 3rd/4th selector shaft sleeve

11.14 Fitting the reverse selector shaft

mode. This is indicated when the synchro sleeves are fully covering the synchro hubs. *Failure to do this will prevent the selectors working and gears will not be obtainable once the transmission is fitted.*

19 Stick the spacers which were selected (refer to paragraphs 3 to 8 of Section 10) with thick grease into the final drive bearing recess in the transmission casing. Hold the casing over the gear train assemblies and slide it into position complete with a new flange gasket. Insert the securing bolts and tighten to the specified torque (photos).

20 The spacers should now be fitted to their original locations on the shaft bearing outer tracks. If new bearings or other components have been fitted, then discard the original spacers and select new ones using the following method. Check that the bearings are fully home in their seats and then using a depth gauge, measure the distance that the bearing outer tracks are below the face of the transmission casing. Now measure the depth of the bearing recesses in the rear cover. Subtract one dimension from the other and fit spacers which are 0.004 in (0.1 mm) thicker than the difference calculated. Spacers are

available in a very wide range of thicknesses for the purpose (photo).

21 Smear the cover mating surfaces and bolt threads with jointing compound, fit the cover and tighten the bolts to the specified torque (photo).

22 Insert the reverse lamp switch ball and screw the switch into position. Make sure that the sealing washer is in good condition and tighten to the specified torque (photo).

23 Bolt the mounting/clutch cable bracket onto the transmission casing (photo).

24 With a piece of rod connected to the gearchange control rod, select all gears in turn to ensure that they move smoothly and engage positively. Once each gear is engaged, turn the input shaft and check that power is being transmitted to the differential/driveshaft splines.

25 If the clutch release bearing and mechanism have been dismantled, refer to Chapter 5 for details of reassembly.

26 Refer to Section 4 and refit the transmission. The transmission is best filled with lubricant after it has been fitted in the car.

11.15 Fitting the reverse gear selector lever

11.16 Fitting the reverse idler shaft and gear

11.17a Selector shaft detent balls and springs

11.17b Fitting the detent springs and balls.
A 1st/2nd   B 3rd/4th   C Reverse

11.17c Detent retaining plugs

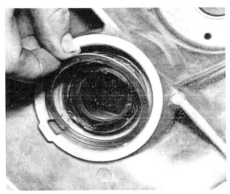
11.19a Transmission casing final drive bearing spacer

11.19b Fitting the transmission casing

11.20 Shaft bearing spacers

11.21a Fitting the transmission casing rear cover

11.21b Rear cover and reverse lamp lead clips

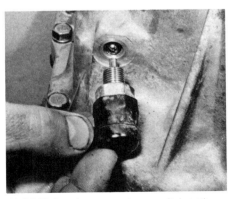
11.22 Fitting the reverse lamp switch and ball

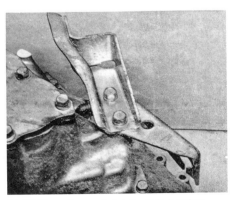
11.23 Mounting and clutch cable bracket

12 Fault diagnosis – manual transmission

Symptom	Reason(s)
Ineffective synchromesh	Worn baulk rings, synchro hubs or sleeves
Jumps out of one or more gears (on drive or over-run)	Weak detent springs, worn selector forks, worn gears or worn synchro sleeves
Noisy, rough, whining and vibration	Worn bearings and/or gear bushes resulting in extended wear generally due to play and backlash
Noisy and difficult engagement of gears	Clutch fault (See Chapter 5), worn selector mechanism

Note: *It is sometimes difficult to decide whether it is worthwhile removing and dismantling the gearbox for a fault which may be nothing more than a minor irritant. Gearboxes which howl, or where the synchromesh can be 'beaten' by a quick gearchange, may continue to perform for a long time in this state. A worn gearbox usually needs a complete rebuild to eliminate noise because the various gears, if re-aligned on new bearings will continue to howl when different wearing surfaces are presented to each other*

The decision to overhaul therefore, must be considered with regard to time and money available, relative to the degree of noise or malfunction that the driver has to suffer

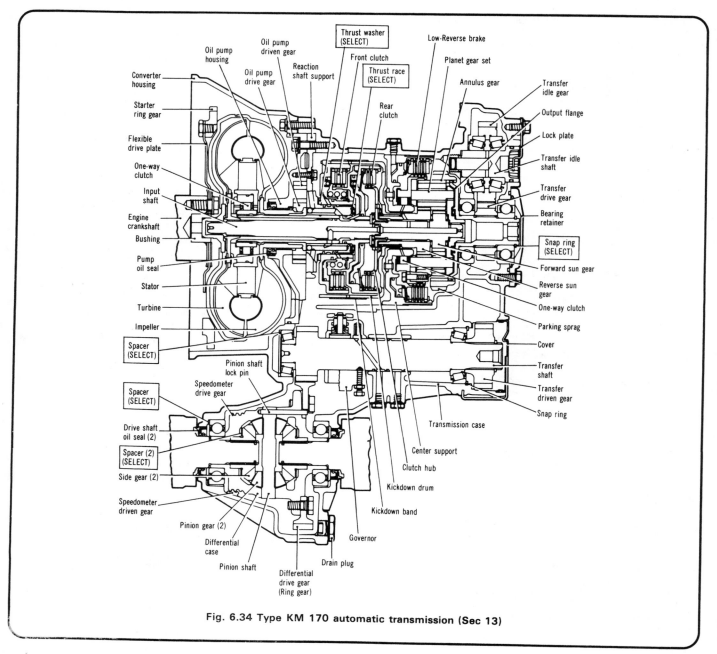

Fig. 6.34 Type KM 170 automatic transmission (Sec 13)

Part B Automatic transmission

13 General description

The automatic transmission is designed to operate with the engine at the front of the car as is the case with manual transmission versions.

This type of transmission is fully automatic and incorporates a torque converter and planetary gear set, also the final drive/differential.

The lubrication system is combined for the transmission and the final drive. Fluid cooling is by means of a heat exchanger located in the base of the engine cooling system radiator.

Due to the complex nature of the automatic transmission and to the need for special tools and equipment, it is recommended that servicing operations should be limited to those described in this Chapter and other work left to your dealer or automatic transmission specialists.

14 Fluid – checking

1   Checking the fluid level and topping up is probably the most important maintenance task essential for reliable operation of the automatic transmission. Check at the specified intervals (see Routine maintenance).

2   Have the fluid at the normal operating temperature after having completed at least 5 miles (8 km) running on the road. Move the selector lever through all positions.

3   With the engine idling and the speed selector lever in N, withdraw the dipstick, wipe it clean, re-insert it and withdraw it for the second time. The fluid level should be between the LOW and HIGH marks on the HOT side of the dipstick. Add fluid if necessary through the dipstick hole making sure that it is of the correct type. 1 Imp pt (0.57 litres, 0.6 US qt) of fluid will raise the level from the LOW to HIGH marks.

4   Refit the dipstick and switch off the engine.

15 Fluid – renewal

1   The fluid should be renewed at the intervals specified in the Routine maintenance Section.

2   Raise the front of the car on ramps or place it over an inspection pit.

3   Place a large container under the drain plugs which are located at the base of the final drive housing and the transmission fluid sump pan. Remove the plugs and allow the fluid to drain into the container. If it is being drained after having come in off the road, the fluid will be very hot and could scald.

4   When all the fluid has drained, refit the drain plugs and tighten to the specified torque.

5   If the drained fluid appears to be badly discoloured or contains dirt or other debris, it is recommended that the fluid sump pan is removed and the filter renewed. This is quite straightforward but make sure that all bolts are tightened to the specified torque and a new gasket is used.

6   When the automatic transmission fluid is drained, there will always remain a quantity of fluid in the torque converter so that the quantity required to refill the transmission will be less than that required to fill a new unit from dry.

7   Pour 8 Imp.pts (4.5 litres, 4.8 US qts) of the specified fluid into the transmission through the transmission dipstick hole.

8   Start the engine and allow it to idle for a minimum of two minutes. Move the speed selector lever to each position in turn locating it finally in the N position.

9   Check the fluid level on the dipstick, adding fluid if necessary to bring it to the LOW mark.

10 Now run the car on the road for at least 5 miles (8 km) and check and top up the fluid again as described in Section 13.

16 Inhibitor switch – adjustment

1   This switch is designed to prevent the starter motor operating unless the speed selector lever is in N or P.

2   If the ignition key will actuate the starter motor with the selector lever not positioned as specified, the inhibitor switch must be adjusted in the following way.

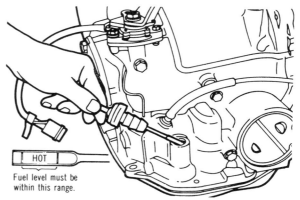

Fig. 6.35 Fluid dipstick (Sec 14)

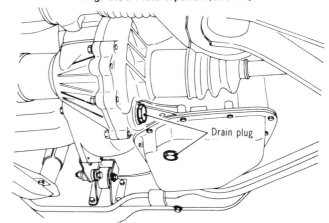

Fig. 6.36 Drain plugs (Sec 15)

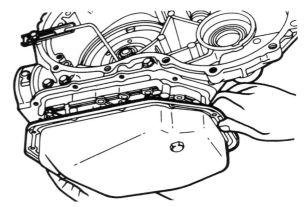

Fig. 6.37 Removing fluid sump pan (Sec 15)

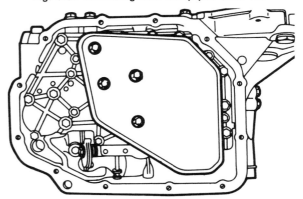

Fig. 6.38 Fluid filter (Sec 15)

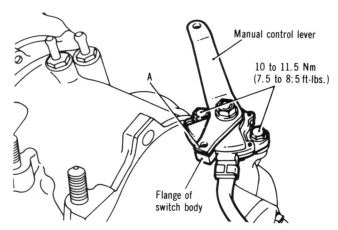

Fig. 6.39 Transmission speed control lever and inhibitor
switch (Sec 16)

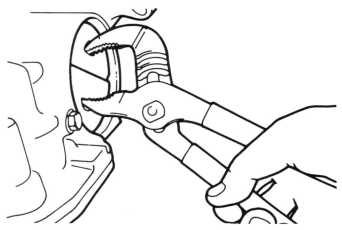

Fig. 6.41 Removing transmission servo cover (Sec 18)

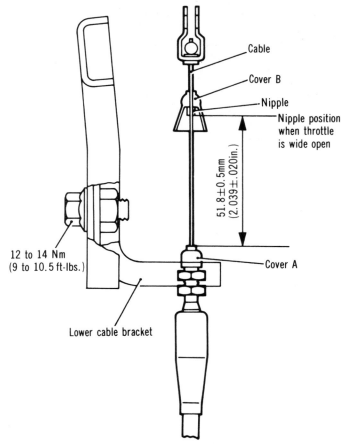

Fig. 6.40 Throttle cable adjustment diagram (Sec 17)

3   Set the console mounted selector control lever in N.
4   Release the inhibitor switch mounting screws and turn the switch
until the projection on the switch body aligns with the 0.472 in (12.0
mm) wide arm of the control lever.
5   Retighten the mounting screws without disturbing the setting.
6   Check that the starter motor will only operate in the N and P
position.

17 Throttle control cable – adjustment

1   Turn the operating lever on the throttle valve plate to the fully
open position.
2   Loosen the throttle cable lower mounting bracket bolt and move
the bracket until the cable distance (cover to nipple) is as shown in Fig
6.40.
3   Tighten the bracket bolt.
4   With the throttle lever still held in the wide open position, check
that the cable still has a little free movement by pulling it upward
gently.

18 Kickdown band – adjustment

1   Clean away all dirt and mud from the servo cover on the
transmission casing.
2   Prise out the circlip and remove the cover.
3   Release the exposed locknut.
4   Hold the kickdown servo piston from turning and tighten the
adjuster screw to a torque of 7 lbf ft (10 Nm). If a torque wrench of
a suitable calibration is not available, attach a spring balance to the

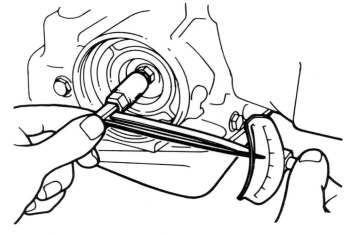

Fig. 6.42 Adjusting kickdown band (Sec 18)

end of a socket wrench which must be exactly one foot in length to
give the same result in lbf ft.
5   Release the screw completely and then tighten to the torque
wrench setting again and then release once more. These operations
ensure that the kickdown band seats properly on the kickdown drum.
6   Now tighten the adjuster screw to a torque of 3.5 lbf ft (5 Nm) and
then unscrew it exactly 3½ turns. Without moving the adjuster screw,
tighten the locknut to between 11 and 15 lbf ft (15 and 21 Nm).
7   Refit the cover, using a new sealing ring if necessary and fit the
retaining circlip.

19 Speed selector control linkage – dismantling and reassembly

1   Working inside the car, remove the knob from the control handle using an Allen key to extract the retaining grub screw.
2   Extract the screws and withdraw the centre console, disconnecting the indicator lamp leads as it is removed.
3   Disconnect the control cable from the base of the selector handle.
4   Working under the car, disconnect the control cable from the arm on the transmission.
5   Disconnect the control cable from the conduit support brackets.

6   Unscrew the pivot bolt and then remove the control handle from inside the car.
7   Renew worn or damaged components, apply grease to all rubbing surfaces and reassemble by renewing the dismantling operations.
8   Once reassembly is completed, carry out the following adjustments.
9   Set the control handle in N and then depress the knob. Turn the handle, which will in turn adjust the height of the rod adjusting cam, until there is a clearance between the detent plate and pin as shown in Fig 6.48.
10 Set the control handle in N and then align the operating arm of the

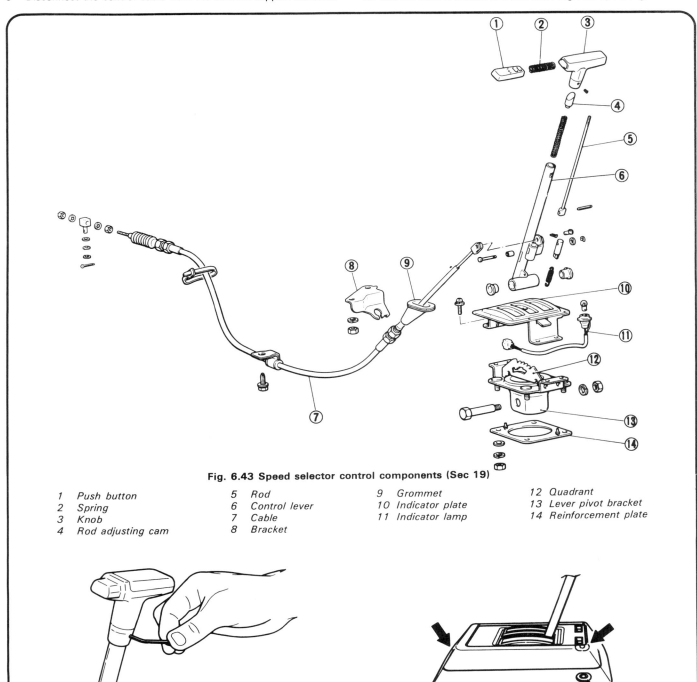

Fig. 6.43 Speed selector control components (Sec 19)

1 Push button	5 Rod	9 Grommet	12 Quadrant
2 Spring	6 Control lever	10 Indicator plate	13 Lever pivot bracket
3 Knob	7 Cable	11 Indicator lamp	14 Reinforcement plate
4 Rod adjusting cam	8 Bracket		

Fig. 6.44 Extracting control knob screw (Sec 19)

Fig. 6.45 Centre console securing screws (Sec 19)

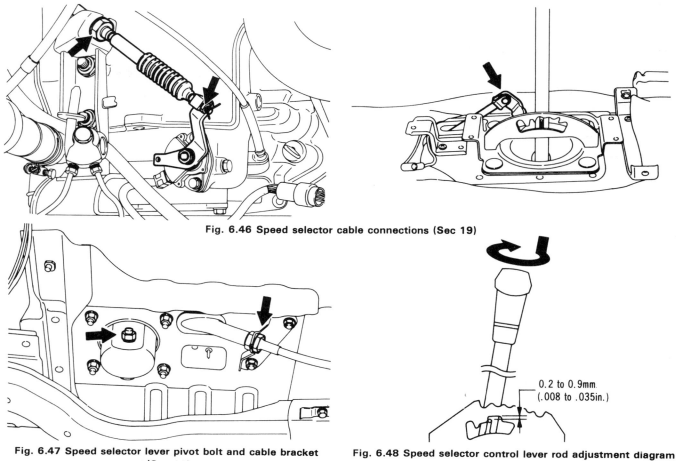

Fig. 6.46 Speed selector cable connections (Sec 19)

Fig. 6.47 Speed selector lever pivot bolt and cable bracket
(Sec 19)

Fig. 6.48 Speed selector control lever rod adjustment diagram
(Sec 19)

0.2 to 0.9mm.
(.008 to .035in.)

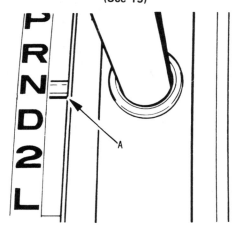

Fig. 6.49 Speed position indicator alignment (Sec 19)

Fig. 6.50 Transmission front damper strut (Sec 20)

lever on the transmission with the projection on the inhibitor switch. Slacken the cable locknuts as necessary to achieve this.

11 Using the adjuster nuts, eliminate the slack from the speed selector cable.

12 Check that the starter operates correctly in all positions and that the position indicator is in alignment with the required speed number or letter. If not, adjust the cable and the inhibitor switch as necessary.

20 Automatic transmission – removal and refitting

1   If the engine is to be the subject of major overhaul at the same

time as the automatic transmission is to be repaired or exchanged, then the engine/transmission should be removed together and separated as described in Chapter 1.

2   If the transmission is to be overhauled or exchanged and the engine does not require major overhaul then the transmission should be removed in the following way leaving the engine in position in the car.

3   Working inside the engine compartment, disconnect the battery negative lead.

4   Disconnect the throttle cable from the carburettor.

5   Disconnect the speed selector control linkage from the operating arm on the transmission also release the locknuts and detach the linkage from the support bracket.

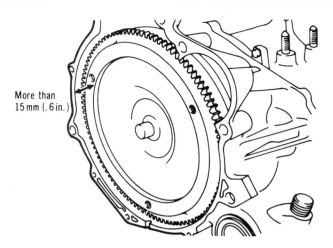

More than
15mm (.6in.)

Fig. 6.51 Torque converter fully installed in housing (Sec 20)

6   Disconnect the electrical leads from the transmission inhibitor switch.

7   Disconnect the fluid cooler hoses from the base of the radiator and quickly plug or cap the hoses and openings to prevent loss of fluid and the entry of dirt.

8   Unscrew and remove the four upper mounting bolts which hold the torque converter housing to the engine crankcase.

9   Raise the front of the car and support it under the body side members so that the suspension hangs free. Remove the under engine splash guard.

10   Drain the transmission fluid.

11   Withdraw the left and right-hand driveshafts from the transmission. To do this, first disconnect the suspension lower balljoints from the track control arms by unscrewing the two bolts from each side of the car. One of each pair of these bolts also secures the end of the radius rod. Release the inboard ends of the driveshaft by inserting a flat blade (the end of the car hub cap remover will do) between the transmission casing and the driveshaft ball track casing and lever the blade sharply to overcome the tension of the circlip.

12   The hub carrier/driveshafts can now be pulled outwards sufficiently to enable the driveshaft ends to be disconnected from the transmission. Support the driveshafts on blocks or tie them up with wire and take great care during the disconnection operations that the flexible brake hoses are not strained.

13   Disconnect the speedometer drive cable from the transmission.

14   Unbolt and remove the starter motor.

15   Disconnect the damper strut from the body and transmission.

16   Unbolt and remove the cover plate from the lower half of the torque converter housing.

17   The three special bolts which hold the torque converter to the engine driveplate will now be accessible but in order to bring each bolt into view for unscrewing, the crankshaft will have to be turned. Do this with a ring spanner applied to the crankshaft pulley centre bolt. The starter ring gear can be jammed to prevent the driveplate turning as each bolt is released.

18   Support the engine on a jack or a hoist and remove all the remaining bolts which hold the transmission to the engine.

19   Support the automatic transmission on a second jack or hoist and unbolt the transmission mounting bracket. The help of an assistant will be required.

20   Keep the torque converter prised fully towards the transmission using a piece of wood as a lever and then pull the transmission away from the engine off its locating dowels, lower it and remove it from under the car.

21   Once removed, it is important that the torque converter is retained fully into its housing to keep the oil pump drive tangs in full engagement, to prevent loss of fluid and to avoid damage to the oil seal.

22   With the transmission removed, clean away all external dirt. If a new or reconditioned unit is to be fitted, check with the supplier to make sure that parts left on the old unit will not be required for the new. These could include damper amd mounting brackets, selector control operating arm and inhibitor switch.

23   Refitting is a reversal of removal but make quite sure that the torque converter is fully fitted in the bellhousing otherwise it will not be in mesh with the oil pump drivegear. To verify this, measure the distance between the face of the starter ring gear and the converter housing mating face. The distance should exceed 0.6 in (15.0 mm). If it is less, turn the converter and at the same time maintain pressure on it until it is felt to drop into engagement with the oil pump drivegear. If the torque converter has been displaced or a new one is to be fitted, examine the oil seal at the oil pump carefully for damage. Apply transmission fluid to the shaft of the torque converter and to the seal lips before pushing the torque converter into position.

24   Only tighten the damper strut bolts after the transmission has been fitted and the car has been lowered onto its roadwheels.

25   Check the adjustment of the inhibitor switch, the speed selector control linkage and the throttle cable as described in earlier Sections of this Chapter.

26   Refill the transmission with the specified fluid remembering that the quantity required will vary depending upon whether a new dry torque converter has been fitted or the original one is used which will still contain fluid.

See overleaf for 'Fault diagnosis – automatic transmission'

21 Fault diagnosis – automatic transmission

Symptom	Reason(s)
Engine will not start in N or P	Faulty starter or ignition circuit Incorrect linkage adjustment Incorrectly installed inhibitor switch
Engine starts in selector positions other than N or P	Incorrect linkage adjustment Incorrectly installed inhibitor switch
Severe bump when selecting D or R and excessive creep when released	Idling speed too high
Poor acceleration and low maximum speed	Incorrect fluid level Incorrect linkage adjustment
No drive in D or R	Throttle control cable requires adjustment Low fluid level Selector linkage requires adjustment Internal fault
No upshift to 2 or at incorrect speed	Throttle control cable requires adjustment Low fluid level Kickdown band requires adjustment
Delayed 1 to 2 upshift	Throttle control cable requires adjustment Low fluid level Kickdown band requires adjustment
No upshift to 3 or at incorrect speed level	Throttle cable requires adjustment Low fluid level Internal fault
Delayed 2 to 3 upshift	Throttle control cable requires adjustment Low fluid level
Overheating	Faulty torque converter Transmission casing caked with mud Fluid cooler lines blocked or hoses collapsed
No downshift D to L	Speed selector linkage incorrectly adjusted Kickdown band requires adjustment
Slip or judder in L	Throttle control requires adjustment Low fluid level Speed selector linkage incorrectly adjusted Internal faults
Upshifts when L selected	Speed selector linkage incorrectly adjusted
Severe shock at kickdown	Throttle control cable requires adjustment Low fluid level Kickdown band requires adjustment
General noise or clatter	Driveplate cracked Driveplate bolts loose

The most likely causes of faulty operation are incorrect oil level and linkage adjustment. Any other faults or mal-operation of the automatic transmission unit must be due to internal faults and should be rectified by your dealer. An indication of a major internal fault may be gained from the colour of the oil which under normal conditions should be transparent red. If it becomes discoloured or black then burned clutch or brake bands must be suspected

Chapter 7 Driveshafts

Contents

Specifications

Type .... Solid, open type with double offset joint at inboard end and Birfield joint at outboard end

Shaft diameter .... 0.87 in (22.0 mm)

Torque wrench settings

	lbf ft	Nm
Driveshaft to hub nut	120	163
Suspension lower balljoint bolts	70	95

1 General description

The driveshafts are of the solid construction type transmitting power from the final drive to the front roadwheels.

The shafts are of unequal length due to the offset nature of the final drive housing.

The joints used at the ends of the driveshaft differ. The one at the inboard end is of the ball, double offset type while the outboard one is of the Birfield type.

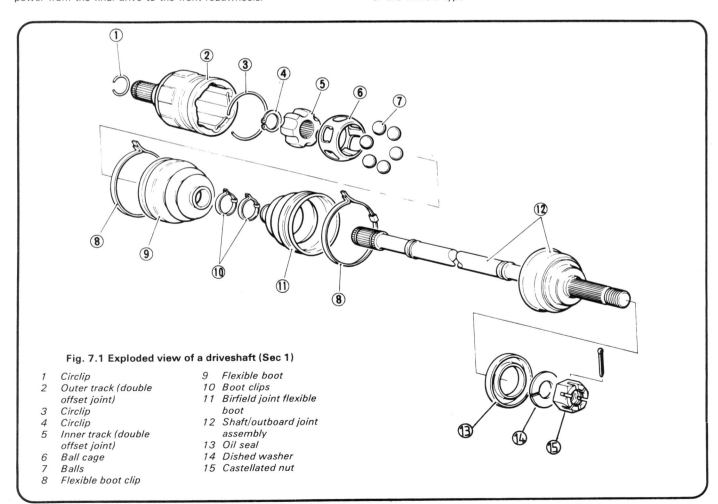

Fig. 7.1 Exploded view of a driveshaft (Sec 1)

1 Circlip
2 Outer track (double offset joint)
3 Circlip
4 Circlip
5 Inner track (double offset joint)
6 Ball cage
7 Balls
8 Flexible boot clip
9 Flexible boot
10 Boot clips
11 Birfield joint flexible boot
12 Shaft/outboard joint assembly
13 Oil seal
14 Dished washer
15 Castellated nut

2 Maintenance

1   Maintenance consists simply of checking the condition of the flexible boots. If there is any sign of a split from which lubricant is escaping, then the boot must be renewed immediately and fresh lubricant injected into the joint; refer to Section 4.

3 Driveshaft – removal and refitting

1   Prise out the centre cap from the front roadwheel using the flat-bladed tool provided in the car tool kit.
2   Loosen but do not remove the driveshaft nut which is now exposed. This is very tight and will require a socket with a long knuckle bar to release it.
3   Loosen the roadwheel nuts, raise the front of the car and support it securely on axle stands placed under the side frame members or front jacking points.
4   Remove the front roadwheel and then unbolt and remove the splash shield from under the engine compartment.
5   Disconnect the suspension lower balljoint from the track control arm by unscrewing the two securing bolts. One of these two bolts also secures the end of the radius rod.
6   Drain the transmission oil.

7   Insert the tapered end of a lever (the roadwheel centre cap removal tool is ideal) into the small gap between the inboard driveshaft joint and the transmission casing. Prise the lever sharply to release the driveshaft from the transmission by overcoming the resistance of the retaining circlip. Do not insert the tool too far or the oil seal may be damaged.
8   Now push the driveshaft splined stub out of the hub carrier. A small two-legged extractor may be necessary for this job if it is tight.
9   Do not allow the driveshaft to drop to the floor as it is released but withdraw it carefully from under the car.
10 Refitting is a reversal of removal but observe the following essential requirements:

Lightly smear the shaft splines with grease
Check that the circlip at the inboard end is in position before offering up the shaft
Always renew the inboard flexible boot retainer ring whenever the shaft is disturbed
Make sure that the dished washer at the hub end is correctly fitted under the nut with its convex face to the nut
Tighten all nuts to the specified torque, the large driveshaft nut being left for final tightening until the car is once again lowered onto its roadwheels. Fit a new split pin (photo)
Refill the transmission with oil of the specified grade
Check that each driveshaft is fully home in the transmission and the circlip engaged – refer to Chapter 6, Section 4, Paragraph 23

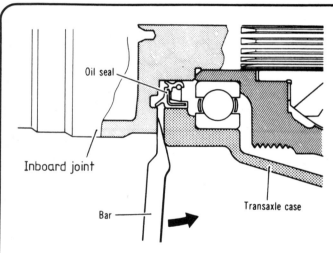

Fig. 7.2 Releasing driveshaft (Sec 3)

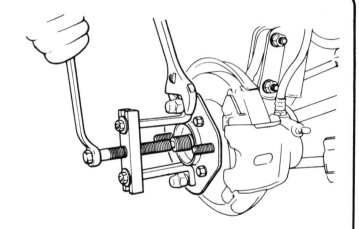

Fig. 7.3 Releasing driveshaft from hub (Sec 3)

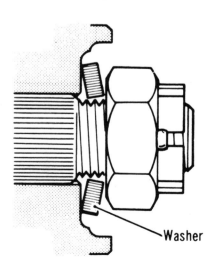

Fig. 7.4 Driveshaft nut and dished washer (Sec 3)

3.10 Driveshaft nut and split pin

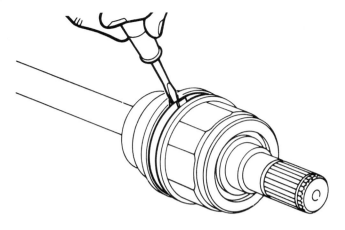

Fig. 7.5 Removing joint boot clip (Sec 4)

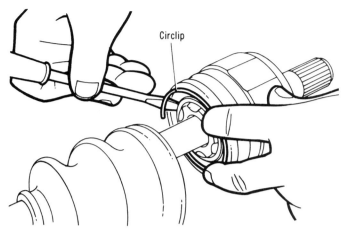

Fig. 7.6 Extracting inboard joint circlip (Sec 4)

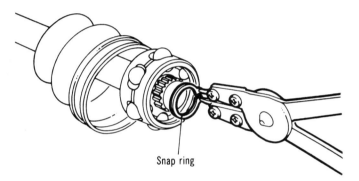

Fig. 7.7 Extracting inboard joint small circlip (Sec 4)

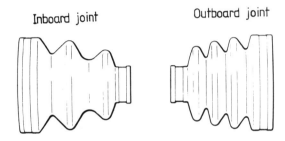

Fig. 7.8 Different contours of driveshaft inboard and outboard flexible boots (Sec 4)

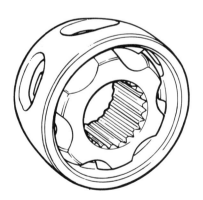

Fig. 7.9 Inner track inserted into ball cage (Sec 4)

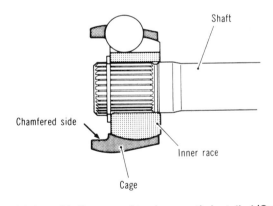

Fig. 7.10 Inboard ball cage and track correctly installed (Sec 4)

4 Driveshaft – overhaul

1 Both joints can be fitted with new flexible boots. The inboard double offset joint can be dismantled, removed and a repair kit fitted but the outboard Birfield joint can only be renewed if worn, as a complete assembly with the shaft.

2 With the complete driveshaft removed as described in the preceding Section, remove the securing clip from the inboard flexible boot.

3 Extract the large circlip by prising it out with a screwdriver.

4 Pull the shaft from the inboard joint and wipe away the lubricant with a clean rag.

5 Extract the small circlip and withdraw the inner track, balls and cage from the joint outer track. Wipe the inner joint components without dismantling them.

6 The flexible boot may now be slid from the shaft.

7 If the outboard flexible boot is to be renewed, detach the securing clip and withdraw the boot from the inboard end of the shaft. Wipe away the lubricant from the outboard Birfield joint with a clean rag.

8 Commence reassembly by fitting the flexible boots onto the shaft. Before doing this, smear the shaft with gear oil and tape over the splines to prevent the boot lips being damaged. Do not push the outboard boot into position yet but delay until the joint is packed with lubricant (see paragraph 15). Make sure that the correct boots are fitted to the correct ends of the shaft.

9 Using the lubricant supplied with the joint repair kit, apply it liberally to the inner track and cage of the double offset joint. Now

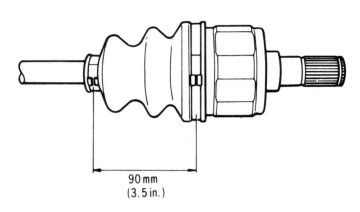

90 mm
(3.5 in.)

Fig.. 7.11 Correct clip positioning of Birfield type joint (Sec 4)

insert the inner track into the cage. This is done by holding the inner track so that the splines are at 90° to the ball cut-outs in the cage. Twist the track as it enters the cage.

10 Apply more lubricant and snap the balls into their cage cut-outs.

11 Hold the track/cage assembly so that the chamfered side of the cage is last to slide on and push the assembly onto the driveshaft.

12 Fit the securing circlip.

13 Pack 1130 to 1700 oz (40 to 60 g) of the lubricant supplied in the repair kit into the outer track of the joint and push the track into position over the ball/cage assembly.

14 Pack another 570 to 850 oz (20 to 30 g) of the lubricant into the driveshaft side of the joint, pull the flexible boot into position and fit a new securing clip.

15 Now turn your attention to the outboard Birfield joint, the flexible boot which has not yet been fitted over the joint.

16 Pack the joint with an equivalent amount of lubricant (from that supplied with the new flexible boot renewal kit) to replenish that which was wiped away.

17 Pull the boot into position and fit new securing clips.

18 In order to prevent air being trapped, or a vacuum being created within the inboard joints which could cause damage to the flexible boots, check that the distance between the two boot clips is as shown in Fig. 7.11. Adjust the position of the smaller clip if necessary.

5 Fault diagnosis – driveshafts

Symptom	Reason(s)
Knock or clicking	Worn joints Worn splines Loose shaft/hub nut
Vibration	Bent shaft Out of balance shaft
Squeaking or grinding	Dry joints due to split flexible boot. Loss of lubricant occurs very rapidly

Chapter 8 Braking system

Contents

Specifications

System type ....

Four wheel hydraulic with servo assistance. Disc front, drum rear. Handbrake mechanical to rear wheels. Pressure-regulating valve in dual hydraulic circuit. Automatic adjusters on rear shoes

Disc brakes
Minimum pad (friction material) thickness .... 0.04 in (1.0 mm)
Minimum disc thickness .... 0.45 in (11.4 mm)
Maximum disc run-out .... 0.006 in (0.15 mm)

Drum brakes
Minimum shoe lining (friction material) thickness .... 0.04 in (1.0 mm)
Internal diameter (new) .... 7.0 in (180.0 mm)
Maximum internal diameter (wear limit) .... 7.2 in (182.0 mm)

Piston diameters
Master cylinder .... 0.813 in (20.64 mm)
Disc brake caliper .... 2.01 in (51.1 mm)
Rear wheel cylinder .... 0.750 in (19.05 mm)
Vacuum servo unit .... 6.0 in (152.4 mm)

Torque wrench settings

	lbf ft	Nm
Driveshaft nut	120	163
Disc caliper bridge bolts	60	82
Caliper mounting bolts	55	75
Disc to hub bolts	35	48
Master cylinder check valve case	35	48
Secondary piston stop bolt	2	3
Master cylinder mounting nuts	9	12
Master cylinder fluid union hollow bolts	24	33
Bleed nipple	7	10
Flexible hose end fitting	12	16
Rigid pipeline flare nut	12	16
Pedal support nuts	9	12
Rear wheel cylinder mounting bolts	9	12
Rear brake backplate bolts	15	20

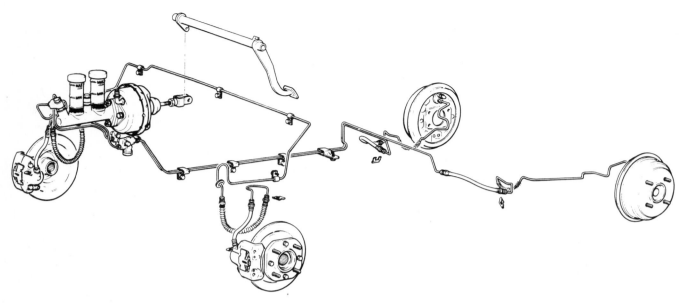

Fig. 8.1 Braking system layout (Sec 1)

1 General description

The braking system is of four wheel hydraulic type using dual circuits.

The front brakes are of single piston disc type while the rear ones are self-adjusting drum type.

A vacuum servo booster is fitted to all models also a pressure regulating valve is incorporated in the hydraulic circuit to prevent rear wheel lock up during heavy brake pedal applications.

The handbrake operates through cables to the rear wheels only, the control lever being floor mounted.

2 Maintenance

1   The system is virtually maintenance-free but regular inspection of all components must be carried out at the mileage intervals specified in the Routine maintenance Section. This visual inspection must include the following:

Check fluid level in master cylinder reservoirs (photo)
Check wear of disc pads and brake shoe linings
Check condition of brake hydraulic flexible hoses and rigid pipelines

2   Detailed descriptions of how to carry out these inspections is to be found in the following Sections.

3 Disc pads – inspection and renewal

1   Jack up the front of the car and support it securely then remove the roadwheels.
2   Remove the small cover plate from the front of the caliper by prising it out with a screwdriver (photo).
3   Now inspect the thickness of the friction material on each pad. If

2.1 Removing the master cylinder reservoir cap

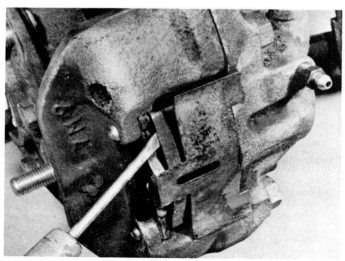

3.2 Removing the disc pad cover plate

it has worn down to 0.039 in (1.0 mm) then the pads must be renewed. Always renew all four pads as an axle set at the same time.

4   Using a pair of pliers, extract the two anti-rattle clips. Note that the inboard clip locates over the square projection of the pad backing plate while the outboard clip passes through the hole in the disc pad backing plate (photo).

5   Tap out the pad retaining pins using a thin punch (photo).

6   Grip the ends of the pad backing plates and withdraw them. Note the anti-squeal shim fitted behind the pad backing plate only on the outboard side (photos).

7   Brush dust and dirt from the disc pad recess paying particular attention to the torque plate shafts (photo).

8   In order to accommodate the new, thicker pads, the caliper piston must be depressed fully into its cylinder. Do this with a piece of flat metal bar or wood but remember that the fluid level in the master cylinder reservoir will rise so anticipate this by syphoning some out beforehand. An old (clean) battery hydrometer is useful for this job.

9   Insert the pads into the caliper making sure that the anti-squeal shim is behind the backing plate of the outboard pad. Check that it is the friction surfaces which are against the disc! Fit the pad retaining pins.

10   Fit the two clips to their correct sides.

11   Snap the cover plate into position.

12   Repeat the operations on the opposite front wheel.

13   Apply the footbrake several times hard to bring the pads up to the disc and then check and top up the brake hydraulic fluid.

3.4 Removing a disc pad anti-rattle clip

3.5 Removing a disc pad retaining pin

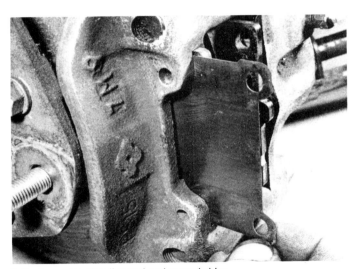

3.6a Removing the disc pad anti-squeal shim

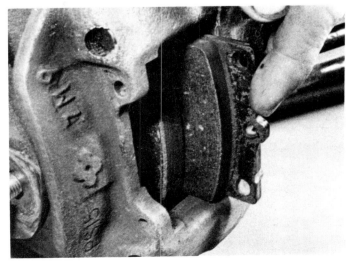

3.6b Removing a disc pad

3.7 Caliper with disc pads removed

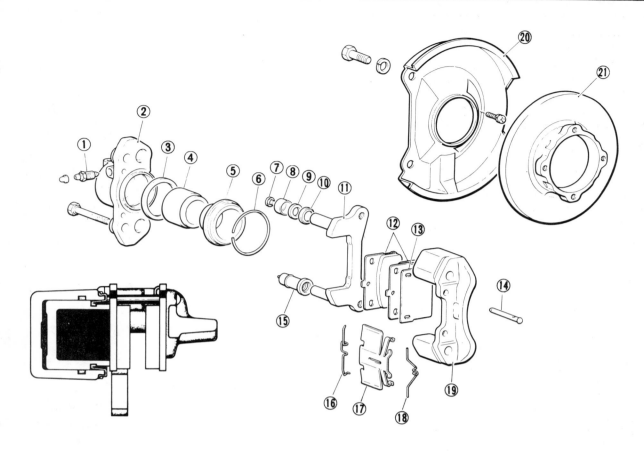

Fig. 8.2 Exploded view of a caliper

1	Bleed nipple	7	Plug	13	Anti-squeal shim
2	Inner housing	8	Cap	14	Pad retaining pin
3	Piston seal	9	Oil seal retainer	15	Bush
4	Piston	10	Oil seal	16	Pad anti-rattle clip (inboard)
5	Dust excluder	11	Torque plate	17	Pad cover plate
6	Retaining ring	12	Disc pads		

18 Pad anti-rattle clip (outboard)
19 Outer housing
20 Disc splash shield
21 Disc

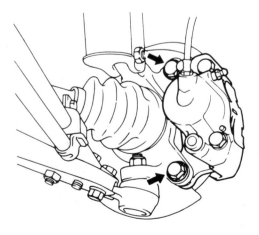

Fig. 8.3 Caliper mounting bolts (Sec 4)

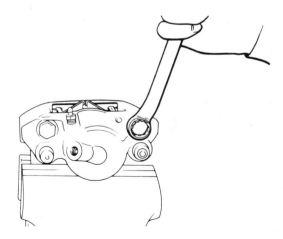

Fig. 8.4 Unscrewing a caliper bridge bolt (Sec 4)

4   Caliper – removal, overhaul and refitting

1   Raise the front of the car and remove the roadwheel.
2   Remove the disc pads as previously described in Section 3.
3   Working under the front wing, pull out the spring clip which retains the brake line to the suspension strut. Uncouple the flexible brake hose from the rigid line using two close-fitting open ended spanners and immediately cap the ends of the pipes to prevent loss of fluid.
4   Unscrew the flexible hose from the caliper.
5   Unscrew the two caliper mounting bolts (not the caliper bridge bolts) and lift the caliper from the hub carrier (knuckle).
6   With the caliper removed, brush away all external dirt.
7   Secure the caliper in the jaws of a vice by means of its mounting eyes and loosen the bridge bolts.
8   Separate the caliper housing inner and outer components and then withdraw the torque plate from the inner caliper housing.
9   Prise out the piston dust excluding seal.
10   Apply low air pressure from a tyre pump and eject the piston. Only quite low pressure is all that is needed for this job, applied at the flexible hose connecting port.
11   Extract the piston seal from its cylinder groove. Take great care not to scratch the cylinder bore when doing this.
12   If the cylinder bore or piston show signs of rubbing, scoring or scratching, renew the caliper complete. If the components are in good condition, discard the rubber seals and obtain a repair kit.
13   Clean everything in methylated spirit or new hydraulic fluid. Pay particular attention to the torque plate shafts and bores, these may require burnishing to remove corrosion.
14   Commence reassembly by fitting the piston seal into its cylinder groove using the fingers only to manipulate it.
15   Dip the piston in hydraulic fluid or apply a little of the *red* rubber grease supplied in the repair kit. Insert the piston into the cylinder using a twisting motion to avoid trapping the lip of the seal. Fit the new dust excluder.
16   Apply the *yellow* grease to the torque plate shafts and connect the torque plate/shafts to the caliper inner housing. Take care not to contaminate the caliper piston or seals with this yellow grease.
17   Tighten the bridge bolts to the specified torque.
18   Fit the caliper, tightening the mounting bolts to the specified torque.
19   Reconnect the flexible hose and fit the disc pads as described in Section 3.
20   Bleed the hydraulic circuit appropriate to the side which was dismantled (refer to Section 12).

5   Disc – inspection and renewal

1   Whenever the disc pads are being inspected for wear, take the opportunity to check the surface of the disc for deep grooving. Light scoring is normal.
2   If as a result of reference to the Fault diagnosis Section, the disc is suspected of being buckled or out of true, it should be measured for run-out using a dial gauge. Where such an instrument is not available, feeler blades may be used between the face of the disc and a fixed point. Turn the disc while measuring and if the run-out exceeds that specified, the disc must be renewed.
3   If as the result of the inspection described in paragraph 1, the disc is badly grooved or has worn thinner than the minimum specified thickness, it should be removed and a new one fitted.
4   To remove a disc, first prise out the cap from the centre of the roadwheel and release the driveshaft to hub nut. This is very tight and will require a socket and long knuckle bar to release it.
5   Now jack up the front of the car and remove the roadwheel.
6   Unbolt the caliper, slide it from the disc and tie it up out of the way. There is no need to disconnect the hydraulic hose.
7   Unscrew and remove the previously loosened driveshaft nut and disconnect the driveshaft from the hub carrier as described in Chapter 7.
8   Using a plastic faced hammer tap the hub out of the hub carrier, taking great care that any bearing pre-load spacers are retained and their exact location recorded.
9   Grip the hub in a vice fitted with jaw protectors and unscrew and remove the disc retaining bolts. Separate the hub and disc.

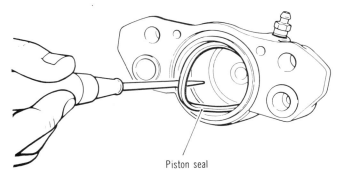
Fig. 8.5 Prising out a caliper piston seal (Sec 4)

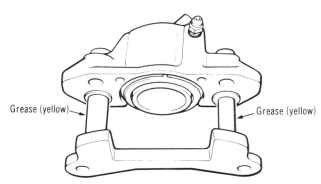
Fig. 8.6 Caliper torque plate shaft greasing points (Sec 4)

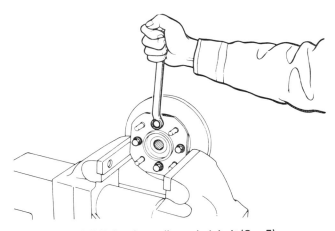
Fig. 8.7 Releasing a disc to hub bolt (Sec 5)

10   Reassembly is a reversal of dismantling but tighten all bolts to the specified torque. The driveshaft nut should be tightened and staked after the car has been lowered onto its roadwheels.

6   Rear shoe linings – inspection and renewal

1   Jack up the rear of the car, remove the roadwheels.
2   Tap off the grease cap, extract the split pin and take off the nut retainer. Unscrew the hub nut and remove the thrust washer. With the handbrake fully off, withdraw the brake drum, catching the outer race as it drops out.
3   The linings fitted as original equipment are of bonded type and if they have worn down to 0.039 in (1.0 mm) then the shoes must be renewed. If on the other hand the linings are in good condition, brush away all dust from the shoes and drum interior taking care not to inhale it and refit the brake drum and roadwheel.
4   If the linings are worn out, always renew them with new or

factory-reconditioned shoes; do not attempt to re-line them yourself.

5   Prise out the spring clips (photo).

6   Remove the shoe return spring. This is the large U-shaped spring anchored at both upper ends (photo).

7   Remove the shoe steady springs and retainers. Do this by gripping the dished retainer with a pair of pliers, depressing it against spring pressure and turning it through 90° to release it from the tee shaped head of the pin (photo).

8   Disconnect the small spring at the bottom of the shoe lower anchorage.

9   Withdraw the shoes and automatic adjuster as an assembly. This

is the time to mark the shoes as to which way up they are fitted and to sketch or mark with quick drying paint the lever and adjuster assembly.

10 Release the handbrake cable from the shoe lever and carry the shoe assembly to the bench.

11 Dismantle the adjuster and the cable lever from the old shoes, clean them and refit them to the new shoes. Circlips are used to retain the components. The automatic adjuster should be cleaned and its friction surfaces smeared with a little high melting point grease. Turn the star wheel on the adjuster so that the strut is in its fully retracted position.

6.5 Shoe return spring retaining clip

6.6 Removing the shoe return spring

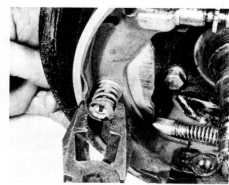
6.7 Removing a steady spring

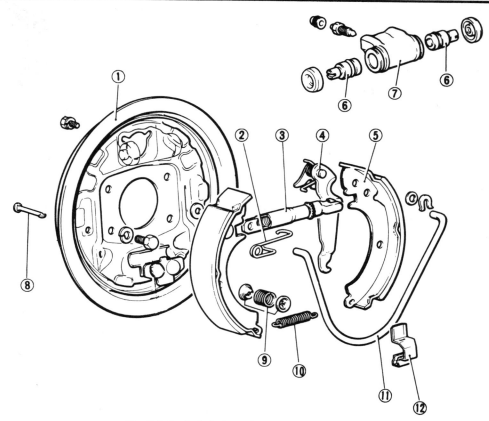

Fig. 8.8 Exploded view of a rear brake (Sec 6)

1 Backplate	5 Shoe	9 Shoe steady spring	11 Shoe return spring
2 Adjuster spring	6 Piston	10 Shoe lower retaining	12 Spring clip
3 Automatic adjuster	7 Cylinder	spring	
4 Handbrake operating lever	8 Shoe steady spring pin		

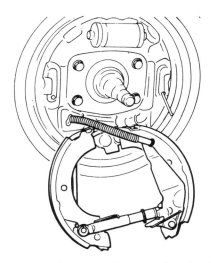

Fig. 8.9 Brake shoes and adjuster withdrawn from backplate (Sec 6)

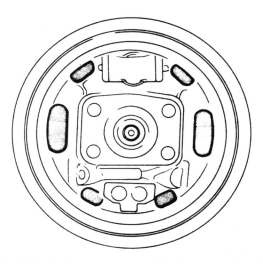

Fig. 8.10 Backplate grease application points (Sec 6)

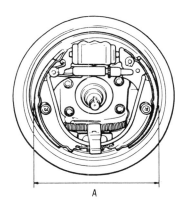

Fig. 8.11 Shoe setting diagram (Sec 6)
A = 7.06 to 7.07 in (179.3 to 179.6 mm)

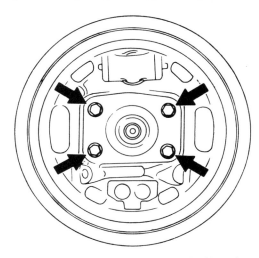

Fig. 8.12 Backplate securing bolts (Sec 7)

12 Apply just a trace of high melting point grease to the shoe rubbing high points on the brake backplate and then locate the new shoe assembly in position having connected the handbrake cable.
13 Fit the small lower shoe spring, the shoe steady springs and the main shoe return spring.
14 The automatic adjuster nut should now be turned to expand the shoes until their outside diameter is between 7.06 and 7.07 in (179.3 and 179.6 mm). This should allow the drum to just slide over the shoes. The shoes may need tapping up or down slightly to centralise them if the drum is difficult to push on.
15 Fit the outer bearing race, the thrust washer and nut. Tighten the nut to 15 lbf ft (20 Nm) while turning the drum. Release the nut and then retighten it to 4 lbf ft (5 Nm). A socket gently tightened by hand will be the approximate setting if a suitable torque wrench is not available. Endfloat should just be eliminated.
16 Fit the nut retainer without disturbing the setting and insert a new split pin, bending its ends over securely.
17 Renew the shoes on the opposite brake.
18 Once the shoes in both rear brakes have been renewed, apply the handbrake and the footbrake alternately several times to actuate the automatic adjuster and to bring the shoes as close as possible to the drums.

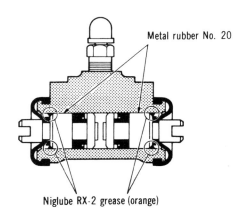

Fig. 8.13 Sectional view of rear wheel cylinder (Sec 7)

---

7   Rear hydraulic wheel cylinder – removal, overhaul and refitting

1   Remove the brake shoes as described in the preceding Section.
2   Disconnect the hydraulic brakeline from the wheel cylinder and

immediately cap the open end of the pipe to prevent loss of fluid and the entry of dirt. A bleed nipple dust cap is useful for this.
3   Unbolt the wheel cylinder from the backplate. If there is any difficulty in reaching these bolts, the backplate can be removed (four bolts) complete with wheel cylinder for later separation.
4   Clean away external dirt from the wheel cylinder and pull off the dust excluding boots.
5   Pull out the pistons.

6   Examine the surfaces of the pistons and the cylinder bore. If they are severely scored or show signs of metal to metal rubbing, renew the wheel cylinder complete.

7   If the components are in good condition, clean them in methylated spirit or clean hydraulic fluid, discard the rubber seals and obtain a repair kit.

8   Anti-rust-and-rubber grease, which should be applied to the cylinder bore and piston, is supplied in the repair kit.

9   Fit the new seals so that the lips face the correct way. Fit the dust excluding boots.

10 Coat the mating surfaces of the wheel cylinder and backing plate with jointing compound and bolt the wheel cylinder into position.

11 Fit the brake shoes and drum (Section 7). Reconnect the hydraulic line to the cylinder.

12 Make sure that all bolts are tightened to the specified torque.

13 Bleed the appropriate hydraulic circuit on completion (see Section 12).

8   Brake drum – inspection and renewal

1   Whenever the brake drum is removed to inspect the wear of the linings, check the condition of the drum interior surface for deep scoring or grooving.

2   Where there is evidence of this, renew the drum.

3   After a high mileage, the inside diameter of the drum may have worn to such an extent that its diameter exceeds that specified.

4   Also the drum may be found to have worn oval in shape if measured with an internal gauge or calipers. Once again, the only remedy is renewal of the drum.

9   Master cylinder – removal, overhaul and refitting

1   The master cylinder may be equipped with a composite type reservoir or separate reservoirs, one for each circuit. Apart from this difference, the construction is identical.

2   To remove the master cylinder, first disconnect the fluid level sensor lead connector plug (photo).

9.2 Brake master cylinder reservoirs

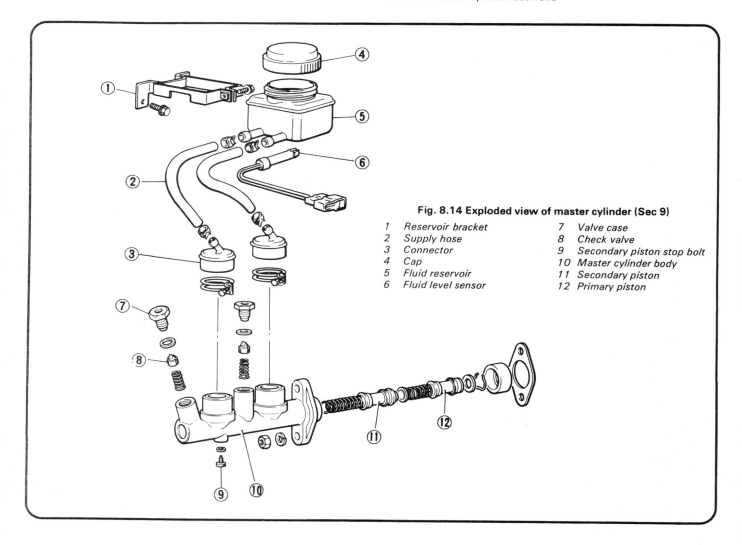

Fig. 8.14 Exploded view of master cylinder (Sec 9)

1   Reservoir bracket
2   Supply hose
3   Connector
4   Cap
5   Fluid reservoir
6   Fluid level sensor
7   Valve case
8   Check valve
9   Secondary piston stop bolt
10 Master cylinder body
11 Secondary piston
12 Primary piston

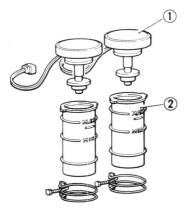

Fig. 8.15 Master cylinder alternative type reservoirs (Sec 9)

1   Fluid level sensor   2   Reservoir

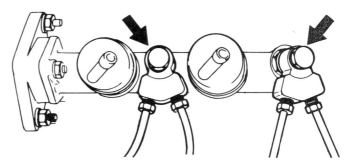

Fig. 8.16 Master cylinder fluid line banjo connectors and hollow bolts (Sec 9)

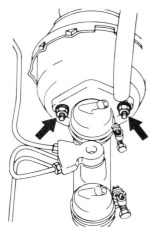

Fig. 8.17 Master cylinder mounting nuts (Sec 9)

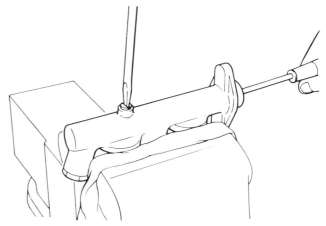

Fig. 8.18 Removing master cylinder secondary piston stop bolt (Sec 9)

3   Disconnect the hydraulic brake lines from the master cylinder and quickly cap or plug the openings to prevent loss of fluid or the entry of dirt. Do not allow hydraulic fluid to come into contact with the bodywork as it acts as an effective paint stripper.
4   Unscrew the mounting nuts and pull the master cylinder from the servo unit, taking care not to bend or damage the hydraulic circuit rigid pipelines.
5   With the master cylinder removed from the car, tip out the hydraulic fluid and discard it. Brush away all external dirt and then secure the master cylinder in a vice fitted with soft protective jaws, so that the piston stop bolt is uppermost. Remove the dust excluding boot.
6   Apply pressure to the end of the primary piston using a screwdriver to relieve the end pressure of the secondary piston on the stop bolt. Unscrew and remove the stop bolt.
7   Extract the circlip from the end of the master cylinder.
8   The primary piston, the secondary piston and return spring should now be ejected. Do not attempt to separate the primary piston and its spring, nor the seals from the pistons.
9   Inspect the surfaces of the pistons and the cylinder bore for scoring or metal to metal rubbing areas. If evident, renew the master cylinder complete.
10   If the components are in good condition, clean them in clean hydraulic fluid or methylated spirit — nothing else!
11   Unscrew the valve cases, extract the check valve and spring, clean the parts and refit them.
12   Obtain a repair kit which will contain new primary and secondary pistons and springs with the pistons already fitted with new seals.
13   Fit the secondary piston and spring into the cylinder having applied the rubber grease supplied in the kit or dipped the parts in clean hydraulic fluid.

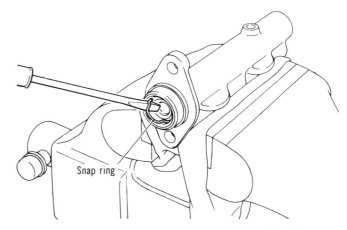

Fig. 8.19 Extracting master cylinder circlip (Sec 9)

14   Fit the primary piston/spring assembly in the same way and retain it in the cylinder by fitting the circlip.
15   Using a screwdriver applied to the end of the primary piston depress it into the cylinder as far as it will go, hold it in this position and screw in the secondary piston stop bolt.
16   Fit the dust excluder.
17   Before fitting the master cylinder to the servo unit check the servo pushrod to primary piston clearance as described in Section 13.
18   Fit the master cylinder, reconnect the pipelines and the reservoir hoses.
19   Fill the hydraulic fluid reservoirs and bleed both hydraulic circuits as described in Section 12.
20   Reconnect the fluid level sensor connecting plug.

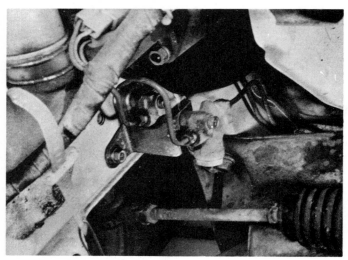

10.1 Brake pressure regulating valve

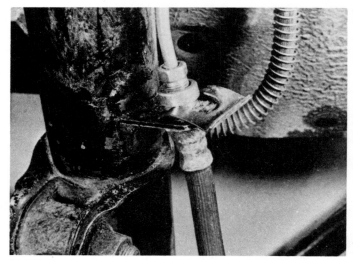

11.3 Brake pipe clip and bracket on front suspension strut

10 Pressure regulating valve – removal and refitting

1   This is a twin valve unit located on the right-hand side of the engine compartment (photo).
2   To remove the regulator first note the connecting sequence of the pipelines and then uncouple them. Cap them quickly to prevent loss of fluid. Bleed nipple rubber caps are very suitable for capping the pipelines.
3   Unscrew and remove the mounting bolts and withdraw the unit.
4   The pressure regulator is set during production and should not be dismantled but if a fault is suspected it should be renewed as a complete assembly.
5   Refitting is a reversal of removal, bleed the complete hydraulic system on completion as described in Section 12.

11 Flexible and rigid hydraulic lines – inspection and renewal

1   Inspect the condition of the flexible hydraulic hoses. If they are swollen, perished or chafed, they must be renewed.
2   To remove a flexible hose, hold the flats on its end-fitting in an open-ended spanner and unscrew the union nut which couples it to the rigid brake line.
3   Disconnect the flexible hose from the rigid line and support bracket by pulling out the U-shaped spring clip then unscrew the hose from the caliper or wheel cylinder circuit as the case may be (photo).
4   Refitting is a reversal of removal. The flexible hoses may be twisted not more than one quarter turn in either direction if necessary to provide a 'set' to ensure that they do not rub or chafe against any adjacent component.
5   At regular intervals wipe the steel brake pipes clean and examine them for signs of rust or denting caused by flying stones.
6   Examine the securing clips which are plastic coated to prevent wear to the pipe surface. Bend the tongues of the clips if necessary to ensure that they hold the brake pipes securely without letting them rattle or vibrate.
7   Check that the pipes are not touching any adjacent components or rubbing against any part of the vehicle. Where this is observed, bend the pipe gently away to clear.
8   Although the pipes are rustproof any section of pipe may become rusty through chafing and if so should be renewed. Brake pipes are available to the correct length and fitted with end unions from most dealers and can be made to pattern by many accessory suppliers. When fitting the new pipes use the old pipes as a guide to bending and do not make any bends sharper than is necessary.

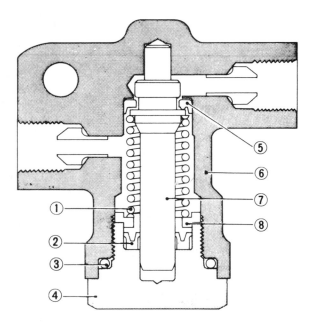

Fig. 8.20 Sectional view of pressure regulating valve (Sec 10)

1	Spring	5	Seal
2	Seal	6	Valve body
3	O-ring	7	Plunger
4	Plug	8	Spring retainer

12 Hydraulic system – bleeding

1   The two independent hydraulic circuits are as follows; the front right-hand caliper and left rear wheel cylinder and the front left-hand caliper and right rear wheel cylinder.
2   If the master cylinder or the pressure regulating valve have been disconnected and reconnected then the complete system (both circuits) must be bled.
3   If only a component of one circuit has been disturbed then only the particular circuit need be bled.

Bleeding – two man method

4   Gather together a clean jar and a suitable length of clear plastic tubing which is a tight fit over the bleed screw. Engage the help of an assistant.
5   Before commencing the bleeding operation, check that all rigid pipes and flexible hoses are in good condition and that all hydraulic

unions are tight. Take great care not to allow hydraulic fluid to come into contact with the vehicle paintwork, otherwise the finish will be seriously damaged. Wash off any spilled fluid immediately with cold water.

6   If hydraulic fluid has been lost from the master cylinder, due to a leak in the system, ensure that the cause is traced and rectified before proceeding further or a serious malfunction of the braking system may occur.

7   To bleed the system, clean the area around the bleed screw at the wheel cylinder to be bled. If the hydraulic system has only been partially disconnected and suitable precautions were taken to prevent further loss of fluid, it should only be necessary to bleed that part of the system. However, if the entire system is to be bled, start at the wheel furthest away from the master cylinder.

8   Remove the master cylinder filler cap and top up the reservoir. Periodically check the fluid level during the bleeding operation and top up as necessary.

9   Destroy the vacuum in the servo by giving several applications of the brake pedal in rapid succession.

10 Connect one end of the plastic tubing to the bleed screw and immerse the other end in the glass jar containing sufficient clean hydraulic fluid to keep the end of the tube submerged in the fluid. Open the bleed screw half a turn and have your assistant depress the brake pedal to the floor and then slowly release it. Tighten the bleed screw at the end of each downstroke to prevent expelled air and fluid from being drawn back into the system. Repeat this operation until clean hydraulic fluid, free from air bubbles, can be seen coming through the tube. Now tighten the bleed screw and remove the plastic tube.

Bleeding – using one-way valve kit

11 There are a number of one-man, do-it-yourself, brake bleeding kits currently available from motor accessory shops. It is recommended that one of these kits should be used wherever possible as they greatly simplify the bleeding operation and also reduce the risk of expelled air and fluid being drawn back into the system.

12 If a one-man brake bleeding kit is being used, connect the outlet tube to the bleed screw and then open the screw half a turn. If possible position the unit so that it can be viewed from the car, then depress the brake pedal to the floor and slowly release it. The one-way valve

in the kit will prevent dispelled air from returning to the system at the end of each stroke. Repeat this operation until clean hydraulic fluid, free from air bubbles, can be seen coming through the tube. Now tighten the bleed screw and remove the outlet tube.

Bleeding – using a pressure bleeding kit

13 These too are available from motor accessory shops and are usually operated by air pressure from the spare tyre.

14 By connecting a pressurised container to the master cylinder fluid reservoir, bleeding is then carried out by simply opening each bleed nipple in turn and allowing the fluid to run out, rather like turning on a tap, until no air is visible in the fluid.

15 Using this system, the large reserve of hydraulic fluid provides a safeguard against air being drawn into the master cylinder during the bleeding operation.

16 This method is particularly effective when bleeding 'difficult' systems and when bleeding the entire system at the time of the routine fluid renewal.

All systems

17 If the entire system is being bled the foregoing procedures should now be repeated at each wheel, finishing at the wheel nearest to the master cylinder. Do not forget to recheck the fluid level in the master cylinder at regular intervals and top up as necessary.

18 When completed, recheck the fluid level in the master cylinder, top up if necessary and refit the cap. Check the 'feel' of the brake pedal which should be firm and free from any 'sponginess' which would indicate air still present in the system.

19 Discard any expelled hydraulic fluid as it is likely to be contaminated with moisture, air and dirt which makes it unsuitable for further use. Clean fluid should always be stored in an airtight container as it absorbs moisture which will lower its boiling point.

13 Vacuum servo unit (booster) – removal and refitting

1   Remove the master cylinder as described in Section 9.

2   Disconnect the vacuum hose from the angled pipe fitting on the brake servo unit.

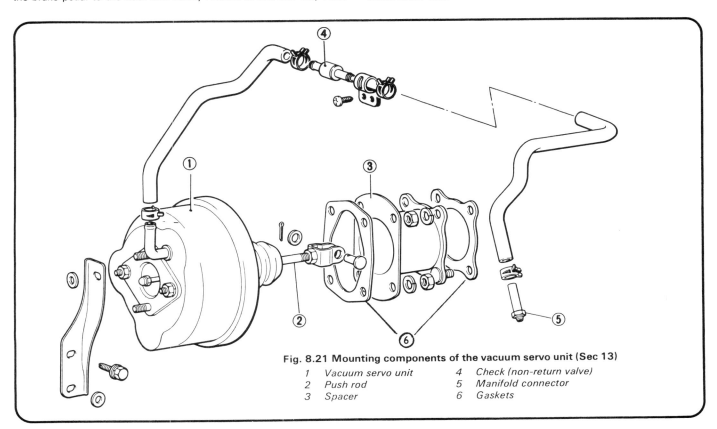

Fig. 8.21 Mounting components of the vacuum servo unit (Sec 13)

1   Vacuum servo unit   4   Check (non-return valve)
2   Push rod   5   Manifold connector
3   Spacer   6   Gaskets

3 Disconnect the pushrod from the arm of the brake pedal by extracting the split pin and the clevis pin.

4 Unscrew and remove the brake servo unit mounting nuts and lift the unit from the car.

5 The servo unit should not be dismantled but in the event of the unit becoming faulty, it should be renewed complete.

6 It should be appreciated that a faulty servo unit will not affect the safety of the hydraulic system, the only indication being that higher pedal pressures will be required for the same levels of retardation.

7 If a fault is suspected in the vacuum servo unit, first check the vacuum non-return valve. Do this by holding the thumb over the open end of the non-return valve on the side of the valve which is nearest to the servo unit. Turn the engine on the starter and feel for a vacuum (suction). If none can be felt renew the valve, reconnect it in accordance with the label on the valve and then test the operation of the servo again.

8 When refitting the servo unit it is very important that there is a clearance between the rear face of the master cylinder primary piston and the front of the domed nut on the servo pushrod of between 0 and 0.03 in (0 and 0.75 mm). To calculate this, use a depth gauge at the rear end of the master cylinder and then measure the projection of the servo pushrod. Both of the measurements must be taken from the flange mating faces. By simple calculation it can be decided whether the projection of the pushrod must be altered to achieve the correct clearance. If necessary, turn the domed nut while holding the pushrod stationary.

9 When fitting the servo, renew the gaskets one each side of the spacer and note that the pressure regulating valve support bracket is attached to the master cylinder mounting stud.

10 Bleed the complete hydraulic system as described in Section 12.

14 Handbrake – adjustment

1 The handbrake is normally adjusted by the action of the hand and footbrake being applied and the consequent actuation of the rear drum adjuster mechanism.

2 However, due to cable stretch and wear in the linkage, additional adjustment may be required under the following conditions.

3 Pull the handbrake control lever slowly from the fully off to the fully on position and count the number of 'clicks' as the ratchet passes over the notches in the quadrant.

4 If it is more than six or seven, the cables require adjustment. Five or less indicate over-adjustment which will prevent the automatic adjusters operating correctly.

5 To adjust, remove the cover from the base of the handbrake control lever. This will expose the cable ends and equaliser.

6 Adjust each nut until the cables appear to be equally taut and the hand control lever passes over the specified number of notches to apply the handbrake fully. The nuts may not be equally tightened to achieve this as the cables stretch at different rates.

7 Now jack up the rear of the car and with the handbrake fully off, check that the rear roadwheels do not bind when turned.

8 If the adjustment is correct, lower the car and then switch on the ignition and check that the handbrake 'ON' indicator lamp goes out when the lever is fully released but comes on when the lever is pulled over one notch. Adjust the position of the switch to achieve this situation.

15 Handbrake cable – renewal

1 Working inside the car, remove the cover from the base of the handbrake control lever.

2 Disconnect the cable from the equaliser by unscrewing the nuts.

3 Unscrew and remove the handbrake lever mounting bolts.

4 Release the cable clamp inside the car interior.

5 Working under the car, disconnect the cable clamp from the rear suspension arm.

6 Jack up the rear of the car and remove the roadwheel, the brake drum and the shoes as described earlier in this Chapter.

7 Unhook the handbrake cable from the shoe lever.

8 Prise off the E-ring that retains the handbrake cable to the brake backplate.

9 Withdraw the handbrake cable into the car interior and remove it. Note the direcion of fitting the grommet.

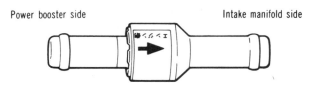

Power booster side   Intake manifold side

Fig. 8.22 Servo check (non-return) valve (Sec 13)

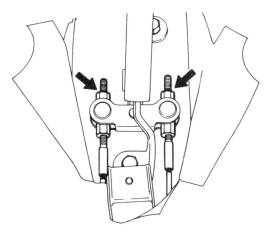

Fig. 8.23 Handbrake cable adjusting nuts (Sec 14)

Fig. 8.24 Handbrake 'ON' switch positioning bolt (Sec 14)

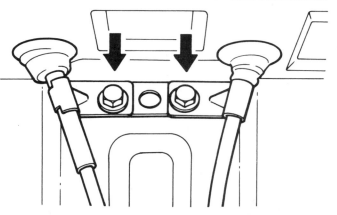

Fig. 8.25 Handbrake cable interior clamps (Sec 15)

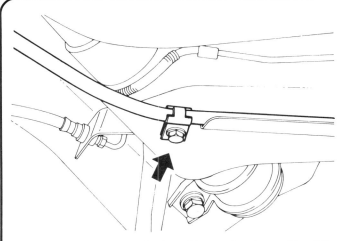

Fig. 8.26 One of the handbrake cable exterior clamps (Sec 15)

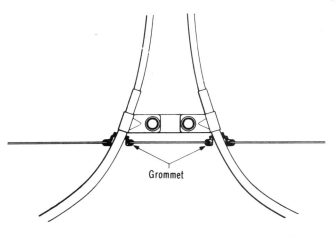

Fig. 8.27 Handbrake cable sealing grommets (Sec 15)

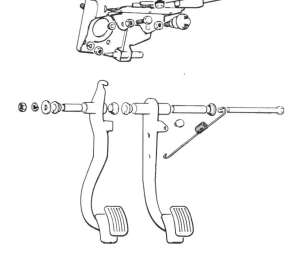

Fig. 8.28 Clutch and brake pedal (RHD) (Sec 16)

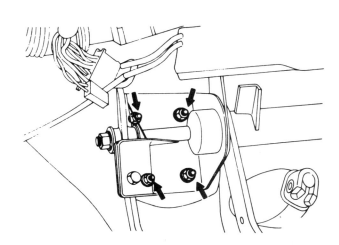

Fig. 8.29 Pedal cross-shaft support (LHD) (Sec 16)

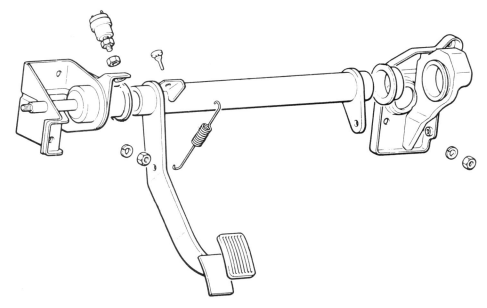

Fig. 8.30 Brake pedal and cross-shaft (LHD) (Sec 16)

10 Fit the new cable by reversing the removal operations. Take care that the cables are not twisted before tightening the clamps.
11 Adjust the shoes when refitted, by repeated applications of the footbrake pedal, then adjust the handbrake cable as described in the preceding Section.

16 Brake pedal – removal, refitting and adjustment

Right-hand drive models – removal

1 Working inside the car, remove the parcels tray.
2 Unhook the brake pedal return spring.
3 Disconnect the pushrod from the brake pedal arm by extracting the split pin and clevis pin.

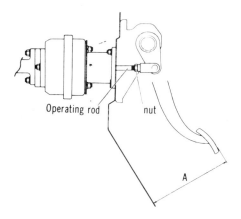

Fig. 8.31 Brake pedal setting diagram (Sec 16)

A = 7.1 to 7.3 in (180 to 185 mm)

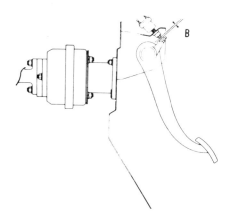

Fig. 8.32 Stop lamp switch setting diagram (Sec 16)

B = 0.020 to 0.039 in (0.5 to 1.0 mm)

4 Refer to Chapter 5 and disconnect the clutch operating cable from the clutch pedal arm.
5 Unscrew and remove the nut from the end of the pedal cross-shaft and withdraw the shaft towards the right-hand side, taking off the clutch pedal and then the brake pedal.
6 In the rare event of the pedal support requiring removal, the steering column will first have to be removed as described in Chapter 10.

Left-hand drive models – removal

7 Working inside the car, remove the parcels tray and the left-hand demister duct (Chapter 2).
8 Remove the steering column/shaft as described in Chapter 10.
9 Disconnect the clutch cable from the clutch pedal (Chapter 5).
10 Unhook the brake pedal return spring and disconnect the pushrod from the brake pedal by extracting the split pin and clevis pin.
11 Remove the nuts from the left-hand pedal support, withdraw the support complete with clutch pedal.
12 Remove the brake pedal towards the left-hand side.

All models – refitting and adjustment

13 This is a reversal of the removal procedure on all models but apply grease to the shaft bushes and linkage pivots.
14 On completion, adjust the pedal travel in the following way.
15 Release the stop lamp switch locknut and unscrew the switch several times.
16 Release the pushrod locknut at the brake pedal arm clevis fork and turn the pushrod until the distance between the top of the pedal rubber and the toe board is between 7.1 and 7.3 in (180 to 185 mm).
17 Now screw the stop lamp switch in until a clearance exists between the end of the switch plunger and the brake pedal arm of between 0.020 and 0.039 in (0.5 and 1.0 mm). Tighten the switch locknut.
18 The pedal free play should now be between 0.4 and 0.6 in (10.0 to 15.0 mm) assuming that the vacuum servo pushrod to primary piston clearance is correct (refer to Section 13).
19 With the footbrake pedal fully applied, the lower edge of the pedal pad should not be closer to the toe board than 1.6 in (40.0 mm).

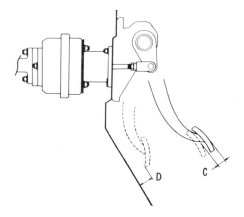

Fig. 8.33 Brake pedal free play and stroke diagram (Sec 16)

C = 0.4 to 0.6 in (10.0 to 15.0 mm)
D = 1.6 in (40.0 mm) minimum

17 Fault diagnosis – braking system

Symptom	Reason(s)
Pedal travels almost to floor before brakes operate	Brake fluid too low Caliper leaking Wheel cylinder leaking Master cylinder leaking (bubbles in master cylinder fluid) Brake flexible hose leaking Brake line fractured Brake system unions loose Rear brake adjuster seized
Brake pedal feels springy	New linings not yet bedded-in Brake discs or drums badly worn or cracked Master cylinder securing nuts loose
Brake pedal feels spongy and soggy	Caliper or wheel cylinder leaking Master cylinder leaking (bubbles in master cylinder reservoir) Brake pipe line or flexible hose leaking Union in brake system loose Blocked reservoir cap vent hole
Excessive endfloat required to brake car	Pad or shoe linings badly worn New pads or shoes recently fitted – not yet bedded-in Harder linings fitted than standard causing increase in pedal pressure Linings and brake drums contaminated with oil, grease or hydraulic fluid Servo unit inoperative or faulty Scored drums, discs or seized wheel cylinders
Brakes uneven and pulling to one side	Linings and discs or drums contaminated with oil, grease or hydraulic fluid Tyre pressures unequal Brake caliper loose Brake pads or shoes fitted incorrectly Different type of linings fitted at each wheel Anchorages for front suspension or rear suspension loose Brake discs or drums badly worn, cracked or distorted Incorrect front wheel alignment Incorrectly adjusted rear hub bearings
Brakes tend to bind, drag or lock-on	Air in hydraulic system Wheel cylinders seized Handbrake cables too tight Weak shoe return spring Incorrectly set foot pedal or pushrod Master cylinder seized Front disc distorted (excessive run-out) Rear brake adjusters seized

Chapter 9 Electrical system

Contents

Specifications

System type .... 12V negative earth

Battery
Capacity at 20 hr rate .... 32, 45 or 60 Ah according to operating territory

Alternator
Output 12V-45A
Rotation .... Clockwise
Voltage regulator .... Electronic integral with brush holder

Starter motor
Type .... Pre-engaged
Number of pinion teeth 9
No load characteristics:
    Terminal voltage 10.5V
    Current .... Less than 53A
    Speed .... More than 5000 rpm

Bulbs (except North America)

	Wattage
Headlight	45/40
Front parking light	5
Side repeater light	10
Front direction indicator light	21
Reversing lights	21
Rear direction indicator light	21
Stop/tail light	21/5
Rear number plate light	4
Interior light (front)	10
Interior light (rear)	5
Instrumentation light	3.4
Heater panel light	1.4
Ashtray light	3.4

Bulbs (North America)

	Wattage
Headlight (sealed beam)	65/55
Front direction indicator/parking light	27/8
Front side marker light	3.8
Stop/tail light	27.8
Rear direction indicator light	27
Rear side marker light	3.8
Reversing light	27
Rear number plate light	7.5
Interior light (front)	10
Interior light (rear)	5
Instrumentation light	3.4
Heater panel light	1.4
Ashtray light	3.4
Combination gauge light	3.4

Fuses

For precise circuits protected refer to the diagram on the fuse cover

Torque wrench settings

	lbf ft	Nm
Starter motor mounting bolts	22	30
Windscreen wiper arm nut	12	16
Tailgate wiper arm nut	4	6
Alternator mounting bolt	18	25
Alternator link bolt	10	14

1 General description

The electrical system is 12 volt negative earth and the major components comprise a 12 volt battery, an alternator which is driven from the crankshaft pulley and a starter motor.

The battery supplies a steady current for the ignition, lighting, and other electrical circuits and provides a reserve of electricity when the current consumed by the electrical equipment exceeds that being produced by the alternator.

The alternator has a regulator which ensures a high output if the battery is in a low state of charge or the demand from the electrical equipment is high, and a low output if the battery is fully charged and there is little demand for the electrical equipment.

When fitting electrical accessories to cars with a negative earth system it is important, if they contain silicone diodes or transistors, that they are connected correctly, otherwise serious damage may result to the components concerned.

2 Battery – maintenance and precautions

1 The battery is located on a platform within the engine compartment.

2 Maintenance consists of visually checking that the electrolyte level is between the low and high levels. The electrolyte level can be seen through the translucent case of the battery.

3 Due to the efficiency of the electronic voltage regulator the battery is normally kept in a fully charged condition but without being overcharged so that the need for frequent topping up with electrolyte does not occur. However, the weekly visual check of the electrolyte level should not be overlooked in case the battery case develops a leak or a fault does occur in the voltage regulator.

4 If it is necessary to top up the electrolyte, add only distilled or purified water. Lift up the battery cover and unscrew and remove the plugs from all the cells. Pour in sufficient water to give an even level in each cell within the high and low marks (photo).

5 Periodically check the security of the battery lead terminals and smear them with petroleum jelly to prevent corrosion. If the white fluffy condition which indicates corrosion is evident at the terminals or generally in the area of the battery, clean it away and neutralise it with ammonia or a solution of baking soda.

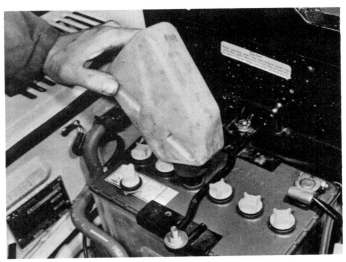

2.4 Topping up the battery

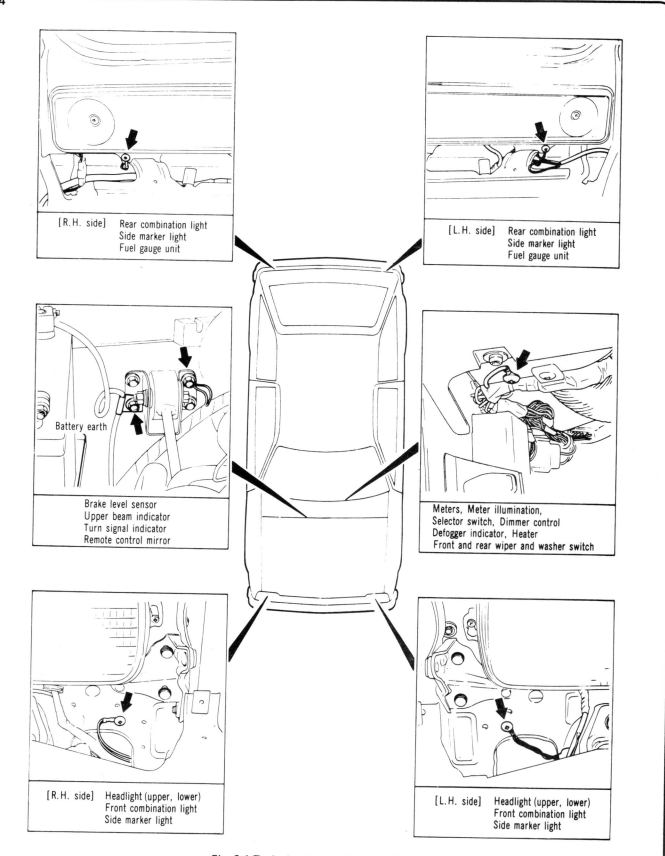

[R.H. side]   Rear combination light
              Side marker light
              Fuel gauge unit

[L.H. side]   Rear combination light
              Side marker light
              Fuel gauge unit

Battery earth

Brake level sensor
Upper beam indicator
Turn signal indicator
Remote control mirror

Meters, Meter illumination,
Selector switch, Dimmer control
Defogger indicator, Heater
Front and rear wiper and washer switch

[R.H. side]   Headlight (upper, lower)
              Front combination light
              Side marker light

[L.H. side]   Headlight (upper, lower)
              Front combination light
              Side marker light

Fig. 9.1 Typical wiring earth points (Sec 1)

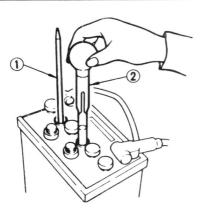

Fig. 9.2 Measuring battery specific gravity and electrolyte temperature (Sec 2)

1   Thermometer   2   Hydrometer

6   Never disconnect a battery lead when the engine is running and never reverse the leads.
7   A battery may be charged from a trickle charger without the need to remove the battery from the car but disconnect the vehicle battery leads before connecting the charger.
8   Never use a naked light, or smoke, near a battery particularly if it is being, or has just been, charged as the gas being produced from it may cause an explosion.
9   If the battery is to be boosted from a unit in another vehicle, connect the positive lead from the battery of the rescue vehicle to the positive terminal of the discharged battery.
10   Connect the negative lead from the battery of the rescue vehicle to a good connection on the engine block of the vehicle with the discharged battery. Do not connect this lead direct to the discharged battery negative terminal.
11   Once the engine starts, remove the negative lead first.
12   It is a wise precaution to cover the battery cell vent plugs with a cloth whenever terminal-connecting operations might cause a spark.
13   Although it is rare these days for owners to check the specific gravity of their batteries, the possession of a hydrometer is still a useful tool for the following purposes.

(i)   To check for a single discharged cell indicating the failure of a battery
(ii)   To check when a battery being charged by a mains charger is fully charged

14   Use the hydrometer in conjunction with the following table.

15   The specific gravity of the electrolyte for fully charged conditions at the electrolyte temperature indicated, is listed in Table A. The specific gravity of a fully discharged battery at different temperatures of the electrolyte is given in Table B.

Table A
Specific gravity – Battery Fully Charged

1.268 at 100°F or 38°C electrolyte temperature
1.272 at 90°F or 32°C electrolyte temperature
1.276 at 80°F or 27°C electrolyte temperature
1.280 at 70°F or 21°C electrolyte temperature
1.284 at 60°F or 16°C electrolyte temperature
1.288 at 50°F or 10°C electrolyte temperature
1.292 at 40°F or 4°C electrolyte temperature
1.296 at 30°F or -1.5°C electrolyte temperature

Table B
Specific Gravity – Battery Fully Discharged

1.098 at 100°F or 38°C electrolyte temperature
1.102 at 90°F or 32°C electrolyte temperature
1.106 at 80°F or 27°C electrolyte temperature
1.110 at 70°F or 21°C electrolyte temperature
1.114 at 60°F or 16°C electrolyte temperature
1.118 at 50°F or 10°C electrolyte temperature
1.122 at 40°F or 4°C electrolyte temperature
1.126 at 30°F or -1.5°C electrolyte temperature

16   The need for adding acid to a battery should never arise. It can only be lost by spillage, in which case have your dealer make good any deficiency.

3   Battery – removal and refitting

1   Remove the cover from the battery.
2   Disconnect the negative lead followed by the positive lead.
3   Remove the battery hold down nuts and retainer and lift the battery from its tray.
4   If a new battery is being purchased, make sure that the new terminal posts are compatible with the existing terminal clamps otherwise a cheap battery may not be quite such a bargain after all.
5   When fitting the battery, make sure that the terminals are positioned correctly to accept the leads of appropriate polarity.

4   Alternator – general description and maintenance

1   Briefly, the alternator comprises a rotor and stator. Current is generated in the coils of the stator as soon as the rotor revolves. This

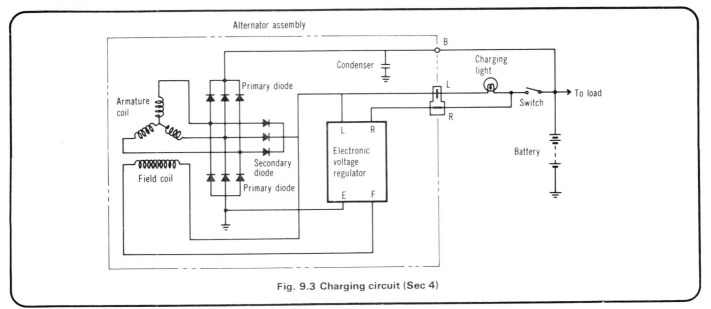

Fig. 9.3 Charging circuit (Sec 4)

current is three-phase alternating which is then rectified by positive and negative silicon diodes and the level of voltage required to maintain the battery charge is controlled by an integral regulator unit.

2   Maintenance consists of occasionally wiping away any oil or accumulated dirt which may have accumulated on the outside of the unit.

3   No lubrication is required as the bearings are grease sealed for life.

4   Check the drivebelt tension periodically to ensure that its specified deflection is correctly maintained.

5   The belt is correctly tensioned when at the mid-point of its longest run it can be deflected with moderate thumb pressure through 0.38 in (9.5 mm).

6   The belt is adjusted by releasing the alternator lower pivot bolt and the upper adjuster link bolt and moving the alternator towards or away from the engine.

5   Alternator – special precautions

Take extreme care when making circuit connections to a vehicle fitted with an alternator and observe the following. When making connections to the alternator from a battery always match correct polarity. Before using electric-arc welding equipment to repair any part of the vehicle, disconnect the connector from the alternator and disconnect the positive battery terminal. Never start the car with a battery charger connected. Always disconnect both battery leads before using a main charger. If boosting from another battery, always connect in parallel using heavy cable.

6   Alternator in-car testing

1   Although it is preferable in every way to have a faulty alternator tested by your dealer or auto electrician, for those home mechanics who possess the necessary gauges and testers, the information in the following Sections will be a guide to the feasibility of repair or whether a new or factory reconditioned unit is an economic alternative. A new unit should always be decided upon rather than repair if the original alternator has covered a high mileage.

Charging voltage test

2   With the ignition switch off, disconnect the battery positive lead and interpose an ammeter between the end of the lead and the battery terminal.

3   Now connect a voltmeter between the 'L' terminal on the alternator and earth. If the voltmeter does not indicate zero then a defective alternator or wiring is indicated.

4   Switch on the ignition but do not start the engine. The reading on the voltmeter should be much lower than the 12V of the battery. If it is around 12V then a faulty alternator is indicated.

5   Short-circuit the terminals of the ammeter and start the engine. Remove the short-circuit when the engine is running.

6   Increase the engine speed to between 2000 and 3000 rpm. If the ammeter indicates 5A or less, check the voltmeter reading without altering the engine speed. The reading should be between 14.1 and 14.7V at 68°F (20°C); this is the specified charging voltage.

7   If the ammeter indicates a reading in excess of 5A, continue to hold the engine speed and to charge the battery until the reading falls below 5A. Alternatively change the battery for a fully charged one. Recheck the charging voltage. If the charging voltage is not within the specified range, then the alternator is faulty.

Output check

8   With the ignition switched off, disconnect the battery negative lead.

9   Disconnect the lead from the B terminal on the alternator and connect an ammeter between the B terminal and the end of the disconnected lead.

10 Unless the car is already equipped with a tachometer, connect one in accordance with the maker's instructions.

11 Reconnect the battery lead to the negative terminal.

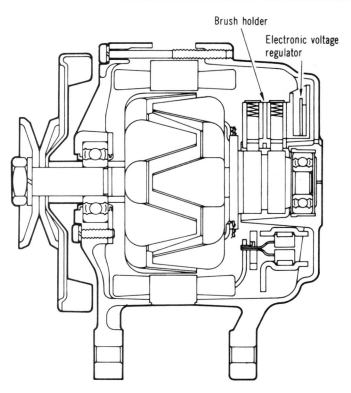

Fig. 9.4 Sectional view of alternator (Sec 4)

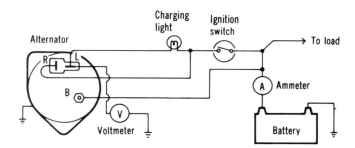

Fig. 9.5 Charging voltage test diagram (Sec 6)

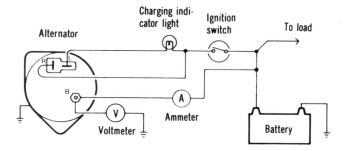

Fig. 9.6 Output check diagram (Sec 6)

12 Connect a voltmeter between the B terminal of the alternator and earth.

13 Start the engine and immediately turn on the headlamps and increase the engine speed to 1300 rpm when the output current should be between 13 and 16A at 13.5V shown on the instruments.

14 Where the indicated readings are outside the specified range, the alternator must be faulty.

7.2a Alternator lead and capacitor

7.2b Alternator connecting plugs

7 Alternator – removal, overhaul, refitting

1 Disconnect the battery negative lead.
2 Disconnect the leads from the alternator (photos).
3 Unscrew the adjuster link and pivot mounting bolts, disconnect the drivebelt and lift the alternator from its bracket on the engine.
4 Clean away any external dirt and grease.
5 Unscrew and remove the three tie bolts and pull off the drive end bracket with the rotor. If a screwdriver is used to prise it, do not insert it too deeply or the stator may be damaged.
6 Hold the rotor stationary and unscrew the pulley retaining nut. Take off the pulley, fan spacer and seal.
7 Remove the rotor from the drive end bracket and extract the seal.
8 Unsolder the rectifier from the stator coil leads. Work quickly when doing this to avoid heat transfer to adjacent parts. If the soldered junction is gripped with a pair of pliers as the heat is applied the pliers will act as a heat sink. Remove the stator from the rear end bracket.
9 If only a brush or spring is to be renewed this can be done without further dismantling by prising up the brush holder carefully and then unsoldering the brush pig tail. Make sure that the B and L plates are only bent at their centres.
10 If complete dismantling is to be carried out, remove the condenser from the B terminal.
11 Unsolder the plates B and L from the rectifier again avoiding undue heat transference as previously explained.
12 Remove the mounting screw and the B terminal bolt and withdraw the voltage regulator and brush holder.
13 Remove the rectifier.
14 With the alternator dismantled, carry out the following tests and inspection to determine which components require renewal.
15 Check the condition of the rotor slip rings. If they are discoloured or rough, polish their outer surfaces with fine glasspaper or crocus cloth. If a slip ring has worn down so that its outside diameter is less than 1.2677 in (32.2) it must be removed and a new one fitted.
16 A circuit tester will be required for the following work. With the probes of the tester, check the circuit between the field coil and the slip ring. If there is no continuity then the coil has an open circuit and the rotor must be renewed.
17 Now check for continuity between the slip ring and the rotor core. If there is continuity, then the coil or slip ring is earthed and must be renewed.
18 Now turn your attention to the stator. Check for continuity between the leads of the stator core. If there is no continuity then the coil has an open circuit and the stator requires renewal.
19 Check for continuity between the stator coil leads and the stator core. If continuity is indicated then the stator is earthed and it must be renewed.
20 To test the heat sink, check for continuity between the positive (+) side of the sink and the stator coil lead connecting terminal. If there is

continuity in both directions, the diode is shorted and the rectifier will have to be renewed.
21 Now check for continuity between the negative (-) side of the sink and the stator coil lead connecting terminal. Once again, if there is continuity in both directions, the diode is shorted and the rectifier will have to be renewed.

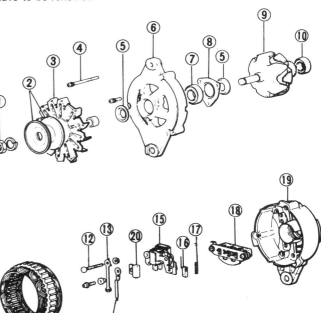

Fig. 9.7 Exploded view of the alternator (Sec 7)

1 Pulley nut
2 Pulley
3 Fan
4 Tie bolt
5 Seal
6 Drive end bracket
7 Ball bearing
8 Bearing retainer
9 Rotor
10 Ball bearing
11 Stator
12 B terminal
13 Plate B
14 Plate L
15 Brush holder and voltage regulator
16 Brush
17 Brush spring
18 Rectifier
19 Rear end bracket
20 Condenser

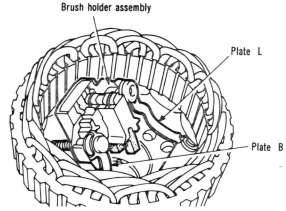

Fig. 9.8 Renewing alternator brush without complete dismantling (Sec 7)

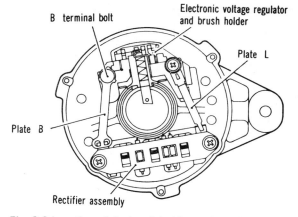

Fig. 9.9 Location of the brush holder and regulator and rectifier (Sec 7)

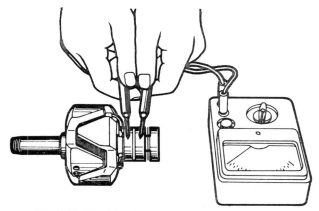

Fig. 9.10 Checking for field coil continuity (Sec 7)

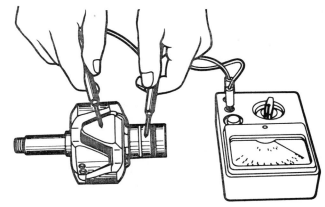

Fig. 9.11 Field coil earth test (Sec 7)

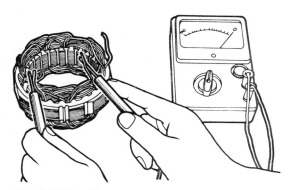

Fig. 9.12 Checking stator coil for continuity (Sec 7)

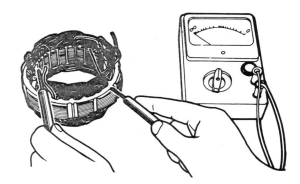

Fig. 9.13 Stator coil earth test (Sec 7)

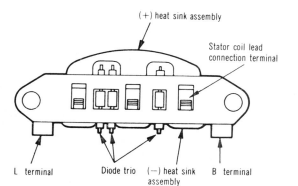

Fig. 9.14 Rectifier heat sink and terminals (Sec 7)

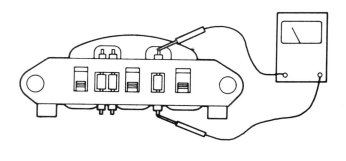

Fig. 9.15 Testing diode trio (Sec 7)

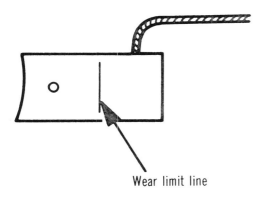

Fig. 9.16 Alternator brush marking (Sec 7)

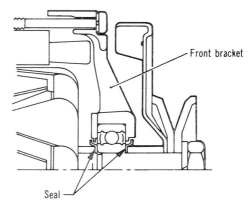

Fig. 9.17 Correct location of alternator front seals (Sec 7)

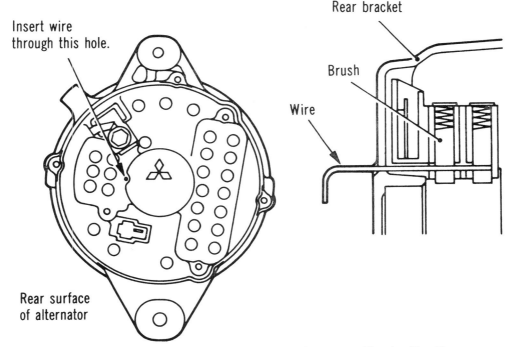

Fig. 9.18 Method of raising brushes to fit rotor into rear end bracket (Sec 7)

22 The diode trio can be tested, again using the circuit tester by placing the tester probes at either end of each diode in turn. If there is continuity or no continuity in both directions then the diode is defective.

23 A worn brush can be detected by referring to the wear limit line on the brush. A new brush is 0.709 in (18.0 mm) in length. Make sure that the brushes move freely in their holders.

24 With all the worn components renewed, reassembly is a reversal of dismantling but observe the following. Make sure that the seals are installed either side of the front bearing as shown in Fig. 9.17. Hold the brushes up out of the way with a piece of wire while fitting the rotor.

25 If the original alternator is being refitted then this is a reversal of removal. Adjust the belt tension as described in Section 4. If a new unit is being installed then carry out the following operations.

26 Offer the alternator to its mounting bracket and insert the pivot bolt through the lug on the drive end bracket. Connect the adjuster link.

27 Slip the drivebelt over the pulleys.

28 Push the alternator towards the timing belt end of the engine and check the gap A (Fig. 9.19) between the lug on the drive end bracket and the mounting bracket. If the clearance exceeds 0.008 in (0.2 mm) then the pivot bolt will have to be withdrawn and a suitable spacer washer inserted to take up the clearance.

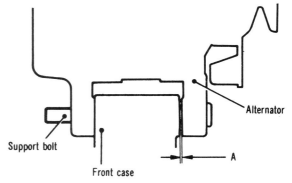

Fig. 9.19 Alternator lower bracket mounting diagram (Sec 7)

A not to exceed 0.008 in (0.2 mm)

29 Adjust the position of the alternator to give the correct belt tension (see Section 4) and then tighten the mounting and adjuster link bolts to the specified torque.

30 Reconnect the alternator leads at the plug. Reconnect the battery.

8 Starter motor – description

1 This type of starter motor incorporates a solenoid mounted on top of the starter motor body. When the ignition switch is operated, the solenoid moves the starter drive pinion, through the medium of the shift lever, into engagement with the flywheel or driveplate starter ring gear. As the solenoid reaches the end of its stroke and with the pinion by now partially engaged with the flywheel ring gear, the main fixed and moving contacts close and engage the starter motor to rotate the engine.

2 This fractional pre-engagement of the starter drive does much to reduce the wear on the flywheel ring gear associated with inertia type starter motors.

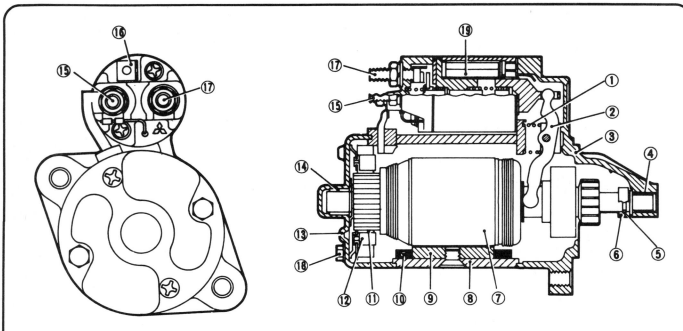

Fig. 9.20 Pre-engaged type starter motor (Sec 8)

1 Coil spring	6 Stop	11 Brush	16 S terminal
2 Shift lever	7 Armature	12 Brush holder	17 B terminal
3 Drive end bracket	8 Yoke	13 Rear cover	18 Tie bolt
4 Bearing	9 Pole	14 Bearing	19 Solenoid switch
5 Circlip	10 Field coil	15 M terminal	

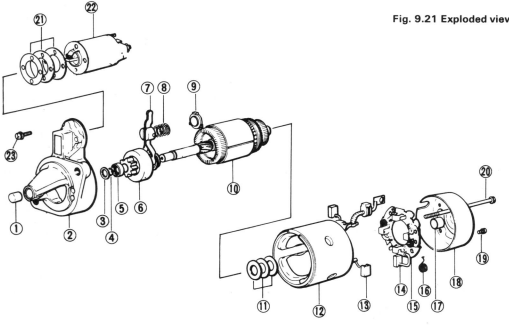

Fig. 9.21 Exploded view of the starter motor (Sec 9)

1 Front bearing
2 Front housing
3 Washer
4 Circlip
5 Stop
6 Overunning clutch and pinion
7 Shift lever
8 Coil spring
9 Spring retainer
10 Armature
11 Washers
12 Yoke
13 Brush
14 Brush
15 Brush holder
16 Brush spring
17 Rear bearing
18 Rear cover
19 Brush holder screw
20 Tie bolt
21 Washers
22 Solenoid switch
23 Solenoid switch screw

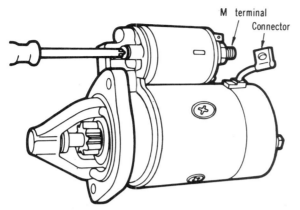

Fig. 9.22 Starter solenoid switch securing screw, 'M' terminal and connector (Sec 9)

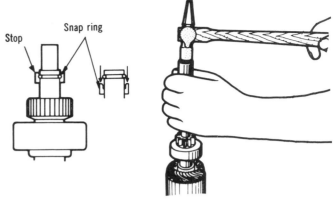

Fig. 9.23 Driving down circlip stop with a piece of tubing (Sec 9)

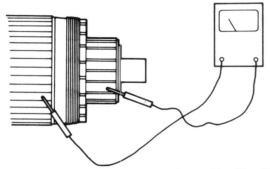

Fig. 9.24 Testing starter armature for earthing (Sec 9)

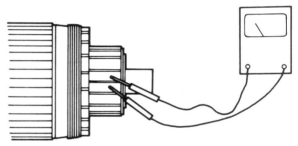

Fig. 9.25 Testing armature for open circuit (Sec 9)

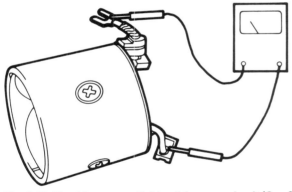

Fig. 9.26 Checking starter field coil for open circuit (Sec 9)

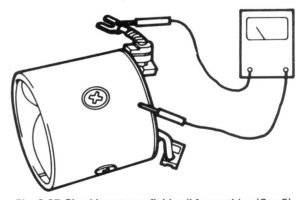

Fig. 9.27 Checking starter field coil for earthing (Sec 9)

9   Starter motor –removal, overhaul, testing and refitting

Removal
1   Disconnect the battery negative lead.
2   Disconnect the leads from the starter motor
3   Unscrew and remove the two starter motor mounting bolts and withdraw the starter.

Dismantling
4   Clean away external dirt and prepare to dismantle and test the unit. As with the alternator, if the starter motor has been in use for a high mileage it will probably be more economical to renew the complete unit for a new or factory reconditioned one, rather than renew individual components.
5   Release the connector from the solenoid A terminal, extract the two solenoid mounting screws and withdraw the solenoid.
6   Remove the two tie bolts and pull the yoke from the armature.
7   Carefully remove the armature and shift lever from the front

housing. Record which way round the shift lever and spring are located.
8   Extract the two screws and remove the rear housing.
9   Remove the brush holder.
10   Using a piece of tubing, drive the pinion stop down the shaft to expose the circlip. Extract this and remove the stop and overrunning clutch from the armature shaft.
11   With the starter motor dismantled, check for wear between the armature shaft and its bearings. If necessary, renew the bearings.
12   Clean the commutator with a fuel-moistened cloth. If it is discoloured, polish it with a piece of fine glasspaper. If the insulators between the commutator segments are level with the segments, then the insulators must be undercut using a thin hacksaw blade. Keep the cut square at its lower corners and to an even depth of between 0.016 and 0.024 in (0.4 and 0.6 mm). If the outside diameter of the commutator has reduced to less than 1.4842 in (37.7 mm) then the armature must be renewed.
13   Electrical faults in the starter motor should be checked in the following way if you possess a circuit tester.

Testing

Testing for earthing (armature)

14 Place one probe of the circuit tester on the commutator and the other on the armature core. If continuity is indicated, renew the armature.

Testing for open circuit (armature)

15 Use the probes of the circuit tester to check for continuity between the commutator segments. If continuity is not indicated, renew the armature.

Testing for open circuit (field coil)

16 Check the field coil as shown in Fig. 9.26. If continuity is not indicated, renew the coil.

Testing for earthing (field coil)

17 Place the probes of the tester as shown in Fig. 9.27. If continuity is indicated, renew the field coil.
18 Renewal of the field coil is best left to your dealer as the retaining screws require a pressure driver to remove them.

Testing the solenoid

19 Push the solenoid plunger in and release it. It should return immediately to its original position.
20 Push the plunger in again and check for continuity between the M and B terminals. If continuity is not indicated, renew the solenoid switch.

Brushes

21 If the brushes are worn below 0.453 in (11.5 mm) renew them. A wear limit line is incorporated on most brushes.

Brush holder

22 Using the tester, check for continuity between the positive (+) side of the brush holder and the base of the assembly. If continuity is indicated, the brush holder must be renewed.

Overrunning clutch/pinnion

23 Check for chipped or worn teeth. Turn the pinion and see that it rotates freely in a clockwise direction but locks when turned anti-clockwise.

Reassembly

24 Commence reassembly by fitting the clutch/pinion to the armature shaft.
25 Fit the pinion stop then the circlip. Using a two-legged puller draw the stop over the circlip.
26 Fit the small washer to the front end of the armature shaft.
27 Engage the shift lever (with spring and retainer) with the armature shaft and locate the assembly in the front housing.
28 Reconnect the yoke.
29 Fit the brush holder and brushes, taking care not to earth the (+) leads.
30 Fit the washer to the rear of the armature shaft.
31 Fit the rear housing and insert and tighten the two tie bolts.
32 Engage the shift lever with the solenoid plunger and fit the solenoid (two screws). Do not reconnect the M terminal connector yet.
33 With the starter motor reassembled, the pinion to stop clearance should now be checked. To do this, make sure that the solenoid M terminal connector is still detached. Connect a 12V supply between the solenoid S terminal and the body of the starter motor as shown in Fig. 9.31. As soon as the circuit is complete, the pinion will move out fully towards its stop. Check the gap between the end of the pinion and the housing stop using feeler gauges. The gap should be between 0.020 and 0.079 in (0.5 and 2.0 mm). If it requires adjustment, add or remove washers between the solenoid and the front housing. It is very important that the foregoing test is completed within 10 seconds to avoid overheating the field coil.
34 Reconnect the M terminal connector on the solenoid.
35 Refitting the starter motor is a reversal of removal.

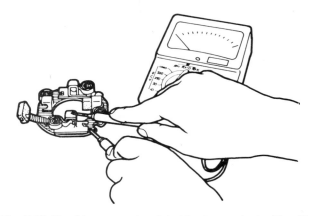

Fig. 9.28 Checking starter brush holder for continuity (Sec 9)

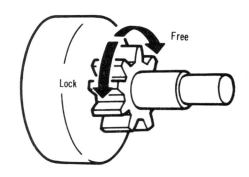

Fig. 9.29 Starter motor clutch/pinion direction of free running and locking (Sec 9)

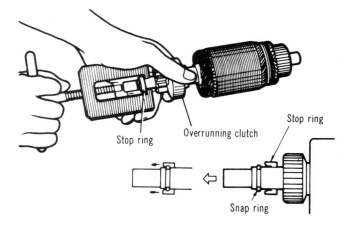

Fig. 9.30 Drawing stop over circlip on armature shaft (Sec 9)

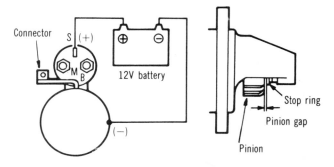

Fig. 9.31 Pinion gap checking circuit (Sec 9)

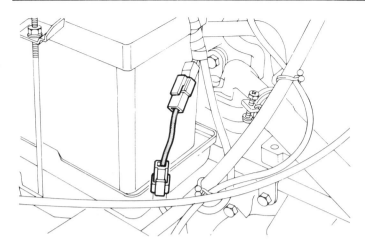

Fig. 9.32 Typical fusible link (Sec 10)

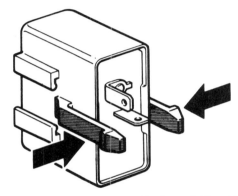

Fig. 9.34 Direction indicator flasher unit (Sec 10)

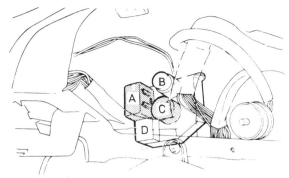

Fig. 9.33 Relay mounting block under instrument panel (Sec 10)

A   Turn signal flasher unit   C   Hazard warning flasher unit
B   Radiator fan relay   D   Seat belt warning buzzer

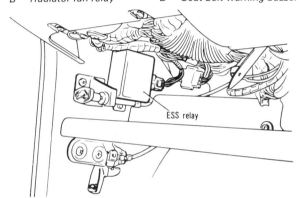

Fig. 9.35 Location of engine speed sensor relay (North America)
(Sec 12)

10 Fuses and fusible links

1   The fuse block is located below the instrument panel on the driver's side.
2   The circuits protected are shown on the lid of the fuse block cover.
3   If a fuse blows, always renew it with one of exactly the same rating. If a fuse blows again immediately after renewal, investigate the cause before renewing it again, the most likely cause being faulty insulation on the circuit wiring.
4   A fusible link is located adjacent to the battery. If the complete electric circuit fails and examination of the fusible link shows the insulation to have swollen and deformed then it must be assumed that a gross short circuit on the power side is responsible. Do not attempt to tape up the defective link or substitute a piece of ordinary wire. The cause of the link fusing must be traced and rectified and a new link of the specified type fitted.

11 Direction indicator/hazard warning units

1   These are independent relays mounted on the relay block under the facia panel.
2   The direction indicator relay is removed by depressing its plastic retaining claws (photo).
3   If the indicator warning lamp and the flasher outside the car commence to flash very rapidly when switched on, a faulty bulb or poor earth connection at the lamp housing may be the cause.

12 Fan and engine speed relays

1   The relay for the radiator electric cooling fan is located on the relay block adjacent to those for the direction indicator and hazard warning circuits.

2   On North American models, an engine speed sensor device is used to detect changes in the ignition circuit pulse voltage. When the engine speed falls to 1600 rpm or less, it causes the fuel cut-off solenoid on the carburettor to close as an integral part of the emission control system.
3   The relay used in this system circuit, is located just behind the bonnet release knob under the facia panel.
4   Refer also to Chapter 3, Section 14.

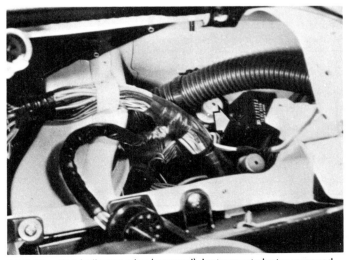

11.2 Direction indicator relay (arrowed). Instrument cluster removed for clarity

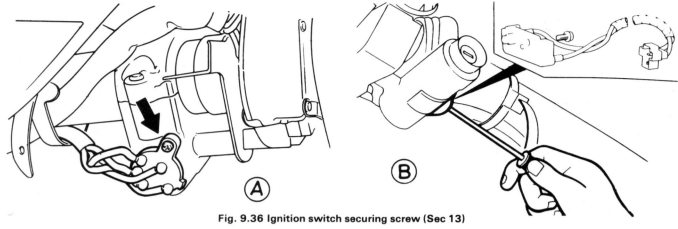

Fig. 9.36 Ignition switch securing screw (Sec 13)

A   Ignition switch

*B   Key reminder (North
      America)*

Fig. 9.37 Ignition switch positions (Sec 13)

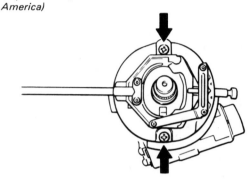

Fig. 9.38 Steering column switch securing screws (Sec 14)

13 Ignition switch – removal and refitting

1   The ignition switch can be removed independently from the
steering column lock.
2   Remove the shroud from the upper column, extract the single
securing screw and pull out the switch.
3   Refitting is a reversal of removal.
4   If a new switch is to be fitted, this is supplied complete with leads
and multi-pin plug, the wires being soldered to the switch contacts.

14 Steering column switch – removal and refitting

1   The steering column switch is of the combination type and
controls the direction indicators and the headlamp main/passing
beams and the dipped beam.
2   Access to the switch is obtained by first removing the steering
wheel and the column shrouds as described in Chapter 10.
3   Extract the switch securing screws, release the switch harness at
the connector and withdraw the switch from the upper end of the
steering shaft.
4   Refitting is a reversal of removal.

15 Lighting switch – removal and refitting

1   Extract the four screws which secure the instrument cluster hood.
2   Remove the corner panel as described in Chapter 12.
3   Disconnect the instrument cluster hood harness and withdraw the
hood.
4   Extract the screw from the lighting switch knob and withdraw the
switch from the rear side of the instrument cluster hood.
5   Refitting is a reversal of removal.

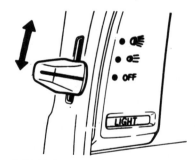

Fig. 9.39 Lighting switch positions (Sec 15)

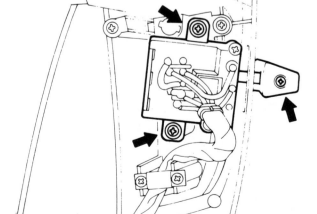

Fig. 9.40 Lighting switch and mounting screws (Sec 15)

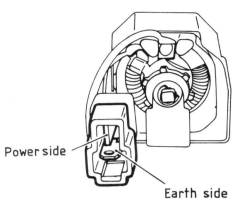

Power side

Earth side

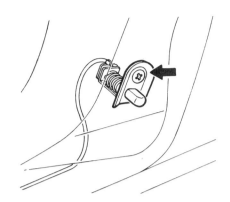

Fig. 9.41 Instrument panel rheostat knob (Sec 16)

Fig. 9.42 Rear view of panel rheostat (Sec 16)

Fig. 9.43 Courtesy lamp switch with cover removed (Sec 17)

16 Panel rheostat – removal and refitting

1   The rheostat switch which controls the intensity of illumination of the instrument panel is accessible for removal by following the procedure described for the lighting switch in the preceding Section.

17 Courtesy lamp switch – removal and refitting

1   Open the door and peel off the rubber cap which covers the switch plunger (photo).
2   Extract the single retaining screw and withdraw the switch from the cavity.
3   If the electrical lead is to be disconnected, take care that it does not drop back inside the body when released.
4   When refitting the switch make sure that the screw is tight and a rust-free earth connection is being made. Smearing the switch spring with petroleum jelly will help to reduce corrosion.

18 Tailgate latch switch – removal and refitting

1   This switch controls the lamp in the luggage compartment and is incorporated in the latch.
2   Remove the rear end trim.
3   Remove the link rod which connects the latch to the lock cylinder.
4   Remove the latch and disconnect the switch leads.
5   When refitting the switch, check that the lamp goes off when the tailgate is closed. If necessary adjust the switch plunger by placing washers between the switch and its mounting bracket.

17.1 Removing the courtesy lamp switch cover

19 Windscreen wiper/washer switch – removal and refitting

1   The operations are as described for the lighting switch except that the switch is mounted on the opposite side of the instrument cluster hood. Refer to Section 14.

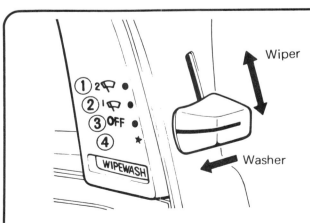

Wiper

Washer

Fig. 9.44 Washer/wiper switch positions (Sec 19)

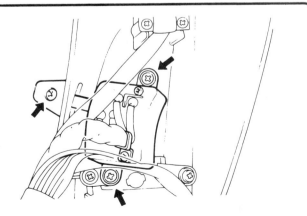

Fig. 9.45 Rear view of wiper switch (Sec 19)

20 Tailgate washer/wiper switch – removal and refitting

1   Reach up under the instrument panel and depress the two plastic retaining claws. Withdraw the switch until the wiring plug can be disconnected and then withdraw the switch.
2   Refitting is a reversal of removal.
3   The tailgate heated window switch is removed and refitted in exactly the same way.

21 Remotely controlled mirror adjusting switch – removal and refitting

1   Remove the gear lever or speed selector lever knob and after extracting the securing screws, remove the centre console.
2   The switches (left and right) are now accessible for disconnection and removal.
3   Refitting is a reversal of the removal procedure.

22 Tailgate demister switch – removal and refitting

1   The switch incorporates an indicator lamp and is removable as described for the tailgate wiper/washer switch in Section 19.

23 Horn switch – removal and refitting

1   The components of the horn switch are accessible after prising off the horn pad from the centre of the steering wheel.
2   If the horn contact ring must be removed, then the steering wheel will first have to be withdrawn as described in Chapter 10.

24 Switches – miscellaneous

1   Due to their integration with other components, the following switches have already been covered in the Chapters indicated to which reference should be made.

   Automatic transmission selector switch (Chapter 6)
   Coolant temperature switch (Chapter 2)
   Oil pressure switch (Chapter 1)
   Parking brake ON switch (Chapter 8)
   Radiator fan switch (Chapter 2)
   Stop lamp switch (Chapter 8)

25 Headlamp sealed beam unit – renewal

1   On cars fitted with this type of headlamp, lamp failure will indicate the need for renewal of the complete lens/reflector assembly.
2   Remove the radiator grille by extracting the securing screws.
3   Remove the headlamp unit ring retaining screws (not the beam adjusting screws).
4   Pull the lamp unit out and disconnect the electrical plug from its rear.
5   Refit the new sealed beam unit by reversing the removal operations.

26 Headlamp bulb – renewal

1   On this type of headlamp, it is possible to remove and refit a bulb and its holder by inserting your hand through the access hole in the wing valance at the side of the engine compartment. However, as it is very difficult to be sure thaat the bulb assembly has been positively refitted, the following method is recommended.
2   Extract the securing screws and remove the radiator grille.
3   Remove the headlamp bezel (two screws).

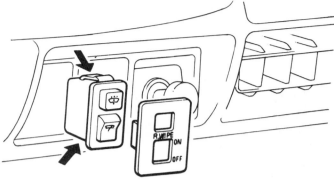

Fig. 9.46 Tailgate wiper/washer switch (Sec 20)

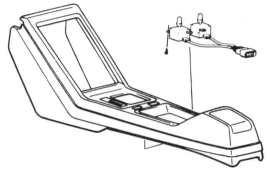

Fig. 9.47 Exterior mirror remote control switches (Sec 21)

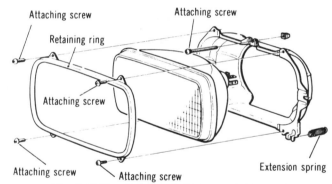

Fig. 9.48 Headlamp sealed beam unit (Sec 25)

26.3 Removing the headlamp bezel

26.4a Headlamp retaining screw

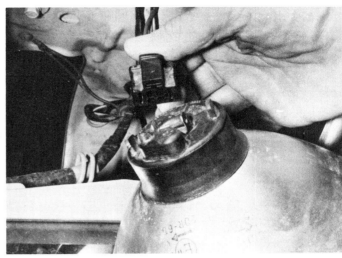

26.4b Detaching the headlamp wiring plug

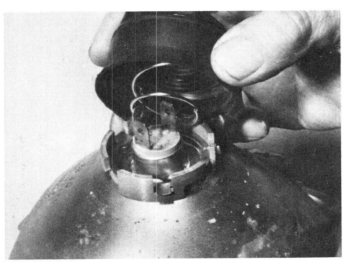

26.4c Removing the bulb holder cover

26.4d Removing the headlamp bulb and holder

4   Push the headlamp in slightly and turn it clockwise. Release the lamp and pull it forward until the bulb and holder can be removed (photos).
5   Renew the bulb and refit the bulb holder and the headlamp. Provided the two beam adjusting screws have not been disturbed, the alignment of the headlamps should not have altered.

27 Headlamp beam – alignment

1   It is recommended that the headlamps are adjusted by a service station using accurate beam setting equipment.
2   In an emergency however, the beams can be adjusted using the screws provided at the front of each lamp.

28 Exterior lamps – bulb renewal

Front parking/indicator lamp
1   Access to the bulbs is obtained by extracting the lens retaining screws and removing the lens (photo).

Side marker/repeater lamp
Front
2   Remove the screws from the lens, pull out the combined lens/lamp body and withdraw the bulb holder (photo).

Rear
3   Remove the trim panel from inside the luggage compartment and pull the lamp holder from its socket (photo).

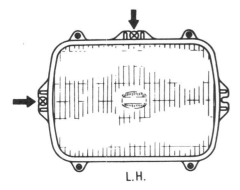

L.H.

Fig. 9.49 Typical headlamp adjusting screws (Sec 27)

28.1 Front parking direction indicator lamps

28.2 Front side marker lamp

28.3a Rear side marker cover panel

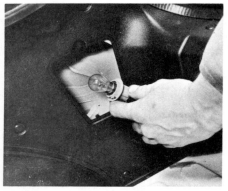

28.3b Removing rear side marker bulb holder

28.4a Rear lamp cluster cover panel

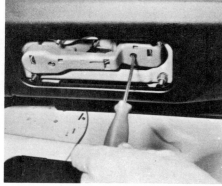

28.4b Extracting the rear lamp cluster bulb holder screws

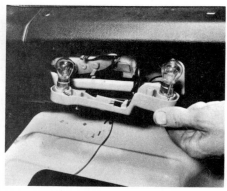

28.4c Withdrawing the rear lamp cluster bulb holder

28.6 Rear number plate lamp

29.1a Removing front interior lamp lens

29.4 Removing an indicator lamp

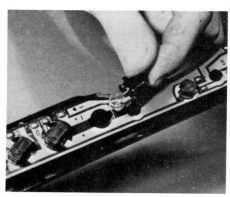

29.1b Front interior lamp switch and bulb holder

Rear lamp holder

4 The bulb holder can be released from the lamp body after reaching into the luggage area and prising off the small trim panel and extracting the two retaining screws (photos).
5 The lamp body with lens can be removed if necessary by extracting the securing nuts.

Rear number plate lamp

6 Two screws hold the lens/body assembly together. Extract the screws for access to the bulb (photo).

29 Interior lamps – bulb renewal

Front compartment roof lamp

1 Use a screwdriver carefully to prise the lens from its base. Pull the festoon type bulb from its contact springs (photo).

Rear compartment roof lamp

2 Press the sides of the lens in with the fingers and pull it from the lamp base. Pull the festoon type bulb from its contact springs.

Instrument panel

3 To renew an indicator or warning lamp bulb on the instrument panel, first withdraw the panel as described in the next Section.
4 The bulbs are of wedge base type and their holders may be simply pulled from their locations (photo).

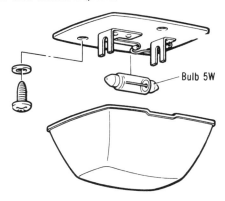

Fig. 9.50 Interior (rear) roof lamp (Sec 29)

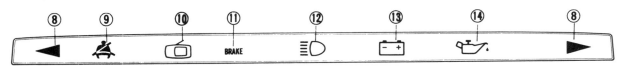

Fig. 9.51 Indicator and warning lamps (Sec 29)

8 Direction indicators
9 Seat belt reminder
10 Door open lamp

11 Handbrake 'ON', low fluid level or pressure
12 Main beam (headlamps)

13 Charge system (ignition warning)
14 Oil pressure

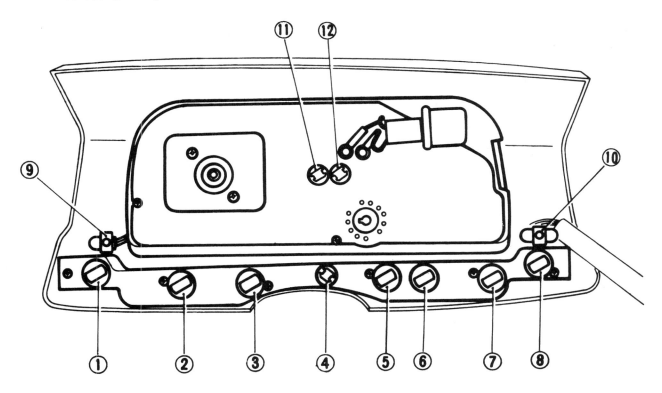

Fig. 9.52 Instrument panel indicator and warning lamp bulb holder identification (Sec 29)

1 Direction indicator
2 Oil pressure
3 Charge (ignition)
4 Headlamp main beam

5 Brake warning
6 Door open
7 Seat belt

8 Direction indicator
9 Wiper switch
10 Lighting switch

11 Power (transmission ratio)
12 Economy (transmission ratio)

30.1 Extracting an instrument cluster hood screw

30.2 Extracting an instrument cluster securing screw

30.4 Speedometer cable and instrument panel wiring harness plug disconnected

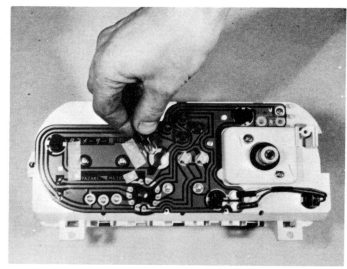

30.5 Instrument cluster lamp

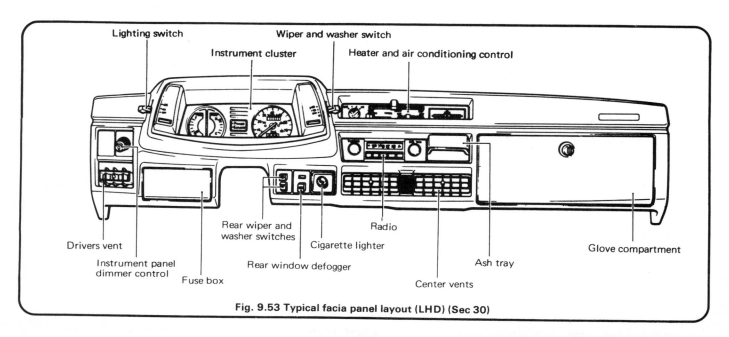

Lighting switch

Wiper and washer switch

Instrument cluster

Heater and air conditioning control

Drivers vent

Instrument panel dimmer control

Fuse box

Rear wiper and washer switches

Rear window defogger

Cigarette lighter

Radio

Center vents

Ash tray

Glove compartment

Fig. 9.53 Typical facia panel layout (LHD) (Sec 30)

30 Instrument panel – removal and refitting

1   Disconnect the battery and then inside the car, extract the four screws from the instrument cluster hood and remove the hood (photo).
2   Extract the five screws which secure the corner panels. Remove the instrument cluster screws (photo).
3   Gently withdraw the instrument panel towards you and at the same time have an assistant feed the speedometer cable through the grommet in the engine compartment rear bulkhead to provide greater flexibility for movement of the panel.
4   As soon as they are accessible, disconnect the cable from the speedometer by depressing the retaining claw and disconnect the multi-pin wiring connector (photo).
5   With the panel removed it may be dismantled as necessary and the individual instruments removed (photo).

Fig. 9.54 Instrument cluster hood screws (Sec 30)

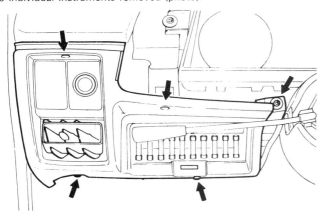

Fig. 9.55 Corner panel securing screws (Sec 30)

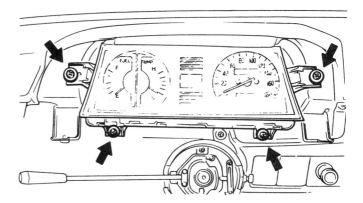

Fig. 9.56 Instrument cluster securing screws (Sec 30)

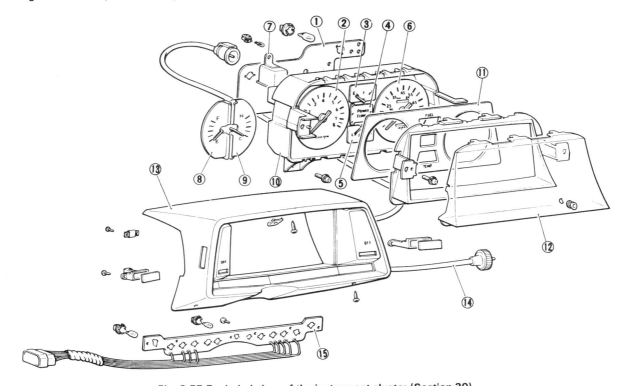

Fig. 9.57 Exploded view of the instrument cluster (Section 30)

1 Printed circuit board	4 Ratio selector indicator	8 Fuel gauge (subject to model)
2 Tachometer (where fitted)	5 Coolant temperature gauge (subject to model)	9 Coolant temperature gauge (subject to model)
3 Fuel gauge (subject to model)	6 Speedometer	10 Case
	7 Buzzer	11 Panel

12 Glass
13 Hood
14 Speedometer cable
15 Printed circuit board (indicator lamps)

6　If the fuel gauge and the coolant temperature gauges have both started to indicate incorrect readings at the same time, suspect the instrument voltage regulator. As this is built into the fuel gauge, renewal of this instrument should correct both instruments.

7　If the speedometer cable is to be renewed, disconnect it from the transmission. When fitting the new cable, make sure that there are no sharp bends, that it is not trapped anywhere and that it is securely engaged in transmission and speedometer head on completion of refitting.

8　Refitting is a reversal of removal.

31 Combination gauges – removal and refitting

1　Certain models have gauges fitted into the sloping face of the centre console.

2　The gauges can be removed if the console is first released and moved back so that the gauge securing screws can be extracted from their rear.

3　Refitting is a reversal of the removal procedure.

32 Horns

1　These are located behind the radiator grille (photo).

2　The tone of the horns is adjustable by means of the screw provided. Seal the screw on completion to prevent it moving due to vibration.

33 Windscreen wiper blades and arms – removal and refitting

1　A wiper blade can be removed by pulling the wiper arm from the glass until it locks and then prising aside the small clip so that the blade can be slid from its pivot (photo).

2　Before removing a wiper arm it is recommended that its angle on the windscreen is marked with a piece of masking tape to provide a guide to refitting.

3　Prise up the plastic cover from the wiper arm securing nut, unscrew the nut and pull the arm from the spindle splines (photo).

4　Refitting is a reversal of removal, do not overtighten the wiper arm nuts.

34 Windscreen wiper motor and linkage – removal and refitting

1　Disconnect the battery.

2　Disconnect the electrical leads from the wiper motor by pulling apart the connecting plug.

3　Unscrew and remove the wiper motor mounting bolts (photo).

4　Using a screwdriver, prise the wiper linkage from the ball pin on the motor crankarm and then withdraw the wiper motor (photo).

5　To remove the linkage, withdraw the blades and arms as described in Section 33.

6　Remove the heater air intake grille panel from just below the windscreen.

7　Unbolt the wheel boxes from their mounting brackets and withdraw the linkage (photo).

8　It will be obvious that the wiper linkage can be removed without first having to withdraw the wiper motor if there is no reason to remove the motor.

9　It is not recommended that the wiper motor is dismantled but rather a new or exchange unit is obtained. Do not remove the motor crankarm unless its relationship to the motor driveshaft is first marked.

10　When the motor is refitted, switch on the ignition and then actuate the wiper motor by means of the wiper switch. Switch off the wiper motor by means of the wiper switch so that the motor is automatically in its parked position. Failure to observe this operation may cause the wiper arms to be fitted incorrectly to their driving spindles with subsequent damage occurring to the arms, blades or bodywork once they are switched on.

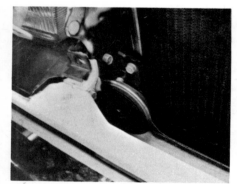

32.1 Horn location

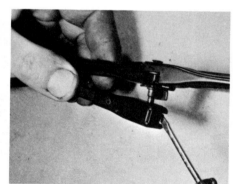

33.1 Disconnecting wiper blade

33.3 Wiper arm fixing

34.3 Windscreen wiper motor

34.4 Windscreen wiper motor crank arm

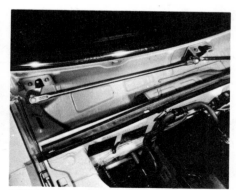

34.7 Windscreen wiper linkage and wheelboxes

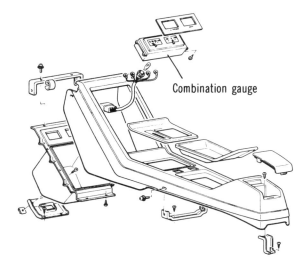

Fig. 9.58 Combination gauges fitted to centre console (Sec 31)

Combination gauge

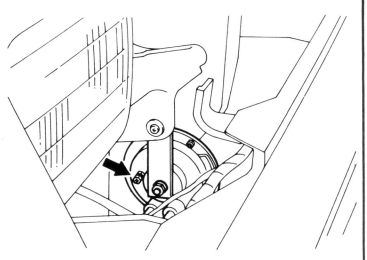

Fig. 9.59 Horn adjusting screw (Sec 32)

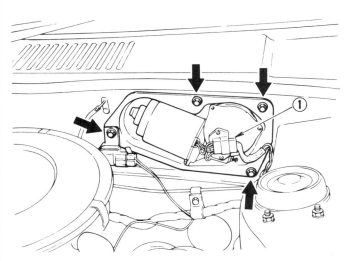

Fig. 9.60 Wiper motor mounting bolts (Sec 34)

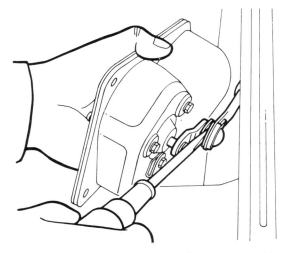

Fig. 9.61 Separating wiper linkage from motor crankarm (Sec 34)

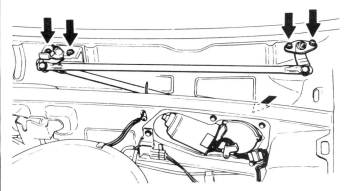

Fig. 9.62 Wiper linkage wheelbox mountings (Sec 34)

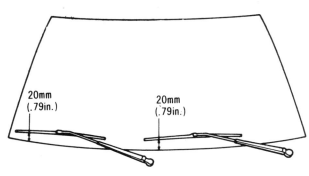

20mm
(.79in.)

20mm
(.79in.)

Fig. 9.63 Windscreen wiper arm parked position (Sec 34)

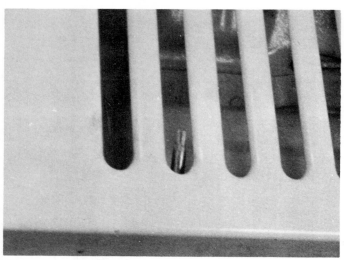

35.2 Windscreen washer jet

36.5 Tailgate wiper motor

35 Windscreen washer – description and adjustment

1   The washer reservoir is located within the engine compartment and incorporates an electric pump. A fault in the pump can only be rectified by fitting a new sealed unit.

2   The washer jets are located between the grille openings and their angles can be adjusted by bending their support brackets on the engine compartment rear bulkhead. The fluid should strike the windscreen at the points shown in Fig. 9.65 (photo).

36 Tailgate wiper motor – removal and refitting

1   The motor is located within the tailgate.

2   Remove the wiper blade and arm as described for a windscreen wiper arm in Section 33.

3   Unscrew the driveshaft nut and remove the spacers.

4   Remove the tailgate trim panel. This is held by plastic studs and the fingers should be inserted between the panel and the frame of the tailgate and the panel jerked sharply away.

5   Disconnect the motor electrical leads by pulling the connector plug apart (photo).

6   Unscrew and remove the wiper motor mounting bolts and remove the motor.

7   If the wiper motor is faulty, it is recommended that a new or reconditioned unit is fitted rather than dismantle the original motor.

8   Refitting is a reversal of removal but push the motor by means of the wiper operating switch, not the ignition key and then fit the wiper arm/blade in accordance with the diagram.

37 Tailgate washer – description and adjustment

1   On models equipped with this facility, the fluid reservoir which serves the windscreen washer also serves the tailgate window but with the inclusion of an additional electric pump at the side of the reservoir.

2   A ball type non-return valve is fitted in the fluid pipe under the instrument panel. If this is ever removed, make sure that it is refitted the right way round.

3   Plastic washer fluid pipes are easier to remove and refit and are less likely to damage the components to which they are connected if the pipe ends are first warmed in very hot water.

4   If the jet requires adjustment to make the fluid striking point match that shown in the diagram, insert a pin into the jet and move it on its ball seating.

38 Heated tailgate window – precautions and repair

1   Care should be taken not to scratch the electrical grid lines on the interior surface of the tailgate glass.

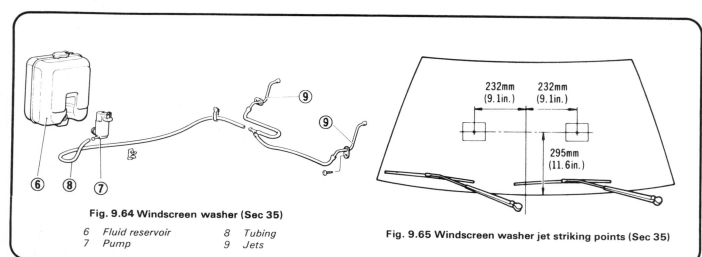

Fig. 9.64 Windscreen washer (Sec 35)

| 6 | Fluid reservoir | 8 | Tubing |
| 7 | Pump | 9 | Jets |

Fig. 9.65 Windscreen washer jet striking points (Sec 35)

232mm (9.1in.)   232mm (9.1in.)   295mm (11.6in.)

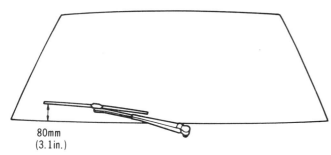

Fig. 9.66 Tailgate wiper arm setting diagram (Sec 36)

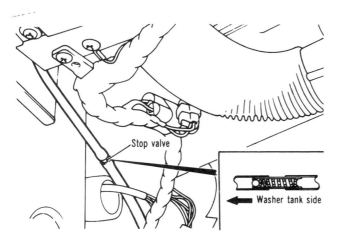

Fig. 9.68 Washer tube non-return valve (Sec 37)

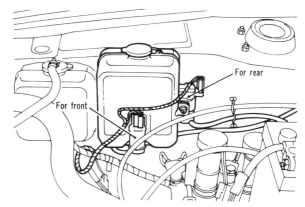

Fig. 9.67 Combined washer reservoir for windscreen and tailgate
(Sec 37)

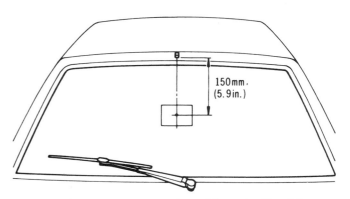

Fig. 9.69 Tailgate washer jet striking point (Sec 37)

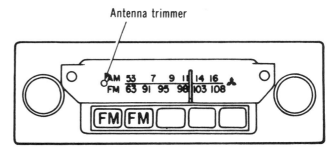

Fig. 9.70 Radio aerial trimmer screw (typical) (Sec 40)

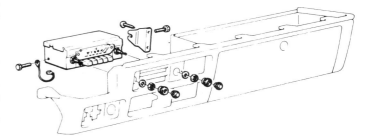

Fig. 9.71 Radio mounting (Sec 40)

2   Clean the glass with a cloth and water to which a little household washing-up liquid has been added. Clean along the grid lines not across them.
3   Do not stick self-adhesive labels over the grid lines as when they are removed they are likely to damage them.
4   Repair of a broken grid can be carried out using a conductive paint repair kit available from your dealer. Clean the ends of the remaining grid lines and the glass on the area where the paint is to be applied with steel wool and then with methylated spirit.
5   To obtain a straight grid line, stick masking tape to the glass leaving a centre gap as wide as the grid line and then paint in with a fine brush. Allow the paint to dry and then remove the tape.

39 Seat belt warning system (North America)

1   This system operates in the following way; if the driver sits in his seat and turns the ignition key to the ON position without having fastened the safety belt, a warning buzzer and lamp are actuated for a four to eight second period.
2   The front passenger seat safety belt does not incorporate the warning device.
3   The buzzer also serves the anti-theft system which sounds if an attempt is made to open the driver's door from the inside without having first withdrawn the ignition key.
4   The main components of the system are a microswitch built into the safety belt buckle and a timer plugged into the relay block.

40 Radios (as fitted as factory option) – removal and refitting

1   To remove this type of radio, first detach the instrument panel trim then pull off the control knobs from the radio. Unscrew the two nuts from behind the knobs.

2   Remove the radio mounting bolts (one from each side) and withdraw the radio until the power supply, aerial and speaker leads can be disconnected. Remove the radio.
3   To remove the speaker, withdraw the instrument cluster hood,

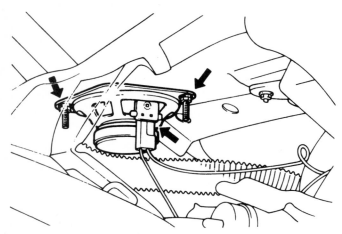

Fig. 9.72 Radio speaker mounting (Sec 40)

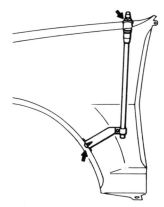

Fig. 9.73 Radio aerial mounting (Sec 40)

corner panel and instrument cluster as described in Section 29 of this Chapter.

4   To remove the aerial, jack up the front of the car, remove the roadwheel and the splash shield, unbolt the aerial and withdraw it, pulling its connecting lead ·carefully through the grommets after disconnecting it from the radio.

41 Radios and tape players – fitting (general)

A radio or tape player is an expensive item to buy and will only give its best performance if fitted properly. If you do not wish to do the fitting yourself there are many in-car entertainment specialists who can do the fitting for you.

Make sure the unit purchased is of the same polarity as the car and ensure that units with adjustable polarity are correctly set before commencing installation.

It is difficult to give specific information with regard to fitting, as final positioning of the radio/tape player, speakers and aerial is entirely a matter of personal preference. However, the following paragraphs give guidelines, which are relevant to all installations.

Radios

Most radios are a standardised 7 in wide by 2 inches deep – this ensures that they will fit into the radio aperture provided in the car. If your car does not have such an aperture, the radio must be fitted in a suitable position either in, or beneath, the dashpanel. Alternatively, a special console can be purchased which will fit between the dashpanel and the floor, or on the transmission tunnel. These consoles can also be used for additional switches and instrumentation if required. Where

no radio aperture is provided, the following points should be borne in mind before deciding where to fit the unit:

(a)   *The unit must be within easy reach of the driver wearing a seat belt*

(b)   *The unit must not be mounted in close proximity to an electric tachometer, the ignition switch and its wiring, or the flasher unit and associated wiring*

(c)   *The unit must be mounted within reach of the aerial lead and in such a place that the aerial lead will not have to be routed near the component detailed in the preceding paragraph 'b'*

(d)   *The unit should not be positioned where it might cause injury to the car occupants in an accident; for instance, under the dashpanel above the driver's or passenger's legs*

(e)   *The unit must be fitted really securely*

Some radios will have mounting brackets provided, together with instructions: others will need to be fitted using drilled and slotted metal strips, bent to form mounting brackets. These strips are available from most accessory shops. The unit must be properly earthed by fitting a separate earthing lead between the casing of the radio and the vehicle frame.

Use the radio manufacturer's instructions when wiring into the vehicle's electrical system. If no instructions are available, refer to the relevant wiring diagram to find the location of the radio 'feed' connection in the vehicle's wiring circuit. A 1 to 2 amp 'in-line' fuse must be fitted in the radio's 'feed' wire; a choke may also be necessary (see next Section).

The type of aerial used and its fitted position, is a matter of personal preference. In general, the taller the aerial, the better the reception. It is best to fit a fully retractable aerial — especially, if a mechanical car-wash is used or if you live where cars tend to be vandalised. In this respect, electrical aerials which are raised and lowered automatically when switching the radio on or off are convenient, but are more likely to give trouble than the manual type.

When choosing a site for the aerial, the following points should be considered:

(a)   *The aerial lead should be as short as possible – this means that the aerial should be mounted at the front of the car*

(b)   *The aerial must be mounted as far away from the distributor and HT leads as possible*

(c)   *The part of the aerial which protrudes beneath the mounting point must not foul the roadwheels, or anything else*

(d)   *If possible, the aerial should be positioned so that the coaxial lead does not have to be routed through the engine compartment*

(e)   *The plane to the panel on which the aerial is mounted should not be so steeply angled that the aerial cannot be mounted vertically (in relation to the 'end-on' aspect of the car). Most aerials have a small amount of adjustment available*

Having decided on a mounting position, a relatively large hole will have to be made in the panel. The exact size of the hole will depend upon the aerial being fitted, although, generally, the hole required is of $\frac{3}{4}$ inch (19 mm) diameter. On metal bodied cars, a 'tank-cutter' of the relevant diameter is the best tool to use for making the hole. This tool needs a small diameter pilot hole drilled through the panel, through which the tool clamping bolt is inserted. On GRP bodied cars a 'hole-saw' is the best tool to use. Again, this tool will require the drilling of a small pilot hole. When the hole has been made the raw edges should be de-burred with a file and then painted, to prevent corrosion.

Fit the aerial according to the manufacturer's instructions. If the aerial is very tall, or if it protrudes beneath the mounting panel for a considerable distance, it is a good idea to fit a stay between the aerial and the vehicle frame. This can be manufactured from the slotted and drilled metal strips previously mentioned. The stay should be securely screwed or bolted in place. For best reception it is advisable to fit an earth lead between the aerial body and the vehicle frame – this is essential for GRP bodied cars.

It will probably be necessary to drill one or two holes through bodywork panels in order to feed the aerial lead into the interior of the car. Where this is the case ensure that the holes are fitted with rubber grommets to protect the cable, and to stop possible entry of water.

Positioning and fitting of the speaker depends mainly on its type. Generally, the speaker is designed to fit directly into the aperture already provided in the car (usually in the shelf behind the rear seats, or in the top of the dashpanel). Where this is the case, fitting the speaker is just a matter of removing the protective grille from the aperture and screwing or bolting the speaker in place. Take great care not to damage the speaker diaphragm whilst doing this. It is a good idea to fit a 'gasket' between the speaker frame and the mounting panel, in order to prevent vibration — some speakers will already have such a gasket fitted.

If a 'pod' type speaker was supplied with the radio, the best acoustic results will normally be obtained by mounting it on the shelf behind the rear seat. The pod can be secured to the panel with self-tapping screws.

When connecting a rear mounted speaker to the radio, the wires should be routed through the vehicle beneath the carpets, or floor mats — preferably in the middle, or along the side of the floorpan, where they will not be trodden on by passengers. Make the relevant connections as directed by the radio manufacturer.

Ensure that all the electrical connections have been made properly, so that there is a good electrical contact and that all the wiring is installed neatly and secured to the car with wiring clips, or PVC tape.

After completing the installation of the radio, it will be necessary to trim the radio to suit the aerial. If specific instructions on this are not given by the manufacturer of the radio, proceed as follows. Find a medium waveband station with a low signal strength and turn the trim screw on the radio in or out until the signal is received at maximum strength.

Tape players

Fitting instructions for both cartridge and cassette stereo tape players are the same and in general the same rules apply as when fitting a radio. Tape players are not usually prone to electrical interference like radios — although it can occur — so positioning is not so critical. If possible the player should be mounted on an 'even keel'. Also, it must be possible for a driver wearing a seat belt to reach the unit to change or turn over tapes.

For the best results from speakers designed to be recessed into a panel, mount them so that the back of the speaker protrudes into an enclosed chamber within the car (eg door interiors or the boot cavity).

To fit recessed type speakers in the front doors, first check that there is sufficient room to mount a speaker in each door without fouling the latch or window winding mechanism. Hold the speaker against the skin of the door, and draw a line around the periphery of the speaker. With the speaker removed draw a second 'cutting' line, within the first, to allow enough room for entry of the speaker back, but at the same time providing a broad seat for the speaker flange. When you are sure that the 'cutting-line' is correct, drill a series of holes around its periphery. Pass a hacksaw blade through one of the holes and cut through the metal between the holes until the centre section of the panel falls out.

De-burr the edges of the hole and paint the raw metal to prevent corrosion. Cut a corresponding hole in the door trim panel — ensuring that it will be completely covered by the speaker grille. Now drill a hole in the door edge and a corresponding hole in the door surround. These holes are to feed the speaker leads through — so fit grommets. Pass the speaker leads through the door trim, door skin and out through the holes in the side of the door and door surround. Refit the trim panel and then secure the speaker to the door using self-tapping screws. **Note:** *If the speaker is fitted with a shield to prevent water dripping on it, ensure that this shield is at the top.*

Pod type speakers can be fastened to the shelf behind the rear seat, or anywhere else offering a corresponding mounting point. If the pod speakers are mounted on each side of the shelf behind the rear seat, it is a good idea to drill several large diameter holes through to the boot cavity beneath each speaker — this will improve the sound reproduction. Pod speakers sometimes offer a better reproduction quality if they face the rear window — which then acts as a reflector — so it is worthwhile to do a little experimenting before finally fixing the speaker.

42 Radios and tape players – suppression of interference (general)

To eliminate unwanted noises costs very little and is not as difficult as is sometimes thought. With common sense and patience and following the instructions in the following paragraphs, interference can be virtually eliminated.

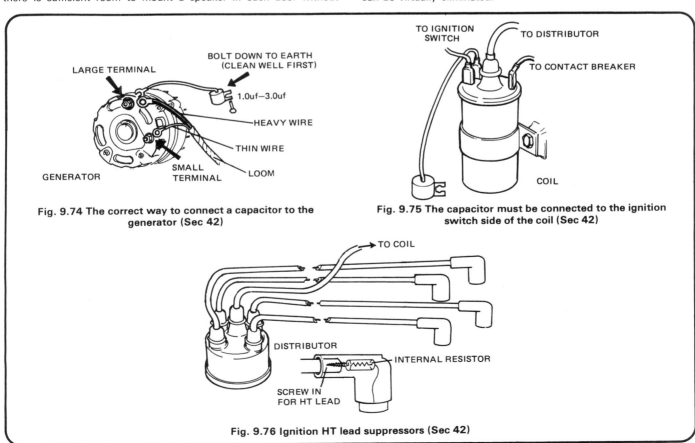

Fig. 9.74 The correct way to connect a capacitor to the generator (Sec 42)

Fig. 9.75 The capacitor must be connected to the ignition switch side of the coil (Sec 42)

Fig. 9.76 Ignition HT lead suppressors (Sec 42)

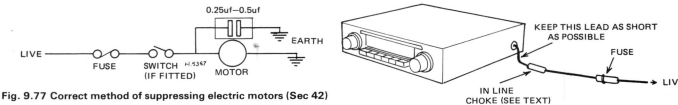

Fig. 9.77 Correct method of suppressing electric motors (Sec 42)

Fig. 9.79 Fitting an 'in-line' choke (Sec 42)

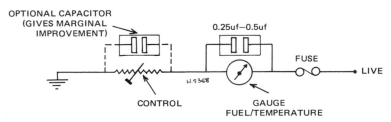

Fig. 9.78 Method of suppressing instrument voltage controls (Sec 42)

The first cause for concern is the generator. The noise this makes over the radio is like an electric mixer and the noise speeds up when you rev up (if you wish to prove the point, you can remove the drivebelt and try it). The remedy for this is to connect a 1.0 uf-3.0 uf capacitor between earth, probably the bolt that holds down the generator base, and the *large* terminal on the dynamo, or alternator. If you connect it to the small terminal, you will probably damage the generator permanently (see Fig. 9.74).

A second common cause of electrical interference is the ignition system. Here a 1.0 uf capacitor must be connected between earth and the 'SW' or '+' terminal on the coil (see Fig. 9.75). This may stop the tick-tick-tick sound that comes over the speaker. Next comes the spark itself.

There are several ways of curing interference from the ignition HT system. One is to use carbon film HT lead, but this is liable to internal breaks, causing erratic ignition. The second and more successful method is to use resistive spark plug caps (see Fig. 9.76) of about 10 000 ohm to 15 000 ohm resistance. If, due to lack of room, these cannot be used, an alternative is to use 'in-line' suppressors (Fig. 9.76) – if the interference is not too bad, you may get away with only one suppressor in the coil to distributor line. If the interfeerence continues (a 'clacking' noise), fit suppressor to all the HT leads.

Check that the case of the radio and the fixings for the aerial make good electrical contact with the metalwork of the car. Ensure that the aerial plug is pushed fully into the socket in the radio and that the radio

has been trimmed (see preceding Section). Make sure that the radio has an in line fuse and that the rating of the fuse cartridge is not higher than 2 amps.

Although the ignition system is the principal cause of interference, unwanted noises on the radio can also be produced by the electric motors of the windscreen wiper, windscreen washer, heater fan and electric aerial, if fitted. Other sources of interference are electric fuel pumps, flashing turn signals and instrument voltage stabilizers: Fig. 1.77 shows the way to suppress interference from an electric motor and Fig. 9.78 shows instrument voltage stabilizer suppression. Turn signals are not normally suppressed.

Modern car radios usually have a choke as well as a fuse in the live line, as shown in Fig. 9.79. If your installation lacks one of these, put one in as shown. For a transistor radio, a choke having a current carrying capacity of 2 amps is adequate. For any other equipment, use a choke of the same current rating as the protective fuse. Components for radio interference suppression are available from radio and car accessory shops.

An electric clock should be suppressed by a connecting of 0.5 uf capacitor across it as shown for a motor in Fig. 9.77.

If the car is fitted with electronic ignition, it is not recommended that spark plug resistors and contact breaker capacitors are fitted. Most electronic ignition units have built-in suppression and the addition of external components may have adverse effects upon the operation of the ignition system.

43 Fault diagnosis – electrical system

Symptom	Reason(s)
Starter fails to turn engine	Battery discharged Battery defective internally Battery terminal leads loose or earth lead not securely attached to body Loose or broken connections in starter motor circuit Starter motor switch or solenoid faulty Starter brushes badly worn, sticking, or brush wires loose Commutator dirty, worn or burnt Starter motor armature faulty Field coils earthed
Starter turns engine very slowly	Battery in discharged condition Starter brushes badly worn, sticking or brush wires loose Loose wires in starter motor circuit
Starter spins but does not turn engine	Pinion or flywheel gear teeth broken or worn Battery discharged
Starter motor noisy or excessively rough engagement	Pinion or flywheel gear teeth broken or worn Starter motor retaining bolts loose

Symptom	Reason(s)
Battery will not hold charge for more than a few days	Battery defective internally Electrolyte level too low or electrolyte too weak due to leakage Plate separators no longer fully effective Battery plates severely sulphated Drivebelt slipping Battery terminal connections loose or corroded Alternator not charging Short in lighting circuit causing continual battery drain Alternator integral, regulator unit not working correctly
Ignition light fails to go out, battery runs flat in a few days	Drivebelt loose and slipping or broken Alternator brushes worn, sticking, broken or dirty Alternator brush springs weak or broken Internal fault in alternator

Failure of individual electrical equipment to function correctly is dealt with alphabetically, item-by-item, under the headings listed below

Horn

Horn operates all the time	Horn push either earthed or stuck down Horn cable to horn push earthed
Horn fails to operate	Cable or cable connection loose, broken or disconnected Horn has an internal fault
Horn emits intermittent or unsatisfactory noise	Cable connections loose Horn incorrectly adjusted

Lights

Lights do not come on	If engine not running, battery discharged Wire connections loose, disconnected or broken Light switch shorting or otherwise faulty
Lights come on but fade out	If engine not running battery discharged
Lights give very poor illumination	Lamp glasses dirty Lamps badly out of adjustment
Lights work erratically – flashing on and off, especially over bumps	Battery terminals or earth connection loose Lights nor earthing properly Contacts in light switch faulty

Wipers

Wiper motor fails to work	Blown fuse Wire connections loose, disconnected or broken Brushes badly worn Armature worn or faulty Field coils faulty
Wiper motor works very slowly and takes excessive current	Commutator dirty, greasy or burnt Armature bearings dirty or unaligned Armature badly worn or faulty
Wiper motor works slowly and takes little current	Brushes badly worn Commutator dirty, greasy or burnt Armature badly worn or faulty
Wiper motor works but wiper blades remain static	Wiper motor gearbox parts badly worn

44 Fault diagnosis – radio interference

Noise	Source	Remedy
'Machine gun' rattle when engine running	Ignition system coil or HT lead	Install a capacitor to + (switch) terminal of ignition coil
Undulating whine according to engine speed	Alternator	Install a capacitor to alternator terminal

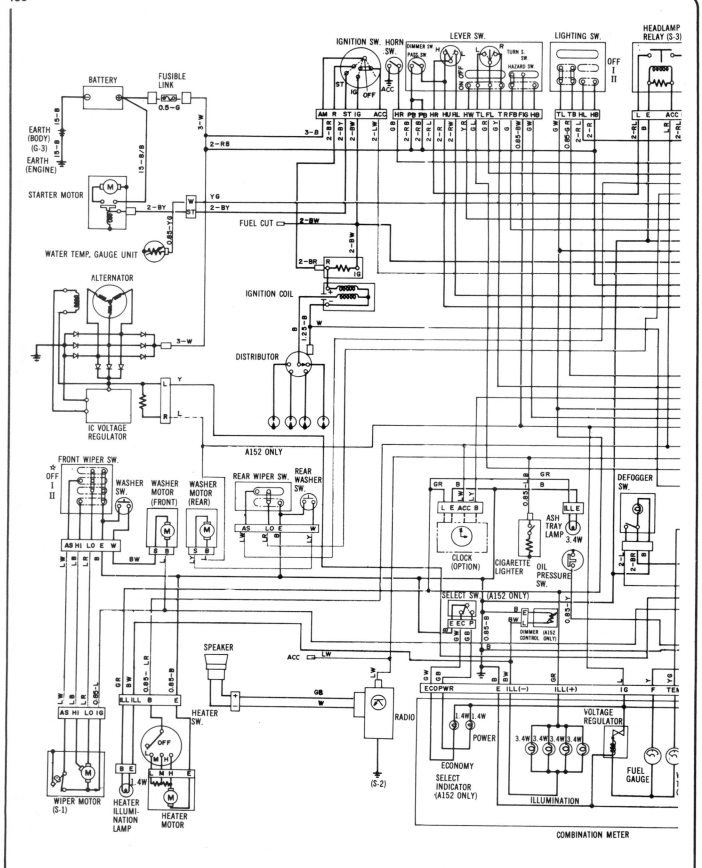

Fig. 9.80 Wiring diagram for right-hand drive cars

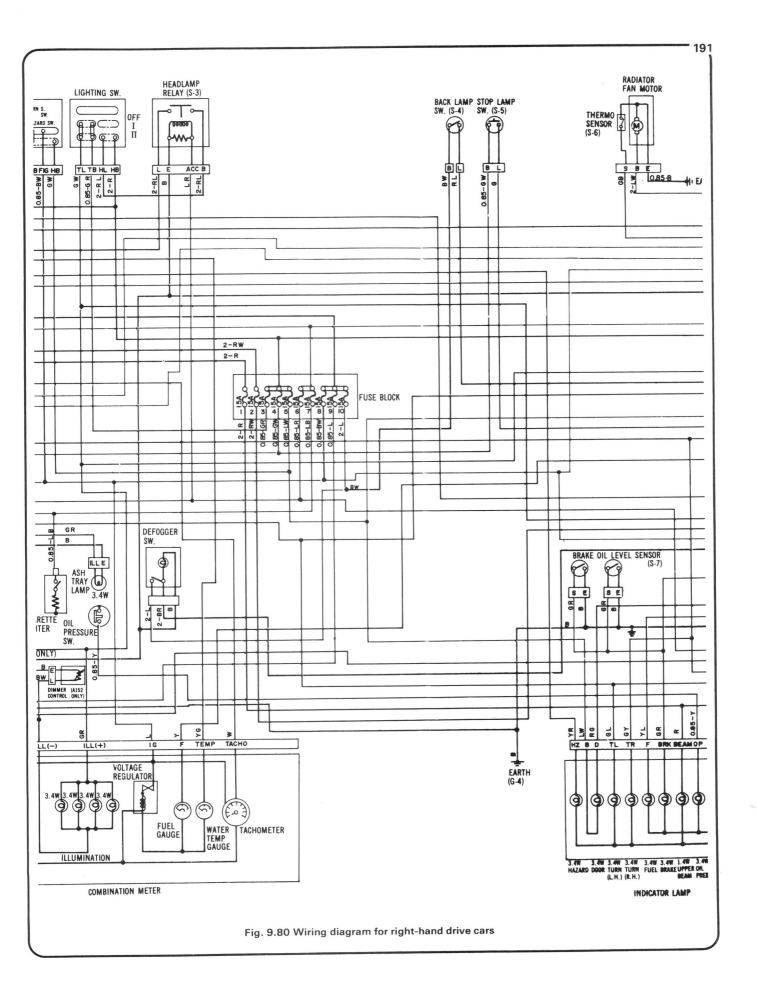

Fig. 9.80 Wiring diagram for right-hand drive cars

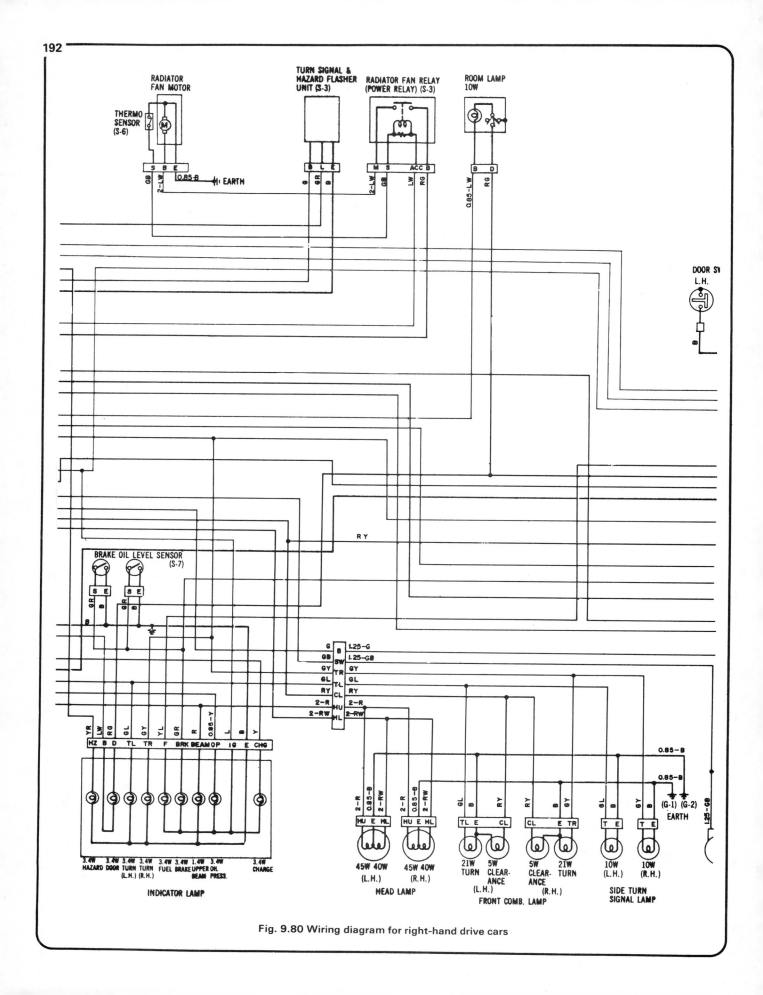

Fig. 9.80 Wiring diagram for right-hand drive cars

Fig. 9.80 Wiring diagram for right-hand drive cars

Key to Fig. 9.80

Symbol	Colouring	Connected circuit	System
B	Black	Earth	Starting
BW	Black/white	Ignition	
W	White	Charging	
WR	White/red	Armature	Charging
WB	White/black	Field	
R	Red	Headlamp, upper beam	
RW	Red/white	Headlamp, lower beam and fog lamp	
RB	Red/black	Interior lamp	Lighting
RY	Red/yellow	Instrument lamp	
RL	Red/blue	Backup lamp	
G	Green	Stoplamp switch	
GW	Green/white	Tail lamp and license lamp	
GR	Green/red	Parking lamp	
GY	Green/yellow	Turn signal lamp, right	Signal
GB	Green/black	Horn	
GL	Green/blue	Turn signal lamp, left	
Y	Yellow	Fuel gauge	
YR	Yellow/red	Upper beam indicator lamp	
YB	Yellow/black	Oil pressure indicator lamp	Gauge and indicator
YG	Yellow/green	Temperature and parking brake indicator lamps	
YL	Yellow/blue	Turn signal indicator lamp	
YW	Yellow/white	Charging indicator lamp	
L	Blue	Windshield wiper	
LW	Blue/white	Radio, cigarette lighter, wipe and clock	Others
LR	Blue/red	Windshield wiper	

Symbol	Part name	Location
S-1	Wiper motor (front)	Dash panel
S-2	Earth	Tightening with cigarette lighter bracket
S-3	Headlamp relay, turn signal and hazard flasher unit, radiator fan relay	Relay box on toeboard forward of corner panel on driver's side
S-4	Back lamp switch	Transaxle
S-5	Stoplamp switch	Brake pedal bracket
S-6	Thermosensor	Lower tank of radiator
S-7	Brake oil level sensor	Brake master cylinder
S-8	Door switch	Lower forward corner of each rear side panel
S-9	Fuel gauge unit	Fuel tank
S-10	Parking brake switch	Under parking brake
S-11	Wiper motor (rear)	Inside of tail gate

Key to Fig. 9.81

Symbol	Colouring	Connected circuit	System
B	Black	Grounding	Starting
BW	Black/white	Ignition	
BY	Black/yellow	Starter motor	
BR	Black/red	Ignition coil (R)	
W	White	Charging, tachometer, ESS relay	Charging
WB	White/black	Ammeter	
WR	White/red	Turn signal flasher unit	
R	Red	Headlight, upper beam	Lighting
RW	Red/white	Headlight, lower beam	
RB	Red/black	Seat belt switch, passing switch	
RY	Red/yellow	Headlight lower beam	
RL	Red/blue	Inhibitor switch	
RG	Red/green	Door switch, door indicator, upper beam lever switch	
G	Green	Stoplight switch, luggage compartment light, handle lock switch	Signal
GW	Green/white	Tail light, license light, select switch (economy), side marker light	
GR	Green/red	Brake warning light, brake level sensor, parking brake	
GY	Green/yellow	Turn signal light (RH)	
GB	Green/black	Select switch (power), horn	
GL	Green/blue	Turn signal light (LH)	
GO	Green/orange	Hazard warning switch	
Y	Yellow	Fuel gauge, oil pressure indicator light, charging indicator	Gauge and indicator
YR	Yellow/red	Remote control mirror switch (S) – (RH)	
YB	Yellow/black	Remote control mirror switch (M^2) – (RH)	
YG	Yellow/green	Temperature indicator, remote control mirror switch (M^1) – (RH), seat belt indicator	
YW	Yellow/white	Seat belt buzzer	
L	Blue	Voltage regulator, wiper motor (rear), windshield washer motor, remote control mirror switch (M^1) – (LH)	Others
LW	Blue/white	Heater switch (low), wiper switch (AS), radio, cigarette lighter, remote control mirror switch (M^2) – (LH)	
LB	Blue/black	Wiper switch (high), remote control mirror switch (B)	
LR	Blue/red	Wiper switch (low), remote control mirror switch (S)	
LY	Blue/yellow	Rear washer switch	

Symbol	Part name	Location
CB-1	Earth	Rear roll rod mounting bracket
CB-2	Earth	Rear roll rod mounting bracket
CB-3	Stoplight switch	Brake pedal bracket
CB-4	Earth	Radiator fan shroud
CB-5	Thermo sensor	Left of radiator lower tank
CB-6	Idle-up solenoid	Hood latch
CB-7	Diode	Back of ignition coil
CB-8	Earth	Underside of RH headlight
CB-9	Earth	Underside of LH headlight
CB-10	Earth	Right of rear end panel inside surface
CB-11	Earth	Left of rear end panel inside surface
CB-12	Earth	Upper left side of lift gate
CB-13	Luggage compartment light switch	Inside lift gate latch
CE-1	Earth	RH side of engine block
CE-2	Solenoid valve	Inside carburettor
CE-3	Backup light switch	Front of transaxle
C1-1	Earth	Bottom of driver's side instrument panel
C1-2	Seat belt timer	Innermost part of driver's side instrument panel
C1-3	Turn signal flasher unit	Innermost part of driver's side instrument panel
C1-4	Hazard flasher unit	Innermost part of driver's side instrument panel
C1-5	Radiator fan motor relay	Innermost part of driver's side instrument panel
C1-6	ESS relay	Above parcel tray on driver's side
C1-7	Buzzer	Rear side of instrument cluster
C1-8	Connector	Under side of instrument panel

All these four parts are in a relay box

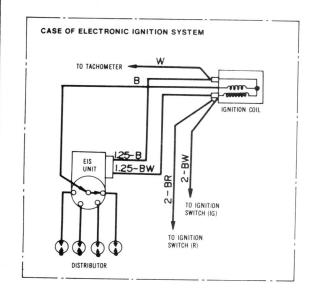

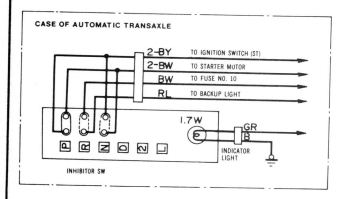

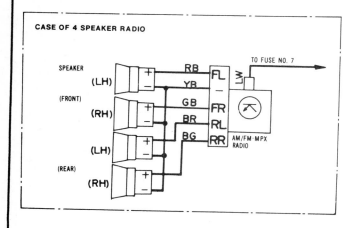

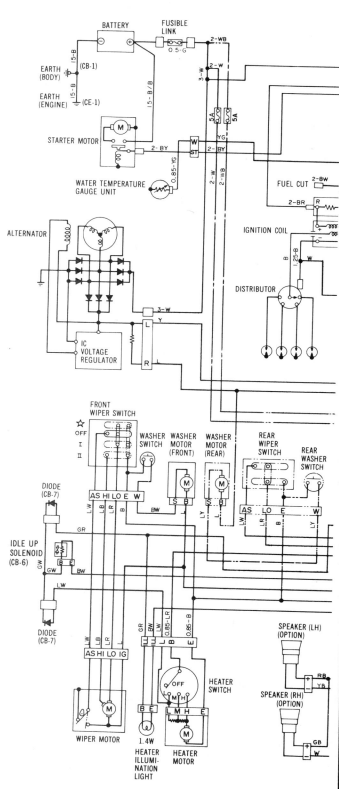

Fig. 9.81 Wiring diagram for left-hand drive cars

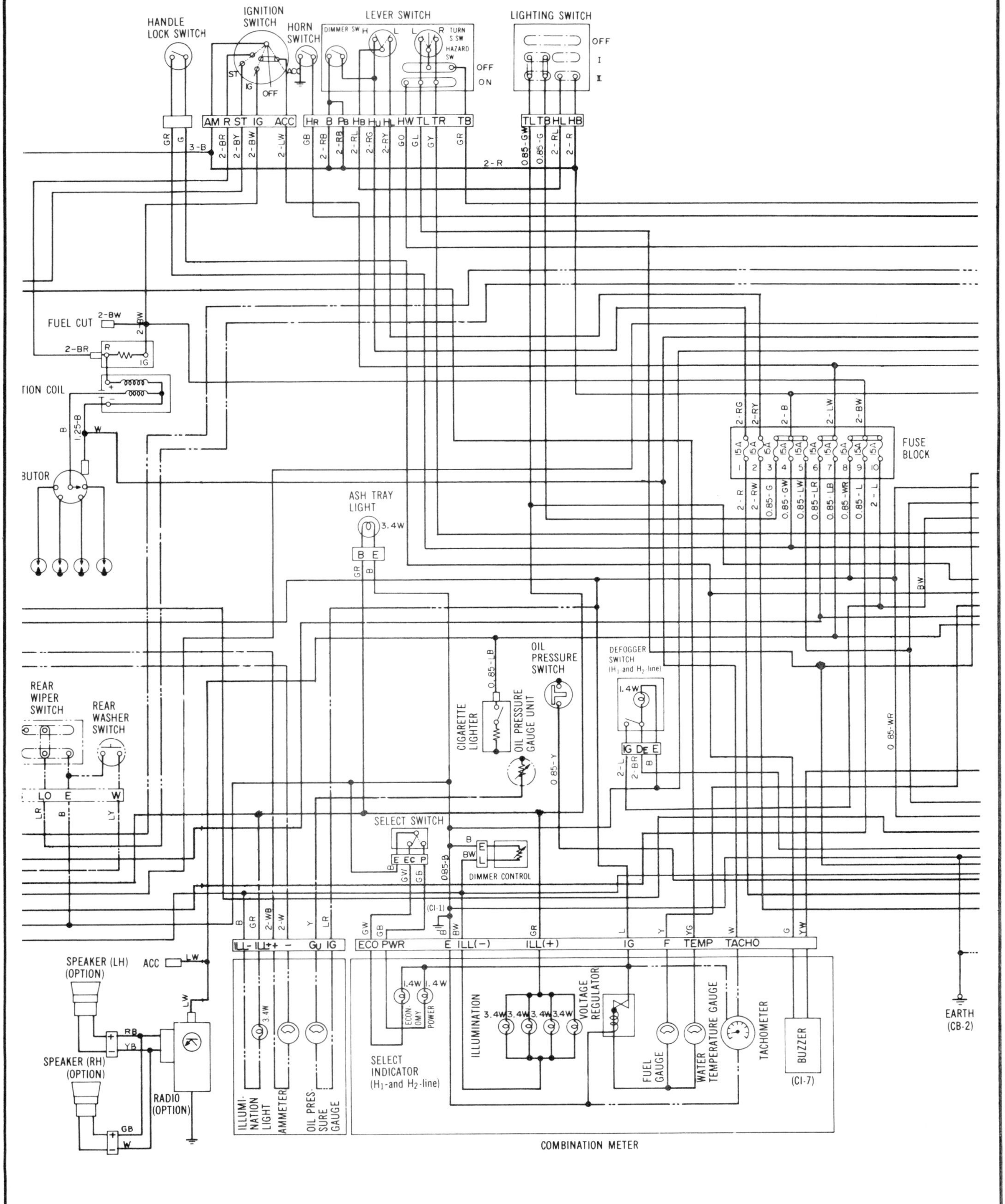

HANDLE LOCK SWITCH

IGNITION SWITCH

HORN SWITCH

LEVER SWITCH

DIMMER SW

TURN S. SW

HAZARD SW

OFF

ON

LIGHTING SWITCH

OFF

I

II

ST

IG

OFF

ACC

AM R ST IG ACC

Hr B Pb HB Hu HL HW TL TR TB

TL TB HL HB

GR

G

3-B

2-BR

2-BY

2-BW

2-LW

GB

2-RB

2-RL

2-RG

GO

GL

GY

GR

2-R

0.85-GW

0.85-G

2-RL

2-R

FUEL CUT

2-BW

2-BW

2-BR

R

IG

TION COIL

B

1.25-B

W

BUTOR

FUSE BLOCK

2-RG

2-RY

2-B

2-LW

2-BW

15A × 10

2-R

2-RW

0.85-G

0.85-LW

0.85-LR

0.85-LB

0.85-WR

0.85-L

2-L

ASH TRAY LIGHT

3.4W

B E

GR

B

OIL PRESSURE SWITCH

0.85-B

OIL PRESSURE GAUGE UNIT

0.85-Y

DEFOGGER SWITCH (H₁ and H₂ line)

1.4W

IG D E E

2-L

2-BR

B

0.85-WR

REAR WIPER SWITCH

REAR WASHER SWITCH

LO E W

LR

B

LY

SELECT SWITCH

E EC P

BI

GV/

GB

0.85-B

B

E

BW

DIMMER CONTROL

(CI-1)

B

BW

SPEAKER (LH) (OPTION)

ACC

LW

LW

RB

YB

SPEAKER (RH) (OPTION)

GB

W

RADIO (OPTION)

B

GR

2-WB

2-W

Y

LR

GW

GB

B

BW

GR

YG

W

G

Y-W

ILL- ILL++ - Gu IG

ECO PWR

E ILL(-)

ILL(+)

IG

F

TEMP

TACHO

ILLUMI-NATION LIGHT

3.4W

AMMETER

OIL PRESSURE GAUGE

1.4W

1.4W

ECONOMY

POWER

SELECT INDICATOR (H₁-and H₂-line)

ILLUMINATION

3.4W 3.4W 3.4W 3.4W

VOLTAGE REGULATOR

FUEL GAUGE

WATER TEMPERATURE GAUGE

TACHOMETER

BUZZER

(CI-7)

EARTH (CB-2)

COMBINATION METER

CIGARETTE LIGHTER

Fig. 9.81 Wiring diagram for left-hand drive cars

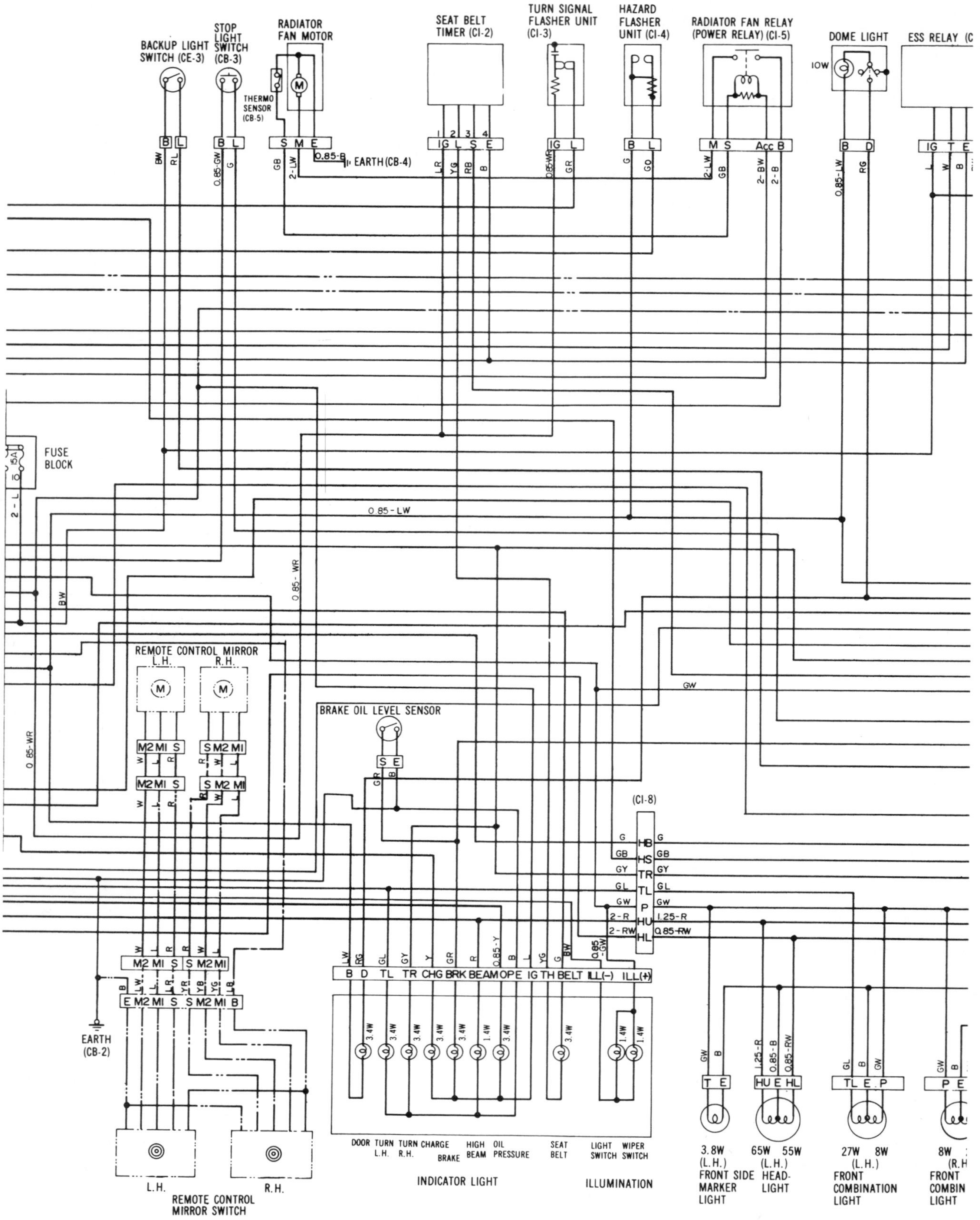

Fig. 9.81 Wiring diagram for left-hand drive cars

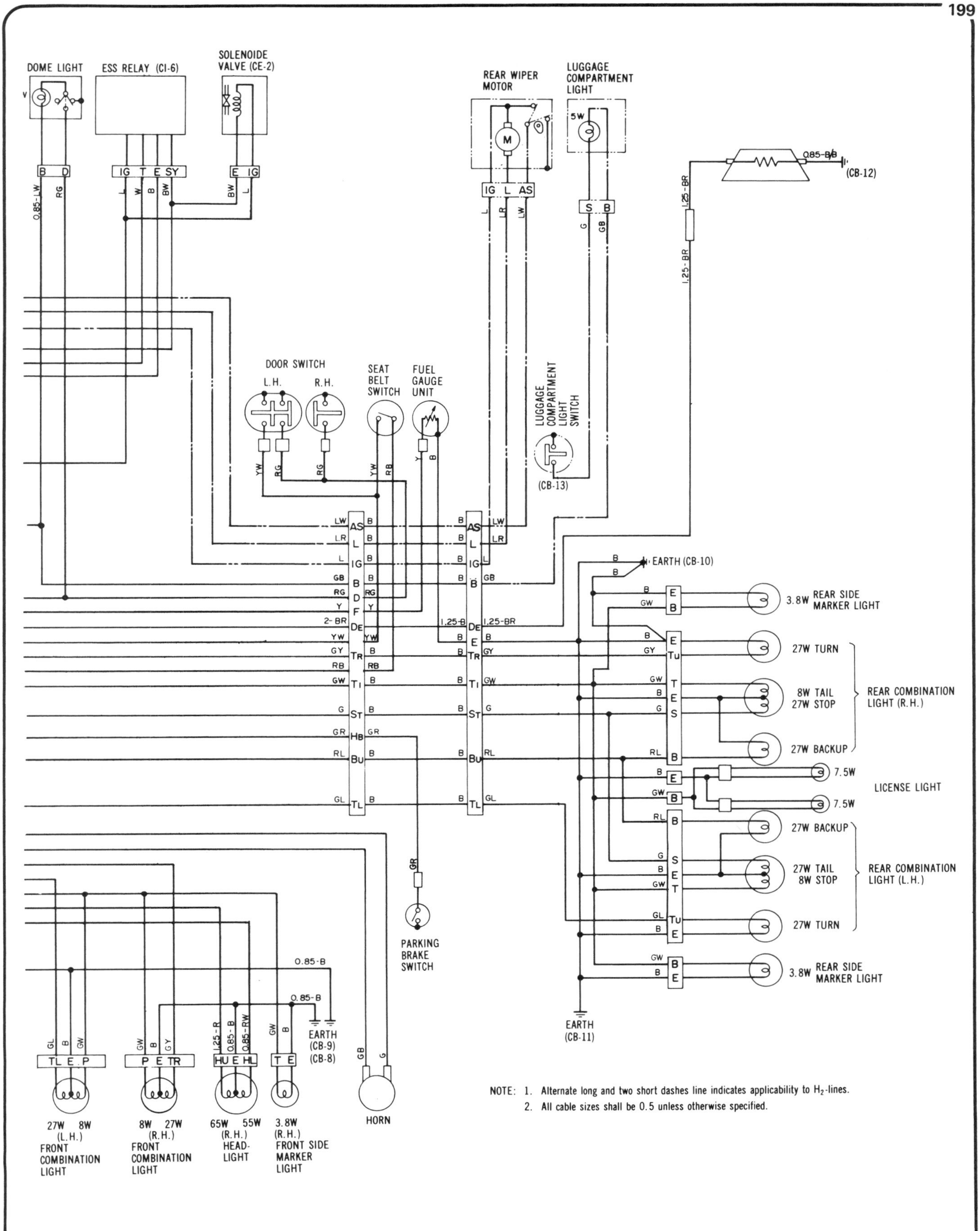

Fig. 9.81 Wiring diagram for left-hand drive cars

Chapter 10 Steering

Contents

Specifications

Type .... Rack and pinion with collapsible type column

Steering angles

Camber	0 to 1° positive
Castor	0° 30' to 0° 70'
King pin inclination	12° 42'
Toe	0.16 in (4.0 mm) toe-in to 0.08 in (2.0 mm) toe-out

Torque wrench settings

	lbf ft	Nm
Column bracket mounting bolts	7	10
Shaft joint pinch bolts	14	19
Steering wheel nuts	34	46
Rack housing mounting bolts	25	34
Damper plug locknut	50	68
Tie-rod balljoint castellated nut	24	33
Tie-rod inner swivel to rack	70	95
Tie-rod locknut	38	52

1 General description

The steering gear is of the rack and pinion type transmitting movement to the arms on the hub carrier (knuckle) through ball jointed tie-rods.

The steering column is of the collapsible type with the shaft at its lower end incorporating two universal joints.

2 Maintenance and inspection

1 The steering system is maintenance-free but regular inspection of all components must be carried out at the intervals specified in the Routine maintenance Section.

2 Inspect the condition of the steering rack bellows for splits. If any are found, renew the bellows immediately as described in Section 4.

3 Inspect the dust excluding rubber seals on the tie-rod balljoints. If they are split, then they must be renewed. It is often difficult to obtain a new seal without buying the complete balljoint assembly – a breakers yard may be able to help here.

4 Check the tie-rod end balljoints for wear. To do this, try and compress the balljoint with a pair of gland nut pliers or similar. If the movement exceeds 0.06 in (1.5 mm) then the joint is worn and must be renewed.

5 Finally, go over all the steering nuts and bolts with a torque wrench occasionally and see that they are correctly tightened.

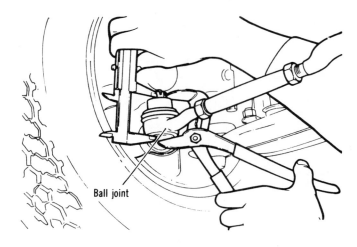

Fig. 10.1 Checking tie-rod and balljoint for wear (Sec 2)

Ball joint

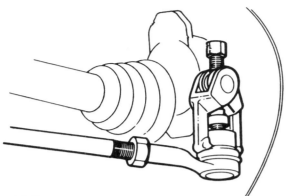

Fig. 10.2 Typical extractor for disconnecting a tie-rod balljoint (Sec 3)

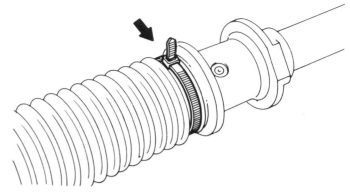

Fig. 10.3 Bellows securing clip (Sec 4)

3 Tie-rod end balljoints – renewal

1   To renew a balljoint or just the dust excluder, raise the front of the car and remove the roadwheel.
2   Pull out the split pin from the castellated nut on the balljoint taper pin (photo). Unscrew the nut. It sometimes happens that the taper pin starts to turn within the eye of the steering arm making it impossible to unscrew the nut. Should this happen, locate a jack under the balljoint and apply pressure to force it into the eye.
3   A balljoint separator will now be required to separate the taper pin from the eye of the steering eye. Several types are available from motor accessory shops. Striking the eye with hammers to dislodge the taper pin is not recommended and will probably only cause damage to adjacent components.
4   Hold the tie-rod quite still using an open-ended spanner on the flats provided and then release the tie-rod end locknut.
5   Unscrew and remove the balljoint counting the number of turns required to disconnect it.
6   If only the balljoint dust excluding seal is to be renewed, change it. If the complete balljoint assembly is to be renewed, obtain the new one, making sure it is of the correct type.
7   Screw the balljoint onto the tie-rod by the equivalent number of turns as was recorded at removal.
8   Reconnect the balljoint to the steering arm, tighten the nut to the specified torque and fit a new split pin.
9   Refit the roadwheel and lower the car.

10 The front wheel alignment must now be checked and adjusted as described in Section 10. If this work is to be carried out by your dealer, tighten the balljoint locknut and the bellows smaller securing band so that the car can be driven to his premises at the earliest opportunity.

4 Steering rack bellows – renewal

1   Remove the tie-rod end balljoint and its locknut as described in the preceding Section.
2   Remove the securing bands from the rack bellows. These are of the nylon ratchet type.
3   Withdraw the bellows and remove them.
4   If any dirt has entered through the defective bellows, wipe clean and apply some of the specified lubricant.
5   Fit the new bellows; fit and tighten the large clip but only locate, do not tighten the smaller one yet.
6   Screw the balljoint onto the tie-rod by the same number of turns as was recorded at removal, reconnect it and check the front wheel alignment as described in Section 10.
7   Tighten the smaller clip.

5 Steering wheel – removal and refitting

1   Prise off the horn pad from the centre of the steering wheel (photo).

3.2 Tie-rod end balljoint

5.1 Removing the horn pad

5.2 Unscrewing the steering wheel nut

5.4 Reverse side of steering wheel hub

7.3 Steering column switches

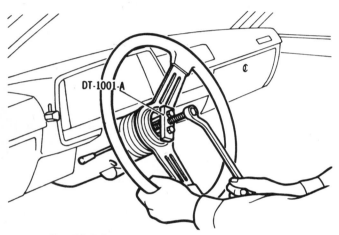

Fig. 10.4 Removing the steering wheel (Sec 5)

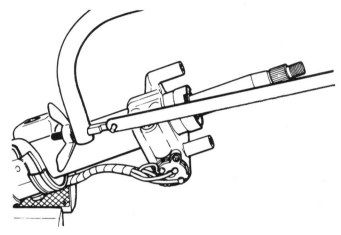

Fig. 10.5 Cutting slot in steering column lockbolt (Sec 6)

2   Unscrew and remove the steering wheel retaining nut which is now exposed (photo).
3   The steering wheel should now be drawn off the shaft using a suitable puller. Two small tapped holes are provided in the steering wheel hub for this purpose. Attempting to jar the wheel off the shaft with the hands may damage the inbuilt collapsible feature of the shaft.
4   Refitting is a reversal of removal but make sure that the front roadwheels are in the straight ahead position when the steering wheel is offered to the shaft (wheel spokes horizontal in lower half of rim) (photo).

6   Steering column lock – removal and refitting

1   Remove the steering wheel as described in the preceding Section.
2   Shear head bolts are used to retain the lock to the column and to be able to remove them, a slot must be cut in their heads. Do this with a hacksaw which will also mean damaging the lock clamp but as the purpose of the operation is to renew the lock anyway this is not important.
3   Withdraw the lock and detach the ignition switch (one screw).
4   When fitting the new lock, align it with the boss on the column and test its operation with the ignition key before fully tightening the new screws until their heads break off.

7   Steering column – removal, overhaul and refitting

1   Remove the steering wheel as described in Section 5.
2   Remove the steering column shroud.
3   Disconnect the wiring harness plugs and withdraw the column switches (two screws) (photo).

4   Working at the lower end of the column, unscrew and remove the coupling pinch bolt.
5   Unscrew and remove the steering column bracket mounting bolts and withdraw the shaft/column from the car interior.
6   To remove the lower universally jointed section of the shaft, extract the pinch bolt that secures the lower coupling to the pinion shaft of the steering gear.
7   Unscrew the dust cover bolts and withdraw the shaft/cover into the car interior.
8   Withdraw the bearing from the dust cover and carefully remove the dust cover from the shaft joint. Apart from renewing the bearing or dust cover, wear in the universal joints can only be rectified by complete replacement of the lower shaft/joint assembly.
9   To dismantle the main column/shaft, extract the circlip from the upper end and unlock the column lock using the ignition key. Tap the shaft out of the column tube using a plastic faced hammer applied to the upper end of the shaft.
10 Where necessary, remove the steering column lock as described in Section 6.
11 The steering column bracket is secured with a plain headed screw and a slot must be cut in it in order to be able to remove it with a screwdriver.
12 The column bearing can be removed but wear in the shaft itself or deformation of the collapsible convoluted section will mean purchasing new components. Never attempt to straighten the shaft or column tube.
13 Reassemble by inserting the shaft into the column and secure with the circlip.
14 If the column bracket was removed, fit it using a new shear head bolt, tightening it until the head breaks off.
15 Apply grease to the lower bearing and fit it into the bottom of the column tube.
16 Fit the column lock as described in Section 6.
17 Fit the bearing and dust cover to the jointed shaft section. Make

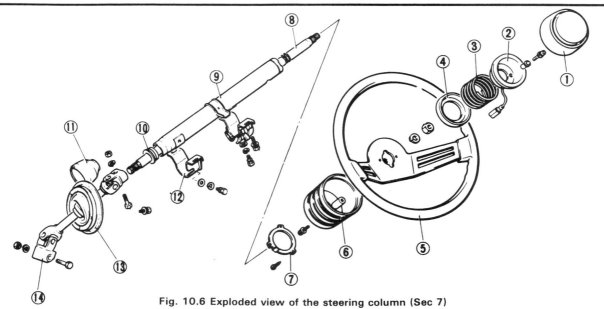

Fig. 10.6 Exploded view of the steering column (Sec 7)

1	Horn button	5	Steering wheel	9	Steering column tube	12 Clamp
2	Contact plate	6	Cover	10	Lower bearing	13 Dust excluding cover
3	Horn spring	7	Horn contact	11	Boot	14 Universal joint
4	Seat	8	Steering shaft			

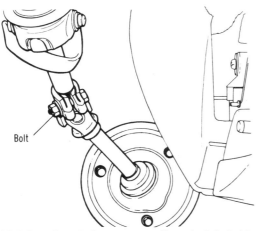

Fig. 10.7 Steering shaft upper coupling pinch bolt (Sec 7)

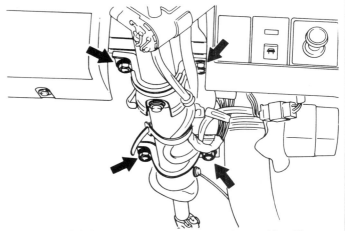

Fig. 10.8 Steering column retaining clamps (Sec 7)

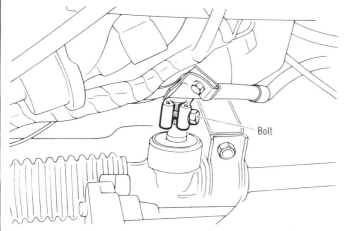

Fig. 10.9 Steering shaft lower coupling pinch bolt (Sec 7)

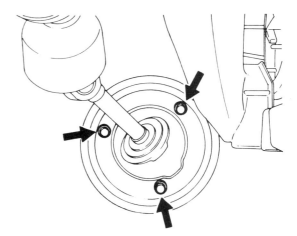

Fig. 10.10 Dust cover securing bolts (Sec 7)

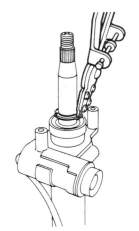

Fig. 10.11 Extracting the steering shaft circlip (Sec 7)

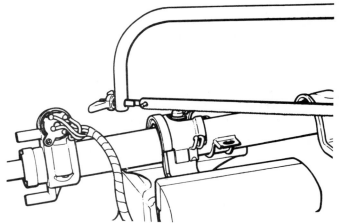

Fig. 10.12 Cutting slot in column clamp screw (Sec 7)

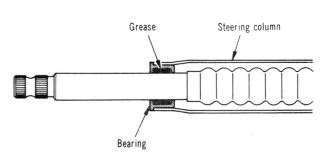

Fig. 10.13 Lubrication of shaft/column bearing (Sec 7)

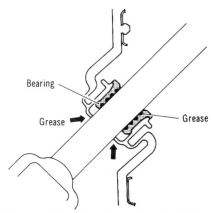

Fig. 10.14 Correct orientation of steering shaft/dust cover bearing
and dust excluding cover (Sec 7)

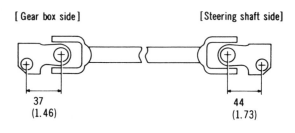

mm (in.)

Fig. 10.15 Correct orientation of steering shaft and jointed pivots
(Sec 7)

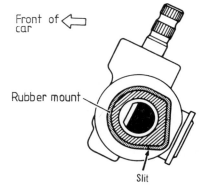

Fig. 10.16 Fitting diagram for steering rack housing mounting
rubber insulator (Sec 8)

sure that the bearing is the correct way round and pack grease into the
lips of the dust cover and into the bearing grooves.
18 Fit the jointed shaft section to the rack pinion making quite sure
that the shaft is the right way round by measuring the distances
between the centres of the joint pivot pin and the pinch bolt (Fig.
10.15). Tighten the coupling pinch bolt.
19 Fit the main column/shaft, connecting the lower end of the shaft
to the joint coupling splines and the upper clamps (bolts only finger
tight).
20 Adjust the position of the main column as necessary to allow the
pinch bolt of the upper coupling to pass through the groove in the
steering shaft.
21 Tighten the pinch bolts and the column bracket bolts to the
specified torque.

22 Fit and tighten the dust cover bolts.
23 Check that the front roadwheels are in the straight ahead position
and fit the steering wheel as described in Section 5.

8 Steering rack and pinion – removal and refitting

1 Jack up the front of the car and remove the front roadwheels.
2 Unscrew and remove the pinch bolt which secures the universal
joint of the lower steering shaft to the pinion of the steering gear.
3 Disconnect both tie-rod balljoints from the steering arms of the
hub carriers (knuckles) using a balljoint extractor as described in
Section 3.

4   Unbolt and remove the steering gear from the crossmember at the bottom of the engine compartment rear bulkhead (photo).
5   Refitting is a reversal of removal but make sure that the mounting clamp rubber insulators are positioned with their slits facing downward.
6   Tighten all bolts to the specified torque, no tighter, or the rack housing may distort.

9   Steering rack and pinion – overhaul

1   With the rack removed from the car, clean away any external dirt using paraffin and a stiff brush or a water soluble solvent.
2   If the steering gear has been in use for a high mileage, it may be more economical to purchase a complete new or factory reconditioned assembly rather than overhaul the old unit.
3   If the gear is to be overhauled, gently grip the tubular section of the housing in a vice well padded with rags.
4   Release the securing locknuts and unscrew the tie-rod balljoint assemblies as described in Section 3.
5   Release the right-hand bellows securing clip (fitted position) and pull off the bellows.
6   Relieve the staking at the rack end ball swivel.
7   Extend the rack fully so that it can be gripped carefully in a vice fitted with jaw protectors.

8.4 Steering rack mountings

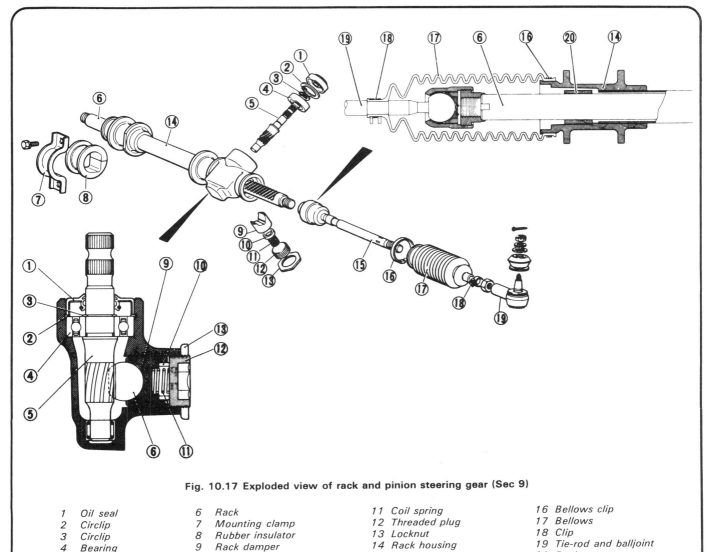

Fig. 10.17 Exploded view of rack and pinion steering gear (Sec 9)

1 Oil seal	6 Rack	11 Coil spring	16 Bellows clip
2 Circlip	7 Mounting clamp	12 Threaded plug	17 Bellows
3 Circlip	8 Rubber insulator	13 Locknut	18 Clip
4 Bearing	9 Rack damper	14 Rack housing	19 Tie-rod and balljoint
5 Pinion	10 Rubber cushion	15 Tie-rod	20 Bush

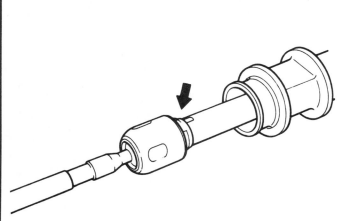

Fig. 10.18 Rack and ball swivel staking (Sec 9)

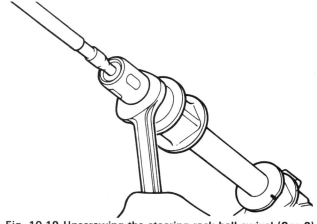

Fig. 10.19 Unscrewing the steering rack ball swivel (Sec 9)

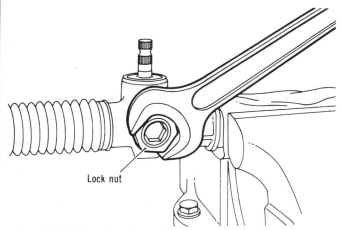

Lock nut

Fig. 10.20 Releasing the rack damper plug locknut (Sec 9)

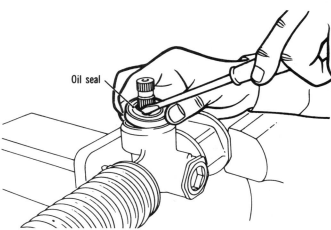

Oil seal

Fig. 10.21 Removing the pinion oil seal (Sec 9)

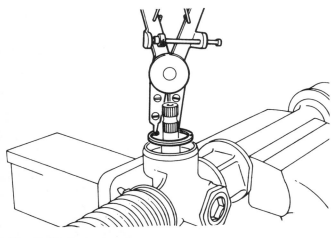

Fig. 10.22 Extracting the pinion bearing large circlip (Sec 9)

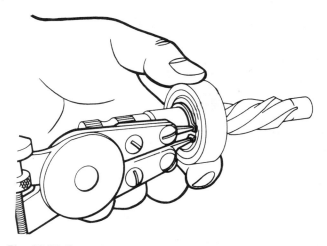

Fig. 10.23 Extracting the pinion bearing small circlip (Sec 9)

8   Using an open-ended spanner, unscrew the ball swivel from the end of the rack.

9   Hold the tubular part of the rack housing once again in the vice and unscrew the locknut from the damper plug.

10 Unscrew and remove the damper plug. This will require a special socket but one can be fabricated from a large nut using a little imagination and welding it to a suitable extension bar.

11 Extract the damper spring, the cushion rubber and the rack damper from the pinion housing.

12 Prise out the pinion oil seal.

13 Extract the circlip and push out the pinion complete with bearing.

14 Extract the bearing retaining circlip. Support the bearing centre track and press the pinion from it. If the bearing is to be renewed then a two-legged extractor can be used to remove it but after removal, it will not be fit for further service.

15 Grip the tie-rod which is still attached to the rack and withdraw the rack from the housing. Take care not to damage the bushes.

16 Inspect all components for wear and damage and renew as necessary. The free length of the damper spring should be 0.55 in (13.9 mm); if it has been compressed below this, fit a new one.

17 Renew the oil seal as a matter of routine.

18 Commence reassembly by pressing the new bearing onto the pinion. Apply pressure only to the inner track. Fit the circlip.

19 Apply some of the recommended grease to the rack, the pinion, bush and needle roller bearing. Take care not to seal the air passage in the housing bush with grease.

20 Insert the rack into the pinion housing end of the rack tube.

21 Fit the pinion so that it meshes with the rack and fit a securing circlip. Select a circlip from one of the three sizes available to give the minimum pinion endfloat.

22 Grease the lips of the oil seal and fit it squarely. Set the rack centrally.

23 Fit the pinion damper cushion, spring and damper plug. Pack the pinion damper with grease.

24 Tighten the damper plug to between 5 and 11 lbf ft (7 and 15 Nm). Back off the plug between 30° and 60° and then tighten the locknut.

25 Screw the tie-rod ball swivel to the end of the rack, tightening to the specified torque. At this stage, check the ball swivels for wear. The correct swivel torque with a spring balance attached to the end of the tie-rod should be between 1.4 and 3.6 lbf ft (2.0 and 4.9 Nm). This can be judged fairly accurately to be correct if the tie-rod does not fall under its own weight neither is it very stiff to deflect with hand pressure.

26 If the ball swivels are loose or very stiff when tightened to the correct torque then they must be renewed, no adjustment is provided.

27 If the ball swivel torque is correct, stake it to the rack.

28 Smear the ball swivel with grease and fit the bellows. Tighten the inner securing clip but not the outer (smaller) one yet.

29 With the steering rack assembled, the starting force required to turn the pinion from the centre rack position should be checked. This can be done by winding a cord round the splines of the pinion and attaching the cord to a spring balance. A force of between 11 and 66 lb (5 to 30 kg) will be required to start it turning. To measure the pinion preload over the full rack travel will require the use of a special torque wrench. The preload should be between 3.6 and 9.6 lbf in (0.4 to 1.1 Nm) to keep the pinion turning once it has started.

30 If these settings are not complied with, try minor adjustment of the rack damper plug.

31 Tighten the bellows outer securing clip.

10 Front wheel alignment and steering angles

1   Accurate front wheel alignment is essential for good steering behaviour and even tyre wear. Before considering the steering angles, check that the tyres are correctly inflated, that the front wheels are not buckled, the hub bearings are not worn or out of adjustment and that the steering linkage is in good order without slackness or wear in the joints or bushes.

2   Wheel alignment consists of three factors:

Camber is the angle at which the wheels are inclined from the vertical when viewed from the front of the car. The camber angle is positive when the tops of the wheels are tilted outboard. The camber angle is set in production and is not adjustable.

Castor is the angle between the steering axis and a vertical line

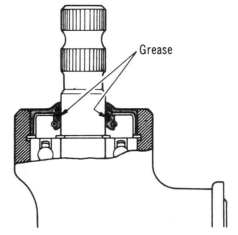

Fig. 10.24 Pinion oil seal installed (Sec 9)

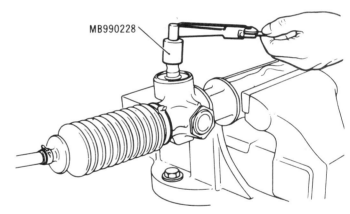

Fig. 10.25 Measuring pinion preload (Sec 9)

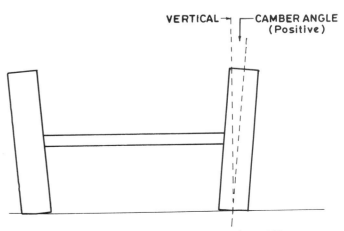

Fig. 10.26 Camber angle diagram (Sec 10)

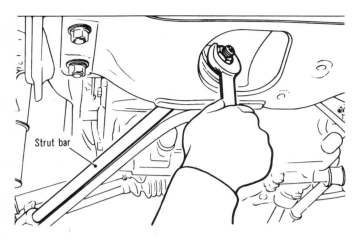

Fig. 10.27 Adjusting a radius rod (strut lever) for castor correction (Sec 10)

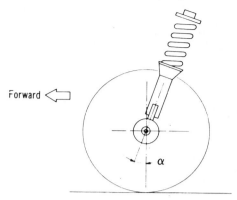

Fig. 10.28 Castor angle diagram (Sec 10)

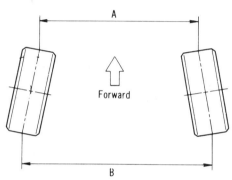

Fig. 10.29 Toe-in diagram (A less than B) (Sec 10)

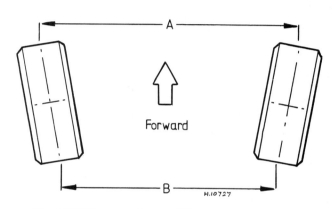

Fig. 10.30 Toe-out diagram (B less than A) (Sec 10)

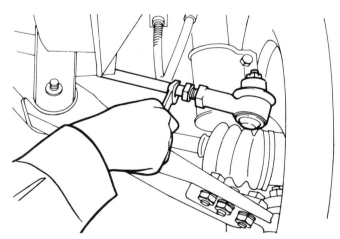

Fig. 10.31 Adjusting the length of a tie rod (Sec 10)

when viewed from each side of the car. Very slight variations in castor can be made by turning the anchor nut on the end of the radius rod (strut bar) but as very accurate equipment is required to measure the castor angle, leave this work to your dealer.

Toe-in is the amount by which the distance between the front inside edges of the roadwheel rims (measured at hub height) varies from the dimension measured at the rear inside edges of the wheel rim.

3   Toe-in or toe-out checks are best carried out with modern setting equipment but a reasonably accurate alternative checking and adjustment procedure can be carried out in the following way.

4   Position the car on level ground with the front wheels set in the straight ahead attitude.

5   Obtain or make up a tracking gauge. These are available from motor accessory stores or one can be made up from a length of tubing, cranked to clear the engine/transmission lower surfaces and fitted with a setscrew and locknut at one end.

6   Using the gauge, measure the distance between the inner rims of the wheels (at hub height) at the rear of the wheels.

7   Push the car in its forward direction of travel so that the roadwheels turn through half a turn (180°), then measure the distance between the inside edges of the rims (at hub height) at the front of the roadwheels. This last measurement should differ from the previous one by the amount given in the Specifications.

8   Where the toe is found to be incorrect, slacken the locknuts on both tie-rods and rotate the rods equally until on rechecking, the alignment is found to be correct. Do not turn the tie-rods by more than $\frac{1}{4}$ turn before rechecking. Turn both rods in the same direction (clockwise or anti-clockwise) when the rod is viewed from the centre of the steering rack housing.

9   Tighten the tie-rod locknuts at the same time holding the tie-rod

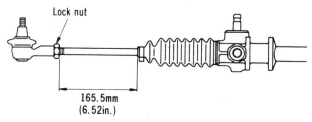

Fig. 10.32 Tie rod basic setting diagram (Sec 10)

with an open ended spanner fitted to its flats and the balljoint at the centre of its arc of travel.

10 It is very important to keep the lengths of the track rods equal otherwise the position of the steering wheel spokes will alter and the roadwheel steering angles on turns will be incorrect causing scrubbing of the tyre treads. If new components have been fitted, the tie-rods can be set equally as shown in Fig. 10.32 to provide a basic starting point for adjustment. The measurement is between the end face of the

locknut and the end of the rubber bellows assuming that the neck of the bellows is correctly seated in the groove in the tie-rod.

11 After setting the wheel alignment in this way, adjust the front wheel alignment using a tracking gauge, again rotating the tie-rods equally.

12 When alignment is correct, ensure that the bellows are not twisted and tighten the tie-rod locknuts without moving the tie-rod and holding the balljoint in the centre of its arc of travel.

11 Fault diagnosis – steering

Symptom	Reason(s)
Stiff steering	Dry rack or column bushes Soft tyres Corroded tie-rod balljoints Rack housing bolts overtightened Incorrect pinion preload
Car wanders or pulls to one side	Excessive play in rack, tie-rod end balljoints Incorrect tyre pressures Binding brake Incorrect wheel alignment Bent track control arm or hub carrier (knuckle)
Poor self centring action	Soft tyres Rack housing bolts overtightened Excessive pinion preload Incorrect wheel alignment Corroded tie-rod end balljoints

Chapter 11 Suspension

Contents

Specifications

Front suspension type .... Macpherson strut, coil spring with anti-roll bar

Rear suspension type .... Trailing arm, telescopic hydraulic shock absorbers and coil springs. Anti-roll bar according to model

Roadwheels
Type .... Steel or aluminium according to model
Size .... 4.5J x 13

Tyres
Size .... 155 SR13 or 175/70 SR13 according to model. A few models may be fitted with 6.15-13-4PR crossply for operation in certain territories

Pressures:
Radial ply .... 24 lbf/in² (17 kgf/cm²)
Crossply .... 28 lbf/in² (1.9 kg/cm²)

Torque wrench settings	lbf ft	Nm
Front suspension		
Driveshaft nut	120	163
Radius rod nuts	60	82
Track control arm to balljoint	70	95
Hub to disc	35	48
Hub carrier to suspension strut	60	82
Tie-rod balljoint to hub carrier	24	33
Anti-roll bar to crossmember	18	25
Anti-roll bar to radius rod	5	7
Suspension strut piston rod nut	35	48
Suspension strut upper mounting nuts	10	14
Track control arm inner pivot bolt	5	7
Crossmember securing bolts	60	82
Rear suspension		
Crosstube end nuts	50	68
Crosstube to body clamp bolts	50	68
Shock absorber mounting bolts	55	75
Roadwheels		
Roadwheel nuts:		
Steel wheels	55	75
Aluminium wheels	65	88

1 General description

The front suspension is of the MacPherson strut type with track control arms located by radius rods (drag struts).

An anti-roll bar is fitted to control roll on cornering.

The driveshaft/hubs are supported in a hub carrier (knuckle) which is bolted to the base of the suspension strut and the track control arm balljoint.

The rear suspension is of the trailing arm type and incorporates coil springs and telescopic hydraulic dampers. An anti-roll bar is also fitted at the rear of the car on some models.

The roadwheels may be of steel or aluminium construction according to model and the tyres are radial ply type, except for certain territories.

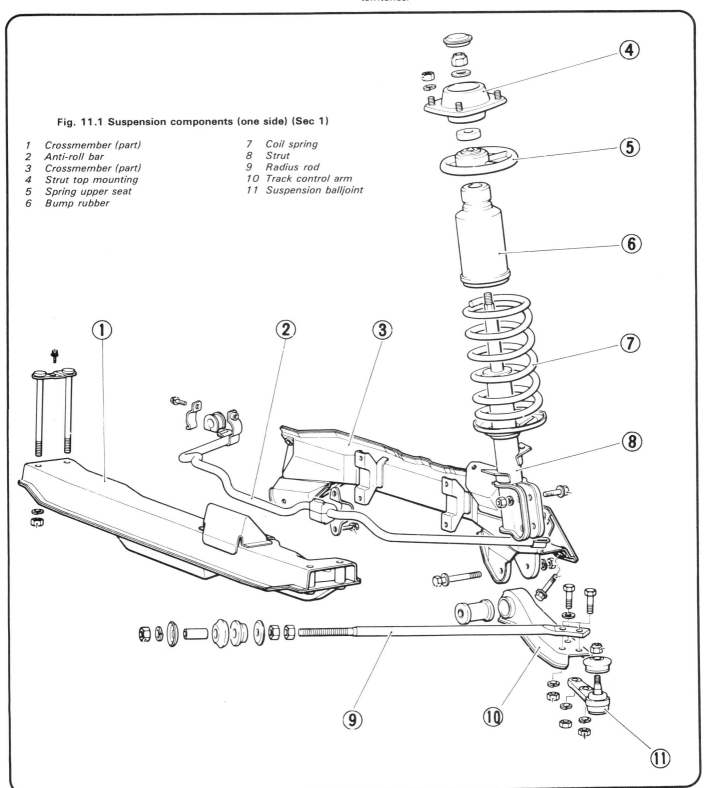

Fig. 11.1 Suspension components (one side) (Sec 1)

1	Crossmember (part)	7	Coil spring
2	Anti-roll bar	8	Strut
3	Crossmember (part)	9	Radius rod
4	Strut top mounting	10	Track control arm
5	Spring upper seat	11	Suspension balljoint
6	Bump rubber		

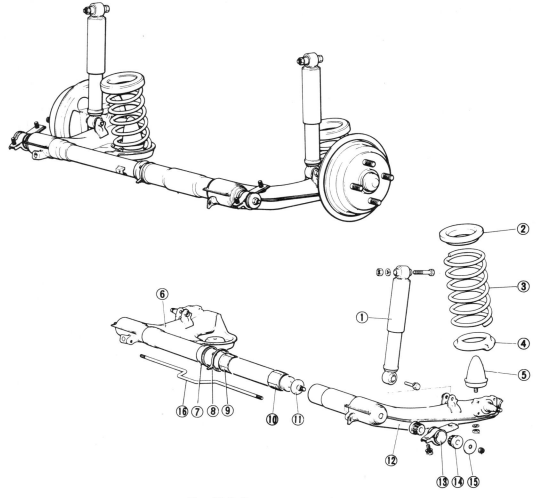

Fig. 11.2 Rear suspension (Sec 1)

1 Shock absorber	5 Bump rubber	9 Bush	13 Attachment clamp
2 Spring upper seat	6 Suspension arm (right)	10 Bush	14 Flexible bush
3 Coil spring	7 Dust cover	11 Stop	15 Washer
4 Spring lower seat	8 Clip	12 Suspension arm (left)	16 Anti-roll bar

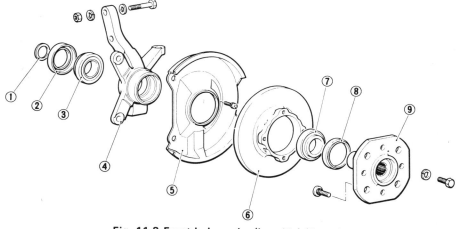

Fig. 11.3 Front hub carrier (knuckle) (Sec 2)

1 Spacer	4 Hub carrier (knuckle)	7 Outboard bearing
2 Oil seal	5 Disc shield	8 Oil seal
3 Inboard bearing	6 Disc	9 Hub

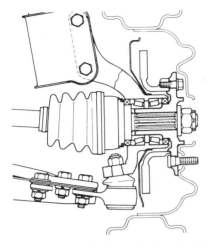

Fig. 11.4 Part-sectional view of a front hub (Sec 2)

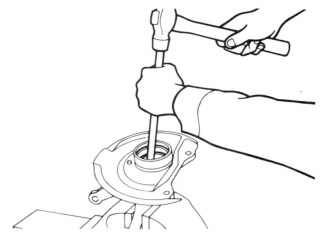

Fig. 11.5 Fitting a bearing track to hub carrier (Sec 2)

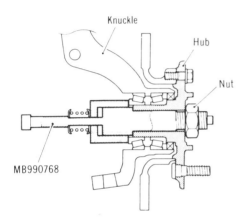

Fig. 11.6 Hub bearing preload spacer tool (Sec 2)

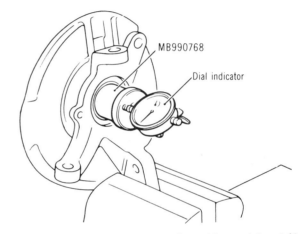

Fig. 11.7 Dial gauge fitted in conjunction with special tool (Sec 2)

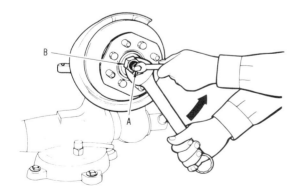

Fig. 11.8 Checking hub bearing preload (Sec 2)

For A and B see text

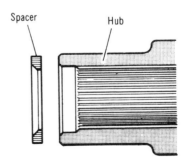

Fig. 11.9 Hub bearing preload spacer (Sec 2)

2 Front hub carrier (knuckle) – removal, overhaul and refitting

1   Remove the driveshaft as described in Chapter 7. Retain the bearing spacers.
2   Unbolt the disc brake caliper, slide it off the disc and tie it up out of the way without disconnecting the hydraulic flexible hose.
3   Disconnect the tie-rod end balljoint from the steering arm on the hub carrier.
4   Disconnect the track control arm balljoint from the hub carrier.

5   Unscrew the two bolts which secure the hub carrier to the base of the suspension strut.
6   Remove the carrier complete with disc and hub.
7   Tap the hub out of the carrier using a plastic faced hammer.
8   Unbolt and remove the brake disc from the hub.
9   The bearings should now be wiped clean and the oil seals prised from their seats and discarded.
10 If the bearings are in good condition, pack them with fresh grease and reassemble the disc, hub and hub carrier. Fit new oil seals.
11 The hub carrier can be refitted using the original preload spacers.

12 If the bearings are worn or the hub or carrier is to be renewed, proceed as follows.

13 Remove the bearing tracks using a drift and hammer.

14 Clean out the bearing recesses and drive the outer tracks of the new bearings into position in the hub carrier.

15 Apply lubricant generously to the bearing tracks.

16 Bolt the disc and hub together.

17 Fit the inner race of the outboard bearing to the hub carrier and then fit the outboard oil seal.

18 Support the inner race of the bearing just fitted and fit the hub into the carrier, preferably using a press.

19 Fit the inner race of the inboard bearing.

20 The thickness of the new bearing preload spacers must now be determined in the following way.

21 A special tool (MB 990768) must now be borrowed or purchased. Fit the tool as shown in Fig. 11.6 and tighten the nut to a torque of 14 lbf ft (20 Nm).

22 Stop the tool from rotating by holding the flats on its end. Rotate the hub to settle the bearings.

23 Fit a dial gauge to the tool and load it with 0.2 in (5.0 mm) of travel. Now zero the gauge.

24 Hold the special tool (A) from rotating and unscrew the nut (B) noting the total dial gauge reading (Fig. 11.8). Repeat the measuring operation aand take the average. Select a spacer from the following table and fit it to the inboard end of the hub, chamfered side to hub carrier. The hub bearings will now be correctly preloaded when the driveshaft nut is tightened to torque.

Dial gauge reading	Spacer thickness	Colour code	Part number
0.137 to 0.141 in (3.4 to 3.59 mm)	0.139 in (3.55 mm)	Red	MB 109126
0.141 to 0.146 in (3.59 to 3.71 mm)	0.144 in (3.67 mm)	White	MB 109127
0.146 to 0.151 in (3.71 to 3.83 mm)	0.149 in (3.79 mm)	Black	MB 109128
0.151 to 0.156 in (3.83 to 3.95 mm)	0.154 in (3.91 mm)	Yellow	MB 109129
0.156 to 0.160 in (3.95 to 4.07 mm)	0.159 in (4.03 mm)	Blue	MB 109165

25 Refitting the hub carrier is a reversal of removal; tighten all bolts to the specified torque.

26 The driveshaft nut should be tightened fully after the weight of the car is on its roadwheels.

3　Front anti-roll bar and radius rod – removal and refitting

1　Unbolt and remove the splash shield from under the engine compartment.

2　Unscrew and remove the two bolts which secure the anti-roll bar to the track control arm on each side of the car. On each side one of these bolts holds the track control arm and suspension balljoints together so do not move the car once the bolts have been removed (photo).

3　Measure the length of exposed thread on the forward end of each radius road and record it.

4　Unscrew the nuts from the radius rods and remove the rods and anti-roll bar (photo).

5　Refitting is a reversal of removal. If a new radius rod is being fitted, note that the left-hand one is marked with an 'L'.

6　If the original components have been refitted, set the exposed part of the radius rod threads to the length recorded at dismantling and the castor angle (see Chapter 10) should not be altered. If new components have been fitted, have the castor angle checked by your dealer.

7　Tighten all nuts and bolts to the specified torque with the weight of the car on its roadwheels.

3.2 Front suspension lower balljoint disconnected

3.4 Radius rod and anti-roll bar mountings

Fig. 11.10 Left-hand radius rod identification (Sec 3)

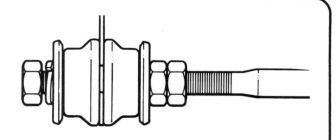

Fig. 11.11 Radius rod bush arrangement (Sec 3)

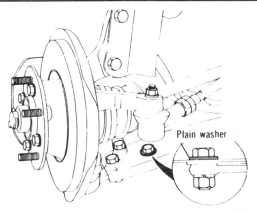

Fig. 11.12 Location of balljoint bolt plain washer (Sec 4)

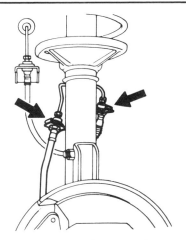

Fig. 11.13 Brake line attachment to front strut (Sec 5)

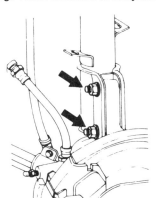

Fig. 11.14 Hub carrier attachment to suspension strut (Sec 5)

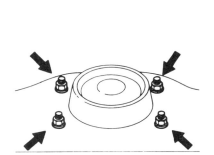

Fig. 11.15 Strut upper mounting nuts (Sec 5)

5.4 Strut to hub carrier (knuckle) bolts

4 Front suspension track control arm – removal and refitting

1 Unbolt the radius rod and anti-roll bar from the track control arm.
2 Unscrew and remove the remaining bolt which holds the balljoint to the track control arm.
3 Unscrew and remove the pivot bolt which secures the inner end of the track control arm to the crossmember. Remove the control arm.
4 Take the opportunity to check the balljoint for wear. If it turns very freely in its seat or up and down movement can be detected, it must be renewed after removing it from the hub carrier with a balljoint extractor.
5 If the flexible bush in the track control arm is worn, a new one can be fitted. Although a press will simplify removal and refitting the bush, the use of a bolt, nuts and distance pieces will accomplish the same result especially if the bush is smeared with soapy water to ease fitting.
6 Refitting is a reversal of removal. Make sure that the plain washer is fitted under the inboard securing bolt of the balljoint.

5 Front suspension strut – removal and refitting

1 Jack up the front of the car and support it securely on stands placed under the frame members.
2 Remove the roadwheel.
3 Disconnect the flexible hoses from the rigid brake hydraulic lines at the strut brackets. Plug the openings to prevent loss of fluid and the entry of dirt.
4 Support the base of the track control arm and then remove the bolts which hold the hub carrier (knuckle) to the base of the strut (photo).
5 Remove the nuts from the strut top mounting.
6 Withdraw the complete strut assembly from under the wing.
7 Refitting is a reversal of removal, tighten all bolts to the specified torque and bleed the hydraulic system as described in Chapter 8.

6 Front suspension strut – overhaul

1 With the strut removed from the car as described in the preceding Section, clean away external dirt.
2 The coil spring must now be compressed. Suitable compressors can be obtained from most motor accessory stores.
3 With the spring compressed, hold the spring upper seat with a special tool (MB 990775) or a substitute device while the nut at the top of the strut piston rod is unscrewed.
4 Remove the spring upper seat, the spring (still compressed) and the bump rubber.
5 A choice is now available before proceeding. If the unit is simply leaking fluid, it can be repaired. If it is badly worn after having been in

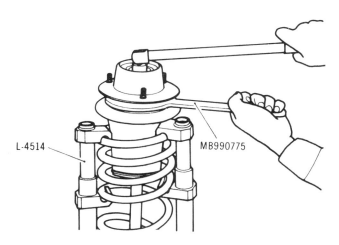

Fig. 11.16 Removing strut piston rod nut (Sec 6)

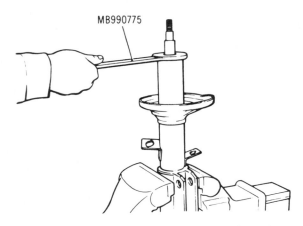

Fig. 11.17 Unscrewing strut gland nut (Sec 6)

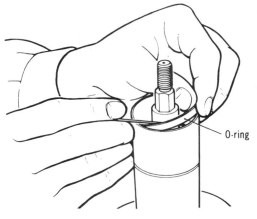

Fig. 11.18 Removing strut oil seal (Sec 6)

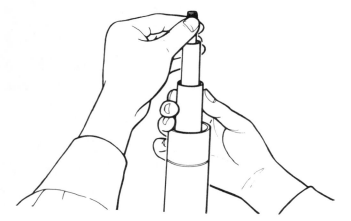

Fig. 11.19 Withdrawing strut piston rod/guide (Sec 6)

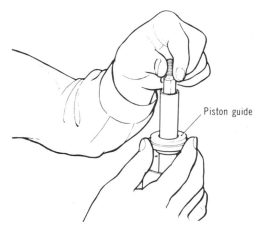

Fig. 11.20 Refitting strut piston guide (Sec 6)

service for a high mileage it can be renewed (less spring and upper mounting) or a cartridge insert can be fitted by following the particular manufacturer's instructions.

Repair
6   Secure the strut vertically in a vice.
7   Using a pin wrench or special tool MB 990775, unscrew the gland nut from the top of the strut.
8   Drain the fluid and discard the small square section sealing ring.
9   Slowly withdraw the piston rod/guide out of the tubular casing of the strut.
10   Repair kits are available to include some or all of the dismantled items as wear dictates the need.
11   Observe absolute cleanliness during reassembly and apply clean fluid to all components as they are refitted.
12   Fit the piston rod into the cylinder and then fit the piston/cylinder into the strut casing.
13   Fill the strut with 240 cc of shock absorber fluid. This must be done slowly while moving the piston rod up and down so that trapped air can escape.
14   Fit the piston guide.
15   Fit a new square section seal.
16   Tape over the threads of the piston rod to prevent damage to the lips of the oil seal nut. Screw in the nut until the nut makes metal to metal contact with the strut tube.
17   Fit the compressed spring, the bump rubber, the spring seat, the insulator and washer.
18   Align the D-shaped hole in the spring seat correctly with the piston rod.
19   Hold the spring upper seat with the special tool and tighten the self-locking nut at the top of the piston rod to the specified torque.

6.21 Front suspension strut upper mounting

20   Gently release the coil spring compressor and remove it, making sure that the ends of the spring coils are correctly seated in their seat grooves.
21   Pack grease into the strut upper bearing, keeping it away from rubber components and then fit the cap (photo).

7 Front crossmember – removal and refitting

1   Raise the front of the car and support it on axle stands placed under the jacking points.
2   Remove the splash shield from under the engine compartment.
3   Remove the anti-roll bar, the radius rods and the suspension track control arms.
4   Remove the transmission gearchange and stabiliser rods.
5   Remove the steering rack and pinion housing with the tie-rods (see Chapter 9).
6   Support the engine/transmission on a jack or by attaching it to a hoist.
7   Disconnect the engine stabiliser/damper and mounting.

8   Raise the engine/transmission slightly and unbolt and remove the crossmember.
9   Refitting is a reversal of removal. Tighten all the bolts to the specified torque when the weight of the car is again on the roadwheels.

8 Rear hubs – overhaul and adjustment

1   Raise the rear of the car and support on axle stands. Remove the roadwheel.
2   Remove the dust cap, extract the split pin and remove the nut retainer (photo).

8.2a Removing the rear hub dust cap

8.2b Rear hub nut retainer and split pin

8.2c Removing the rear hub nut retainer

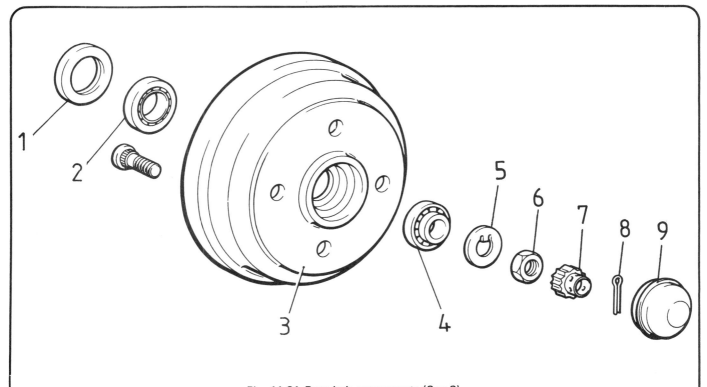

Fig. 11.21 Rear hub components (Sec 8)

1 Oil seal	4 Outboard bearing	7 Nut retainer
2 Inboard bearing	5 Thrust washer	8 Split pin
3 Brake drum	6 Nut	9 Dust cap

8.3 Rear hub bearing thrust washer

8.4 Rear hub outboard bearing

3   Unscrew and remove the nut, take out the thrust washer (photo).
4   Remove the brake drum taking care that the outboard bearing does not fall out (photo).
5   If the bearings are being inspected and repacked with grease at the specified mileage interval (see Routine maintenance) wipe out the old grease and inspect the bearings for wear, scoring or chipping. If they are in good order and the oil seal is not leaking, re-pack the space between the bearings with grease and refit the drum as described in paragraphs 10 to 16 of this Section.
6   If the oil seal is leaking or the bearings are worn, prise out the oil seal and obtain a new one.
7   Using a drift, drive out the bearing outer tracks.
8   Wipe out the bearing track seats and tap the new tracks squarely into position.
9   Fill the space between the bearings with grease, fit the bearing inner races and the new oil seal into its recess.
10 Fit the brake drum. Make sure that the outboard bearing is in position, fit the thrust washer and screw on the nut to a torque of 14

lbf ft (20 Nm) while turning the drum in the normal direction of forward travel to settle the bearings.
11 Release the nut and then tighten to 4lbf ft (5 Nm). In the absence of a torque wrench of suitable calibration, hold a socket spanner in the hand and tighten it gently. All bearing endfloat should now be eliminated.
12 Fit the nut retainer and a new split pin. Make sure that the legs of the pin go round the nut retainer neatly to prevent them rubbing on the inside of the dust cap which should be fitted now.
13 Fit the roadwheel and lower the car.

9   **Rear shock absorber – removal, testing and refitting**

1   Jack up the rear of the car, support both the body frame members and the base of the suspension trailing arm.
2   Remove the roadwheel.

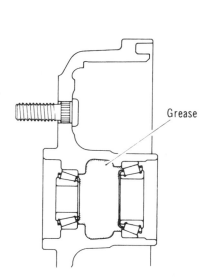

Fig. 11.22 Rear hub grease packing diagram (Sec 8)

Grease

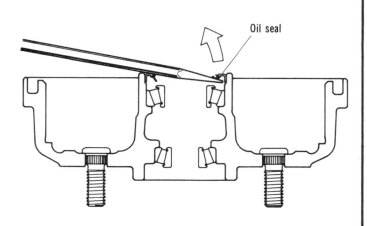

Oil seal

Fig. 11.23 Prising out rear hub oil seal (Sec 8)

9.3a Rear shock absorber lower mounting

9.3b Rear shock absorber upper mounting

11.9 Rear suspension attachment clamp

3   Unscrew the shock absorber lower mounting bolt and then the upper one and remove the unit from the car (photo).
4   To test a shock absorber, grip its lower mounting eye in the jaws of a vice and fully extend and compress is at least six times. If there is any tendency to jerkiness or if there is a seizure or lack of resistance then the unit must be renewed.
5   Refitting is a reversal of removal but before fitting a new unit which may have been stored horizontally, prime it by carrying out exactly the same procedure as described for testing until smooth action is obtained with good damping action.

10 Rear coil spring – removal and refitting

1   Raise the rear of the car and support it under the frame member.
2   Place a jack under the suspension trailing arm and remove the roadwheel.
3   Disconnect the shock absorber lower mounting.
4   Carefully lower the jack under the trailing arm, taking care not to strain the brake hydraulic hoses until the coil spring can be removed.
5   Refit by reversing the removal operations but make sure that the spring ends are correctly located against the stops of their seats.

11 Rear suspension – removal, dismantling and refitting

1   The rear suspension should be removed from the car for dismantling in the following way.
2   Raise the rear of the car and support it on axle stands placed under the bodyframe side members.
3   Remove both rear brake assemblies as described in Chapter 8.
4   Remove the exhaust rear section.
5   Support the suspension arms and disconnect the lower mountings of the shock absorbers as described in Section 9 of this Chapter.

6   Remove the roadsprings as described in Section 10 of this Chapter.
7   Temporarily reconnect the shock absorbers.
8   Disconnect the hydraulic brake lines from their brackets on the suspension arms.
9   Support the weight of the suspension annd unbolt the attachment clamps from the body (photo).
10 Withdraw the suspension.
11 Clean away any external dirt and then unscrew and remove the nuts from the outer ends of the crosstube.
12 Withdraw the attachment clamps and the rubber bushes.
13 Remove the clip from the dust cover on the centre joint of the

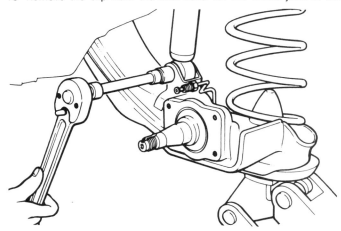

Fig. 11.24 Releasing rear shock absorber lower mounting (Sec 11)

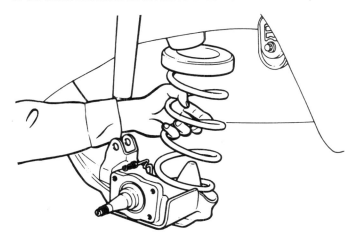

Fig. 11.25 Removing a rear coil spring (Sec 11)

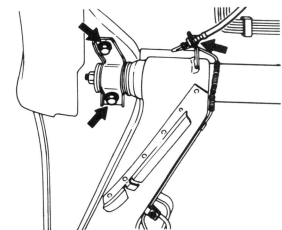

Fig. 11.26 Suspension attachment clamp and brakeline bracket (Sec 11)

220

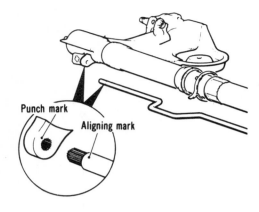

Fig. 11.27 Rear anti-roll bar alignment (Sec 11)

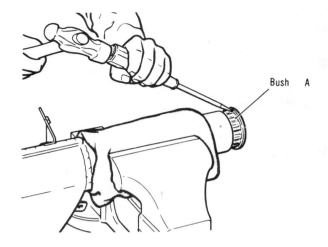

Fig. 11.28 Removing crosstube bush (Sec 11)

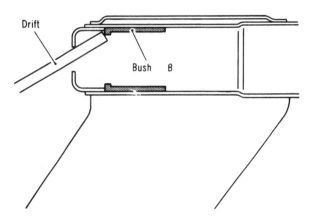

Fig. 11.29 Removing left-hand crosstube bush (Sec 11)

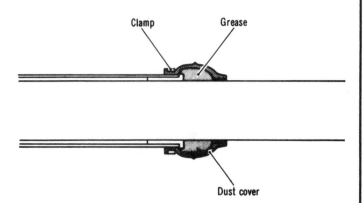

Fig. 11.30 Crosstube dust cover (Sec 11)

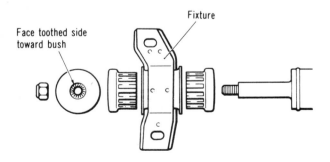

Fig. 11.31 Suspension arm bush arrangement (Sec 11)

11.14 Rear suspension crosstube dust cover

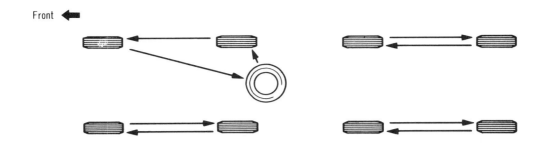

Fig. 11.32 Roadwheel rotation (radial ply tyres) (Sec 12)

crosstube and then (where fitted) mark the alignment of both ends of the anti-roll bar to the anchor brackets. A punch mark will be found on the bracket but the anti-roll bar is best marked in relation to this with a spot of quick drying paint.

14 Pull the two sections of the crosstube complete with suspension arms apart. The dust cover should remain on the right-hand section of the crosstube (photo).

15 Extract the plastic stop from the right-hand crosstube and then tap off the bush.

16 With a drift, drive out the bush from the opposite crosstube.

17 Renew worn components as necessary, apply grease to the bushes and fit them using pieces of suitable diameter tubing.

18 Assemble the two suspension sections making sure that the dust cover is fitted the correct way round and packed with grease. Tighten the clip.

19 Ensure that the anti-roll bar is corrrectly aligned with its bracket marks.

20 The bushes and washer either side of the suspension attachment clamp must be assembled as shown in the diagram.

21 All nuts and bolts must be finally tightened to the specified torque when the weight of the car is again on the roadwheels.

22 Bleed the brake hydraulic system as described in Chapter 8.

12 Roadwheels and tyres

1 The roadwheels may be of steel or aluminium construction according to model.

2 Whenever the roadwheels are removed from the car for inspection of the brakes or other work, check that the securing nut recesses in the wheels are not becoming enlarged or deformed. In the case of steel wheels, check for rust and neutralise and repaint where it is evident.

3 As well as the regular tyre pressure check, frequently inspect the treads and walls for cuts and blisters. If any are found, have the tyre inspected and repaired by a tyre specialist.

4 An uneven wear pattern on the tyre tread will probably be due to incorrect steering angles (see Chapter 10) or to the front wheels at least, if not all wheels, requiring balancing. Front wheel out-of-balance is usually detected by the 'flutter' of the steering wheel at various roadspeeds.

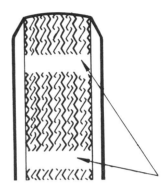

Fig. 11.33 Typical tyre tread wear indicators (Sec 12)

5 To even out the wear in the tyre treads which occurs at different rates between front and rear tyres because of the differing characteristics of the front and rear suspension and the effect of the steering, it is worth moving the roadwheel positions every 5000 miles (8000 km).

6 With the radial tyres fitted, move the wheels front to rear and rear to front on the same side of the car only. Do not move the wheels from side to side of the car as this will introduce some curious characteristics into the roadholding behaviour if the tyres have been in use for some time and have acquired an in-built carcass 'set'.

7 If the spare wheel is brought into the pattern of movement, mark it so that it can be used on the same side of the car each time it is brought into use.

8 The tyres fitted as original equipment incorporate tread wear indicators. As soon as these become visible the tyre must be renewed. On other tyres, a safe wear limit should be regarded as preferably 2.0 mm, with an absolute minimum of 1.0 mm of tread still showing.

13 Fault diagnosis – suspension

Symptom	Reason(s)
Pitching during braking, rolling on corners	Defective front struts or rear shock absorbers. Cracked anti-roll bar
Wheel wobble and vibration	Roadwheels out of balance Loose wheel nuts or bearings
Steering wander*	Incorrectly adjusted rear hub bearings Loose suspension attachment bolts and nuts Uneven tyre pressures (side to side)

*Refer also to Fault diagnosis, Chapter 10.

Chapter 12 Bodywork and fittings

Contents

Specifications

Type .... Steel, welded, integral construction. Three or five door hatchback

Dimensions and weights .... These are tabulated in the Introductory Section to this manual

Torque wrench settings

	lbf ft	Nm
Seat belt anchor bolts	17	23
Impact absorbing bumpers	40	54
Shock absorber to body	25	34
Bumper bar to shock absorber	45	61
Door hinge bolts	18	25
Tailgate hinge bolts	16	22

1 General description

The bodywork is of an all steel welded construction without a separate chassis frame.

Three or five door hatchback versions are available and the specification is dependent upon the particular model in the range.

In the interest of economy, the front wings can be removed by unbolting them in the event of damage.

A laminated windscreen is fitted as standard.

2 Maintenance – bodywork and underframe

1   The general condition of a car's bodywork is the thing that significantly affects it value. Maintenance is easy but needs to be regular. Neglect, particularly after minor damage, can lead quickly to further deterioration and costly repair bills. It is important also to keep watch on those parts of the car not immediately visible, for instance the underside, inside all the wheel arches and the lower part of the engine compartment.

2   The basic maintenance routine for the bodywork is washing – preferably with a lot of water, from a hose. This will remove all the loose solids which may have stuck to the car. It is important to flush these off in such a way as to prevent grit from scratching the finish. The wheel arches and underframe need washing in the same way to remove any accumulated mud which will retain moisture and tend to encourage rust. Paradoxically enough, the best time to clean the underframe and wheel arches is in wet weather when the mud is thoroughly wet and soft. In very wet weather the underframe is usually cleaned of large accumulations automatically and this is a good time for inspection.

3   Periodically, it is a good idea to have the whole of the underframe of the car steam cleaned, engine compartment included, so that a thorough inspection can be carried out to see what minor repairs and renovations are necessary. Steam cleaning is available at many garages and is necessary for removal of the accumulation of oily grime which sometimes is allowed to become thick in certain areas. If steam cleaning facilities are not available, there are one or two excellent grease solvents available which can be brush applied. The dirt can then be simply hosed off.

4   After washing paintwork, wipe off with a chamois leather to give an unspotted clear finish. A coat of clear protective wax polish will give added protection against chemical pollutants in the air. If the paintwork sheen has dulled or oxidised, use a cleaner/polisher combination to restore the brilliance of the shine. This requires a little effort, but such dulling is usually caused because regular washing has been neglected. Always check that the door and ventilator opening drain holes and pipes are completely clear so that water can be drained out. Bright work should be treated in the same way as paintwork. Windscreens and windows can be kept clear of the smeary film which often appears, by adding a little ammonia to the water. If they are scratched, a good rub with a proprietary metal polish will often clear them. Never use any form of wax or other body or chromium polish on glass.

3   Maintenance – upholstery and carpets

1   Mats and carpets should be brushed or vacuum cleaned regularly to keep them free of grit. If they are badly stained remove them from the car for scrubbing or sponging and make quite sure they are dry before refitting. Seats and interior trim panels can be kept clean by a wipe over with a damp cloth. If they do become stained (which can be more apparent on light coloured upholstery) use a little liquid detergent and a soft nail brush to scour the grime out of the grain of the material. Do not forget to keep the head lining clean in the same way as the upholstery. When using liquid cleaners inside the car do not over-wet the surfaces being cleaned. Excessive damp could get into the seams and padded interior causing stains, offensive odours or even rot. If the inside of the car gets wet accidentally it is worthwhile taking some trouble to dry it out properly, particularly where carpets are involved. *Do not leave oil or electric heaters inside the car for this purpose.*

4   Minor body damage – repair

The photographic sequences on pages 230 and 231 illustrate the operations detailed in the following sub-sections.

Repair of minor scratches in the vehicle's bodywork

If the scratch is very superficial, and does not penetrate to the metal of the bodywork, repair is very simple. Lightly rub the area of the scratch with a paintwork renovator, or a very fine cutting paste, to remove loose paint from the scratch and to clear the surrounding bodywork of wax polish. Rinse the area with clean water.

Apply touch-up paint to the scratch using a thin paint brush; continue to apply thin layers of paint until the surface of the paint in the scratch is level with the surrounding paintwork. Allow the new paint at least two weeks to harden: then blend it into the surrounding paintwork by rubbing the paintwork, in the scratch area, with a paintwork renovator or a very fine cutting paste. Finally, apply wax polish.

Where the scratch has penetrated right through to the metal of the bodywork, causing the metal to rust, a different repair technique is required. Remove any loose rust from the bottom of the scratch with a penknife, then apply rust inhibiting paint to prevent the formation of rust in the future. Using a rubber or nylon applicator fill the scratch with bodystopper paste. If required, this paste can be mixed with cellulose thinners to provide a very thin paste which is ideal for filling narrow scratches. Before the stopper-paste in the scratch hardens, wrap a piece of smooth cotton rag around the top of a finger. Dip the finger in cellulose thinners and then quickly sweep it across the surface of the stopper-paste in the scratch; this will ensure that the surface of the stopper-paste is slightly hollowed. The scratch can now be painted over as described earlier in this Section.

Repair of dents in the vehicle's bodywork

When deep denting of the vehicle's bodywork has taken place, the first task is to pull the dent out, until the affected bodywork almost attains its original shape. There is little point in trying to restore the original shape completely, as the metal in the damaged area will have stretched on impact and cannot be reshaped fully to its original contour. It is better to bring the level of the dent up to a point which is about $\frac{1}{8}$ in (3 mm) below the level of the surrounding bodywork. In cases where the dent is very shallow anyway, it is not worth trying to pull it out at all. If the underside of the dent is accessible, it can be hammered out gently from behind, using a mallet with a wooden or plastic head. Whilst doing this, hold a suitable block of wood firmly against the outside of the panel to absorb the impact from the hammer blows and thus prevent a large area of the bodywork from being 'belled-out'.

Should the dent be in a section of the bodywork which has double skin or some other factor making it inaccessible from behind, a different technique is called for. Drill several small holes through the metal inside the area – particularly in the deeper section. Then screw long self-tapping screws into the holes just sufficiently for them to gain a good purchase in the metal. Now the dent can be pulled out by pulling on the protruding heads of the screws with a pair of pliers.

The next stage of the repair is the removal of the paint from the damaged area, and from an inch or so of the surrounding 'sound' bodywork. This is accomplished most easily by using a wire brush or abrasive pad on a power drill, although it can be done just as effectively by hand using sheets of abrasive paper. To complete the preparation for filling, score the surface of the bare metal with a screwdriver or the tang of a file, or alternatively, drill small holes in the affected area. This will provide a really good 'key' for the filler paste.

To complete the repair see the Section on filling and re-spraying.

Repair of rust holes or gashes in the vehicle's bodywork

Remove all paint from the affected area and from an inch or so of the surrounding 'sound' bodywork, using an abrasive pad or a wire brush on a power drill. If these are not available a few sheets of abrasive paper will do the job just as effectively. With the paint removed you will be able to gauge the severity of the corrosion and therefore decide whether to renew the whole panel (if this is possible) or to repair the affected area. New body panels are not as expensive as most people think and it is often quicker and more satisfactory to fit a new panel than to attempt to repair large areas of corrosion.

Remove all fittings from the affected area except those which will act as a guide to the original shape of the damaged bodywork (eg headlamp shells etc). Then, using tin snips or a hacksaw blade, remove all loose metal and any other metal badly affected by corrosion. Hammer the edges of the hole inwards in order to create a slight depression for the filler paste.

Wire brush the affected area to remove the powdery rust from the surface of the remaining metal. Paint the affected area with rust inhibiting paint; if the back of the rusted area is accessible treat this also.

Before filling can take place it will be necessary to block the hole in some way. This can be achieved by the use of Zinc gauze or Aluminium tape.

Zinc gauze is probably the best material to use for a large hole. Cut a piece to the approximate size and shape of the hole to be filled, then position it in the hole so that its edges are below the level of the surrounding bodywork. It can be retained in position by several blobs of filler paste around its periphery.

Aluminium tape should be used for small or very narrow holes. Pull a piece off the roll and trim it to the approximate size and shape required, then pull off the backing paper (if used) and stick the tape over the hole; it can be overlapped if the thickness of one piece is insufficient. Burnish down the edges of the tape with the handle of a screwdriver or similar, to ensure that the tape is securely attached to the metal underneath.

Bodywork repairs – filling and re-spraying

Before using this Section, see the Sections on dent, deep scratch, rust holes and gash repairs.

Many types of bodyfiller are available, but generally speaking those proprietary kits which contain a tin of filler paste and a tube of resin hardener are best for this type of repair. A wide, flexible plastic or nylon applicator will be found invaluable for imparting a smooth and well contoured finish to the surface of the filler.

Mix up a little filler on a clean piece of card or board – measure the hardener carefully (follow the maker's instructions on the pack) otherwise the filler will set too rapidly or too slowly.

Using the applicator apply the filler paste to the prepared area; draw the applicator across the surface of the filler to achieve the correct contour and to level the filler surface. As soon as a contour that approximates the correct one is achieved, stop working the paste – if you carry on too long the paste will become sticky and begin to 'pick up' on the applicator. Continue to add thin layers of filler paste at twenty-minute intervals until the level of the filler is just proud of the surrounding bodywork.

Once the filler has hardened, excess can be removed using a metal plane or file. From then on, progressively finer grades of sandpaper should be used, starting with a 40 grade production paper and finishing with 400 grade wet-and-dry paper. Always wrap the abrasive paper around a flat rubber, cork, or wooden block – otherwise the surface of the filler will not be completely flat. During the smoothing of the filler surface the wet-and-dry paper should be periodically rinsed in water. This will ensure that a very smooth finish is imparted to the filler at the final stage.

At this stage the 'repair area' should be surrounded by a ring of bare metal, which in turn should be encircled by the finely 'feathered' edge of the good paintwork. Rinse the repair area with clean water, until all of the dust produced by the rubbing-down operation has gone.

Spray the whole repair area with a light coat of primer – this will show up any imperfections in the surface of the filler. Repair these imperfections with fresh filler paste or bodystopper, and once more smooth the surface with abrasive paper. If bodystopper is used, it can be mixed with cellulose thinners to form a really thin paste which is ideal for filling small holes. Repeat this spray and repair procedure until you are satisfied that the surface of the filler, and the feathered edge of the paintwork are perfect. Clean the repair area with clean water and allow to dry fully.

The repair area is now ready for final spraying. Paint spraying must be carried out in warm, dry, windless and dust free atmosphere. This condition can be created artificially if you have access to a large indoor working area, but if you are forced to work in the open, you will have to pick your day very carefully. If you are working indoors, dousing the floor in the work area with water will help to settle the dust which would otherwise be in the atmosphere. If the repair area is confined to one body panel, mask off the surrounding panels; this will help to minimise the effects of a slight mis-match in paint colours. Bodywork fittings (eg chrome strips, door handles etc) will also need to be masked off. Use genuine masking tape and several thicknesses of newspaper for the masking operations.

Before commencing to spray, agitate the aerosol can thoroughly, then spray a test area (an old tin, or similar) until the technique is mastered. Cover the repair area with a thick coat of primer; the thickness should be built up using several thin layers of paint rather than one thick one. Using 400 grade wet-and-dry paper, rub down the surface of the primer until it is really smooth. While doing this, the work area should be thoroughly doused with water, and the wet-and-dry paper periodically rinsed in water. Allow to dry before spraying on more paint.

Spray on the top coat, again building up the thickness by using several thin layers of paint. Start spraying in the centre of the repair area and then, using a circular motion, work outwards until the whole repair area and about 2 inches of the surrounding original paintwork is covered. Remove all masking material 10 to 15 minutes after spraying on the final coat of paint.

Allow the new paint at least two weeks to harden, then, using a paintwork renovator or a very fine cutting paste, blend the edges of the paint into the existing paintwork. Finally, apply wax polish.

5   Major body damage – repair

1   Because the car is built without a separate chassis frame and the body is therefore integral with the underframe, major damage must be repaired by competent mechanics with the necessary welding and hydraulic straightening equipment.
2   If the damage has been serious it is vital that the body is checked for correct alignment as otherwise the handling of the car will suffer and many other faults such as excessive tyre wear and wear in the transmission and steering may occur.
3   There is a special body jig which most large body repair shops have, and to ensure that all is correct it is important that the jig be used for all major repair work.

6   Bonnet – removal and refitting

1   Open the bonnet fully and prise off the clip which retains the stay to the body (photo).
2   Mark the position of the hinges to the bonnet, unbolt them and with the help of an assistant, lift the bonnet from the car (photo).

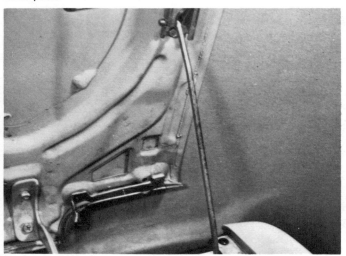

6.1 Bonnet stay

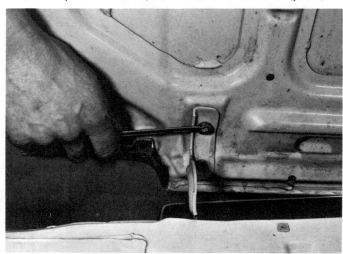

6.2 Removing the bonnet hinge bolt

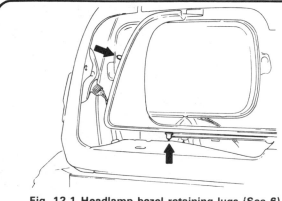

Fig. 12.1 Headlamp bezel retaining lugs (Sec 6)

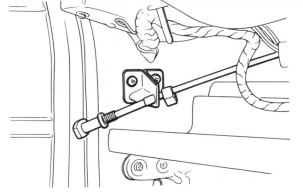

Fig. 12.2 Bonnet release control handle (Sec 6)

6.3 Radiator grille upper screw

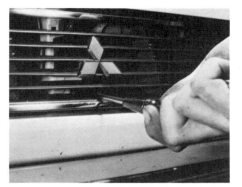
6.3b Radiator grille lower screw

6.6 Bonnet latch

3   If the hinges must be removed, the radiator grille and headlamp bezel must now be removed (photo).
4   Extract the grille securing screws and remove the grille.
5   Take care when withdrawing the headlamp bezel as it has two positioning lugs which can break if it is roughly handled.
6   The bonnet latch is bolted to the engine compartment rear bulkhead and it and the release cable can be removed if the latch bolts and the release cable support bracket bolts (inside the car) are unscrewed (photo).
7   Refitting is a reversal of removal. Do not fully tighten the hinge or latch bolts until the bonnet is checked for closure. Any adjustment can be carried out by using the hinges or latch within the limits of their elongated bolt holes.
8   Grease the hinge pivots and the latch.

7 Front wing – removal and refitting

1   Remove the radiator grille and the headlamp bezel from the side on which the wing is to be detached.
2   Disconnect the wiring from the front side marker lamp (if fitted).
3   On models without impact absorbing bumpers, remove the embellisher strip and the corner.
4   On models with impact absorbing bumpers, unbolt the bumper from the shock absorbing struts.
5   Unbolt and remove the plastic stoneguard from under the wing. It will probably be easier to carry out this job if the roadwheel is first removed.
6   If the radio aerial is on the side of the car being worked upon,

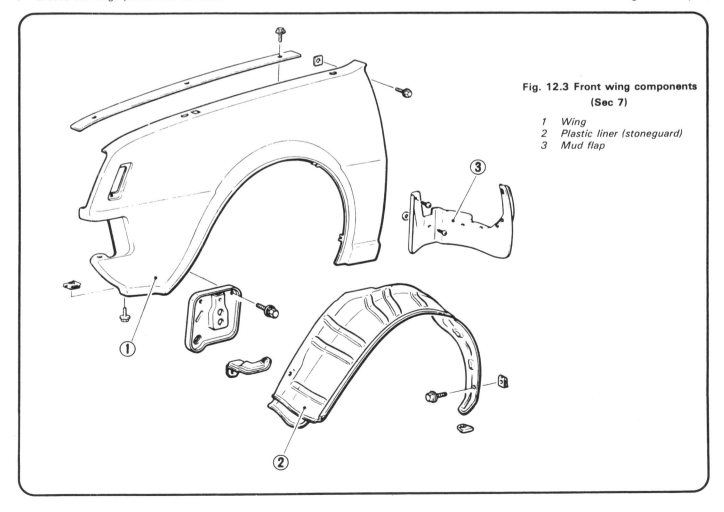

Fig. 12.3 Front wing components
(Sec 7)

1   Wing
2   Plastic liner (stoneguard)
3   Mud flap

release its bracket which will be visible now that the stoneguard has been removed.

7   Unscrew all the wing securing bolts and remove the wing. The sealing mastic along the top edge may require cutting with a sharp knife.

8   Refitting is a reversal of removal, apply mastic to the top mating flange.

9   Apply protective coating to the underwing surface and refinish the upper surface to the original body colour.

8   Bumpers (non-impact absorbing type) – removal and refitting

1   Prise off the embellisher strip from its securing clips.
2   Remove the corner mouldings.
3   Unbolt the main bumper bar from the support brackets and withdraw it. With the front bumper, disconnect the lamp connecting leads at the plugs.
4   Refitting is a reversal of removal.

9   Bumpers (impact absorbing type) – removal and refitting

1   Working under the bumper bar, unscrew the bolts which hold it to the shock absorbing struts. Remove the bumper bar.
2   The individual silicone rubber filled struts can be unbolted and removed.
3   Refitting is a reversal of removal but tighten all the bolts to the specified torque.

10   Front door window regulator and glass – removal and refitting

1   From the door interior trim panel, remove the armrest (two screws) (photo).
2   Using a piece of wire with a small hook at its end, insert it behind the window regulator handle and extract the securing clip. Remove the handle.

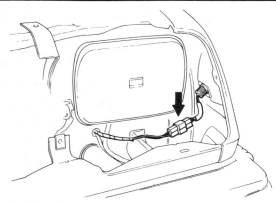

Fig. 12.4 Front side marker wiring (Sec 7)

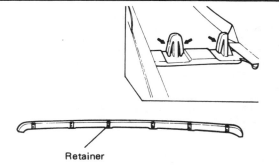

Fig. 12.5 Bumper embellishment strip and clips (Sec 7)

Retainer

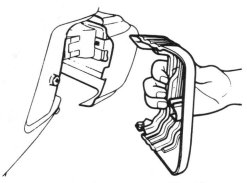

Fig. 12.6 Bumper cover (Sec 7)

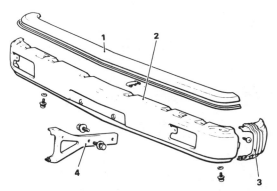

Fig. 12.7 Bumper components (non-impact absorbing) (Sec 8)

1   Embellishment strip   3   Corner
2   Main bar   4   Mounting bracket

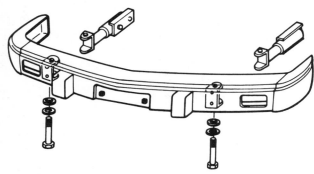

Fig. 12.8 Front bumper (impact absorbing type) (Sec 9)

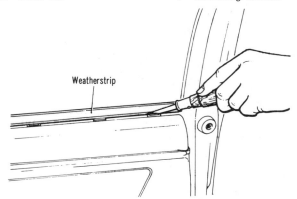

Weatherstrip

Fig. 12.9 Removing the door inner weatherstrip (Sec 10)

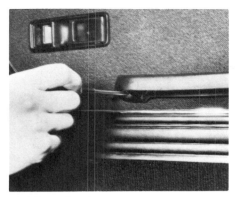
10.1 Extracting the armrest screw

10.3a Door lock interior handle screw

10.3b Removing the door lock interior handle cover plate

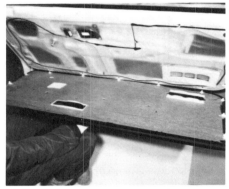
10.4 Removing the door trim panel

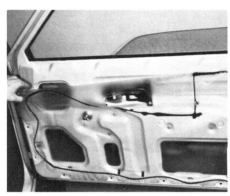
10.5 Removing the door waterproof sheet

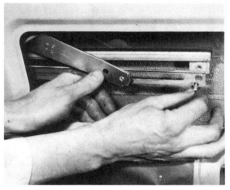
10.8a Removing the rear glass holder to regulator arm screw

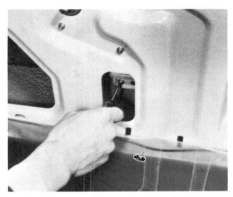
10.8b Removing the front glass holder to regulator arm screw

10.11 Removing the window regulator mechanism

10.18 Window regulator handle ready for refitting

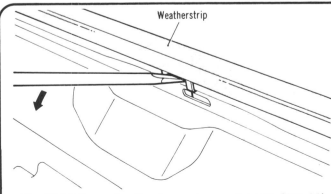
Fig. 12.10 Removing the door outer weatherstrip (Sec 10)

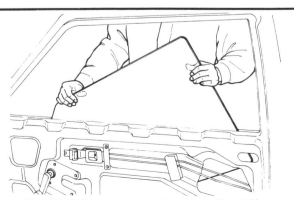
Fig. 12.11 Removing the door glass (Sec 10)

3   Extract the screw from the door lock interior remote control handle and remove the cover plate (photos).
4   Insert a flat blade or the fingers between the trim panel and the door and pull the panel securing clips out of the holes in the door(photo).
5   Carefully peel away the self-adhesive waterproof sheet (photo).
6   Working at the base of the window opening, prise out the inner weatherstrip.
7   Temporarily refit the window regulator handle and lower the glass fully.
8   Remove the screws which hold the glass holder to the regulator arm (photos).
9   Prise out the outer weatherstrip with a screwdriver.
10 Pull the door glass upward and remove it from the door cavity by turning it.
11 Extract the roller guide and regulator mounting screws and withdraw the complete regulator assembly from the lower aperture in the door interior panel (photo).
12 Renew the regulator if it is worn.
13 If a new glass is being fitted, fit the holder to its bottom edge in accordance with Fig. 12.12.
14 Grease the regulator before refitting it.
15 Refitting is a reversal of removal. If the clip on the inner weatherstrip has separated from the trim panel, turn the clip through 90° with a screwdriver to reconnect it.
16 To provide smooth operation of the window regulator and glass, three points of adjustment are provided.

    (a) The roller guide mounting screws
    (b) The glass holder to regulator arm screws
    (c) The front and rear glass slide channel screws

17 Release the screws and move the components until a combined adjustment at all three points makes the glass move up and down smoothly without judder or lack of alignment.
18 When refitting the regulator handle, fit the clip into the handle and then bang the handle onto the splined spindle of the regulator with the hand (photo).

---

11 Front door lock and handle – removal and refitting

---

1   Remove the door glass and regulator as described in the preceding Section.
2   Detach the interior remote control handle and the two control rods from the handle.
3   Disconnect the short link rod (A), pull out the securing clip and remove the lock cylinder (Fig. 12.16).
4   Disconnect the longer link rod (B), unscrew the two securing nuts and remove the door exterior handle (Fig. 12.16).

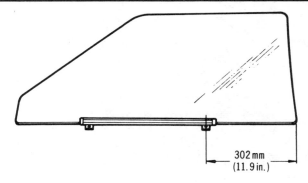

Fig. 12.12 Window glass holder installation diagram (Sec 10)

302 mm
(11.9 in.)

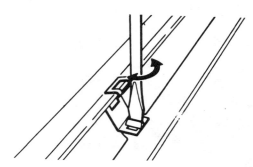

Fig. 12.13 Reconnecting door weatherstrip clip (Sec 10)

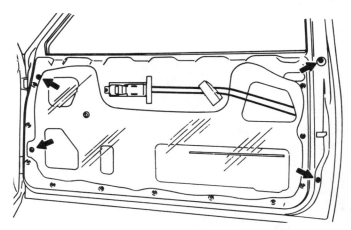

Fig. 12.14 Door glass slide channel screws (Sec 10)

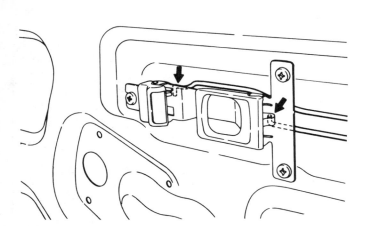

Fig. 12.15 Interior remote control handle (Sec 11)
Operating rods arrowed

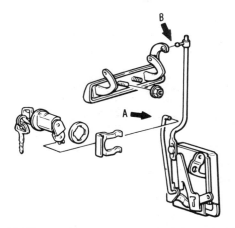

Fig. 12.16 Exterior lock cylinder and handle (Sec 11)
For A and B see text

11.5 Door latch screws

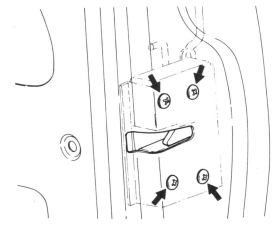

Fig. 12.17 Door lock retaining screws (Sec 11)

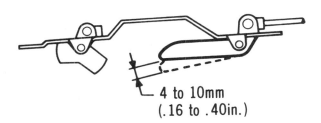

4 to 10mm
(.16 to .40in.)

Fig. 12.18 Door interior handle adjustment diagram (Sec 11)

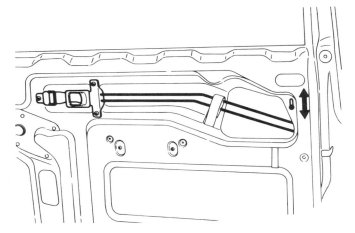

Fig. 12.19 Door lock knob adjusting screw (Sec 11)

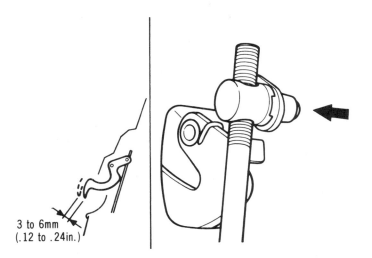

3 to 6mm
(.12 to .24in.)

Fig. 12.20 Door exterior handle adjustment diagram (Sec 11)

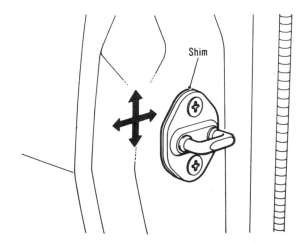

Shim

Fig. 12.21 Door lock striker (Sec 11)

5   Unscrew and remove the four screws from the latch and withdraw the latch with the two control rods (photo).

6   Refitting is a reversal of removal but observe the following points.

   (a) Apply grease to all friction surfaces
   (b) Fit the lock cylinder so that its drain hole faces down

7   Once fitted, adjust the play of the lock interior handle to between

0.16 and 0.40 in (4.0 and 10.0 mm) by sliding the handle mounting plate within the limits of its elongated mounting plate.

8   The length of travel of the lock button can be adjusted by releasing the screw shown in Fig. 12.19.

9   The plug in the exterior handle is adjustable by means of the trunnion on the threaded rod. It should be between 0.12 and 0.24 in (3.0 to 6.0 mm).

This sequence of photographs deals with the repair of the dent and scratch (above rear lamp) shown in this photo. The procedure will be similar for the repair of a hole. It should be noted that the procedures given here are simplified - more explicit instructions will be found in the text

In the case of a dent the first job - after removing surrounding trim - is to hammer out the dent where access is possible. This will minimise filling. Here, the large dent having been hammered out, the damaged area is being made slightly concave

Now all paint must be removed from the damaged area, by rubbing with coarse abrasive paper. Alternatively, a wire brush or abrasive pad can be used in a power drill. Where the repair area meets good paintwork, the edge pf the paintwork should be 'feathered', using a finer grade of abrasive paper

In the case of a hole caused by rusting, all damaged sheet-metal should be cut away before proceeding to this stage. Here, the damaged area is being treated with rust remover and inhibitor before being filled

Mix the body filler according to its manufacturer's instructions. In the case of corrosion damage, it will be necessary to block off any large holes before filling - this can be done with zinc gauze or aluminium tape. Make sure the area is absolutely clean before ...

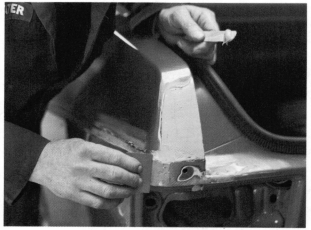

... applying the filler. Filler should be applied with a flexible applicator, as shown, for best results: the wooden spatula being used for confined areas. Apply thin layers of filler at 20-minute intervals, until the surface of the filler is slightly proud of the surrounding bodywork

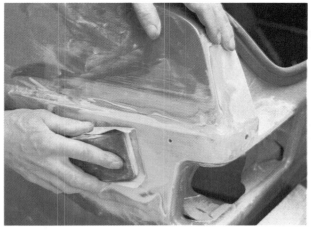

Initial shaping can be done with a Surform plane or Dreadnought file. Then, using progressively finer grades of wet-and-dry paper, wrapped around a sanding block, and copious amounts of clean water, rub-down the filler until really smooth and flat. Again, feather the edges of adjoining paintwork

Again, using plenty of water, rub down the primer with a fine grade of wet-and-dry paper (400 grade is probably best) until it is really smooth and well blended into the surrounding paintwork. Any remaining imperfections can now be filled by carefully applied knifing stopper paste

The top coat can now be applied. When working out of doors, pick a dry, warm and wind-free day. Ensure surrounding areas are protected from over-spray. Agitate the aerosol thoroughly, then spray the centre of the repair area, working outwards with a circular motion. Apply the paint as several thin coats.

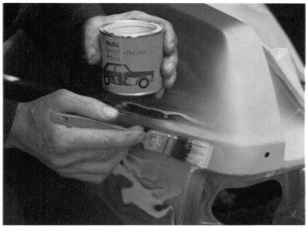

The whole repair area can now be sprayed or brush-painted with primer. If spraying, ensure adjoining areas are protected from over-spray. Note that at least one-inch of the surrounding sound paintwork should be coated with primer. Primer has a 'thick' consistency, so will fill small imperfections

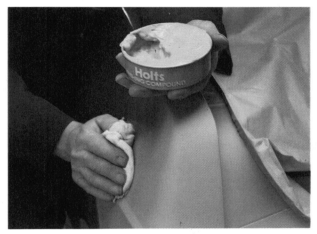

When the stopper has hardened, rub-down the repair area again before applying the final coat of primer. Before rubbing-down this last coat of primer, ensure the repair area is blemish-free - use more stopper if necessary. To ensure that the surface of the primer is really smooth use some finishing compound

After a period of about two-weeks, which the paint needs to harden fully, the surface of the repaired area can be 'cut' with a mild cutting compound prior to wax polishing. When carrying out bodywork repairs, remember that the quality of the finished job is proportional to the time and effort expended

12.2a Door lower hinge

12.2b Door upper hinge

12 Front door – removal and refitting

1   Open the door and support it on blocks or jacks under its bottom edge, suitably padded with rag to prevent damage to the paintwork.
2   Unscrew and remove the bolts which secure the hinge plates to the door (photos).
3   Lift the door from the car.
4   If the hinges must be removed from the body pillars, mark their position first to facilitate refitting.
5   Refitting is a reversal of removal. Adjust the position of the door within the body frame by loosening the hinge bolts. Check also that with the door closed, the door exterior panel is flush with the adjacent body panels.
6   The door striker can be adjusted to provide smooth positive closure by releasing its screws. Sometimes additional shims are required under the striker to provide correct alignment.

13 Rear door – removal, dismantling, reassembly and refitting

1   On five door cars the operations on the rear doors are very similar to those described for the front doors except that there are design variations in some of the components.

14 Tailgate – removal and refitting

1   Open the tailgate fully.
2   Using a flat blade or the fingers inserted between the trim panel and the tailgate prise the trim panel securing clips from their holes and remove the panel.
3   Disconnect the wiring connector plugs which are now exposed.
4   For ease of refitting, tie a length of string to the connector and

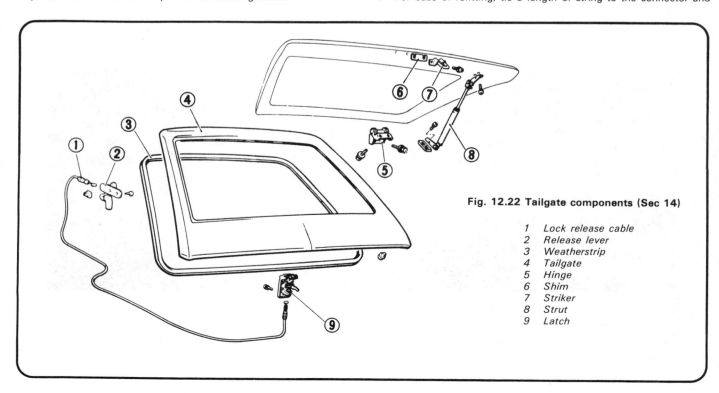

Fig. 12.22 Tailgate components (Sec 14)

1   *Lock release cable*
2   *Release lever*
3   *Weatherstrip*
4   *Tailgate*
5   *Hinge*
6   *Shim*
7   *Striker*
8   *Strut*
9   *Latch*

draw the wiring harness out of the tailgate. Retain the string within the tailgate for use at refitting.

5   Disconnect the washer tube.

6   With an assistant supporting the tailgate, disconnect the support struts from the tailgate.

7   Mark the position of the hinges to the tailgate and unbolt them from the tailgate. Lift the tailgate away.

8   If the hinges are to be renewed, unbolt them from the body.

9   Refitting is a reversal of removal. If the hinges were removed, apply sealing compound to the hinge to body mating surfaces before fitting.

10 Do not tighten the hinge bolts fully until the alignment of the tailgate has been checked. There should be an even gap at the top and sides of the tailgate when it is closed.

11 Adjustment is provided for at the hinge support strut anchor plates and the striker by means of their elongated bolt holes.

15 Tailgate lock – removal and refitting

1   Remove the trim panel from the tailgate as described in the preceding Section.

2   Disconnect the lock link rod from the lock cylinder.

3   Extract the three latch securing screws and disconnect the operating cable.

4   Remove the lock cylinder.

5   Unhook the cable from the release lever and remove the lever.

6   If the operating cable is to be renewed then the front and rear seats, the floor carpet and items of trim will first have to be removed.

7   Refitting is a reversal of removal. The operating cable is adjusted by moving the position of the striker. Make sure that the release lever returns fully when the operating cable is released.

16 Windscreen and tailgate glass – removal, refitting

Windscreen

1   Although it is recommended that screen removal and refitting is left to the specialist fitting companies, for those who are determined to carry out the work themselves follow the operations described in this Section.

2   Remove the wiper arms and blades, the interior rear view mirror and the sun visors.

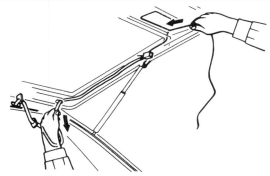

Fig. 12.23 Withdrawing tailgate electrical harness (Sec 14)

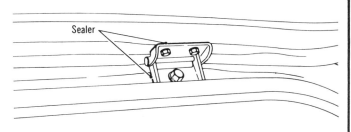

Fig. 12.24 Tailgate hinge sealant application points (Sec 14)

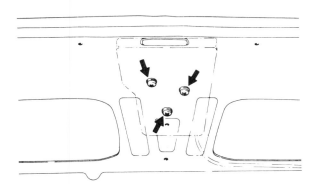

Fig. 12.25 Tailgate latch screws (Sec 15)

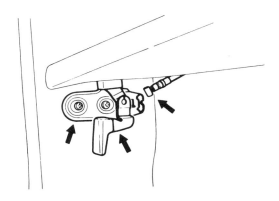

Fig. 12.26 Tailgate latch cable connection (Sec 15)

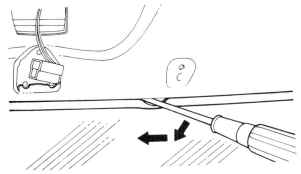

Fig. 12.27 Peeling back windscreen weatherstrip (Sec 16)

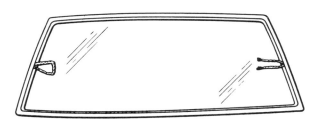

Fig. 12.28 Windscreen cord (Sec 16)

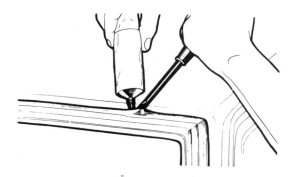

Fig. 12.29 Sealing windscreen weatherstrip (Sec 16)

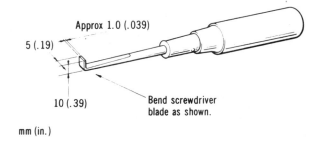

Fig. 12.30 Weatherstrip trim installing tool (Sec 16)

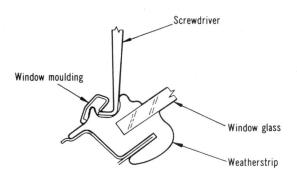

Fig. 12.31 Method of installing weatherstrip trim (Sec 16)

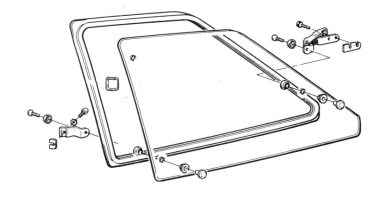

Fig. 12.32 Rear quarter window (Sec 17)

3   Protect the paintwork and prise out the bright moulding strip from the groove in the weatherstrip.
4   Working inside the car, use a screwdriver to peel back the lip of the weatherstrip and then apply even pressure to push the windscreen outwards. Have an assistant help to retain the screen as it is pushed out.
5   The windscreen on all models is of the laminated type and so there will not be a problem of glass crystals to clear up.
6   Remove the rubber weatherstrip from the old glass and fit it to the new glass. Make sure that it is free from even the smallest glass fragment and old sealant and that the rubber has not hardened. If it has, fit a new weatherstrip.
7   Clean the flange on the bodywork.
8   Insert a piece of cord about 0.13 in (3.2 mm) all round the body flange groove so that the ends overlap at one side.
9   Apply soap solution to the body flange and then locate the screen in position.
10   With an assistant applying gentle pressure to the outside of the glass, pull the ends of the cord from inside the car so that the lip of the weatherstrip engages over the body flange.
11   If the weatherstrip is not in new condition or if it has been inclined to leak, inject a suitable sealant between the glass and the weatherstrip and the body flange.
12   Refit the bright moulding. This job will be made easier if a blade is made up and slid along the weatherstrip groove, at the same time maintaining pressure on the moulding (Fig. 12.30).

Tailgate glass
13   The operations are similar to those just described for the windscreen but remember to disconnect the leads from the heating element.
14   The tailgate glass is of toughened type not laminated.

---

17 Rear quarter window glass – removal and refitting

---

1   Slide off the hinge cover using a flat bladed screwdriver.
2   Extract the hinge and latch screws and remove the window complete with hinges and latch still attached.

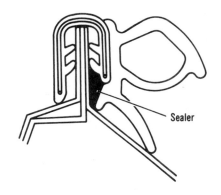

Fig. 12.33 Sectional view of quarter window weatherstrip (Sec 17)

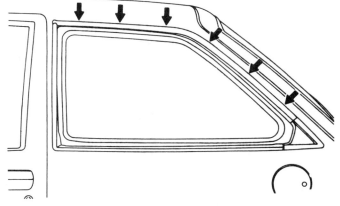

Fig. 12.34 Quarter window upper moulding screws (Sec 17)

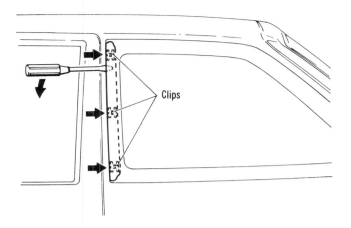

Fig. 12.35 Quarter window front moulding clips (Sec 17)

3 The body weatherseal if renewed, must have sealant injected all round its outer edge.
4 The hinges and the latch can be packed out with shims and the glass moved about within the limit of the elongated hinge and latch screw holes to provide correct alignment and watertight closure.
5 The decorative moulding on the body around the quarter window can be removed by extracting the screws hidden under the weatherstrip. The quarter window should be removed before this job is attempted.
6 The front and lower moulding sections are held by plastic clips which incorporate an expansion pin.

18 Front seat – removal and refitting

1 The seats are mounted on runners which in turn are bolted to the floor.
2 Extract the bolts and remove the seat from the car interior.
3 Refitting is a reversal of removal.

19 Rear seat – removal and refitting

1 Unlock the seat back and fold it down.
2 Detach the shelf trim from the seat back (if fitted).

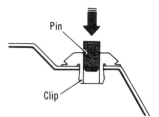

Fig. 12.36 Plastic clip with expansion pin (Sec 17)

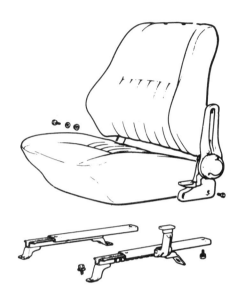

Fig. 12.37 Front seat components (Sec 18)

3 Detach the carpet from the seatback.
4 Remove the screws which hold the lower edge of the seat cushion also those which hold the rear of the cushion and the seatback hinge.
5 Remove the seat from the car.
6 Refitting is a reversal of removal.

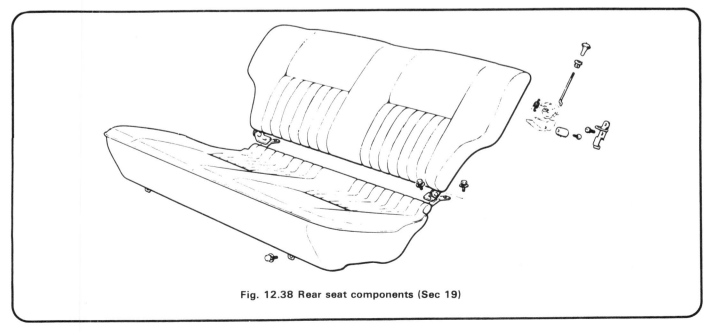

Fig. 12.38 Rear seat components (Sec 19)

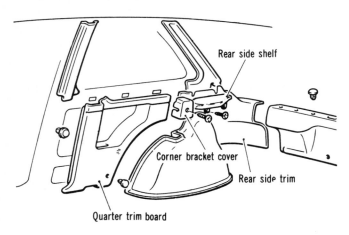

Fig. 12.39 Quarter trim panel (Sec 20)

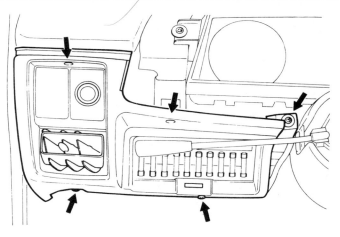

Fig. 12.40 Facia corner panel screws (Sec 21)

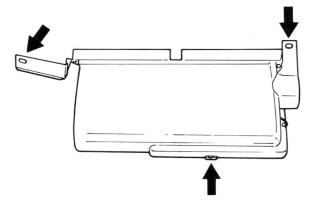

Fig. 12.41 Centre ventilator duct (Sec 21)

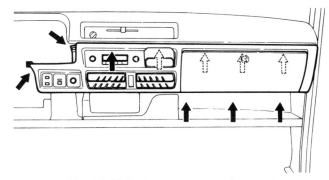

Fig. 12.42 Facia panel screws (Sec 21)

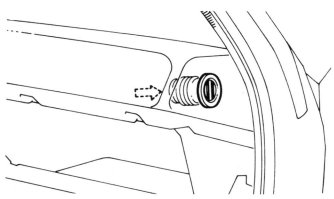

Fig. 12.43 Side demister nozzle (Sec 22)

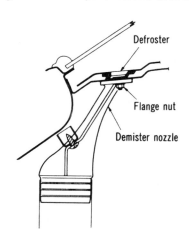

Fig. 12.44 Windscreen demister grille (Sec 22)

20 Interior rear quarter trim panel – removal and refitting

1   Remove the rear seat complete as described in the preceding Section.
2   Remove the corner bracket cover.
3   Remove the rear shelf screws and the side trim.
4   Remove the moulding from the centre body pillar.
5   Prise the trim panel away, releasing its mounting clips.
6   Refitting is a reversal of removal.

21 Facia panel – removal and refitting

1   Extract the four screws which secure the instrument cluster hood.
2   Extract the corner panel securing screws, pull the panel away until

the rheostat switch wiring connector can be separated. Remove the corner panel.
3   Release the wiring and withdraw the instrument cluster hood.
4   Remove the centre ventilator duct (three screws).
5   From the rear of the facia panel disconnect the wiring plugs for the rear wiper switch, rear screen demister switch and the cigar lighter.
6   Extract the facia panel mounting screws and pull the panel towards you.

22 Facia panel crash pad – removal, refitting

1   This is removed independently of the facia panel which must be withdrawn first as described in the preceding Section.
2   Remove the instrument cluster as described in Chapter 9.

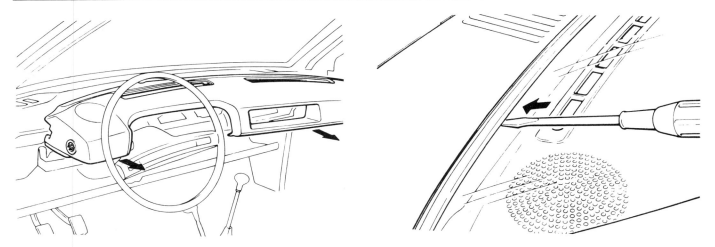

Fig. 12.45 Removing facia crash pad (Sec 22)   Fig. 12.46 Refitting facia crash pad (Sec 22)

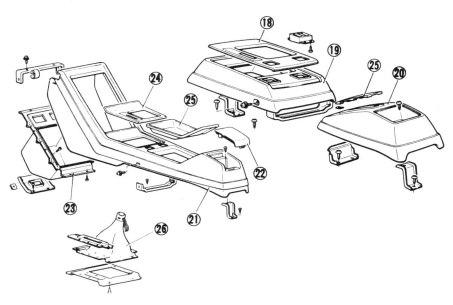

Fig. 12.47 Centre console assemblies (Sec 23)

18 Escutcheon plate	21 Centre console (front –	23 Cubby hole liner	25 Handbrake control
19 Centre console (front)	alternative type)	24 Escutcheon plate	lever cover
20 Centre console (rear)	22 Ash tray lid		26 Gearchange lever cover

3   Remove the heater motor electrical harness and the control panel as described in Chapter 2.
4   Disconnect the side demister outlet nozzle.
5   Reach under the crash pad and remove the nuts which hold the windscreen demister outlet grilles. Remove the grilles.
6   Withdraw the crash pad towards you.
7   Refitting is a reversal of removal, engage the edge of the pad below the lower edge of the windscreen weatherstrip using a screwdriver.

23 Centre console – removal and refitting

1   The type of console fitted depends upon the model and the transmission (manual or automatic).

Centre console (front)
2   Remove the gearchange lever knob and the ratio selector knob (Chapter 6).

3   Remove the screws from the sides of the console and withdraw the console only far enough to be able to disconnect the wiring harness from the switches and any instrumentation, before lifting the console away completely. Refitting is a reversal of removal.

Centre console (rear)
4   Access to the mounting screws is obtained after removing the ashtray and the handbrake control lever cover.
5   Refitting is a reversal of removal.

24 Parcels shelf – removal and refitting

1   Remove the centre console as described in the preceding Section.
2   Disconnect the control lever brackets under the facia panel for the tailgate latch and the bonnet release.
3   On North American cars so fitted, unbolt the relay for the engine speed sensor (ESS) device (Chapter 9, Section 12).

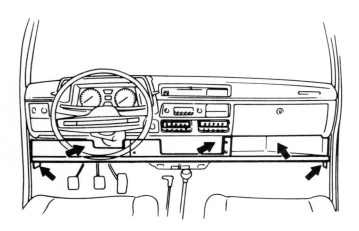

Fig. 12.48 Parcels shelf securing screws (Sec 24)

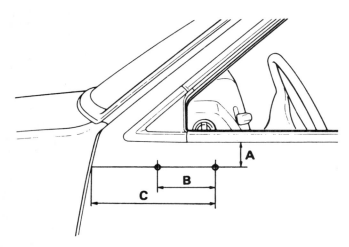

Fig. 12.49 Exterior mirror mounting plate hole diagram (early type mirror) (Sec 26)

A   1.6 in (40.0 mm)   C   7.1 in (180.0 mm)
B   3.19 in (81.0 mm)   Hole diameter 0.18 in (4.7 mm)

4   Extract the screws which secure the parcels shelf in position and remove it.
5   Refitting is a reversal of removal.

25 Seat velts – inspection and maintenance

1   Periodically inspect the seat belts for fraying or damage. If evident, always renew the belt, never attempt to repair it.
2   Dirt on a seat belt should be removed by wiping it with a damp cloth to which a little household detergent has been added.
3   If the car has been involved in a front end collision and the belts were in use, it is wise to discard them and fit complete new assemblies as the belts and the reel mechanism may have been strained when the impact occurred.
4   Periodically check the torque of the mounting bolts. Never attempt to alter the arrangement of the anchorage components with regard to the positioning of the washers and spacers.

26 Exterior rear view mirror

1   On some models, the door mounted mirror is secured to a mounting plate.
2   The plate is held to the door with two self-tapping screws while the mirror is secured to the plate with a single screw.
3   If a mirror is being fitted to a new door, see Fig. 12.49 for positioning and drilling the holes.
4   On other models, the mirror is retained by a projection from the door corner moulding and a single screw.

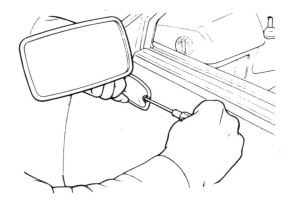

Fig. 12.50 Door mirror securing screw (early type mirror) (Sec 26)

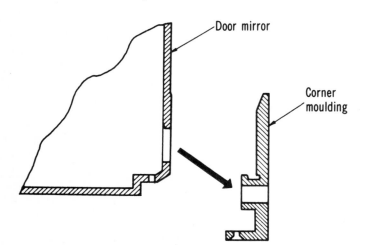

Fig. 12.51 Door mirror retaining lug (later type mirror) (Sec 26)

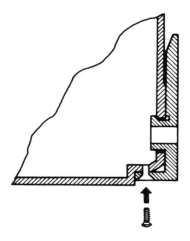

Fig. 12.52 Door mirror securing screw (later type mirror) (Sec 26)

27 Interior rear view mirror

1   This is of dipping type and has an in-built safety device to protect the occupants if it is struck during forward impact.

2   Under these circumstances, the mirror head and stem break off from the mounting plate, due to the release of a circlip.

3   The mirror can be reassembled if the mounting plate is removed and the screw extracted from the end of the stem of the mirror (photos).

4   Fit the stem to the mounting plate, locate the circlip and screw in and tighten the screw.

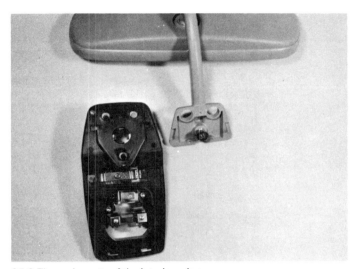

27.3 The main parts of the interior mirror

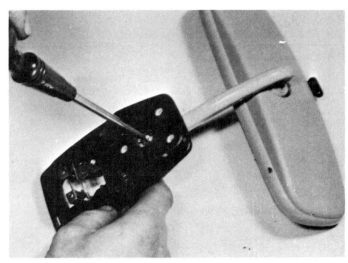

27.4 Reconnecting the interior mirror

Conversion factors

Length (distance)

Inches (in)	X	25.4	= Millimetres (mm)	X 0.039	= Inches (in)
Feet (ft)	X	0.305	= Metres (m)	X 3.281	= Feet (ft)
Miles	X	1.609	= Kilometres (km)	X 0.621	= Miles

Volume (capacity)

Cubic inches (cu in; in^3)	X	16.387	= Cubic centimetres (cc; cm^3)	X 0.061	= Cubic inches (cu in; in^3)
Imperial pints (Imp pt)	X	0.568	= Litres (l)	X 1.76	= Imperial pints (Imp pt)
Imperial quarts (Imp qt)	X	1.137	= Litres (l)	X 0.88	= Imperial quarts (Imp qt)
Imperial quarts (Imp qt)	X	1.201	= US quarts (US qt)	X 0.833	= Imperial quarts (Imp qt)
US quarts (US qt)	X	0.946	= Litres (l)	X 1.057	= US quarts (US qt)
Imperial gallons (Imp gal)	X	4.546	= Litres (l)	X 0.22	= Imperial gallons (Imp gal)
Imperial gallons (Imp gal)	X	1.201	= US gallons (US gal)	X 0.833	= Imperial gallons (Imp gal)
US gallons (US gal)	X	3.785	= Litres (l)	X 0.264	= US gallons (US gal)

Mass (weight)

Ounces (oz)	X	28.35	= Grams (g)	X 0.035	= Ounces (oz)
Pounds (lb)	X	0.454	= Kilograms (kg)	X 2.205	= Pounds (lb)

Force

Ounces-force (ozf; oz)	X	0.278	= Newtons (N)	X 3.6	= Ounces-force (ozf; oz)
Pounds-force (lbf; lb)	X	4.448	= Newtons (N)	X 0.225	= Pounds-force (lbf; lb)
Newtons (N)	X	0.1	= Kilograms-force (kgf; kg)	X 9.81	= Newtons (N)

Pressure

Pounds-force per square inch (psi; lbf/in^2; lb/in^2)	X	0.070	= Kilograms-force per square centimetre (kgf/cm^2; kg/cm^2)	X 14.223	= Pounds-force per square inch (psi; lbf/in^2; lb/in^2)
Pounds-force per square inch (psi; lbf/in^2; lb/in^2)	X	0.068	= Atmospheres (atm)	X 14.696	= Pounds-force per square inch (psi; lbf/in^2; lb/in^2)
Pounds-force per square inch (psi; lbf/in^2; lb/in^2)	X	0.069	= Bars	X 14.5	= Pounds-force per square inch (psi; lbf/in^2; lb/in^2)
Pounds-force per square inch (psi; lbf/in^2; lb/in^2)	X	6.895	= Kilopascals (kPa)	X 0.145	= Pounds-force per square inch (psi; lbf/in^2; lb/in^2)
Kilopascals (kPa)	X	0.01	= Kilograms-force per square centimetre (kgf/cm^2; kg/cm^2)	X 98.1	= Kilopascals (kPa)

Torque (moment of force)

Pounds-force inches (lbf in; lb in)	X	1.152	= Kilograms-force centimetre (kgf cm; kg cm)	X 0.868	= Pounds-force inches (lbf in; lb in)
Pounds-force inches (lbf in; lb in)	X	0.113	= Newton metres (Nm)	X 8.85	= Pounds-force inches (lbf in; lb in)
Pounds-force inches (lbf in; lb in)	X	0.083	= Pounds-force feet (lbf ft; lb ft)	X 12	= Pounds-force inches (lbf in; lb in)
Pounds-force feet (lbf ft; lb ft)	X	0.138	= Kilograms-force metres (kgf m; kg m)	X 7.233	= Pounds-force feet (lbf ft; lb ft)
Pounds-force feet (lbf ft; lb ft)	X	1.356	= Newton metres (Nm)	X 0.738	= Pounds-force feet (lbf ft; lb ft)
Newton metres (Nm)	X	0.102	= Kilograms-force metres (kgf m; kg m)	X 9.804	= Newton metres (Nm)

Power

Horsepower (hp)	X	745.7	= Watts (W)	X 0.0013	= Horsepower (hp)

Velocity (speed)

Miles per hour (miles/hr; mph)	X	1.609	= Kilometres per hour (km/hr; kph)	X 0.621	= Miles per hour (miles/hr; mph)

Fuel consumption*

Miles per gallon, Imperial (mpg)	X	0.354	= Kilometres per litre (km/l)	X 2.825	= Miles per gallon, Imperial (mpg)
Miles per gallon, US (mpg)	X	0.425	= Kilometres per litre (km/l)	X 2.352	= Miles per gallon, US (mpg)

Temperature

Degrees Fahrenheit (°F) $= (°C \times \frac{9}{5}) + 32$

Degrees Celsius (Degrees Centigrade; °C) $= (°F - 32) \times \frac{5}{9}$

*It is common practice to convert from miles per gallon (mpg) to litres/100 kilometres (l/100km), where mpg (Imperial) x l/100 km = 282 and mpg (US) x l/100 km = 235

Index

Printed by
Haynes Publishing Group
Sparkford Yeovil Somerset
England